The Change Maker – We Do Recover
A Journey of Transformation
By C. Michael Welsh

A Journey of Transformation

COPYRIGHT PAGE

© 2024 by The Change Maker Press All rights reserved. No part of this publication may be reproduced, distributed, or transmitted in any form or by any means, including photocopying, recording, or other electronic or mechanical methods, without the prior written permission of the publisher, except in the case of brief quotations embodied in critical reviews and certain other noncommercial uses permitted by copyright law. For permission requests, write to the publisher, addressed "Attention: Permissions Coordinator," at the email address below.

The Change Maker Press
chris@thechangemaker.biz
www.thechangemaker.biz

The Change Maker Press books may be purchased for educational, business, or sales promotional use.

Publisher's Cataloging-in-Publication Data
Names: C. Michael Welsh
Title: The Change Maker – We Do Recover – A Journey of Transformation
The Change Maker Press, 2024
Identifiers: ISBN 978-1-964122-10-6
First Edition
2024

The views and opinions expressed in this book are those of the author(s) and do not necessarily reflect the official policy or position of The Change Maker Press.

The Change Maker Press and the associated logo are trademarks of The Change Maker Press. Other product and company names mentioned herein may be the trademarks of their respective owners.

The Change Maker Press

A Journey of Transformation

Table of Contents

Embracing the Change Maker Within 12

Part I: Understanding Change 13
I: Understanding Change 15
II. Defining Change 21
III. The Dynamics of Change 27
IV. The Drivers of Change 39
V. The Psychological Impact of Change 51
VI. The Paradox of Resistance and Acceptance 63
VII. The Cycle of Change 77
VIII. Change as A Catalyst for Personal Growth 95

Part II: The Principles of Being a Change Maker 111
I. Introduction 113
II. Principle 1: Self-Awareness 119
III. Principle 2: Empathy and Compassion 131
IV. Principle 3: Vision and Purpose 139
V. Principle 4: Resilience And Adaptability 149
VI. Principle 5: Collaboration and Community 159
VII. Principle 6: Authenticity and Integrity 169
VIII. Principle 7: Patience and Persistence 183
IX. Principle 8: Innovation and Creativity 193
X. Principle 9: Mindful Action 201

Part III: The Steps of Transformation 217
I: The Steps of Transformation 219
II. Self-Reflection as the Starting Point 227
III. Setting Clear Goals for Personal Change 239

IV. Cultivating a Vision for Transformation 251
V. Personal States of Being 263
VI. Energy, Vibration, and Frequency 275
VII. Manifestation as a Catalyst for Transformation 289
VIII. Goals and Alignment 299
IX. Celebrating Successes Along the Way 311
X. Turning Change into a Lifestyle 321
XI. Prioritizing Self-Care and Well-Being 335

Part IV: How and Why, We Change 347
I. How and Why, We Change 349
II. The Intrinsic Motivations for Change 361
III. The Extrinsic Factors Influencing Change 369
IV. The Science of Behavior Change 383
V. The Stages of Change 397
VI. The Role of Beliefs and Mindset 415
VII. The Connection Between Emotions and Change 429
VIII. The Importance of Self-Reflection 443

In an era where transformation is not just desired but essential, "The Change Maker: We Do Recover" emerges as a beacon of hope and a manual for those seeking long-term recovery from addiction. This book is more than just a collection of words; it's a journey, a mentor, and a mirror that reflects our deepest potential for growth and self-realization.

At the heart of this book lies a profound understanding of the human spirit - its resilience, its yearning for purpose, and its incredible capacity for change. The author, C. Michael Welsh, with wisdom and compassion, guides us through the intricate maze of addiction and recovery, revealing how we can become architects of our destiny and catalysts for positive change in our lives and the lives of others.

Each chapter is meticulously crafted, offering a harmonious blend of practical advice, psychological insights, and soul-stirring wisdom. From confronting the shadows of our addiction to embracing the luminous potential of our recovery, this book is a comprehensive guide to personal transformation on the challenging path of recovery. It recognizes that recovery is not a linear journey but a complex dance of growth, setbacks, and breakthroughs.

What sets this book apart is its unwavering belief in the power of the individual in the context of addiction and recovery. It inspires us to look within, to find the change maker that resides in each of us, even when we may have lost sight of it amidst the struggles of addiction. This book does not just speak to us; it listens to the unspoken stories of our hearts, encouraging us to be brave, to be vulnerable, and, most importantly, to be our authentic selves.

As you turn these pages, you will find yourself on a transformative journey towards recovery. You will encounter chapters that resonate with the core of your being, offering insights into making peace with your past, overcoming trauma, setting meaningful goals, and cultivating a plethora of positive emotional states essential for recovery. Each lesson is a step towards a more fulfilling life, a life lived with purpose, joy, and an unwavering commitment to personal growth in the context of recovery.

"The Change Maker: We Do Recover" is more than just a book; it's a companion for those who dare to dream of a life beyond addiction, for those who seek to make a difference in their lives and the lives of others who are also on the path of recovery. It is an invitation to embark on the most important journey you will ever take - the journey towards your truest self in sobriety.

So, dear reader, as you embark on this journey of recovery, remember that the path of transformation is unique for each one of us. May this book light your way, challenge you, comfort you, and inspire you to become the change maker in your own life, charting a course towards long-term recovery.

Welcome to your journey of transformation. Your recovery starts here.

C. Michael Welsh

A Journey of Transformation

Embracing the Change Maker Within

Welcome to a transformative journey like no other, one that will empower you to recover from addiction and embrace a life of lasting change. "The Change Maker- We Do Recover" by C. Michael Welsh is not just a book; it's your trusted companion on the path to long-term recovery, offering you guidance, wisdom, and a roadmap for transformation.

In an era where the need for personal change is not just desired but essential, we embark on a journey of profound significance. This book is more than just a collection of words; it's an invitation to delve deep into the heart of your own transformation. It's a mirror reflecting your potential for growth, a mentor guiding you through the intricate maze of addiction and recovery, and a beacon of hope illuminating the way towards a brighter future.

At its core, this book understands the human spirit- its resilience, its yearning for purpose, and its remarkable capacity for change. With wisdom and compassion, C. Michael Welsh will walk beside you, offering insights and support as you become the architect of your own destiny and a catalyst for positive change in your life and the lives of others.

Our journey together is divided into several parts, each carefully crafted to address the various aspects of personal transformation and long-term recovery. We'll start by understanding the essence of change and the principles of being a change maker. We'll explore the steps of transformation, understanding why and how we change.

But what sets this book apart is its unwavering belief in the power within each of us. It inspires us to look within, to find the change maker that resides in our souls, even when addiction has dimmed its light. This book doesn't just speak to us; it listens to the unspoken stories of our hearts, encouraging us to be brave, vulnerable, and, most importantly, authentic.

As you journey through these pages, you'll encounter chapters that resonate with the core of your being. You'll gain insights into making peace with your past, overcoming trauma, setting meaningful goals, and cultivating a plethora of positive emotional states vital for recovery. Each lesson is a step towards a more fulfilling life- a life lived with purpose, joy, and an unwavering commitment to personal growth within the context of recovery.

"The Change Maker- We Do Recover" is more than a book; it's a companion for those who dare to dream of a life beyond addiction, for those who aspire to make a difference in their lives and the lives of others. It invites you to embark on the most important journey you will ever take- the journey towards your truest self in sobriety.

So, dear reader, as you begin this journey of recovery, remember that your path of transformation is unique, yet you are never alone. May this book light your way, challenge you, comfort you, and inspire you to become the change maker you were always meant to be.

A Journey of Transformation

Recovery from addiction is a journey that demands a profound transformation from the very core of your being. It requires you to become a change maker within yourself, to let go of the past that drags you down and to take that big leap forward into a brighter and sober future. As the saying goes, "If you want to fly in the sky, you need to leave the earth." In this book, we will explore the significance of embracing the change maker within and the necessity of letting go of the past in the pursuit of long-term recovery from addiction.

Addiction is often rooted in the past, a complex web of experiences, traumas, and choices that have led to a cycle of dependency. It's a burden that keeps you tethered to the ground, preventing you from soaring freely in the sky of a healthy and fulfilling life. To break free from the chains of addiction, you must summon the courage to let go of the past that has been holding you captive.

Letting go is never easy. It means accepting the things we don't want to happen but must, knowing the truths we'd rather avoid, and even separating from people we can't imagine living without, especially those who might enable our addiction. It is, however, in these very moments of release that we find the path to recovery.

One of the most profound aspects of recovery is the transformation it demands. You must be willing to change your perspective, your habits, and your entire way of life. It's a journey that takes you from the darkness of addiction into the light of sobriety, from despair to hope, from self-destruction to self-realization.

The process of letting go is akin to shedding old skin. It's the recognition that the past cannot be altered, and holding onto it only perpetuates suffering. Why let go of yesterday? Because yesterday has already let go of you. The past no longer defines you; it is the present and the future that hold the promise of a new beginning.

Recovery is not a journey of erasing the past but rather making peace with it. It is about understanding the past's influence on your addiction, acknowledging the mistakes, and using them as stepping stones toward a brighter future. When you let go of the past, you create space for personal growth, healing, and the development of new, healthier habits.

As you embark on your journey towards long-term recovery, consider these self-reflection questions. A best practice is to keep a journal of your answers to the self-reflection questions in this book.

> What aspects of my past have contributed to my addiction, and how can I make peace with them?
>
> Am I ready to let go of the people, habits, and memories that keep me anchored to my addiction?
>
> What does being a change maker within myself mean to me, and how can I embrace this role?

In what ways can I cultivate the courage to move forward without constantly looking back?

How can I use my past experiences as lessons to propel me towards a brighter and sober future?

Remember, embracing the change maker within is a courageous step towards lasting recovery. Letting go of the past doesn't mean forgetting it; it means acknowledging its presence and choosing not to be defined by it. As you leave the earth of addiction behind and aim to fly in the sky of recovery, know that the journey ahead is one filled with challenges but also with immense opportunities for growth, healing, and transformation.

Part I: Understanding Change

Understanding Change

The journey of long-term recovery from addiction is a path laden with the weight of the past. It's a journey where we confront our regrets, acknowledge our limitations, and wrestle with the fear of failure. Yet, within this complex terrain lies the opportunity for transformation, growth, and the creation of a brighter future. In this book, we delve into the importance of understanding change as the first step on the road to recovery.

The past can often feel like an anchor, tethering us to our old selves and reminding us of who we once were. It's a constant presence, unalterable and unerasable. It's easy to get caught in the trap of dwelling on what could have been, but this rumination only keeps us locked in a prison of regret. The key to breaking free is acceptance.

Acceptance, in the context of recovery, means acknowledging the past without letting it define our future. It means recognizing the actions and choices that led us down the path of addiction while understanding that we can choose a different direction moving forward.

Every step we take on the road to recovery is an act of forging our own path. It's a journey where we weave the tapestry of our lives with both our weaknesses and our strengths. Within the depths of our minds, there may be seeds of limitations, but there also lies the immense power to replace negativity with positivity, to nurture growth, and to cultivate resilience.

To embark on the path of recovery is to long for success more than we fear failure. It is to recognize that mistakes and pain have been formidable companions on our journey, etching wisdom upon our souls and forging the strength within us. Regret should not be for the actions we've taken but for the opportunities we've missed. It's a reminder that inaction is the truest form of regret.

It's essential to trust that we are precisely where we need to be in our recovery journey, guided by a higher force that orchestrates the circumstances required for our growth and transformation. Have faith, for the divine is ever-present, weaving miracles into the fabric of our existence. But the secret to unlocking the door of success lies not in idle wishes; it lies in the courageous act of doing.

Self-Reflection Questions:

How does the weight of the past impact my present and my journey towards recovery?

What does acceptance mean to me in the context of my addiction and recovery?

In what ways have my limitations held me back, and how can I replace negativity with positivity?

How can I shift my focus from fearing failure to longing for success in my recovery journey?

A Journey of Transformation

> What role have mistakes and pain played in shaping my character, and how can I turn them into sources of strength?

Remember, understanding change is the first step towards lasting recovery. It's about acknowledging your past, accepting it, and using it as a foundation upon which you can build a brighter future. Your journey may be challenging, but it's also a journey of self-discovery, growth, and the realization of your true potential.

Setting the Stage for the Exploration of Change

Recovery from addiction is a profound journey of transformation, one that requires us to confront our past, understand our present, and embrace our future. As we embark on this path towards long-term recovery, it is crucial to set the stage for the exploration of change. This stage is marked by the willingness to see things as they truly are, the commitment to applying knowledge, and the courage to let go of the past while holding onto its lessons. In this book, we will explore the importance of setting the stage for change in the context of addiction recovery.

In our pursuit of recovery, we must remember never to let our feelings obstruct our view of reality. Addiction often distorts our perception, leading us to make choices that serve immediate gratification but do not align with our long-term well-being. Seeing things as they truly are requires us to confront the harsh truths of our addiction, the consequences it has brought into our lives, and the damage it has inflicted on ourselves and our loved ones.

Knowledge alone is not enough; we must apply it to effect change. This applies not only to understanding the nature of addiction but also to the practical steps required for recovery. It means seeking help, utilizing coping strategies, and making deliberate choices that support sobriety. Recovery is not a passive endeavor; it demands active participation and the application of the insights we gain.

Wishing for recovery is not enough; we must take action. It's easy to harbor the desire for change, but real progress occurs when we translate that desire into concrete steps. Recovery requires us to do the hard work, to confront our triggers and cravings, to develop healthier habits, and to cultivate resilience in the face of challenges.

A fundamental aspect of setting the stage for change is the ability to forgive what has hurt us in the past while never forgetting what it has taught us. Our past, marked by addiction and its repercussions, can be a source of shame and regret. However, it also holds valuable lessons. It teaches us about the consequences of our actions, the depths of our vulnerabilities, and the strength we can muster to overcome adversity.

Accepting the past without regret is a powerful act of self-compassion. It means acknowledging that we cannot change what has already transpired but can shape our future through our choices and actions. It is about letting go of the burden of guilt and self-blame, which can hinder our progress, and instead using the past as a stepping stone towards recovery.

Handling the present with confidence involves making daily choices that align with our recovery goals. It's recognizing that each moment is an opportunity for growth and sobriety. Facing the future without fear requires us to approach it with hope, optimism, and a commitment to continued self-improvement.

Sometimes, things must go very wrong before they can be set right. Our addiction may have led us down a dark path, but it is within our power to change our trajectory. By looking forward, we mature; by looking back, we gain wisdom from our experiences, and by looking up, we find the guidance and strength needed to navigate the challenges ahead.

Self-Reflection Questions:

> How have my feelings and emotions affected my perception of addiction and recovery?
>
> What knowledge have I gained about addiction, and how can I apply it to my recovery journey?
>
> In what ways can I transform my wishes for recovery into concrete actions and strategies?
>
> What valuable lessons has my past taught me about addiction and myself?
>
> How can I accept my past without regret and use it as a foundation for my recovery?

Remember, setting the stage for change is an essential step on the path to long-term recovery. It involves embracing the present, learning from the past, and confidently facing the future. Your journey may be challenging, but it is also a journey of empowerment, growth, and transformation.

The Fundamental Role of Change in Life and Personal Growth

Change is an inherent part of life, and it plays a fundamental role in our personal growth and recovery journey, especially when seeking long-term recovery from addiction. In this book, we will explore the significance of change, both in the context of life as a whole and the recovery process, emphasizing the importance of self-validation, forgiveness, resilience, and the ability to let go of the past.

Often, we seek validation from others to affirm our self-worth and identity. We look for approval and acceptance, hoping that external validation will fill the void within us. However, this external reliance can be a precarious foundation. As the statement suggests, seeking validation from others can set us up for disaster. True self-worth and completeness come from within. No one else can provide it. It is essential to know who we are and understand that what others say or think about us is irrelevant to our self-worth. This realization is a pivotal point in personal growth and recovery, as it allows us to focus on self-acceptance and self-validation rather than depending on external sources.

A Journey of Transformation

Forgiveness is another crucial aspect of personal growth. It's relatively easy to forgive the mistakes of others, but rebuilding trust once it's been shattered can be exceptionally challenging, especially in the context of addiction and recovery. Forgiveness, in this case, may also extend to forgiving ourselves for the harm we've caused and the mistakes we've made during our addiction. Recognizing that forgiveness is a complex and ongoing process can be a powerful catalyst for personal growth. It's a process that requires patience, empathy, and a commitment to healing.

Change often demands that we move on from the past. Life is continually evolving, and so must we. Holding onto past hurts, regrets, or grudges can hinder personal growth and recovery. The statement reminds us that there's no point in dwelling on the past because it's impossible to change it. The past, with all its challenges and hardships, can serve as a valuable teacher. It offers lessons and opportunities for growth. It teaches us resilience, adaptability, and the strength to overcome adversity.

Embracing change and personal growth is not always easy, but it is not impossible. The statement encourages us to remember that just because something is hard does not mean it is unattainable. It highlights the importance of self-determination and perseverance. In the context of addiction recovery, this means recognizing that change is possible, even when it seems difficult. It's about believing in our ability to overcome addiction, no matter how challenging the journey may be.

Self-focus and positivity are also critical in the pursuit of personal growth. It is easy to be influenced by negative opinions or attitudes of others. Some people may be perpetually negative, but we should not let their negativity affect our own progress. Instead, we should concentrate on ourselves, our goals, and our self-improvement. Staying positive and cultivating a resilient mindset are essential components of personal growth.

Self-Reflection Questions:

How has seeking validation from others influenced my sense of self-worth, especially in the context of addiction and recovery?

What role does forgiveness play in my personal growth and recovery journey? How do I navigate forgiving myself and others for past mistakes?

How can I embrace change and let go of the past in my pursuit of long-term recovery from addiction?

What challenges have I faced in believing that change is possible, and how can I maintain a positive and resilient mindset?

In what ways can I prioritize self-focus and positivity in my personal growth and recovery journey?

Remember, personal growth and recovery are ongoing processes, and change is a constant companion on this journey. Embrace change as a tool for transformation and healing, and believe in your capacity to evolve and thrive.

The Importance of Understanding the Essence of Change

In the journey towards long-term recovery from addiction, understanding the essence of change holds paramount importance. It is through this understanding that we can truly grasp the transformative power of recovery, learn to leave the past behind, and embrace a future filled with promise and self-empowerment. In this book, we will explore the significance of comprehending the essence of change, with a focus on letting go of the past, recognizing our self-worth, and acknowledging our uniqueness.

Often, the hardest battles we face are the ones we choose to walk away from. Addiction can be a relentless adversary, but it is essential to remember that the past does not define our present or future. The pain, struggles, and mistakes of yesterday need not haunt us today. We must remind ourselves that the past cannot hurt us unless we allow it to. It is, after all, a collection of memories and experiences that reside within our minds.

The act of looking back can sometimes be a trap, drawing us into a never-ending cycle of regret and sorrow. What lies behind us, no matter how significant, is dwarfed by the vastness of what lies ahead. It's essential to focus on the journey ahead, to fix our gaze on the potential for growth, healing, and self-discovery that the future holds. This shift in perspective allows us to see the path of recovery as a promising and uncharted territory.

Understanding the essence of change means recognizing our intrinsic worth. Each of us is unique and possesses inherent value. The belief in our self-worth is a cornerstone of recovery. We are not defined by our addiction or past mistakes. We are somebody, and we have the capacity for greatness. Recovery is not about becoming someone different; it's about rediscovering and embracing the greatness that has always resided within us.

You are the only version of "you" to ever exist in the universe. This realization is both empowering and humbling. It highlights our individuality and the irreplaceable role we play in the world. Our journey of recovery is a testament to our unique experiences, challenges, and triumphs. No one else can walk in our shoes or understand our journey in the same way.

Embracing our Uniqueness Can Be a
Source of Strength and Motivation.

In the pursuit of recovery, it takes a strong person to chart their own course and not wait for external validation. Others may have their opinions and expectations, but our recovery journey is deeply personal. It is a reflection of our commitment to self-improvement and well-being. We should not rely on others to validate our existence or the choices we make on the path to recovery.

A Journey of Transformation

As we strive towards recovery, we may encounter our greatest opposition when we are closest to achieving our most significant goals and witnessing miracles. This opposition can take various forms, including self-doubt, external challenges, or the pull of old habits. It is imperative to stay resolute in doing what is right for our individual journeys. The path of recovery is uniquely ours, and no one else can navigate it for us.

Self-Reflection Questions:

How has my past influenced my present perception of self and my recovery journey?

What strategies can I employ to let go of the past and focus on the promising future of recovery?

How can I nurture my self-worth and recognize my uniqueness as a source of strength in my recovery?

In what ways can I take ownership of my recovery journey and not rely on external validation?

How can I stay resolute in doing what is right for me, especially when facing opposition or challenges in recovery?

Understanding the essence of change is a cornerstone of long-term recovery. It allows us to release the burdens of the past, embrace our uniqueness, and confidently walk the path towards a brighter and sober future. Your recovery journey is a testament to your strength and individuality, and it holds the promise of growth, self-discovery, and lasting transformation.

Defining Change: A Key to Long-Term Recovery

Long-term recovery from addiction is a journey that demands unwavering faith, resilience, and the courage to face each new day with hope and determination. To truly embrace this journey, it is crucial to define the concept of change and understand its role in our recovery process. In this book, we will explore the significance of defining change, focusing on finding strength in adversity, maintaining a positive attitude, and letting go of the past.

Some days, the greatest act of faith is the simple act of getting out of bed and facing another day. Addiction can weigh us down with despair, regret, and self-doubt. However, choosing to rise each morning, despite the challenges, is an act of resilience and belief in the possibility of change. It signifies our commitment to the journey of recovery, one day at a time.

Defining change also means shifting our mindset from talking endlessly about the problems associated with addiction to actively seeking solutions. Addiction can often trap us in a cycle of dwelling on the negative consequences and struggles. However, real progress occurs when we shift our focus towards solutions. Recovery is about taking concrete steps to address the root causes of addiction and learning healthier coping mechanisms.

Strength is not solely found in moments of success and ease but often emerges from the struggles we face. The statement highlights the transformative power of adversity. Every challenge and hardship we've endured has shaped us into the person we are today. It is through these experiences that we develop resilience, empathy, and the determination to overcome addiction.

Whenever we contemplate giving up, it's essential to reflect on why we've persevered for as long as we have. This introspection can reveal the inner strength and motivations that drive us towards recovery. It serves as a reminder of the progress we've made and the goals we aim to achieve.

A crucial aspect of defining change is understanding that happiness is not determined by external circumstances but by our attitudes and perspectives. Even in the face of addiction and recovery, we have the power to maintain a positive outlook. Cultivating a positive attitude involves focusing on gratitude, resilience, and the belief that each day brings new opportunities for growth.

Our most valuable assets are not solely found in intellectual knowledge but in the qualities that connect us with others. A heart full of love, a listening ear, and a helping hand are invaluable resources in the journey of recovery. They strengthen our connections, provide support, and foster a sense of community that can be instrumental in maintaining sobriety.

Finally, change often necessitates letting go of the burdens of the past. We cannot reach for new possibilities if our hands are still clinging to the remnants of yesterday's struggles and regrets. The past should be viewed as a source of lessons, not as an anchor that holds us back. Starting each day with a fresh perspective, unburdened by past mistakes, is essential for cultivating a positive and hopeful future.

A Journey of Transformation

Self-Reflection Questions:

How does the act of facing each new day contribute to my resilience and faith in recovery?

What strategies can I employ to shift my focus from problems to solutions in my recovery journey?

How have the challenges and struggles I've faced during addiction made me stronger and more determined in recovery?

What motivates me to continue on the path of recovery, even when the journey is difficult?

How can I maintain a positive attitude and outlook on life, even in the face of addiction and recovery challenges?

In what ways can I leverage my heart full of love, listening ear, and helping hand to support my own recovery and the recovery of others?

What steps can I take to let go of the burdens of the past and embrace each new day with hope and optimism?

Defining change is a critical step on the road to long-term recovery. It involves recognizing the transformative power of resilience, positivity, and letting go of the past. Each new day presents an opportunity to move closer to a life free from addiction, filled with hope and the promise of a brighter tomorrow.

A Comprehensive Definition of Change

For those on the path to long-term recovery from addiction, understanding the concept of change is not merely an academic exercise but a lifeline to transformation and healing. In this book, we will delve into a comprehensive definition of change, encompassing the themes of perseverance, determination, self-belief, and the ever-present potential for personal growth.

"Don't get discouraged by what you're going through. Your time is coming. Where you are is not where you're going to stay." This statement encapsulates the essence of change. It reminds us that change is not only possible but inevitable. No matter how challenging our circumstances may be in the present, they do not dictate our future. Recovery is a journey that requires patience and perseverance, and the belief that better days lie ahead.

Change demands that we refrain from making excuses for why we can't get things done and instead focus on the compelling reasons why we must make it happen. Addiction often thrives on excuses and rationalizations, perpetuating destructive behaviors. In recovery, we must shift our mindset from finding reasons to continue down the wrong path to finding compelling motivations for positive change.

The idea that "no matter how long you have traveled in the wrong direction, you can always turn around" is at the heart of the recovery journey. Addiction may have led us down a dark and destructive path, but it is never too late to make a U-turn towards recovery and healing. This recognition is a testament to our inner strength and the resilience of the human spirit.

Living in the past can be a significant barrier to change. Addiction often ties us to regrets, guilt, and shame from our past actions. However, we are not promised tomorrow, and dwelling on the past can hinder our ability to move forward. The key to change is to embrace the present moment and focus on becoming the person we were meant to be.

To truly understand change, we must ignite our inner fire and follow our heart's desire. This involves identifying our innermost aspirations, values, and passions. Recovery is not merely about abstaining from substances but about rediscovering our authentic selves and aligning our actions with our deepest desires.
As we reflect on this comprehensive definition of change, consider the following self-reflection questions:

> How has discouragement affected my journey towards recovery, and how can I maintain hope and perseverance in the face of challenges?
>
> What excuses have I made for not taking positive steps in my recovery, and how can I shift my focus to the compelling reasons for change?
>
> How does the concept of turning around and changing direction resonate with my recovery journey? What steps can I take to make positive changes in my life?
>
> In what ways have I been living in the past, and how can I shift my focus to the present moment to facilitate personal growth and change?
>
> What are the inner desires and passions that I wish to pursue in my journey towards becoming the person I was meant to be?

A comprehensive definition of change encompasses the recognition of our potential for transformation, the importance of perseverance, and the need to embrace the present moment. It reminds us that recovery is not just about overcoming addiction; it is about rediscovering our true selves and pursuing our deepest desires. With determination and self-belief, we can navigate the path towards long-term recovery and a brighter future.

The Inevitability of Change in All Aspects of Life

Change is an undeniable force that permeates every facet of our existence. For those embarking on the path to long-term recovery from addiction, understanding the inevitability of change is not just a philosophical concept but a practical and empowering reality. In this book, we will explore

A Journey of Transformation

the profound nature of change, emphasizing the importance of self-understanding, embracing the journey, overcoming fears, and finding joy in life.

"The most difficult phase of our life is not when no one understands us. It's when we don't understand ourselves." Addiction often disconnects us from our true selves, leaving us feeling lost and alienated. Recovery necessitates deep self-reflection and self-understanding. It involves unraveling the layers of addiction to reconnect with our authentic identity, desires, and aspirations. Recognizing that change begins from within is a pivotal step on the path to recovery.

Our tendency to fixate on the finish line can obscure the beauty of the journey itself. Recovery is not a race; it is a transformative process filled with lessons, growth, and self-discovery. It is essential to cherish each step along the way, acknowledging that change unfolds gradually and that the journey is as valuable as the destination.

"Too many of us are not living our dreams because we are living our fears." Addiction is often intertwined with fear—fear of facing the underlying issues, fear of sobriety, and fear of change itself. Conquering addiction requires confronting these fears head-on. It entails embracing the uncertainty of recovery with courage and determination. Realizing that change involves discomfort and fear is the first step towards conquering them.

Change is not always about external circumstances; it also involves transforming our perspectives and attitudes. "When life changes to be harder, change yourself to be stronger." In the face of adversity and life's challenges, we have the power to adapt and grow stronger. Recovery equips us with resilience and the ability to navigate life's ups and downs with newfound strength.

"The trick is to enjoy life. Don't wish away your days waiting for better ones ahead." Recovery offers the opportunity to rekindle the joy of living. It encourages us to appreciate the present moment, rather than yearning for an idealized future. By embracing the changes inherent in the recovery journey, we can find fulfillment and contentment in the here and now.

"Do what you love and love what you do!" This mantra underscores the importance of aligning our actions and choices with our passions and values. Recovery provides a second chance to pursue our true interests and purpose in life. It invites us to engage in activities and relationships that bring fulfillment and joy, fostering a sense of purpose that supports sobriety.

Self-Reflection Questions:

How has my understanding of myself evolved during my journey towards recovery, and how has self-awareness influenced my progress?

In what ways can I shift my focus from the finish line of recovery to appreciating the transformative journey itself?

What fears have I encountered on my path to recovery, and how have I worked to overcome them?

How has recovery empowered me to adapt and become stronger in the face of life's challenges?

What steps can I take to find joy in the present moment and embrace the changes that come with it?

How can I align my actions with my passions and values in my ongoing recovery journey?

The inevitability of change is a fundamental truth of life, and recognizing its transformative potential is a cornerstone of long-term recovery. By understanding ourselves, embracing the journey, conquering fears, and finding joy in each moment, we can navigate the changes of life with resilience and a renewed sense of purpose.

How Change Manifests in Various Forms

Change is a dynamic and multifaceted force that permeates our lives in countless ways. For those embarking on the path to long-term recovery from addiction, understanding the diverse manifestations of change is essential. In this book, we will explore how change takes shape in various forms, emphasizing the power of acceptance, living in the present, embracing challenges, cultivating positivity, and unleashing our potential.

"Embrace the power of acceptance and compassion, looking beyond religious scriptures and past scars to connect with the essence of a person's heart." Change often begins with acceptance—acceptance of ourselves and others. In recovery, it is crucial to accept our past mistakes and recognize that they do not define our worth. By extending compassion to ourselves and others, we forge connections that support our journey to sobriety.

"Let go of the past, seize the uniqueness of each moment, and focus on the present to shape a brighter future." Change is embodied in the act of letting go. Addiction is often intertwined with dwelling on past regrets and traumas. Recovery invites us to release the burdens of the past, allowing us to fully engage with the present moment. Each moment is unique and holds the potential to shape a brighter future if we seize it with intention.

"Embrace challenges as stepping stones, knowing that struggles don't define us." Change often presents itself as challenges and obstacles. These challenges, though formidable, are not indicative of our worth or identity. In fact, they are stepping stones that propel us toward personal growth and resilience. Embracing challenges with determination can lead to transformative change.

"Free yourself from overthinking, occupy your mind with positivity, and believe in your strength." Change is profoundly influenced by our thought patterns. Overthinking and negative self-talk can hinder our progress. To manifest positive change, we must occupy our minds with positivity and self-belief. Believing in our inherent strength empowers us to overcome addiction and achieve lasting recovery.

"Release judgment, embrace potential, and seize the opportunities for success and happiness that await." Change is also about shifting our perspectives and letting go of judgment, both of ourselves and others. Recovery entails embracing our potential for growth and seizing the opportunities that lead to success and happiness. By releasing judgment, we create a supportive environment for personal transformation.

Self-Reflection Questions:

> How has the power of acceptance and compassion influenced my relationships, both with myself and with others, in my recovery journey?
>
> What strategies have I employed to let go of the past and fully engage with the present moment to shape a brighter future?
>
> How have I approached challenges and setbacks in my recovery, and in what ways have they contributed to my personal growth?
>
> What techniques or practices have helped me free myself from overthinking and cultivate a mindset of positivity and self-belief?
>
> How has releasing judgment, embracing potential, and seizing opportunities played a role in my pursuit of success and happiness in recovery?

Change manifests in diverse forms, from acceptance and letting go of the past to embracing challenges, cultivating positivity, and releasing judgment. By recognizing these manifestations and integrating them into our recovery journey, we can navigate the path towards long-term sobriety with resilience and a renewed sense of purpose.

The Dynamics of Change

Change is a dynamic and ever-present force that shapes the course of our lives. For those on the path to long-term recovery from addiction, understanding the complex dynamics of change is essential. In this book, we will explore the multifaceted nature of change, focusing on the lessons learned from wounds, the value of simplicity, the importance of honesty, the preciousness of life, and the guiding light of hope.

"Remember that our wounds can be our greatest teachers." Change often emerges from the lessons we glean from our wounds and hardships. Addiction can be a profound wound, but it also offers the opportunity for transformation and growth. By reflecting on the lessons learned from our struggles, we can harness the power of change and move toward healing.

"True wealth is found in simplicity, not material possessions." The dynamics of change often lead us to reevaluate our priorities. Recovery challenges the materialistic mindset that can fuel addiction. True wealth lies in simplicity—cultivating meaningful connections, finding contentment in the present moment, and nurturing our inner well-being.

"Being honest about our desires, needs, and feelings helps us form genuine connections." Change often involves a shift in our interpersonal dynamics. Honesty, both with ourselves and others, is a cornerstone of recovery. It enables us to form genuine connections built on trust and authenticity. By being true to ourselves, we can foster supportive relationships that facilitate change.

"Life is a precious gift, and every moment is worth cherishing." The dynamics of change prompt us to reevaluate our relationship with life itself. Addiction can rob us of the ability to cherish each moment. In recovery, we rediscover the preciousness of life and embrace the opportunities for growth and joy that each moment holds.

"When we face challenges, hope is our guiding light. We can overcome anything and find the sun's rays again." Change often brings challenges and adversity. Hope serves as a guiding light that propels us forward. It reminds us that, even in our darkest moments, we have the inner strength to overcome obstacles and find the brightness of hope once more.

Let us embrace these truths in our journey toward long-term recovery. Finding peace in simplicity, being true to ourselves and others, and cherishing the gift of life are all essential components of change. As you reflect on the dynamics of change, consider the following self-reflection questions:

> How have my wounds and struggles in addiction served as teachers in my recovery journey? What lessons have I learned from them?
>
> In what ways have I reevaluated my understanding of wealth and simplicity during my recovery? How has this reevaluation affected my priorities?

A Journey of Transformation

> How has honesty played a role in forming genuine connections in my life, both within and outside of my recovery journey?
>
> How has my perception of life as a precious gift evolved during my recovery, and in what ways do I cherish each moment?
>
> How has hope guided me through the challenges and setbacks in my recovery? How do I cultivate and maintain hope in my daily life?

Understanding the dynamics of change involves recognizing the transformative power of our wounds, finding wealth in simplicity, nurturing honest connections, cherishing life, and embracing the guiding light of hope. By integrating these principles into our recovery journey, we can navigate the path toward lasting sobriety with resilience and an unwavering sense of purpose.

Understanding the Nature of Change

Change, like a relentless river, flows through the landscape of our lives, shaping the contours of our existence. For those embarking on the path to long-term recovery from addiction, comprehending the intricate nature of change is vital. In this book, we will delve into the profound understanding of change, emphasizing the power of the present and the future, the acceptance of each individual's essence, cherishing every moment, releasing apprehensions about the unknown, cultivating resilience, and nurturing optimism.

"Let us grasp the boundless power of the present and future, and let our hearts overflow with a profound acceptance of each individual's true essence, unfettered by their past or beliefs." Change invites us to embrace the limitless potential of the present and future. Recovery teaches us to see beyond a person's past or beliefs and connect with the essence of their true self. By accepting individuals unconditionally, we create an environment conducive to change.

"In every passing moment lies an extraordinary opportunity, so let us cherish it dearly." Change is not an abstract concept; it is embedded in the fabric of every moment. In recovery, we learn to cherish each moment as a unique opportunity for growth and transformation. Recognizing the value of these moments can profoundly shape our journey.

"Release all apprehensions about the unknown future and anchor our focus in the present, knowing that everything else will fall into place effortlessly." Change often triggers apprehensions about the unknown future. Recovery encourages us to relinquish these anxieties and anchor our focus in the present. By doing so, we trust that, as we navigate the present with intention and commitment, the future will align effortlessly.

"May we cultivate unyielding resilience and a steadfast optimism, for it is through the crucible of adversity that we truly thrive." Change often presents challenges and adversities. Recovery equips us with the tools to cultivate unyielding resilience, enabling us to face adversity with strength and determination. Optimism becomes our compass, guiding us through the most challenging moments.

"The perils of excessive contemplation can sow seeds of discontent; hence, let our minds be filled with thoughts that exude positivity and boundless potential." Change can provoke excessive contemplation and self-doubt. Recovery encourages us to fill our minds with thoughts that radiate positivity and boundless potential. By maintaining a positive mindset, we facilitate the transformative power of change.

Self-Reflection Questions:

> How has my understanding of the present and future evolved during my recovery journey, and how has this impacted my ability to accept others unconditionally?
>
> In what ways have I learned to cherish each moment as an opportunity for growth and transformation in my recovery?
>
> How have I navigated apprehensions about the unknown future and anchored my focus in the present? How has this trust in the process influenced my recovery?
>
> What strategies have I developed to cultivate unyielding resilience in the face of adversity, and how has optimism guided me through challenging times?
>
> How has maintaining a positive mindset and filling my mind with thoughts of boundless potential supported my journey of change in recovery?

Understanding the nature of change involves embracing the power of the present and future, accepting others unconditionally, cherishing each moment, releasing apprehensions about the unknown, cultivating resilience, and nurturing optimism. By integrating these principles into our recovery journey, we can navigate the path toward lasting sobriety with grace and an unwavering sense of hope.

Continuous vs. Episodic Change

In the journey towards long-term recovery from addiction, the concept of change is a constant companion. However, change itself can take on different forms and durations, leading us to contemplate the distinction between continuous and episodic change. This book explores the nuances of these two types of change and the significance they hold in the context of addiction recovery.

"It is during our darkest moments that we must focus to see the light." Episodic change often emerges from moments of darkness and crisis. These episodes can serve as catalysts for transformation in addiction recovery. They compel us to seek help, make significant changes, and embark on the path to recovery.

A Journey of Transformation

"Don't judge each day by the harvest you reap but by the seeds that you plant." Continuous change, on the other hand, centers on the daily cultivation of positive habits and choices. In long-term recovery, it's not solely about the immediate results but the consistent efforts to plant the seeds of recovery through commitment, self-care, and resilience.

"The best and most beautiful things in the world cannot be seen or even touched, they must be felt with the heart." Continuous change invites us to connect with the intangible but profound aspects of recovery—the emotional and spiritual growth, the healing of relationships, and the restoration of inner peace. These beautiful transformations are felt deep within our hearts.

"The keys to being patience are acceptance and faith. Accept things as they are, and look realistically at the world around you. Have faith in yourself and in the direction you have chosen." Continuous change requires patience, and it thrives on acceptance and faith. Accepting the reality of addiction and our own vulnerabilities is the foundation of recovery. Faith in ourselves and our chosen path sustains us as we navigate the daily challenges.

"It doesn't matter how much you want. What really matters is how much you want it." Episodic change often involves a powerful desire for immediate transformation—a moment of clarity or crisis that drives us to seek help. However, continuous change underscores the importance of sustained commitment and resilience. It's not about the intensity of desire but the enduring dedication to recovery.

"The extent and complexity of the problem does not matter as much as does the willingness to solve it." Whether change is episodic or continuous, what truly matters is the willingness to confront addiction and embrace recovery. The extent and complexity of the problem may vary, but the unwavering determination to overcome it is the common thread.

Self-Reflection Questions:

How have moments of crisis or darkness in my life influenced my episodic changes in recovery, and what pivotal moments have catalyzed my commitment to sobriety?

In what ways have I cultivated continuous change in my recovery journey through daily habits, self-care, and resilience?

How have I experienced the intangible beauty of recovery, such as emotional healing and spiritual growth, and how do these aspects contribute to my journey?

How has my patience in recovery been shaped by acceptance and faith in myself and my chosen path?

What motivates me in both episodic and continuous change? How do I sustain my commitment to recovery over time?

Understanding the dynamics of continuous and episodic change in addiction recovery empowers us to navigate the path towards lasting sobriety with awareness and resilience. It reminds us that change can take various forms, and each form plays a unique role in our journey to heal and grow.

Gradual vs. Abrupt Change

In the realm of addiction recovery, the journey towards long-term sobriety is often marked by the distinction between gradual and abrupt change. This book explores these two modes of transformation and their significance in the recovery process, drawing inspiration from the metaphor of a frog at the bottom of a well and the pursuit of living a purposeful life.

"We think too small. Like a frog at the bottom of a well. He thinks the sky is only as big as the top of the well. If he surfaced, he would have an entirely different view." Gradual change, akin to the frog's ascent from the well, involves a gradual shift in perspective and behavior. It encompasses the steady process of transformation, where small, consistent steps accumulate to create profound change. This incremental approach allows individuals in recovery to gradually acclimate to a sober life, building resilience along the way.

"The great and glorious masterpiece of a person is to know how to live and fulfill their purpose." Abrupt change, on the other hand, can manifest as a sudden awakening or a moment of clarity—an epiphany that propels individuals to embark on a path of immediate transformation. Such moments often bring a profound understanding of one's purpose and a resolute commitment to living a life aligned with that purpose.

"The ability to convert ideas to things is the secret to outward success." Gradual change encompasses the patient process of converting intentions into tangible actions. It involves turning recovery aspirations into daily habits and practical strategies. This steady transformation allows individuals to build a foundation for lasting sobriety and success in life.

"Change your thoughts, and you change your world." Both gradual and abrupt change involve a fundamental shift in mindset. Gradual change encourages individuals to continuously reshape their thoughts and beliefs over time, leading to lasting transformation. Abrupt change often sparks a radical shift in perspective, catapulting individuals into a new world of possibilities.

Self-Reflection Questions:

How has gradual change played a role in my recovery journey, and what small steps have I taken to build resilience and sobriety over time?

Have I experienced moments of abrupt change or epiphany in my recovery journey that led to a profound shift in perspective or commitment to sobriety?

How have I transformed my recovery intentions into practical actions and daily habits, thus converting ideas into tangible success?

A Journey of Transformation

> In what ways have I actively changed my thoughts and beliefs to create a more positive and fulfilling world for myself?

Understanding the interplay between gradual and abrupt change in addiction recovery empowers individuals to navigate their unique paths towards lasting sobriety. Both modes of transformation offer valuable insights and tools to foster personal growth and build a meaningful, purpose-driven life in recovery.

The Interconnectedness of Change in Different Areas of Life

In the pursuit of long-term recovery from addiction, it becomes apparent that change is not confined to a single facet of life. Instead, it ripples through various dimensions, intertwining them in a dance of transformation. This book explores the interconnectedness of change in different areas of life and the profound impact it has on the recovery journey.

"Embrace the thrill of taking a leap of faith! When fear arises, gather your courage and jump into the unknown, for it brings incredible growth and endless possibilities." Change in recovery often begins with a leap of faith—a courageous step into the unknown. As we confront our fears and venture into uncharted territory, we find ourselves transformed, gaining strength and resilience along the way.

"Your past, including mistakes, has shaped the remarkable person you are today." Change in recovery acknowledges the role of the past. Our mistakes and experiences have shaped us into unique individuals. By embracing our past with compassion and learning from it, we set the stage for profound personal growth.

"Amid daily distractions, focus on what truly matters: your passions, dreams, and cherished connections." Change extends its influence to our priorities. Recovery encourages us to shift our focus from distractions to what truly matters—our passions, dreams, and meaningful connections. These become our anchors in the turbulent waters of transformation.

"Let love and kindness guide you, giving without expectation and caring for others selflessly." Change in recovery is not limited to self-transformation; it extends to our relationships and interactions with others. Love and kindness become guiding principles, fostering deeper connections and a sense of community in the journey towards lasting sobriety.

"Believe in your capabilities and have faith in your journey. Success requires patience, effort, and unwavering dedication, but it will come." Change touches upon our belief in ourselves and our journey. In recovery, belief and faith become pillars of strength, driving us to persist through challenges and setbacks on the path to success.

"Push forward, embrace challenges, and witness your dreams turning into reality. You possess the strength to conquer any obstacle and craft a life filled with triumph and fulfillment." Change is not passive; it calls for action. Recovery empowers us to push forward, embrace challenges, and turn dreams into reality. We discover within ourselves the strength to overcome obstacles and create a life filled with triumph and fulfillment.

Self-Reflection Questions:

> How have moments of courage and taking leaps of faith influenced the interconnected changes in various aspects of my life in recovery?
>
> In what ways has my past, including mistakes, contributed to shaping the remarkable person I am today, and how has this self-awareness impacted my journey?
>
> How have my shifting priorities, focusing on passions, dreams, and cherished connections, influenced my overall sense of fulfillment and well-being in recovery?
>
> How has the practice of love and kindness, giving without expectation, and caring for others selflessly enriched my relationships and sense of community in recovery?
>
> How does belief in my capabilities and unwavering faith in my journey empower me to persist through challenges and move closer to the realization of my dreams in recovery?

Recognizing the interconnectedness of change in different areas of life provides insight into the holistic nature of the recovery journey. It underscores the profound impact that transformation can have on our personal growth, relationships, priorities, and overall sense of purpose and fulfillment.

Personal Change: The Relentless Pursuit of Excellence

In the pursuit of long-term recovery from addiction, one is invariably confronted with the profound concept of personal change. This book delves into the essence of personal change as it pertains to the relentless pursuit of excellence in all aspects of life, shedding light on the transformative power it holds in the recovery journey.

"Wholeheartedly embrace your perspective on positive the pursuit of excellence." Personal change, especially in recovery, begins with the conscious decision to embrace a perspective centered on the pursuit of excellence. This mindset acts as the catalyst for transformation, urging individuals to strive for their personal best in all endeavors.

"Let us embrace a mindset of constant growth and relentless pursuit of excellence in all areas of our lives, regardless of the magnitude of the task at hand." Personal change thrives in an environment of continuous growth. Recovery teaches us that no task is too small or too large to be infused with excellence. Every area of life, from the mundane to the significant, becomes an opportunity for transformation.

A Journey of Transformation

"By recognizing that our best is a fluid concept that adapts to each situation, we free ourselves from the burden of self-criticism and remorse." Personal change necessitates the recognition that our best is not a fixed benchmark but a fluid concept that adapts to the circumstances we face. Understanding this liberates us from the heavy burden of self-criticism and remorse, allowing us to channel our energy into constructive growth.

"Every mistake we encounter becomes a valuable lesson, propelling us forward instead of hindering our progress." Mistakes, often viewed with trepidation, take on a new role in personal change—they become valuable lessons. Each misstep serves as a stepping stone, propelling us forward on our journey of transformation rather than hindering our progress.

"With each new day, we are gifted a fresh chance to surpass our previous achievements and transform our aspirations into reality." Personal change operates in the realm of limitless possibilities. With each new day comes a fresh chance to surpass our previous achievements, transforming our aspirations into tangible reality. Recovery reminds us that every dawn heralds the potential for growth and transformation.

"Let us seize these opportunities, fuel our determination, and unlock the vast potential that lies within us. You can conquer any challenge that comes your way!" Personal change invites us to seize opportunities, fuel our determination, and unlock the vast reservoir of potential that resides within us. It reinforces the belief that we possess the inner strength to conquer any challenge that comes our way, no matter how daunting it may seem.

Self-Reflection Questions:

How has your perspective on the pursuit of excellence evolved during your recovery journey, and in what ways has it fueled your personal change efforts?

Can you identify specific areas of your life where you have embraced a mindset of constant growth and pursued excellence, regardless of the task's magnitude?

How has your understanding of personal change helped you release the burden of self-criticism and remorse, allowing you to focus on constructive growth?

What valuable lessons have you learned from the mistakes encountered in your recovery journey, and how have they propelled you forward?

How do you approach each new day as an opportunity to surpass previous achievements and transform aspirations into reality, and how does this outlook impact your overall sense of progress in recovery?

Personal change, grounded in the relentless pursuit of excellence, serves as a driving force in the journey towards long-term recovery from addiction. It empowers individuals to embrace growth, learn from mistakes, and unlock their inherent potential, ultimately fostering a life characterized by continuous transformation and personal fulfillment.

Social Change: The Power of Positive Transformation

In the pursuit of long-term recovery from addiction, the concept of social change takes on a unique significance. This book explores the profound impact of social change on the recovery journey and how the power of positivity can shape our interactions, relationships, and ultimately, our lives.

"Embrace the power of a single positive thought in the morning, as it has the potential to transform your entire day." Social change begins with the individual, and it starts with the power of a single positive thought. Each morning presents an opportunity for transformation, as a positive outlook can set the tone for the day ahead, influencing our interactions and decisions.

"Approach each morning with determination, and by the end of the day, you will experience a satisfying sense of accomplishment." The determination to approach each morning with purpose and resolve can lead to a satisfying sense of accomplishment by day's end. Social change is driven by individuals who actively engage with the world and strive to make it a better place.

"Replace excuses with effort and laziness with unwavering determination, while consciously choosing to perceive the world through the lens of optimism." Social change challenges us to replace excuses with effort and laziness with unwavering determination. By consciously choosing to perceive the world through the lens of optimism, we contribute positively to our communities and promote a culture of change.

"Trust that everything will fall into place as you navigate life's journey. Remember, life itself is a precious gift, so release unnecessary stress and worries." Trust plays a pivotal role in social change. Trusting that everything will fall into place as we navigate life's journey allows us to release unnecessary stress and worries, focusing on constructive actions that drive positive change.

"Take a moment to appreciate the blessings that surround you, instead of dwelling on what you lack. Each day you wake up is a remarkable blessing; cherish it and make it count." Social change encompasses gratitude and appreciation. Taking a moment to appreciate the blessings that surround us, even in challenging times, fosters a sense of fulfillment and a commitment to making each day count.

"Even during challenging times, remember that they can be blessings in disguise, providing opportunities for growth and improvement. So, let go of the past and allow it to shape you into a stronger individual." Social change acknowledges that challenges are opportunities for growth and improvement. Embracing these moments as blessings in disguise allows us to let go of the past and emerge as stronger individuals.

A Journey of Transformation

Self-Reflection Questions:

How has the power of positive thinking influenced your interactions and relationships during your recovery journey?

Can you recall instances where your determination to approach each day with purpose led to a sense of accomplishment and contributed to your personal growth?

In what ways have you actively replaced excuses with effort and embraced a mindset of unwavering determination in your pursuit of recovery?

How has perceiving the world through the lens of optimism impacted your ability to effect social change within your community and support others in their recovery?

Reflect on the role of trust in your journey. How has trusting in the process and the potential for positive change influenced your recovery experience?

Social change is not an abstract concept but a tangible force that can shape our lives and communities. It starts with individual actions, attitudes, and positive thinking, ultimately creating a ripple effect that fosters transformation, connection, and recovery.

Environmental Change: Nurturing Happiness and Growth

In the journey toward long-term recovery from addiction, environmental change plays a significant role. This book explores the profound impact of environmental change on the recovery process and emphasizes the importance of nurturing happiness and personal growth within this transformative context.

"Find happiness within by realizing your full potential and focusing on positivity." Environmental change begins within oneself, and it is rooted in the pursuit of happiness. Realizing one's full potential and focusing on positivity are key aspects of this process. Recovery teaches us that true happiness emanates from self-discovery and a positive outlook on life.

"True happiness comes from aligning your thoughts, words, and actions." Environmental change involves aligning thoughts, words, and actions. It underscores the importance of living in harmony with one's values and principles. Recovery reminds us that happiness blossoms when our inner beliefs and outward expressions are congruent.

"Appreciate what you have and take risks to pursue your dreams without fear of failure." A fundamental aspect of environmental change is gratitude—appreciating what we have. Simultaneously, it encourages individuals to take calculated risks in pursuit of their dreams, free from the paralyzing fear of failure. Recovery champions the idea that growth often lies beyond the comfort zone.

"Every experience is a chance to learn and grow." Environmental change views every experience, including setbacks, as an opportunity for learning and growth. Recovery highlights the importance of resilience and adaptability in the face of challenges, emphasizing that adversity can be a stepping stone to a brighter future.

"Live life with no regrets and make the most of every moment because it's not about the years we live, but the life we live in those years." Environmental change invites us to live life without regrets, seizing every moment with purpose and intention. It underscores that the quality of life is measured not by the years we live but by the depth and meaning of those years. Recovery reinforces the notion that each day in recovery is a precious gift, offering an opportunity to lead a life of fulfillment and purpose.

Self-Reflection Questions:

> How has the process of environmental change influenced your pursuit of happiness and personal growth in your recovery journey?
>
> Can you identify specific instances where aligning your thoughts, words, and actions has contributed to a sense of harmony and contentment in your life?
>
> In what ways have gratitude and the willingness to take calculated risks propelled you toward your dreams, and how has this impacted your recovery experience?
>
> Reflect on the lessons you have learned from both positive and challenging experiences in recovery. How have these experiences shaped your personal growth and resilience?
>
> How do you approach each day in recovery as an opportunity to live life with no regrets and make the most of every moment? How does this perspective influence your sense of fulfillment and purpose?

Environmental change is a powerful force in the journey of long-term recovery from addiction. It begins within, fostering happiness, alignment, gratitude, and growth. By embracing this concept, individuals can transform their lives and create an environment conducive to sustained recovery and personal flourishing.

The Drivers of Change: A Path to Transformation

Long-term recovery from addiction is a journey deeply rooted in the concept of change. This book delves into the driving forces behind change and how they shape the recovery process, emphasizing the importance of self-respect, determination, and a positive mindset.

"If you desire to make a difference in the world, you must be different from the world." Change often begins with the aspiration to make a positive impact on the world, but it necessitates being different from the patterns and behaviors that led to addiction. Recovery teaches us that transformation begins within, requiring us to embrace a new way of life and perspective.

"Respect yourself, and others will follow suit." Self-respect is a cornerstone of recovery. It serves as a catalyst for change, influencing how others perceive and treat us. Recovery underscores that the way we value ourselves sets the standard for how we allow others to treat us.

"Most people will not treat you any better than you treat yourself." Recovery emphasizes the reciprocity of self-treatment and external treatment. How we treat ourselves directly affects how we are treated by others. A fundamental shift in self-perception can trigger a cascade of positive change in personal relationships and interactions.

"Don't make excuses and never give up." Change demands accountability and resilience. Recovery encourages individuals to stop making excuses for their actions and to persevere, even in the face of setbacks. It instills the belief that giving up is not an option and that lasting change is possible through determination.

"Believe it's possible, find a way, and make it happen." The power of belief is a driving force in recovery. The conviction that change is possible fuels the journey toward recovery. Recovery teaches us to seek solutions and forge a path to lasting change, even when it seems challenging.
"You'll never know if you stop now." In the pursuit of long-term recovery, persistence is key. Recovery reminds us that giving up prematurely robs us of the opportunity to discover the potential for transformation that lies ahead. Each step taken in recovery is a step closer to lasting change.

"You may have had a negative past, but you don't have to have a negative future. Leave it behind you and stay positive." Recovery encourages individuals to break free from the shadows of their past and focus on creating a positive future. It emphasizes the power of leaving negative experiences behind and cultivating a positive mindset.

Self-Reflection Questions:

> How has your desire to make a positive difference in the world influenced your commitment to change and your recovery journey?

A Journey of Transformation

> Reflect on the role of self-respect in your recovery. How has respecting yourself impacted the way others treat you and your overall sense of well-being?
>
> Can you identify instances where your self-treatment has had a direct impact on how others have treated you? How have these experiences shaped your recovery journey?
>
> How do you approach challenges and setbacks in your recovery? In what ways has resilience and determination played a role in your ability to persevere?
>
> Reflect on the power of belief and its impact on your journey toward lasting change. How has belief in the possibility of change influenced your actions and decisions in recovery?

The drivers of change are powerful motivators in the pursuit of long-term recovery from addiction. By embracing self-respect, determination, and a positive mindset, individuals can create a foundation for lasting transformation and ultimately shape a brighter future.

Identifying the Catalysts for Change: A Journey to Recovery

Recovery from addiction is a profound transformational journey, and identifying the catalysts for change is often the first step towards lasting recovery. This book explores the essential elements that ignite change and emphasizes the importance of action, determination, self-awareness, and the pursuit of personal growth.

"It's not about saying the right things, it's about doing the right things." Recovery underscores the significance of action over mere words. Change begins with taking positive steps towards recovery, such as seeking help, attending therapy, and making healthier choices. The transformation from addiction to recovery is not just about talking the talk; it's about walking the walk.

"The dream only becomes impossible when you let the possibility of failure overtake your need to succeed." A powerful catalyst for change is the unwavering desire to succeed in recovery. It's the understanding that setbacks and challenges are part of the journey but should never overshadow the determination to overcome addiction. Embracing the possibility of success fuels the recovery process.

"Be a witness, not a judge. Focus on yourself, not on others." Recovery emphasizes self-awareness and self-compassion. It encourages individuals to observe their thoughts, behaviors, and emotions without judgment. This self-awareness allows for a deeper understanding of the underlying causes of addiction and paves the way for personal growth.

"Listen to your heart, not to the crowd." Recovery often involves distancing oneself from negative influences and external pressures. It encourages individuals to trust their inner voice and values rather than conforming to societal expectations. This shift towards authenticity is a powerful catalyst for change.

"We're not the same people we were a year ago, a month ago, or a week ago. We're constantly changing. Experiences don't stop. That's life." Change is a fundamental aspect of life, and recovery underscores the dynamic nature of personal growth. It acknowledges that individuals evolve and adapt over time, making lasting change not only possible but also inevitable.

"If we never go after what we want, we will never have it. Live without regrets. If you want it, fight for it. Fight through the hard times and be grateful for the good times." Recovery encourages individuals to pursue their aspirations and desires. It instills the belief that recovery is achievable through determination, resilience, and gratitude for both the challenges and successes along the way.

"When doubts start to creep in, take a moment to pray." For many, spirituality or a higher power is a catalyst for change in recovery. It provides solace, guidance, and a source of strength during challenging times. Prayer or spiritual practices offer a sense of connection and purpose in the journey toward recovery.

Self-Reflection Questions:

What specific actions have you taken to initiate change in your recovery journey? How have these actions influenced your progress?

Reflect on your desire to succeed in recovery. How does the possibility of success fuel your determination to overcome addiction?

How have you practiced self-awareness and self-compassion in your recovery? In what ways has self-awareness contributed to personal growth?

Have you been able to listen to your inner voice and prioritize your values over external influences in your recovery journey? How has this impacted your sense of authenticity?

Consider how you have evolved and changed during your recovery process. How has your evolving self influenced your commitment to change and growth?

How do you approach your aspirations and desires in recovery? In what ways has determination and resilience been essential in your pursuit of recovery?

Reflect on the role of spirituality or a higher power in your recovery. How does it provide support, guidance, and strength during challenging times?

Identifying the catalysts for change is a pivotal step in the journey towards lasting recovery. By understanding the power of action, determination, self-awareness, authenticity, and spirituality, individuals can unlock their potential for transformation and embrace a life free from addiction.

A Journey of Transformation

Internal Factors: The Keys to Long-Term Recovery

Recovery from addiction is a journey filled with challenges and triumphs, and internal factors play a pivotal role in achieving long-term success. This book explores the significance of personal growth and self-awareness as internal catalysts for lasting recovery. It emphasizes the power of positive thought, choice, and vision in shaping the path to a brighter future.

"Every time you are tempted to react to the same old circumstances in the same old way, ask yourself, Do I want to be a prisoner of the past, or a pioneer of the future?" Addiction often keeps individuals trapped in a cycle of destructive behavior. Personal growth begins with the realization that change is possible and that old patterns can be broken. It's about choosing to be a pioneer of the future, where recovery and well-being are the destination.

"It takes but one positive thought when given a chance to survive and thrive to overpower an entire army of negative thoughts." The power of positive thinking cannot be overstated in the context of recovery. It starts with the belief that recovery is attainable and that personal transformation is within reach. Even in the face of negative thoughts and challenges, a single positive thought can be a beacon of hope.

"You write your own destiny through the choices you make." Recovery is a journey of choice. It involves making conscious decisions that align with the goal of sobriety and well-being. Every choice, no matter how small, shapes the path to recovery. Personal growth is about developing the capacity to make positive choices consistently.

"In order to carry a positive action, we must develop a positive vision." Personal growth and self-awareness are intertwined with having a clear and positive vision for the future. A positive vision provides motivation and direction in recovery. It helps individuals set goals, stay focused, and navigate through the challenges of addiction.

Self-Reflection Questions:

How have personal growth and self-awareness influenced your recovery journey? In what ways have you grown as an individual since embarking on this path?

Reflect on a specific instance when you chose to be a pioneer of the future rather than a prisoner of the past. How did this choice impact your recovery?

How do you nurture and cultivate positive thoughts in your daily life? How have these positive thoughts helped you overcome negative thinking patterns?

Think about the choices you have made in your recovery. How have these choices shaped your journey, and what have you learned from them?

Consider your vision for the future in recovery. How does having a positive vision inspire you to stay on the path of sobriety and personal growth?

How do you envision your destiny as you continue on your recovery journey? What role do you see personal growth and self-awareness playing in your future?

Internal factors, such as personal growth and self-awareness, are the foundation of lasting recovery. They empower individuals to break free from the chains of addiction, make positive choices, and envision a future filled with hope and purpose. By fostering these internal catalysts, individuals can embark on a journey of transformation and embrace a life of sobriety and well-being.

External Factors: Navigating the Complexities of a Changing World

Recovery from addiction is a deeply personal journey, but it's also influenced by external factors that shape our lives. In this book, we explore the impact of external factors, such as societal shifts and technological advancements, on long-term recovery. We delve into the relationship between external forces and an individual's disposition, highlighting the role of personal actions in finding happiness and overcoming challenges.

"Be determined to be cheerful and happy in whatever situation you may find yourself." Recovery often involves facing difficult circumstances, but the external factors that contribute to these challenges can be managed with determination and a positive outlook. A commitment to maintaining a cheerful disposition can provide resilience in the face of external stressors.

"You can learn that the greater part of our misery or unhappiness is determined not by our circumstance but by our disposition." It's essential to recognize that external factors, while impactful, don't solely determine our happiness or well-being. Our disposition, shaped by personal growth and self-awareness, plays a significant role in how we perceive and respond to external forces.

"Happiness is not something ready-made. It comes from your own actions." Happiness is an internal state influenced by external circumstances but ultimately driven by personal actions. In recovery, individuals can actively choose to take positive actions that contribute to their happiness, regardless of external challenges.

"Happiness often sneaks in through a door you didn't know you left open." External factors may bring challenges, but they can also present unexpected opportunities for happiness and growth. Keeping an open mind and heart allows individuals to embrace moments of happiness that arise unexpectedly.

"There are no great people, only great challenges that ordinary people are forced by circumstances to meet." Recovery often requires individuals to confront great challenges. External factors may present these challenges, but it's the ordinary individuals who rise to meet them that achieve greatness in their recovery journey.

"Creativity means believing you have greatness." External factors, such as societal shifts and technological advancements, can inspire creativity and innovation in recovery strategies. Believing in one's potential for greatness can drive individuals to explore creative solutions to their unique challenges.

"Greatness does not approach a person who is forever looking down. Don't be afraid of greatness; some are born great, some achieve greatness, and others have greatness thrust upon them, but no great person lives in vain." Recovery is a path where individuals must look forward, not down, and embrace the potential for greatness within themselves. Whether greatness is innate, achieved, or thrust upon, it contributes to a meaningful recovery journey.

"The history of the world is but the biography of great people." The history of recovery is a collection of countless individual biographies of resilience, determination, and personal growth. External factors shape these stories, but it's the individuals who navigate them with strength and purpose that become part of this history.

Self-Reflection Questions:

How have external factors, such as societal shifts or technological advancements, impacted your recovery journey? Have they presented challenges or opportunities for personal growth?

Reflect on a specific situation where your disposition and personal actions played a significant role in maintaining a positive outlook despite external challenges.

How do you actively pursue happiness in your recovery journey? What personal actions contribute to your sense of well-being and contentment?

Have you experienced moments of unexpected happiness or growth that arose from external circumstances? How did you respond to these opportunities?

Consider the challenges you've faced in recovery. How have they shaped your journey and contributed to your personal growth and resilience?

Do you believe in your potential for greatness in your recovery journey? How has this belief influenced your approach to challenges and opportunities?

External factors are an integral part of the recovery journey, and understanding their influence can empower individuals to navigate them with resilience and creativity. By recognizing the interplay between external forces and personal actions, individuals can shape their recovery path and find happiness, growth, and even greatness along the way.

Recognizing the Triggers for Change:
The Power of Internal and External Factors

In the pursuit of long-term recovery from addiction, recognizing the triggers for change is a crucial step. Change often begins with an internal realization, a shift in disposition, and a determination to overcome the grip of addiction. However, external factors also play a significant role in triggering change. In this book, we explore the interplay between internal and external factors in driving transformation and recovery.

"Be determined to be cheerful and happy in whatever situation you may find yourself." The journey to recovery is not always smooth, and individuals may encounter challenging situations that test their determination. Recognizing the need for change often starts with a deep-seated determination to seek happiness and well-being, even in the face of adversity.

"You can learn that the greater part of our misery or unhappiness is determined not by our circumstance but by our disposition." Understanding that our disposition, shaped by personal growth and self-awareness, plays a central role in our happiness is a profound realization. Recovery involves recognizing that change begins from within, where shifts in disposition can lead to lasting transformation.

"Happiness is not something ready-made. It comes from your own actions." Recovery is an active process where individuals take control of their actions and choices. True happiness arises from the positive actions they take to address their addiction and embrace a healthier, sober lifestyle.

"Happiness often sneaks in through a door you didn't know you left open." Change can often occur unexpectedly, and individuals in recovery may find that moments of happiness and personal growth emerge when they least expect them. Keeping an open mind and heart can allow these moments to flourish.

"There are no great people, only great challenges that ordinary people are forced by circumstances to meet." In the journey to recovery, individuals may confront formidable challenges related to addiction and its consequences. These challenges, often triggered by external circumstances, can bring forth the greatness within ordinary individuals who rise to meet them.

"Creativity means believing you have greatness." Believing in one's potential for greatness is a catalyst for creative solutions in recovery. It empowers individuals to explore new approaches to overcoming addiction and building a life of sobriety.

"Greatness does not approach a person who is forever looking down. Don't be afraid of greatness; some are born great, some achieve greatness, and others have greatness thrust upon them, but no great person lives in vain." Change and recovery require individuals to look forward, not down, and to embrace the potential for greatness within themselves. Whether greatness is innate, achieved, or thrust upon, it is a meaningful part of the recovery journey.

A Journey of Transformation

"The history of the world is but the biography of great people." In the context of recovery, the history of addiction and overcoming it is the collective biography of countless individuals who have faced addiction, recognized the triggers for change, and embarked on their journeys to sobriety.

Self-Reflection Questions:

How has your determination to seek happiness and well-being influenced your decision to pursue long-term recovery from addiction?

Reflect on a specific moment when a shift in your disposition played a pivotal role in your journey to recovery. How did this internal change impact your actions and choices?

What positive actions have you taken to foster happiness and sobriety in your recovery journey? How have these actions contributed to your transformation?

Have you experienced unexpected moments of happiness or growth during your recovery journey? How did these moments shape your outlook on change and transformation?

Consider the challenges you've faced in your recovery. How have external circumstances triggered your motivation to change and overcome addiction?

Do you believe in your potential for greatness in your recovery journey? How has this belief influenced your creativity and problem-solving skills in addressing addiction challenges?

Recognizing the triggers for change, whether internal or external, is a pivotal step in the journey to long-term recovery. By understanding the power of disposition, determination, and the interplay of internal and external factors, individuals can navigate the path to sobriety with resilience, hope, and the potential for greatness.

Events and Experiences That Prompt Individuals to Seek Change

Life is a journey filled with a mix of experiences, and not every day is a good day. Sometimes, it's the challenging events and difficult experiences that prompt individuals to seek change, particularly when it comes to overcoming addiction. In this book, we will explore how life's ups and downs can be powerful catalysts for individuals seeking long-term recovery, and we will reflect on the importance of these events in shaping the path to sobriety.

"Some days are just bad days, that's all." Bad days are a universal experience, and they serve as a reminder of the contrast between sadness and happiness. In the context of addiction recovery, these bad days can be especially poignant, as they highlight the need for change and the pursuit of lasting happiness that comes with sobriety.

"You have to experience sadness to know happiness, and you have to remind yourself that not every day is going to be a good day, that's just the way it is." Addiction often leads individuals to a cycle of highs and lows, where the temporary euphoria of substance use is followed by the depths of sadness and despair. These experiences can become a powerful motivator to seek change and break free from addiction.

"You have to remember that the hard days are what make you stronger. The bad days make you realize what a good day is. If you never had any bad days, you would never have that sense of accomplishment!" In recovery, each day without substance use is a triumph. The challenging days, filled with cravings and temptations, become the stepping stones to greater strength and resilience. It's the awareness of the contrast between the bad days and the good days that fuels the sense of accomplishment in sobriety.

"I don't think anybody is immune to experiencing a bad day." Addiction does not discriminate, and individuals from all walks of life can find themselves facing the challenges of addiction. Understanding that bad days are a shared human experience can reduce the stigma associated with seeking help for addiction.

"Sometimes, a simple reminder that you're in control of your happiness is all that's needed to change your attitude and change your outlook." Recovery from addiction often begins with a shift in attitude and outlook. Recognizing that it is possible to take control of one's happiness and well-being is a pivotal moment on the path to change.

"Every day is a good day to be alive, whether the sun's shining or not. If you don't think every day is a good day, just try missing one." The realization that life itself is a precious gift can be a profound motivator for change. It highlights the importance of embracing each day, even in the face of challenges, and valuing the opportunity for recovery and a brighter future.

Self-Reflection Questions:

Can you identify specific events or experiences in your life that have led you to recognize the need for change and recovery from addiction?

How have bad days and challenging moments shaped your understanding of happiness and sobriety?

Reflect on your sense of accomplishment in your journey to recovery. What milestones or achievements have contributed to your sense of strength and resilience?

Do you believe that seeking help for addiction is a shared human experience that transcends judgment or stigma?

How has a shift in your attitude and outlook influenced your approach to recovery and taking control of your happiness?

A Journey of Transformation

> Consider the preciousness of life itself and the opportunity for recovery. How does this perspective motivate you to embrace each day and commit to long-term change?

Events and experiences, both good and bad, are integral parts of the journey to recovery. They serve as catalysts for change, prompting individuals to seek help, embrace sobriety, and ultimately find happiness in a life free from addiction.

The Role of Crisis and Adversity in Sparking Change

Life is a journey filled with twists and turns, and it's often in moments of crisis and adversity that we are compelled to seek change and transformation. When it comes to individuals seeking long-term recovery from addiction, these challenging experiences can be powerful catalysts for change. In this book, we will explore the role of crisis and adversity in sparking change and the profound lessons they offer on the path to recovery.

"Wealth is the ability to fully experience life." While wealth is commonly associated with material possessions, the true wealth lies in our ability to embrace life in its entirety. Addiction can diminish this ability, limiting one's capacity to experience the richness of life's moments. Crisis and adversity can serve as wake-up calls, prompting individuals to seek recovery and regain their ability to fully experience life.

"A wise person should have money in their head, but not in their heart." Money, like addiction, can consume a person's life when it becomes the sole focus. The wisdom lies in recognizing that true wealth is not measured by monetary riches but by the richness of one's experiences, relationships, and well-being. Crisis and adversity can lead to a reevaluation of priorities and a shift away from material pursuits.

"Money has never made a person happy, nor will it, there is nothing in its nature to produce happiness." Addiction can be an attempt to find happiness or escape from unhappiness, but it ultimately leads to deeper unhappiness and despair. Crisis can shatter the illusion that external possessions or substances can provide lasting happiness, prompting individuals to seek inner fulfillment and peace through recovery.

"The more of it one has, the more one wants. Money cannot buy peace of mind." Similarly, addiction often leads to a cycle of craving and seeking more of the substance, without ever achieving peace of mind. Crisis can disrupt this cycle, revealing that true peace of mind and contentment can only be found by addressing the underlying issues through recovery.

"Money won't create success, the freedom to make it will." In the context of addiction recovery, success is not defined by material wealth but by the freedom to make choices that lead to a healthy, fulfilling life. Crisis and adversity can provide the impetus to reclaim this freedom and work towards lasting success in recovery.

"A little thought and a little kindness are often worth more than a great deal of money." The journey to recovery involves self-reflection, self-compassion, and the support and kindness of others. Crisis and adversity can inspire individuals to engage in thoughtful self-examination and seek the kindness and understanding they need to heal.

Self-Reflection Questions:

> Can you identify specific moments of crisis or adversity that prompted you to seek change and recovery from addiction?
>
> Reflect on the concept of wealth and its relationship to experiencing life fully. How has addiction limited your ability to fully embrace life, and how has recovery brought you closer to this ability?
>
> Consider the pursuit of material wealth and its impact on your life before seeking recovery. How has your perspective on wealth evolved since then?
>
> Reflect on the pursuit of happiness and peace of mind through addiction. How have crisis and adversity revealed the limitations of external substances in providing lasting happiness and peace?
>
> Explore the concept of success in your recovery journey. How do you define success now, and how has it shifted from your past views?
>
> Think about the importance of self-reflection, self-compassion, and support in your recovery. How have these elements played a role in your ability to overcome adversity and seek lasting change?

Crisis and adversity can be profound teachers, guiding individuals toward recovery and a deeper understanding of what true wealth, success, and happiness entail. These challenging experiences, when met with resilience and the decision to seek change, can be transformative on the path to long-term recovery.

The Psychological Impact of Change

Change is not merely an external process but also a deeply psychological one. It challenges us to confront our own identity, desires, and the expectations of the world around us. For those seeking long-term recovery from addiction, change can be a transformative journey that requires unwavering self-discovery and resilience.

"Visions are worth fighting for. To be nobody but yourself in a world which is doing its best, night and day, to make you everybody else, means to fight the hardest battle which any human being can fight; and never stop fighting." The psychological impact of change begins with the struggle to assert one's authentic self in a world that often pressures individuals to conform. Recovery demands the courage to break free from the mold society imposes and embrace one's unique journey toward healing.

"Never stop fighting until you arrive at your destined place, that is, the unique you." This journey of recovery involves discovering one's true self, free from the cloud of addiction. It necessitates a relentless commitment to self-discovery and personal growth, even when faced with the challenges of withdrawal, cravings, and societal judgment.

"Have an aim in life, continuously acquire knowledge, work hard, and have perseverance to realize the great life." The psychological impact of change encompasses the pursuit of a meaningful life beyond addiction. Setting and working toward recovery goals, acquiring knowledge about addiction and mental health, and developing the perseverance to overcome setbacks are essential aspects of this journey.

"As we advance in life it becomes more and more difficult, but in fighting the difficulties, the inmost strength of the heart is developed." The psychological impact of change is not without its trials. Recovery often involves facing past traumas, addressing deep-seated emotional wounds, and navigating the complexities of relapse prevention. However, it is in these difficult moments that the strength of the human spirit is forged, leading to profound personal growth.

"Why spend your life making someone else's dreams come true? A dream you don't have to fight for isn't a dream, it's a nap." Recovery is about reclaiming one's life and dreams, rather than living for the fulfillment of someone else's expectations or the temporary escape offered by addiction. It's the willingness to fight for a brighter, sober future.

"Remember one changes your afternoon. The other changes your world. So keep fighting." Finally, the psychological impact of change hinges on recognizing that addiction only provides temporary relief, while recovery has the power to transform an entire life. The struggle to overcome addiction is an investment in a future filled with meaningful change and genuine happiness.

A Journey of Transformation

Self-Reflection Questions:

How has the process of change challenged your sense of self and identity? In what ways have you fought to remain true to your authentic self throughout your recovery journey?

Reflect on the concept of perseverance in recovery. Can you identify moments in your journey where perseverance played a crucial role in your progress?

Consider the challenges and difficulties you've encountered on your path to recovery. How have these challenges contributed to the development of your inner strength and resilience?

Think about the dreams and aspirations you've pursued or rekindled in recovery. How have your goals evolved, and how do they differ from the dreams you may have had during your addiction?

Reflect on the transformative power of change in your life. In what ways has your journey in recovery changed not only your afternoon but your entire world?

The psychological impact of change is a central aspect of the recovery process. It involves confronting societal expectations, discovering one's authentic self, and persevering through challenges to achieve lasting transformation. Embracing these psychological aspects of change can lead to profound personal growth and fulfillment on the path to long-term recovery.

How Change Affects Human Psychology

Change is a force that permeates every aspect of human life, including our psychology. When individuals embark on the journey of long-term recovery from addiction, they are thrust into a world of transformation that profoundly impacts their mental and emotional well-being.

"Lots of bad things happen in people's lives. We create rules for ourselves that tell us 'This is as far as I can go in this direction' or 'This is just how life is.' We accept the limits of our vision for the limits of the world." The process of recovery challenges these self-imposed limits and expands the horizons of what is possible. It forces individuals to confront the deeply ingrained beliefs and rules they've established during their addiction. Change, in this context, dismantles old paradigms and paves the way for new perspectives.

"In life, many things don't go according to plan. If you fall, get back up. If you stumble, regain your balance but, never give up." The unpredictable nature of life and the ups and downs of the recovery journey often prompt shifts in human psychology. Individuals in recovery learn to adapt, build resilience, and develop coping strategies that enable them to navigate the unexpected twists and turns with determination and hope.

"You may never understand why something happened the way it did, so don't drive yourself crazy trying. If something hasn't happened for you, it doesn't mean it's never going to happen. It might mean that you're not ready for it." Change in recovery involves accepting the unchangeable, including past mistakes and losses. This acceptance shifts the psychology of individuals from dwelling on what cannot be altered to focusing on what can be achieved in the present and future.

"Life is all about making choices. Always do your best to make the right ones, and always do your best to learn from the wrong ones. The most honorable people of all are not those who never make mistakes, but those who admit to them when they do, and then go on to do their best to make right the wrongs they made." Change in recovery prompts individuals to reevaluate their decision-making processes. They develop the awareness to make healthier choices, learn from their missteps, and take responsibility for their actions. This transformation of decision-making impacts not only their recovery but also their overall psychology.

"If people are good only because they fear punishment and hope for reward, then we are a sorry lot indeed." Change in recovery touches the very essence of human motivation. It shifts the psychology from external motivators like fear of punishment or the hope for reward to intrinsic motivations rooted in personal growth, self-improvement, and the desire for a fulfilling life.

"Remember, hope is a good thing, maybe the best of things, and no good thing ever dies." Perhaps the most profound psychological impact of change in recovery is the rekindling of hope. Hope is a driving force that empowers individuals to persevere through challenges, to envision a brighter future, and to believe in the possibility of lasting recovery.

Self-Reflection Questions:

How have the shifts in your beliefs and perspectives impacted your psychological well-being during your recovery journey?

Reflect on the adaptability and resilience you've developed as a result of navigating the unpredictability of life in recovery. How have these qualities influenced your psychology?

Consider how you've learned to accept what cannot be changed and focus on the present and future. How has this acceptance transformed your outlook on life?

Reflect on the choices you've made and how your decision-making process has evolved in recovery. In what ways has this impacted your psychology?

Explore the motivations that drive your commitment to recovery. Have you noticed a shift from external motivators to intrinsic motivations? How has this affected your sense of purpose and psychological well-being?

Think about the role of hope in your recovery journey. How has hope empowered you to face challenges and believe in the possibility of a better future?

A Journey of Transformation

Change in the context of long-term recovery is a complex and multifaceted phenomenon that touches every aspect of human psychology. It challenges beliefs, transforms decision-making, and ultimately rekindles the flame of hope, driving individuals toward a brighter, sober future.

The Stress and Anxiety Associated with Change

Change is an inevitable part of life, but it often brings with it a multitude of stressors and anxieties. For someone seeking long-term recovery from addiction, these stressors can be particularly intense and challenging to navigate. The process of recovery itself is a profound journey of change, laden with uncertainty and accompanied by various emotional hurdles.

In the face of change, individuals often encounter a series of stressors that can heighten their anxiety levels. "Lots of bad things happen in people's lives," and the decision to embark on the path to recovery is often prompted by a recognition of the negative consequences of addiction. The very awareness of the need for change can lead to feelings of guilt, shame, and anxiety about the future.

As individuals in recovery start to challenge the patterns and behaviors that sustained their addiction, they inevitably encounter moments when they stumble or falter. "In life, many things don't go according to plan. If you fall, get back up. If you stumble, regain your balance but, never give up." This process of trial and error, while crucial for growth, can be a significant source of stress and anxiety. The fear of relapse or setbacks can loom large, creating emotional turmoil.

The lack of control over external circumstances and the inherent unpredictability of life can also induce stress and anxiety. "You may never understand why something happened the way it did so don't drive yourself crazy trying. If something hasn't happened for you, it doesn't mean it's never going to happen. It might mean that you're not ready for it." In recovery, individuals often grapple with the loss of familiar coping mechanisms like substance abuse, leaving them feeling vulnerable and exposed to life's uncertainties.

Change in recovery requires individuals to make choices that align with their newfound commitment to sobriety. "Life is all about making choices. Always do your best to make the right ones, and always do your best to learn from the wrong ones." The pressure to consistently make the right decisions can create significant stress, as the fear of making mistakes and facing potential relapses looms large.

Moreover, the external motivators that may have initially driven individuals to seek recovery, such as the fear of punishment or hope for rewards, can contribute to anxiety. "If people are good only because they fear punishment, and hope for reward, then we are a sorry lot indeed." The transition from external to internal motivations is a critical aspect of long-term recovery but can be accompanied by anxiety as individuals learn to self-motivate and find intrinsic reasons to stay on the path of sobriety.

As individuals in recovery grapple with the stress and anxiety associated with change, they must remember that "hope is a good thing, maybe the best of things, and no good thing ever dies." Hope can serve as a guiding light, providing solace during the darkest moments of uncertainty. It can inspire individuals to persevere, seek support, and keep moving forward in their recovery journey.

Self-Reflection Questions:

How has the awareness of the need for change in your life impacted your stress and anxiety levels?

Reflect on moments of stumbling or faltering in your recovery journey. How did these experiences affect your emotions, and how did you overcome them?

Consider the stressors related to the lack of control and unpredictability in recovery. How do you cope with the uncertainties of life without resorting to substances?

How do you manage the pressure to make the right choices consistently in your recovery? Are there strategies that have been effective in reducing decision-related stress?

Reflect on the shift from external motivators to internal motivations in your recovery. How has this transition impacted your anxiety levels, and how do you nurture your intrinsic motivation?

In moments of stress and anxiety, how do you turn to hope as a source of strength and resilience? How does hope influence your ability to navigate the challenges of change in recovery?

The Potential for Personal Growth and Resilience

Recovery from addiction is an arduous journey, laden with challenges and hurdles, but it is also a path paved with opportunities for profound personal growth and unwavering resilience. In the pursuit of long-term recovery, individuals discover that the very process of overcoming addiction becomes a catalyst for transformative change.

It's often said that "it's so important to make someone happy, but more important to start with yourself." In the context of addiction recovery, this self-focus is paramount. It involves self-compassion and self-care as foundational principles. Recovery demands a deep understanding and acceptance of oneself, acknowledging past mistakes while embracing the potential for change. This internal shift towards self-nurturing lays the foundation for personal growth.

In recovery, setting ambitious goals is encouraged, even if they seem beyond reach. These goals serve as beacons of hope and purpose. They provide individuals with something to strive for, pushing them beyond their comfort zones. When individuals aim high and aspire to achieve more than they previously thought possible, they embark on a journey of self-discovery and personal growth.

However, it's important to recognize that personal growth isn't solely about monumental achievements. "It is the little things in life that are vital. Little things make big things happen." The small victories and daily progress in recovery accumulate over time, leading to significant transformations. It's in the day-to-day choices, the commitment to sobriety, and the practice of healthier habits that personal growth truly blossoms.

Recovery often involves addressing negative thought patterns and emotional baggage that may have fueled addiction. These internal struggles can be likened to water trying to sink a ship, but as the saying goes, "all the water in the world cannot sink a ship unless it gets inside of it." Similarly, in recovery, all the worries, frustrations, anxieties, and negative emotions cannot overwhelm an individual unless they allow them to infiltrate their mind. Resilience is cultivated by learning to protect one's mental fortress, fortifying it against the destructive forces of self-doubt and negativity.

The recovery journey encourages individuals to shift their focus from fears and frustrations to hopes and dreams. "Consult not your fears but your hopes and your dreams. Think not about your frustrations but about your unfulfilled potential." This reframing of mindset fosters resilience by emphasizing the possibilities of the future rather than dwelling on past mistakes. Recovery becomes a journey of self-discovery, as individuals begin to unearth their unfulfilled potential, rediscovering their passions, dreams, and aspirations.

Moreover, individuals are encouraged to leave behind the regrets of past failures and focus on the endless possibilities that lie ahead. "Concern yourself not with what you tried and failed in but with what it is still possible for you to do." This forward-looking perspective fuels personal growth and resilience, as individuals learn to view each day as a new opportunity for progress.

Self-Reflection Questions:

How do you prioritize self-care and self-compassion in your journey of addiction recovery?

Reflect on the goals you've set for yourself in recovery. How have they pushed you to grow and evolve as an individual?

In what ways have you experienced personal growth in your recovery journey, both in significant milestones and everyday victories?

How do you protect your mind from negative thoughts and emotions that can threaten your recovery? Are there specific strategies or practices that have been helpful?
Consider the shift from focusing on fears and frustrations to hopes and dreams in your recovery. How has this change in mindset impacted your resilience and determination?

Reflect on your past failures and how you've approached them in your recovery. How have you embraced the concept of unfulfilled potential and the endless possibilities for personal growth?

Coping Mechanisms and Strategies for Managing Change

In the tumultuous journey of recovery from addiction, change is the ever-present companion. Life in recovery is marked by transformation, growth, and the constant adaptation to new circumstances. To navigate this path successfully, individuals must develop coping mechanisms and strategies to manage change effectively.

One essential principle to embrace in recovery is that "complaining is draining." Complaining diverts precious energy away from addressing the challenges at hand. Addiction recovery requires a significant amount of inner strength and focus, and complaining only siphons away the mental and emotional resources needed for healing and growth. Instead, individuals are encouraged to channel their energy towards proactive solutions.

Furthermore, it's crucial to recognize that we often can't discern the depth of another person's pain. As the saying goes, "the sad thing is, nobody ever really knows how much anyone else is hurting." In the world of addiction recovery, this insight carries particular significance. It encourages individuals to approach both themselves and others with empathy and understanding. The journey towards recovery is rife with personal struggles, and acknowledging this shared human experience can foster a sense of connection and support.

The mind is a powerful force in recovery, influencing emotions, decisions, and ultimately, the trajectory of one's life. Understanding that "your thoughts affect your emotions, your emotions affect your decisions, and your decisions affect your life" underscores the significance of maintaining a positive and constructive mindset. In the face of change, individuals can harness the power of their thoughts to navigate challenges with resilience and determination.

In the realm of relationships, recovery emphasizes balance. "Give but don't allow yourself to be used. Love but don't allow your heart to be abused. Trust but don't be naive." These principles are essential for maintaining healthy boundaries and self-respect. Recovery often involves rebuilding trust, both in oneself and in others. Learning to strike the right balance between generosity and self-preservation is a vital aspect of the journey.

In the pursuit of sobriety, it's essential to maintain one's individuality and voice. While it's crucial to "listen to others," particularly those who can offer guidance and support, individuals should "not lose their own voice." Personal growth in recovery is about discovering one's identity, values, and aspirations. It's essential to preserve one's authenticity while learning from others' experiences. Finally, recovery underscores the idea that what one truly desires may not come easy. "In life, what you really want never comes easy." This acknowledgment prepares individuals for the reality that recovery is a challenging journey. However, it also empowers them to take charge of their destiny.

A Journey of Transformation

Recovery encourages individuals to take responsibility for their healing and personal growth, as "no one else will make it happen for you."

Self-Reflection Questions:

How do you typically respond to change and challenges in your recovery journey? Are there specific coping mechanisms or strategies you find effective?

Reflect on the role of complaining in your life. How can you redirect your energy towards proactive solutions when faced with difficulties?

Consider the importance of empathy and understanding in recovery, both for yourself and others. How has this perspective influenced your interactions and relationships during your journey?

Reflect on the power of your thoughts and mindset in recovery. How do you maintain a positive and constructive outlook, especially in times of change and uncertainty?

How do you strike a balance between giving, loving, and trusting while preserving your boundaries and self-respect?

In what ways have you maintained your individuality and voice in your recovery journey? How do you integrate the wisdom of others while staying true to yourself?

Reflect on the idea that what you truly desire may not come easy. How has this understanding influenced your determination and commitment to your recovery goals?

Strategies for Reducing Anxiety and Fear in Long-Term Addiction Recovery

Addiction is a complex and challenging struggle that can have a profound impact on every aspect of a person's life. Achieving long-term recovery from addiction is a remarkable accomplishment, but it often comes with its own set of challenges, including anxiety and fear. These emotions can be powerful triggers for relapse, making it essential for individuals in recovery to develop effective strategies for managing them. This book will explore various strategies to reduce anxiety and fear while on the journey to long-term recovery, emphasizing the importance of finding inner happiness and positivity.

Strategies for Reducing Anxiety and Fear

Mindfulness and Meditation: Practicing mindfulness and meditation techniques can help individuals in recovery become more aware of their thoughts and feelings, allowing them to respond to anxiety and fear in a healthier way. By focusing on the present moment and learning to accept their emotions without judgment, individuals can gain greater control over their reactions to stressful situations.

Healthy Lifestyle Choices: Physical well-being is closely connected to emotional well-being. Engaging in regular exercise, maintaining a balanced diet, and getting adequate sleep can help reduce anxiety and fear. These healthy habits promote the release of endorphins and improve overall mood, making it easier to maintain a positive outlook.

Support Systems: Building a strong support network is crucial for those in recovery. Connecting with others who have similar experiences and feelings can provide a sense of belonging and understanding. Attending support group meetings, seeking therapy, and maintaining open communication with loved ones can all contribute to a healthier mindset.

Cognitive-Behavioral Therapy (CBT): CBT is a widely used therapeutic approach that focuses on identifying and challenging negative thought patterns. By working with a trained therapist, individuals can learn to reframe their thoughts and develop more constructive ways of thinking, which can help reduce anxiety and fear.

Stress Management Techniques: Learning how to manage stress effectively is vital in addiction recovery. Techniques such as deep breathing exercises, progressive muscle relaxation, and time management can help individuals cope with stressful situations and prevent them from triggering relapse.

Goal Setting and Planning: Setting realistic goals and creating a structured plan for recovery can provide a sense of purpose and direction. Achieving these goals can boost self-esteem and reduce anxiety, as individuals see tangible progress in their recovery journey.

Gratitude and Positivity: Shifting focus from what's lacking to what's present can greatly influence one's happiness. Practicing gratitude and fostering a positive mindset can help individuals find happiness from within, regardless of their external circumstances.

Self-Reflection Questions

What are some specific triggers for my anxiety and fear in my recovery journey, and how can I proactively address them?

Have I explored mindfulness and meditation as tools for managing my emotions, and if not, am I willing to give them a try?

How can I strengthen my support network and be more open about my struggles with addiction and recovery?

Have I considered seeking professional help, such as therapy or counseling, to address my anxiety and fear more effectively?

A Journey of Transformation

>What specific stress management techniques can I incorporate into my daily routine to reduce anxiety and fear?

>Am I setting achievable goals for my recovery, and do I have a structured plan in place to work towards them?

>How can I shift my focus towards gratitude and positivity in my daily life, finding happiness from within rather than relying on external factors?

Long-term recovery from addiction is an ongoing journey that requires dedication and the implementation of effective strategies to reduce anxiety and fear. By embracing mindfulness, building a support network, seeking professional help when needed, and cultivating positivity, individuals in recovery can enhance their emotional well-being and find happiness from within. Remember, life is a series of unique moments, and each one is an opportunity to choose happiness and make the most of our recovery journey.

Embracing Change as an Opportunity for Transformation in Addiction Recovery

Addiction recovery is a challenging journey that often requires individuals to confront their darkest moments and face the unknown. Change is an integral part of this process, and it can be a source of anxiety and fear. However, change also presents an opportunity for transformation and growth. This book will explore the concept of embracing change as a means of personal transformation in long-term addiction recovery, drawing inspiration from the statement, "When you have come to the edge of all the light that you know and are about to drop off into the darkness of the unknown, Faith is knowing One of two things will happen: There will be something solid to stand on, or you will be taught to fly."

Embracing Change for Transformation

Stepping into the Unknown: Recovery often begins when individuals recognize that their current path is unsustainable. Embracing change means acknowledging that the familiar, though destructive, is no longer an option. This step into the unknown can be frightening, but it is the first step towards transformation.

Faith and Hope: The statement emphasizes having faith and hope in the face of uncertainty. In recovery, faith can mean believing in oneself, the support of loved ones, or a higher power. It's essential to trust that change can lead to something better, even if the path forward is unclear.
Learning and Growth: Change presents an opportunity for learning and personal growth. As individuals let go of their addiction and old habits, they gain valuable insights into themselves and their abilities. This process of self-discovery is transformative and can lead to a more fulfilling life.
Resilience and Adaptability: Embracing change in recovery cultivates resilience and adaptability. When individuals face setbacks or roadblocks, they learn to treat defeat as temporary. This resilience is invaluable in maintaining sobriety and overcoming challenges.

Control over Emotions: Maintaining control over emotions is crucial in addiction recovery. Negative emotions can trigger relapse, making it essential to develop emotional resilience and not allow setbacks to dictate one's state of mind.

Adjustment and Flexibility: Recovery is not a linear path. Sometimes, plans go awry, but individuals must be willing to make necessary adjustments to stay on track. Embracing change includes being flexible and adaptable to new circumstances.

Finding Beauty in Life: The final part of the statement reminds us that life is a mix of joy and pain. In recovery, individuals learn to find moments of beauty and happiness even in the midst of challenges. These moments are a testament to their transformation.

Self-Reflection Questions

> Have I reached a point in my recovery where I'm willing to embrace change as an opportunity for transformation?
>
> What does faith mean to me in the context of my recovery journey? How can I cultivate more faith and hope in the face of uncertainty?
>
> How have I grown and learned during my recovery process? What insights have I gained about myself?
>
> Do I have the resilience to treat defeat as a temporary setback, and how can I strengthen my ability to bounce back from challenges?
>
> How can I maintain control over my emotions, ensuring they don't negatively influence my recovery?
>
> Am I willing to adjust and adapt when necessary to stay on the path of recovery, even if it means stepping into the unknown?
>
> What moments in my recovery journey have taken my breath away, and how can I continue to find beauty and happiness in the midst of life's challenges?

In long-term addiction recovery, embracing change is not just a necessity; it is a powerful opportunity for personal transformation. Through faith, resilience, and a willingness to adapt, individuals can learn to fly when faced with the unknown. As they navigate the uncharted territory of recovery, they discover the beauty and joy that life has to offer, proving that transformation is possible when change is embraced with an open heart and a determined spirit.

The Paradox of Resistance and Acceptance in Long-Term Addiction Recovery

Recovery from addiction is a transformative journey that often involves navigating the paradoxical concepts of resistance and acceptance. The path to long-term recovery is not always straightforward, and individuals may encounter internal and external obstacles. However, embracing the paradox of resistance and acceptance can be a powerful approach to finding happiness and fulfillment in recovery. This book will explore the idea that happiness is not in doing what one likes but in liking what one has to do, and how it relates to the principles of resistance and acceptance in addiction recovery.

The Paradox of Resistance and Acceptance

Resistance: Resistance in addiction recovery often manifests as the struggle against change, denial of the addiction's impact, or an unwillingness to accept help. This resistance can hinder progress and prolong the suffering associated with addiction.

Acceptance: Acceptance, on the other hand, is the acknowledgment of the addiction, the need for change, and the willingness to seek help and support. It is the foundation upon which recovery is built.

Happiness in Resistance: Paradoxically, happiness can be found in resistance when it is directed towards resisting the urge to relapse, resisting negative influences, and resisting self-destructive behaviors. In these instances, resistance becomes a tool for preserving and nurturing one's well-being.

Happiness in Acceptance: Acceptance leads to happiness when individuals embrace their recovery journey with an open heart and mind. It involves finding contentment in the process of change, being grateful for each day of sobriety, and deriving joy from the support and growth that recovery offers.

Contentment vs. Desires: The statement "Happiness is not having what you want, but wanting what you have" underscores the importance of contentment in recovery. True happiness comes from appreciating the progress made, even if it falls short of one's desires.

Active Engagement: The idea that "Happiness is a state of activity" emphasizes that happiness is not passive; it requires active engagement in one's recovery and life. It is the result of actively working on personal growth, relationships, and self-improvement.

Continuous Progress: The final part of the statement reminds us that life is a journey of continuous progress. Recovery is no different. It is about taking small steps each day, even if they seem insignificant, to inch closer to a better tomorrow.

A Journey of Transformation

Self-Reflection Questions

Do I find myself resisting aspects of my addiction recovery, and if so, what specific areas am I resisting?

How can I shift my resistance towards healthier forms, such as resisting the urge to relapse or negative influences?

Have I fully accepted the reality of my addiction and the need for change in my life? If not, what steps can I take to embrace acceptance?

What aspects of my recovery journey bring me happiness and contentment? How can I cultivate a greater sense of joy in the process of change?

How can I actively engage in my recovery, ensuring that I am not merely a passive observer but an active participant in my own transformation?

Do I appreciate the progress I've made in my recovery, even if it falls short of my desires? How can I cultivate contentment with where I am on this journey?

What small steps can I take each day to inch closer to a better tomorrow in my recovery and in life?

The paradox of resistance and acceptance in addiction recovery highlights the importance of finding happiness and contentment in the process of change. While resistance may be directed towards negative influences, acceptance paves the way for personal growth and transformation. Embracing these concepts and actively engaging in recovery allows individuals to derive happiness from the progress they make, ultimately leading to a more fulfilling and meaningful life in sobriety. As the statement suggests, it's not just about the years in your life, but the life in your years, and addiction recovery can be a powerful way to infuse life with meaning and purpose.

Overcoming the Natural Resistance to Change in Long-Term Addiction Recovery

Recovery from addiction is a transformative journey that often involves confronting and overcoming the natural resistance to change. This resistance can be fueled by a desire for instant gratification, fear of the unknown, or a tendency to compare oneself to others. However, recognizing and addressing this resistance is vital for achieving long-term recovery. This book explores the concept of resistance to change in addiction recovery, drawing wisdom from the statement, "We waste so many days waiting for the weekend. So many nights wanting morning. Our lust for future comfort is the biggest thief of life."

Understanding Resistance to Change

Desire for Comfort: Human beings are wired to seek comfort and familiarity. Addiction often provides a false sense of comfort, and the idea of leaving that comfort zone can be daunting.

Fear of the Unknown: Change inherently involves the unknown, and it's natural to fear what lies ahead in recovery. The uncertainty can trigger resistance.

Comparing to Others: Comparing one's progress or struggles to those of others can lead to feelings of inadequacy and resistance. Every recovery journey is unique, and comparisons can be detrimental.

Instant Gratification: Addiction often provides immediate gratification, while recovery requires patience and persistence. The desire for quick fixes can create resistance to the slower, but more sustainable, process of change.

Learning from Mistakes: The statement emphasizes that mistakes are meant for learning, not repeating. However, the fear of making mistakes and the shame associated with them can be a barrier to change.

Self-Worth and Overcoming: Overcoming addiction can lead to a sense of accomplishment and an increase in self-worth. However, individuals may struggle with self-perception based on their past actions and mistakes.

Resilience and Growth: The journey through addiction and recovery provides valuable life lessons and opportunities for growth. Understanding that failure is not final but a chance to start anew can help individuals embrace change.

Navigating Resistance and Embracing Change

Mindfulness: Mindfulness practices can help individuals stay present in the moment, reducing the focus on future comfort. Being mindful of the current step in the recovery journey can alleviate resistance.

Self-Compassion: Self-compassion involves treating oneself with kindness and understanding. It's crucial to acknowledge that everyone's path is unique, and progress should not be compared to others.

Patience and Persistence: Recovery is a gradual process that requires patience and persistence. Instead of seeking instant gratification, individuals should focus on the long-term rewards of sobriety.

Learning and Growth: Mistakes are opportunities for learning and growth. Embracing them as part of the recovery journey can lessen the fear of change.

A Journey of Transformation

Positive Self-Perception: It's essential to recognize that self-worth is not defined by past actions but by the strength and resilience to overcome addiction.

Resilience and Rebirth: Viewing failure as a chance for rebirth and renewal can help individuals find the strength to endure the hardships of recovery and embrace change.

Self-Reflection Questions

What aspects of my addiction recovery journey have I been resisting, and why?

How does my desire for future comfort impact my ability to fully engage in the present moment of my recovery?

Have I found myself comparing my progress or struggles to others in recovery, and how has this affected my mindset?

What strategies can I implement to become more mindful and present in my recovery journey, reducing my focus on future comfort?

How can I cultivate self-compassion and remind myself that my self-worth is not defined by my past actions but by my resilience and growth?

Have I embraced the idea that mistakes are opportunities for learning and growth, and how can I integrate this mindset into my recovery?

In what ways can I see failure as a chance for rebirth and renewal, viewing it as a stepping stone toward lasting recovery?

The natural resistance to change is a common obstacle on the path to long-term addiction recovery. Understanding the reasons behind this resistance and adopting strategies to navigate it is essential for sustained progress. By practicing mindfulness, cultivating self-compassion, embracing patience and persistence, learning from mistakes, and recognizing their own worth and resilience, individuals in recovery can overcome resistance and embark on a journey of transformation. As the statement suggests, we must not waste our days waiting for future comfort but instead focus on living in the present, where the real opportunities for change and growth lie.

Understanding the Resistance to Change in Long-Term Addiction Recovery

Recovery from addiction is a journey that often encounters significant resistance to change. The reluctance to embrace change can stem from a variety of factors, including fear of the unknown and attachment to temporary comforts. This book explores the reasons behind the resistance to change in addiction recovery and provides insights into why individuals often struggle with this process. Drawing inspiration from the statement, "Remember that time when we felt hopeless, got lost, and didn't know where to go? But here we are today. We survived," we will delve into the challenges of breaking free from addiction and the path to lasting happiness in recovery.

The Nature of Resistance to Change

Comfort in the Familiar: Addiction provides a false sense of comfort and familiarity, even if it is destructive. The prospect of change can be unsettling because it disrupts the routines and habits individuals have become accustomed to.

Attachment to Temporary Gratification: Addiction often offers immediate gratification, while recovery demands patience and long-term commitment. The allure of quick-fix solutions can lead to resistance to the slower, more sustainable process of change.

Fear of the Unknown: Change entails uncertainty, and human beings are naturally averse to the unknown. In recovery, individuals may fear losing their identity as an addict or may be anxious about the challenges that sobriety may bring.

Ignoring Truths for Temporary Happiness: Addiction often involves turning a blind eye to the negative consequences in pursuit of temporary happiness. Confronting these truths can be painful and create resistance to change.

The Quest for True Happiness: Many individuals seek true happiness but may not realize that it requires patience and perseverance. The pursuit of instant happiness can lead to resistance when genuine contentment doesn't materialize quickly.

Putting One's Whole Heart In: Recovery is a journey that requires wholehearted commitment and effort. Some may resist putting in the necessary work, preferring to take shortcuts or avoid discomfort.

The Power of Positive Thought: The statement reminds us of the power of positive thinking in overcoming negative thoughts. However, breaking free from addiction often involves challenging deeply ingrained negative thought patterns.

Navigating Resistance and Embracing Change

Self-Reflection: Self-reflection is essential for recognizing the reasons behind resistance to change. Individuals should explore their fears, attachments, and desires to better understand their resistance.

Patience and Persistence: It's crucial to acknowledge that lasting happiness and recovery take time. Patience and persistence are key in overcoming resistance to the slow, yet rewarding, process of change.

A Journey of Transformation

Support System: Building a strong support network is vital. Surrounding oneself with people who understand the challenges of recovery and can provide guidance and encouragement can help alleviate resistance.

Cognitive Behavioral Therapy (CBT): CBT is a therapeutic approach that helps individuals challenge and change negative thought patterns. It can be effective in addressing resistance by promoting more constructive thinking.

Mindfulness and Acceptance: Mindfulness practices and acceptance techniques can help individuals stay present in the moment and cope with the discomfort of change without judgment.

Self-Reflection Questions

> What aspects of my addiction recovery journey have I been resistant to, and what emotions or fears are contributing to this resistance?
>
> Have I recognized my attachment to temporary comforts and the desire for quick gratification in my recovery journey? How is this affecting my willingness to embrace lasting change?
>
> How have I confronted the uncomfortable truths about my addiction, and how can I use this self-awareness to overcome resistance to change?
>
> Do I understand that true happiness and lasting recovery require patience and perseverance? How can I cultivate these qualities in my journey?
>
> Have I put my whole heart into my recovery, or have I been taking shortcuts or avoiding discomfort? What changes can I make to fully commit to the process?
>
> How can I apply the power of positive thought and challenge negative thinking patterns to overcome resistance in my recovery?

Understanding the resistance to change in addiction recovery is essential for making progress toward long-term sobriety and happiness. By acknowledging the comfort of the familiar, recognizing the allure of temporary gratification, and confronting the fear of the unknown, individuals can begin to navigate and overcome their resistance to change. Through self-reflection, patience, persistence, support, therapy, mindfulness, and acceptance, individuals can embrace the transformative journey of recovery with open hearts and minds. The power of positive thought can lead them to discover lasting happiness, breaking free from the chains of addiction and achieving the fulfillment they seek.

Common Barriers to Embracing Change in Long-Term Addiction Recovery

Recovery from addiction is a challenging journey that often encounters common barriers to embracing change. These barriers can be both internal and external, making the path to long-term sobriety difficult. This book explores some of the common barriers individuals face in addiction recovery and how these obstacles can hinder their progress. Drawing inspiration from the statement, "Never let the negativity get to you. There are gonna be a lot of people you have to plow through, but as long you believe in yourself, that's all that matters," we will delve into the challenges of overcoming these barriers and finding the strength to embrace change.

Common Barriers to Change

Negativity from Others: External negativity from friends, family, or society can undermine an individual's belief in their ability to recover. People may express doubt or skepticism, which can be disheartening.

Self-Doubt: Individuals in recovery may struggle with self-doubt, questioning whether they have the strength or willpower to change. This self-doubt can undermine their confidence and motivation.

Fear of Failure: The fear of relapse or the fear of not being able to maintain sobriety can be a significant barrier. This fear can paralyze individuals, making them hesitant to embrace change.

Comfort in Familiarity: Addiction often provides a sense of comfort and familiarity, even if it is destructive. Letting go of these familiar habits and routines can be challenging.

Lack of Self-Belief: Some individuals may lack faith in themselves, believing that they are inherently flawed or incapable of change. This lack of self-belief can be a significant obstacle.

Resistance to New Ideas: Change often involves adopting new perspectives and ideas. Some may resist these new ways of thinking, clinging to old beliefs and behaviors.

External Factors: External factors such as stress, financial difficulties, or strained relationships can create additional barriers to change. These external challenges can be overwhelming.

Navigating Barriers to Embrace Change

Self-Confidence: Building self-confidence is essential. Individuals should focus on their strengths, past achievements, and the support they have received to bolster their belief in themselves.

Positive Self-Talk: Replace negative self-talk with positive affirmations. Encourage individuals in recovery to remind themselves of their capabilities and potential for change.

A Journey of Transformation

Resilience: Encourage resilience in the face of failures. Emphasize that failures are opportunities for learning and growth, not reasons to give up.

Seeking Support: Encourage individuals to seek support from a therapist, counselor, or support group. Sharing experiences and receiving guidance can be invaluable.

Cultivating Openness: Help individuals cultivate openness to new ideas and perspectives. Change often involves adopting healthier beliefs and behaviors, which may challenge old ways of thinking.

Self-Compassion: Encourage self-compassion. Recovery is a journey, and setbacks are a part of it. Being kind and forgiving toward oneself is crucial.

Self-Reflection Questions

>Have I encountered negativity from others regarding my addiction recovery, and how has it affected my self-belief and motivation?

>Do I struggle with self-doubt in my recovery journey, and what steps can I take to build more self-confidence in my ability to change?

>How has the fear of failure or relapse hindered my willingness to embrace change, and how can I develop resilience in the face of these fears?

>Am I holding onto familiar habits and routines from my addiction, and what can I do to let go of these comforts in favor of healthier choices?

>Have I explored and challenged any negative self-beliefs I may hold about my worth and capacity for change?

>Do I resist new ideas and perspectives that could promote positive change in my recovery journey, and how can I become more open to these possibilities?

>How can I practice self-compassion in my recovery, especially when faced with setbacks or challenges along the way?

Embracing change in long-term addiction recovery can be challenging, as individuals often encounter common barriers that impede their progress. External negativity, self-doubt, fear of failure, and comfort in familiarity are among the obstacles that individuals must overcome. However, by building self-confidence, engaging in positive self-talk, cultivating resilience, seeking support, fostering openness to new ideas, and practicing self-compassion, individuals can navigate these barriers and find the strength to embrace change. As the statement suggests, believing in oneself and having faith that there is a plan for recovery are essential steps in the journey towards lasting sobriety and personal transformation.

The Power of Acceptance in Facilitating Change in Long-Term Addiction Recovery

Recovery from addiction is a journey that often hinges on the power of acceptance. Acceptance is the cornerstone of lasting change, as it allows individuals to acknowledge their current situation, embrace their inner selves, and find the strength to overcome addiction. This book explores the profound role of acceptance in addiction recovery and the transformative power it holds. Drawing inspiration from the statement, "Stop looking for answers to your life from strangers. The answers to your life are within you and you only," we will delve into the significance of accepting one's inner truth and the importance of faith and patience in the process.

The Significance of Acceptance

Recognizing the Problem: The first step in addiction recovery is admitting the existence of a problem. Acceptance enables individuals to confront the reality of their addiction and take responsibility for their actions.

Embracing Vulnerability: Acceptance involves embracing vulnerability and acknowledging one's limitations. It encourages individuals to seek help and support, recognizing that they cannot overcome addiction on their own.

Self-Reflection and Inner Truth: Acceptance prompts self-reflection and the exploration of one's inner truth. It encourages individuals to ask the right questions and listen to their inner voice, understanding what truly makes them happy and at peace.

Overcoming Denial: Denial is a common defense mechanism in addiction. Acceptance dismantles this barrier, allowing individuals to see the impact of addiction on their lives and those around them.

Building Resilience: Acceptance fosters resilience by encouraging individuals to face their struggles and challenges head-on. It provides the foundation for lasting change and personal growth.

The Role of Faith and Patience

Faith and Prayer: Faith is a potent force in addiction recovery. It cannot be acquired without prayer and serves as a source of strength during the darkest moments. Faith endures through storms and helps individuals find their way into the light.

Endurance and Perseverance: True faith is enduring and persevering. It helps individuals weather the difficulties of recovery and maintain hope and patience in the face of setbacks.

Staying the Course: Recovery is a lifelong journey, and faith is essential for staying the course. It provides the motivation and belief that enduring sobriety is worth the effort.

A Journey of Transformation

Faith in Self: In addition to faith in a higher power, individuals must have faith in themselves. Believing in their ability to change and finding the inner strength to persevere is crucial.

Patience: Patience complements faith in recovery. It acknowledges that change takes time and that setbacks are part of the process. Patience allows individuals to stay committed to their journey despite challenges.

Self-Reflection Questions

Have I fully accepted the reality of my addiction and the need for change in my life? If not, what steps can I take to embrace acceptance?

How has my inner voice guided me towards understanding what truly makes me happy and at peace? What questions have I asked myself on this journey of self-discovery?

In what ways has denial hindered my progress in recovery, and how can I overcome it through acceptance?

How does faith play a role in my recovery, and what practices can I incorporate to strengthen my faith in both a higher power and myself?

Have I embraced the idea that recovery is a lifelong journey, and how can I cultivate the patience needed to stay the course despite setbacks?

How can I apply the power of acceptance, faith, and patience to navigate the challenges of addiction recovery more effectively?

The power of acceptance in addiction recovery is undeniable. It serves as the foundation for change by allowing individuals to recognize the problem, embrace vulnerability, and explore their inner truth. Acceptance dismantles denial, fosters resilience, and sets the stage for personal growth. Moreover, faith and patience are essential companions on this journey, providing strength, motivation, and endurance. Faith, whether in a higher power or in oneself, is the beacon that guides individuals through the darkest storms. Patience acknowledges the gradual nature of change and helps individuals persevere through challenges. Together, these elements form a potent force that can transform addiction recovery into a journey of healing, self-discovery, and enduring sobriety.

Strategies for Overcoming Resistance in Long-Term Addiction Recovery

Recovery from addiction is a challenging journey that often encounters resistance, both from within and from external factors. Overcoming this resistance is crucial for achieving long-term sobriety. This book explores effective strategies for overcoming resistance in addiction recovery, drawing inspiration from the statement, "You have something to offer that nobody else can offer.

There is something unique about you." We will delve into the importance of recognizing one's uniqueness, embracing happiness, and navigating the road to success in recovery.

Recognizing Your Uniqueness

Self-Appreciation: Recognizing your uniqueness is the first step in overcoming resistance. Understand that you have something valuable to offer the world, and that includes your journey of recovery.

Embracing Individuality: Embrace your individuality, personality, and unique gifts. No one else is quite like you, and your recovery journey is a testament to your strength and resilience.

Self-Worth: Recognize that your worth is not determined by past mistakes or addiction. You are more than your struggles, and acknowledging this can boost your self-esteem and motivation.
Embracing Happiness in Recovery

Letting Go of Expectations: Happiness in recovery comes from letting go of rigid expectations about how life should look. Celebrate your life for what it is, including the progress you've made in recovery.

Gratitude: Cultivate gratitude for the positive aspects of your life, no matter how small they may seem. Focusing on gratitude can shift your perspective and enhance your sense of happiness.

Mindfulness: Practice mindfulness to stay present in the moment. Accept your current circumstances without judgment and find contentment in the journey of recovery.
Navigating the Road to Success

Acknowledging Challenges: Recognize that the road to success is not a smooth, straight path. There will be challenges, setbacks, and obstacles along the way.

Determination and Perseverance: Overcome resistance by cultivating determination and perseverance. View challenges as opportunities for growth and learning rather than as insurmountable barriers.

Faith and Belief: Have faith in yourself and your ability to overcome resistance. Believing in your capacity for change is essential for maintaining motivation and resilience.

Building a Support System: Surround yourself with a supportive network of friends, family, or recovery groups. These connections can provide encouragement and guidance when facing resistance.

A Journey of Transformation

Self-Reflection Questions

How do I view my uniqueness, and how can I use my individuality as a source of strength in my recovery journey?

Have I been overly focused on expectations of what my life should look like in recovery? How can I shift my perspective to embrace the happiness that my journey brings?

What practices can I incorporate into my daily life to cultivate gratitude and mindfulness, enhancing my sense of contentment in recovery?

Am I prepared to acknowledge and confront the challenges that may arise on the road to success in recovery? How can I build determination and perseverance to overcome them?

Do I have faith in my ability to change and recover, and how can I strengthen this belief in myself?

Have I established a supportive network of individuals who can provide guidance and encouragement when I encounter resistance in my recovery journey?

Overcoming resistance in addiction recovery is a transformative process that involves recognizing your uniqueness, embracing happiness, and navigating the challenges on the road to success. By appreciating your individuality, letting go of expectations, and practicing gratitude and mindfulness, you can find contentment in your recovery journey. Additionally, building determination, faith, and a support system will empower you to conquer resistance and achieve long-term sobriety. Remember that your journey is one-of-a-kind, just like you, and that you have the inner strength to overcome any obstacle on the path to success in recovery.

Cultivating a Mindset of Acceptance and Adaptability in Long-Term Addiction Recovery

Long-term recovery from addiction is a journey filled with challenges, setbacks, and moments of growth. Cultivating a mindset of acceptance and adaptability is essential for navigating the twists and turns of this journey successfully. This book explores the significance of adopting such a mindset in addiction recovery, drawing inspiration from the statement, "The mystery of life is not a problem to be solved; it is a reality to be experienced." We will delve into the importance of patience, attitude, and resilience in facing the realities of recovery with grace and gratitude.

The Power of Acceptance and Adaptability

Embracing the Mystery of Life: Addiction recovery, like life itself, is a mystery that cannot be entirely solved. Embracing this mystery means accepting the uncertainties and unpredictabilities of the journey.

Defining Moments: Two defining aspects of your character become evident in recovery: patience during times of scarcity and attitude when abundance surrounds you. Patience allows you to persevere through the challenges, while a positive attitude keeps you grounded in gratitude during moments of success.

Inner Strength: Recognize that you are always stronger than you think you are. Cultivating a mindset of acceptance and adaptability helps you tap into this inner strength when facing adversity in recovery.

Positive Focus: Focusing on the positives in recovery can help overshadow the negatives. It's about shifting your perspective to see the progress you've made, no matter how small, and building on that foundation.

Letting Go of Fear: Fear is a common obstacle in recovery. Replacing fear with understanding allows you to approach challenges with a clear mind and the capacity to learn and grow.

Acknowledging Cycles: Recovery often follows a cyclical pattern, much like the weather. Every time it rains, it eventually stops. Similarly, every time you experience pain or setback in recovery, healing and progress follow.

Impermanence: Recognize the impermanence of both the good and the bad in life and recovery. Just as the night gives way to morning, difficult times will eventually pass.

Living with Love, Grace, and Gratitude: Happiness is not something external that can be obtained; it's a spiritual experience rooted in living each moment with love, grace, and gratitude.

Cultivating Acceptance and Adaptability

Self-Compassion: Practice self-compassion by accepting your imperfections and setbacks without self-judgment. This allows you to move forward with a more positive attitude.

Mindfulness and Presence: Cultivate mindfulness to stay present in the moment and accept the realities of your recovery journey without judgment.

Resilience Building: Develop resilience by viewing setbacks as opportunities for growth. Instead of dwelling on the past, focus on how you can adapt and move forward.

Gratitude Journaling: Maintain a gratitude journal to remind yourself of the positives in your life and recovery. Regularly reflect on the things you are thankful for.

Recovery Reset: Understand that you can restart your day at any time, even if you slip up. Allow yourself the flexibility to adapt and make changes as needed.

A Journey of Transformation

Self-Reflection Questions

How do I currently approach the uncertainties and unpredictabilities of my recovery journey, and how can I embrace the mystery of life more fully?

In what ways does patience manifest in my recovery when faced with scarcity or challenges, and how does my attitude influence my response to moments of abundance?

How can I tap into my inner strength and recognize that I am stronger than I think when confronting the difficulties of addiction recovery?

What strategies can I implement to shift my focus from the negatives to the positives in my recovery journey?

Have I learned to let go of fear and replace it with understanding when facing challenges in recovery? If not, what steps can I take to develop this mindset?

How can I acknowledge and accept the cyclical nature of recovery, understanding that pain and healing are part of the process?

Do I recognize the impermanence of both the good and the bad in my life and recovery? How can I use this awareness to maintain a positive attitude?

What practices can I incorporate into my daily life to live with love, grace, and gratitude, fostering a sense of happiness and contentment?

Cultivating a mindset of acceptance and adaptability is crucial for long-term addiction recovery. Embracing the mystery of life, demonstrating patience and a positive attitude, and tapping into your inner strength are vital components of this mindset. By focusing on the positives, letting go of fear, acknowledging cyclical patterns, understanding impermanence, and living with love, grace, and gratitude, you can navigate the challenges of recovery with resilience and a deep sense of fulfillment. Remember that you have the capacity to endure and adapt, and that each day offers a new opportunity to embrace the mysteries of life and recovery.

The Cycle of Change in Long-Term Addiction Recovery

Long-term recovery from addiction is often described as a journey through the cycle of change. This cycle encompasses stages of self-discovery, growth, and transformation. In this book, we will explore the concept of the cycle of change and how it applies to addiction recovery. Drawing inspiration from the statement, "The strongest force in the universe is a human being living consistently with their identity," we will discuss the importance of self-belief, hard work, resilience, and surrounding oneself with positivity during this transformative journey.

Understanding the Cycle of Change

Self-Identity and Belief: The cycle of change begins with a strong sense of self-identity and belief in oneself. Acknowledging that you have the potential for transformation and believing in your ability to overcome addiction are crucial first steps.

Breaking Limitations: Many individuals limit themselves by underestimating their capabilities. However, it's essential to recognize that your mind plays a significant role in determining how far you can go in your recovery journey.

The Power of Belief: Your beliefs about what you can achieve shape your reality. When you believe in your capacity for change, you are more likely to work hard and persevere through challenges.

Hard Work and Courage: Recovery is not an easy path. It requires hard work, courage, and determination. Achieving lasting sobriety often involves overcoming obstacles and setbacks.

Turning Negativity into Positivity: When faced with criticism or setbacks, it's crucial to turn them into opportunities for growth and positivity. This mindset shift can be a catalyst for change.

Staying Positive and Hopeful: Maintaining a positive outlook and holding onto hope are essential. Recovery may be challenging, but a positive attitude can make the journey more manageable.

Continuous Learning and Self-Improvement: Be open to criticism and keep learning. Recovery is an ongoing process of self-improvement and personal growth.

Surrounding Yourself with Positivity

Choosing Positive Influences: Surround yourself with happy, warm, and genuine people who support your recovery journey. Positive influences can bolster your determination and motivation.

The Scheme of Things: Understand the dynamics of life—good things often require hard work and perseverance, while negative choices can be easy to make. Recognize that the effort you invest in recovery is worthwhile.

A Journey of Transformation

Overcoming Challenges: Accept that recovery will have its challenges, but believe that you can overcome them. Your identity and consistency in living by it will drive you forward.

Resilience and Transformation: Embrace the cycle of change as an opportunity for resilience and transformation. Every stage of the cycle brings you closer to a stronger, more authentic self.

Self-Reflection Questions

Do I believe in my capacity for change and recovery? How can I strengthen my self-identity and self-belief in this journey?

Have I limited myself by underestimating what I can achieve in my recovery? What steps can I take to break through these limitations?

How has my belief in my ability to overcome addiction shaped my actions and determination in recovery?

What role has hard work and courage played in my journey, and how have I persevered through challenges?

Can I recall instances when I turned criticism or setbacks into something positive in my recovery journey?

How do I maintain a positive outlook and hope during difficult times in recovery?

Am I open to criticism and committed to continuous learning and self-improvement in my recovery?

Have I surrounded myself with positive and supportive individuals who enhance my determination and motivation?

What strategies can I implement to stay resilient and embrace the cycle of change as an opportunity for transformation in my recovery?

The cycle of change in long-term addiction recovery represents a transformative journey that begins with self-identity and belief in oneself. Overcoming limitations, working hard, and maintaining resilience are key components of this cycle. Turning negativity into positivity and surrounding oneself with positivity can help individuals persevere through challenges. It is essential to understand the dynamics of life and recognize that recovery may be challenging, but the effort invested is worthwhile. By embracing the cycle of change, individuals can transform themselves, live consistently with their identity, and achieve lasting sobriety and personal growth.

Exploring the Stages of Change in Long-Term Addiction Recovery

Long-term recovery from addiction is a journey that involves distinct stages of change, each marked by unique challenges and opportunities for growth. In this book, we will explore these stages and how they apply to the process of addiction recovery. Drawing inspiration from the statement, "Can you remember who you were before the world told you who you should be?" we will delve into the importance of self-discovery, determination, learning from mistakes, and self-improvement in the recovery journey.

The Stages of Change

Pre-Contemplation: In this stage, individuals may not yet recognize the need for change. They may be unaware of the impact of addiction on their lives and the potential benefits of recovery.

Contemplation: At this point, individuals start to acknowledge the consequences of addiction. They consider the idea of change but may still be ambivalent about taking action.

Preparation: In the preparation stage, individuals actively plan for change. They may seek information about treatment options, support networks, and strategies for recovery.

Action: This stage involves taking concrete steps towards recovery. Individuals may enter treatment programs, therapy, or support groups, and make significant efforts to abstain from substance use.

Maintenance: After achieving initial success in recovery, the maintenance stage focuses on consolidating gains and preventing relapse. Individuals continue to practice new coping skills and strategies.

Termination: While not always reached, the termination stage signifies that the individual has successfully integrated recovery into their life. They no longer struggle with cravings or relapse.

Exploring the Stages

Remembering Your Authentic Self: In the early stages of recovery, it's essential to reconnect with your authentic self, free from the expectations and judgments of others. Who were you before addiction took hold of your life?

Dreaming and Taking Action: Recovery often begins with a dream of a healthier, substance-free life. To make this dream a reality, you must be willing to pay the price, taking action and seeking the help you need.

Seizing Opportunities: Recovery doesn't always require extraordinary opportunities. It's about seizing common occasions, such as seeking support or therapy, and making them significant steps toward a better life.

A Journey of Transformation

Learning from Mistakes: It's crucial to acknowledge that people make mistakes, especially in recovery. Rather than dwelling on past choices, focus on learning from them. Every mistake is an opportunity for growth.

Personal Growth: Recovery is a journey of self-improvement. Doing something today that your future self will be proud of means actively working on personal growth and positive change.

Self-Reflection Questions

At what stage of change am I currently in my recovery journey? Have I progressed through the stages, and if not, what steps can I take to move forward?

Can I recall a time in my life before addiction, when I was more true to my authentic self? How can I reconnect with that person as I work towards recovery?

What dreams and aspirations do I have for my substance-free life, and what concrete actions am I willing to take to make those dreams come true?

How can I identify and seize common occasions in my daily life to strengthen my recovery and build a healthier future?

Have I acknowledged and learned from my past mistakes in recovery? How can I turn these mistakes into opportunities for growth and change?

In what ways can I actively work on personal growth and self-improvement to become the person my future self will be proud of?

Exploring the stages of change in long-term addiction recovery is essential for understanding the journey ahead. Each stage presents unique challenges and opportunities for growth, from reconnecting with your authentic self to actively pursuing your dreams. Seizing common occasions, learning from past mistakes, and committing to personal growth are all vital aspects of the recovery process. Remember that recovery is a transformative journey that allows you to rediscover and shape your true self, making your future self proud of the person you are becoming.

Pre-contemplation:
The First Step Towards Long-Term Addiction Recovery

Long-term recovery from addiction is a journey marked by various stages, each with its unique challenges and opportunities for growth. The first stage, pre-contemplation, is a pivotal point where individuals may not yet recognize the need for change. In this book, we will explore the pre-contemplation stage and its significance in addiction recovery. Drawing inspiration from the statement, "Happiness is letting go of what you think your life is supposed to look like and celebrating it for everything that it is," we will discuss the importance of embracing uncertainty, self-discovery, and the potential for transformation even when change is not yet contemplated.

Understanding Pre-contemplation

Unawareness of the Problem: In the pre-contemplation stage, individuals may not fully realize or acknowledge the extent of their addiction. They may be in denial or believe that their substance use is not problematic.

Lack of Motivation for Change: Individuals in this stage often lack motivation to address their addiction. They may not see the negative consequences or may minimize them.

Resistance to Treatment: People in pre-contemplation are often resistant to treatment or intervention. They may reject offers of help and continue their addictive behaviors.

Embracing Uncertainty: Pre-contemplation is a stage where individuals may not yet see the path to recovery. It's an opportunity to embrace uncertainty and be open to the possibility of change in the future.

Self-Discovery: Despite the resistance to change, the pre-contemplation stage can also be a time for self-discovery. Individuals may reflect on their values, aspirations, and the discrepancies between their current situation and their desired life.

Seeds of Transformation: Even when change is not actively contemplated, the pre-contemplation stage may plant the seeds of transformation. Experiences during this stage can serve as catalysts for future readiness to change.

Embracing Pre-contemplation

Recognizing the Stage: The first step in embracing pre-contemplation is recognizing that you may be in this stage. Acknowledge where you are in your addiction journey without self-judgment.

Self-Reflection: Use this time for self-reflection. Explore your motivations, values, and the impact of addiction on your life. Consider what you may want for your future.

Seeking Support: Even if you're not yet ready to take action, it can be helpful to seek support and information about addiction and recovery. Knowledge can empower you when the time for change comes.

Cultivating Patience: Understand that change is a process, and it may take time for you to progress to the next stages of recovery. Cultivate patience with yourself.

Self-Reflection Questions

> Do I recognize that I may be in the pre-contemplation stage of addiction recovery, and am I open to acknowledging my current situation without judgment?

A Journey of Transformation

> How has my addiction affected my life, and have I taken the time for self-reflection to explore my values and aspirations?
>
> Have I sought support or information about addiction and recovery, even if I'm not yet ready to take action? How can knowledge empower me in the future?
>
> Am I cultivating patience with myself, understanding that change is a process, and I may progress to the next stages of recovery in my own time?

Pre-contemplation is the first stage in the journey of addiction recovery, where individuals may not yet recognize the need for change. It is a pivotal point for self-reflection, self-discovery, and embracing uncertainty. While change may not be actively contemplated, this stage can plant the seeds of transformation that will eventually lead to a readiness for change. Recognizing where you are, seeking support, and cultivating patience with yourself are crucial aspects of navigating the pre-contemplation stage on the path to long-term recovery. Remember that every step in the right direction, no matter how small, has the potential to lead to significant transformation in your life.

Contemplation: A Bridge to Long-Term Addiction Recovery

Contemplation is a critical stage in the journey of addiction recovery, where individuals begin to recognize the need for change and consider their options for a healthier, substance-free life. In this book, we will explore the contemplation stage and its significance in the process of addiction recovery. Drawing inspiration from the statement, "Remember that time when we felt hopeless, got lost, and didn't know where to go? But here we are today. We survived," we will discuss the importance of embracing the pain, self-acceptance, and the determination needed to take the first steps toward recovery.

Understanding the Contemplation Stage

Recognition of Hopelessness: In the contemplation stage, individuals often come to terms with the hopelessness that addiction has brought into their lives. They begin to acknowledge the need for change.

Embracing Pain and Acceptance: It is during this stage that individuals may choose to embrace the pain of their addiction and accept it as a reality. Rather than denying or avoiding it, they confront it.

Desire for Rebirth: Contemplation is marked by a desire for rebirth—a longing to break free from the chains of addiction and experience a renewed sense of self.

Process of Learning and Growth: The contemplation stage is an opportunity for deep learning and personal growth. It involves self-reflection and an exploration of the reasons behind addiction.

Taking Ownership: Individuals in this stage often realize that recovery is something they must do for themselves. It's about self-honor and living life with intention.

Building Resilience: Contemplation is a time to build emotional and mental resilience. It requires a willingness to swim in the deep end of life's challenges and emerge stronger.

Embracing Contemplation

Self-Reflection: Engage in self-reflection to explore your feelings about addiction and the impact it has had on your life. What are your reasons for considering change?

Acceptance of Pain: Instead of fighting pain, embrace it as a part of the healing process. Accept that pain can be a catalyst for transformation and growth.

Self-Compassion: Practice self-compassion and self-acceptance. Understand that taking steps toward recovery is an act of self-love and self-honor.

Setting Intentions: Contemplation is an excellent time to set intentions for your recovery journey. What do you want to achieve, and how do you envision your life without addiction?

Building Support: Seek support from friends, family, or professional resources who can guide you through the contemplation stage and provide assistance when you decide to take action.

Self-Reflection Questions

Have I reached the contemplation stage in my addiction recovery journey, and what factors led me to consider change?

How have I embraced the pain and hopelessness that addiction has brought into my life, and have I accepted it as a catalyst for transformation?

In what ways have I shown self-compassion and self-acceptance as I contemplate my recovery options?

Have I set clear intentions for my recovery journey, and can I envision a life free from addiction?

How have I built a support system to assist me during the contemplation stage and beyond?

The contemplation stage in addiction recovery is a pivotal moment where individuals begin to recognize the need for change and consider their options for a healthier future. It involves embracing pain, accepting hopelessness, and desiring rebirth. During this stage, self-reflection, self-compassion, and setting intentions are crucial for paving the way toward recovery. Embracing the pain and understanding that change is an act of self-love and self-honor can propel individuals

A Journey of Transformation

toward taking action and seeking the support needed to embark on the path of long-term recovery. Remember, you have the resilience and strength to emerge from the deep end of life's challenges stronger than ever before.

Preparation: Equipping Yourself for Long-Term Addiction Recovery

The preparation stage in addiction recovery is a crucial period where individuals actively plan for change and commit to the journey toward lasting sobriety. In this book, we will delve into the significance of the preparation stage and how it empowers individuals seeking long-term recovery from addiction. Drawing inspiration from the statement, "Don't let the concept of change scare you as much as the prospect of remaining unhappy," we will discuss the importance of embracing change, the impact of support systems, and the value of tools and lessons in the recovery process.

Understanding the Preparation Stage

Active Planning: In the preparation stage, individuals move beyond contemplation and take active steps to plan for change. They may seek information about treatment options, support networks, and strategies for recovery.

Acknowledgment of Unhappiness: This stage is marked by the acknowledgment that addiction has led to unhappiness and a desire to break free from its grip. The prospect of remaining unhappy becomes more daunting than the fear of change.

Building a Support System: Individuals in the preparation stage often recognize the importance of building a strong support system. They seek guidance and assistance from friends, family, or professional resources.

Tools for Recovery: Preparation involves acquiring the necessary tools and coping mechanisms to navigate the challenges of addiction recovery successfully. These tools may include therapy, self-help techniques, and relapse prevention strategies.

Learning from Lessons: The preparation stage allows individuals to reflect on their past experiences and the valuable lessons learned from their addiction journey. These lessons serve as motivation for change.

Commitment to Change: Individuals in this stage make a firm commitment to change and embark on their recovery journey with determination and a clear plan.

Embracing the Preparation Stage

Embracing Change: Understand that change is not something to fear but a powerful means to break free from the cycle of addiction and unhappiness. Embrace the opportunity for transformation.

Recognizing Unhappiness: Acknowledge that unhappiness is a driving force for change. Use this realization as motivation to seek a healthier, substance-free life.

Building a Support System: Invest in building a strong support system of friends, family, or professionals who can provide guidance and assistance throughout your recovery journey.

Utilizing Tools for Recovery: Actively engage with the tools and resources available for recovery, such as therapy, support groups, and coping strategies. Recognize their value in helping you maintain sobriety.

Applying Lessons Learned: Reflect on the lessons you've learned from past experiences with addiction. Understand that these lessons have the potential to guide you toward a brighter future. Committing to Change: Make a firm commitment to change and develop a clear plan for your recovery journey. Understand that this commitment is a step toward a more fulfilling life.

Self-Reflection Questions

Have I moved into the preparation stage of my addiction recovery, and what active steps have I taken to plan for change?

How does the acknowledgment of my unhappiness with addiction motivate me to seek lasting sobriety?

Have I built a strong support system to assist me on my recovery journey, and how can I further strengthen this network?

What tools and coping mechanisms have I acquired or plan to use during my recovery, and how do I recognize their importance?

What valuable lessons have I learned from my past experiences with addiction, and how can I apply these lessons to guide me toward a brighter future?

Am I fully committed to change, and have I developed a clear plan for my recovery journey?

The preparation stage in addiction recovery is a pivotal period where individuals actively plan for change and commit to the journey of long-term sobriety. Embracing change and acknowledging the unhappiness caused by addiction serve as powerful motivators for transformation. Building a robust support system, utilizing tools for recovery, and applying lessons learned from past experiences are crucial aspects of this stage. Commitment to change and the development of a clear plan are fundamental for embarking on a fulfilling and substance-free life. Remember that the preparation stage is a bridge that leads to lasting happiness and recovery from addiction.

A Journey of Transformation

Action: The Catalyst for Long-Term Addiction Recovery

The action stage in addiction recovery is a critical turning point, where individuals transition from planning and contemplation to taking concrete steps toward lasting sobriety. In this book, we will explore the significance of the action stage and how it empowers individuals seeking long-term recovery from addiction. Drawing inspiration from the statement, "You build on failure. You use it as a stepping stone," we will discuss the importance of leaving the past behind, embracing emotions, and the necessity of change to achieve personal growth and recovery.

Understanding the Action Stage

Stepping Stones from Failure: The action stage is marked by a willingness to build on past failures and use them as stepping stones toward a brighter future. It involves letting go of the past's burdens while retaining the lessons learned.

Closing the Door on the Past: Individuals in the action stage actively close the door on their addiction past. They recognize that dwelling on past mistakes is unproductive and that it's time to move forward.

Embracing Emotions: In this stage, people give themselves permission to feel a wide range of emotions without shame. They understand that emotions are a natural part of the recovery journey.

Change as a Necessity: The action stage emphasizes the importance of change as a necessary component of personal growth and recovery. It requires a commitment to evolving and leaving behind old habits.

Maintaining Positivity: Even when faced with challenges, individuals in the action stage keep their heads up, focusing on the blessings and opportunities in their lives rather than dwelling on negativity.

Taking Action in Recovery

Learning from Failure: Understand that failure is not a dead-end but a valuable teacher. Use past failures as stepping stones to guide you toward healthier choices and behaviors.

Closing the Door on the Past: Actively work on closing the door on your addiction past. While you don't forget your mistakes, you no longer allow them to consume your energy, time, or space.

Embracing Emotions: Give yourself permission to feel and express your emotions, both positive and negative. Understand that emotional healing is an integral part of the recovery process.

Embracing Change: Embrace change as a necessary part of personal growth and recovery. Recognize that clinging to the past prevents you from evolving and improving yourself.

Maintaining Positivity: Keep your head up and focus on the blessings in your life. A positive outlook can provide the strength and motivation needed to overcome challenges.

Self-Reflection Questions

> Have I transitioned into the action stage of my addiction recovery, and how have I used past failures as stepping stones for growth?
>
> Am I actively working on closing the door on my addiction past, and how do I ensure that I don't dwell on past mistakes while retaining the lessons learned?
>
> Have I given myself permission to embrace and express my emotions, recognizing their importance in my healing process?
>
> How am I embracing change as a necessary component of personal growth and recovery, and what steps have I taken to evolve and leave behind old habits?
>
> Do I maintain a positive outlook, even in the face of challenges, and how does this perspective help me see the blessings in my life?

The action stage in addiction recovery represents a pivotal moment where individuals move from contemplation and planning to taking concrete steps toward lasting sobriety. It involves building on past failures, closing the door on the addiction past, embracing emotions, and embracing change as a catalyst for personal growth. Maintaining a positive outlook helps individuals see the blessings and opportunities in their lives, even in the face of challenges. Remember that taking action is the key to achieving long-term recovery and building a brighter future free from addiction.

Maintenance: Sustaining the Light Within for Long-Term Recovery

The maintenance stage in addiction recovery represents a journey marked by commitment, self-discovery, and the continuous effort to nurture the light from within. In this book, we will explore the significance of the maintenance stage and its role in sustaining long-term recovery from addiction. Drawing inspiration from the statement, "People are like stained-glass windows. They sparkle and shine when the sun is out, but when the darkness sets in, their true beauty is revealed only if there is light from within," we will discuss the importance of self-belief, self-worth, personal growth, and the relentless pursuit of one's best self.

Understanding the Maintenance Stage

Commitment to Recovery: In the maintenance stage, individuals have made significant progress and are committed to maintaining their sobriety. They understand that recovery is an ongoing journey.

A Journey of Transformation

Discovering Inner Light: This stage encourages individuals to discover and nurture their inner light—their unique gifts, strengths, and the qualities that make them special.

Self-Belief: People in the maintenance stage have developed self-belief and recognize that confidence in oneself is a key element of success in recovery.

Self-Worth: The maintenance stage emphasizes the importance of self-worth, emphasizing that feeling worthy and deserving of a better life is foundational to sustained recovery.

Personal Growth: It is during this stage that individuals actively engage in personal growth and self-improvement efforts. They continuously seek opportunities to enhance themselves.

Continuous Self-Reflection: Self-reflection remains a constant companion in the maintenance stage. Individuals assess their progress, identify areas of improvement, and set new goals.

Sustaining the Light Within

Nurturing Inner Light: Continue nurturing your inner light—the qualities that make you unique and valuable. Recognize that your light shines brightest when you believe in yourself.

Self-Belief: Cultivate self-belief as the foundation of your recovery journey. Understand that success in recovery begins with a deep sense of confidence in your abilities.

Self-Worth: Affirm your self-worth daily. Remind yourself that you are deserving of a better life, and believe in your capacity to sustain recovery.

Personal Growth: Stay committed to personal growth and self-improvement. Seek out opportunities for learning and self-enhancement to continue evolving.

Continuous Self-Reflection: Maintain a practice of self-reflection. Regularly assess your progress, set new goals, and adapt to the changing dynamics of your recovery journey.

Relentless Pursuit: Approach recovery as a relentless pursuit of your personal best. Understand that your only competition is yourself, and strive to outwork your past self.

Self-Reflection Questions

> Have I entered the maintenance stage of my addiction recovery, and how have I committed to sustaining my sobriety?

> What qualities within me do I consider my inner light, and how can I nurture and showcase them to maintain my recovery?

How has self-belief played a role in my recovery journey, and how can I further cultivate confidence in myself?

What steps have I taken to affirm my self-worth and maintain a belief in my deservingness of a better life in recovery?

How am I actively engaging in personal growth and self-improvement efforts to continue evolving as a person in recovery?

Do I practice continuous self-reflection to assess my progress, set new goals, and adapt to the changing dynamics of my recovery journey?

The maintenance stage in addiction recovery signifies a commitment to sustaining the light within—the qualities that make individuals unique and valuable. It is a journey marked by self-belief, self-worth, personal growth, and a relentless pursuit of one's best self. By nurturing their inner light, individuals can continue to shine brightly, even in the face of darkness. This stage underscores the importance of self-belief and self-worth as foundational elements of sustained recovery. As individuals continuously engage in personal growth and self-reflection, they empower themselves to maintain their sobriety and make every day count on their path to long-term recovery.

Navigating the Challenges and Opportunities at Each Stage of Addiction Recovery

The journey of addiction recovery is not a linear path but a series of stages, each presenting its own challenges and opportunities for growth. In this book, we will explore the significance of navigating the challenges and seizing the opportunities at each stage of addiction recovery. Drawing inspiration from the statement, "One of the reasons people cling to their hates so stubbornly is because they sense, when hate is gone, they will be forced to deal with pain," we will discuss how facing pain, choosing joy, taking chances, and embracing life are essential elements in the recovery process.

Understanding the Stages of Addiction Recovery

Recognition of Hate and Pain: The initial stage of addiction recovery often involves recognizing the hatred or resentment that may have fueled addiction. This recognition can be painful but is essential for growth.

Character Development: As individuals progress through recovery, how they respond to the challenges and setbacks defines their character. Overcoming adversity strengthens their resilience and character.

Choosing Positivity: Recovery provides individuals with the opportunity to choose positivity over negativity each day. The decision to wake up and embrace joy sets the tone for their journey.

A Journey of Transformation

Embracing Growth: Taking chances and making mistakes are integral to personal growth. Recovery is not about perfection but about learning from failures and practicing courage.

Rising from Pain: Recovery allows individuals to rise from the pain and trauma that may have fueled addiction. It is a transformative process that can lead to a renewed appreciation for life.

Embracing Humanity: Recovery encourages individuals to embrace their humanity, acknowledging their flaws and vulnerabilities while striving for improvement.

Navigating Challenges and Seizing Opportunities

Facing Pain: Acknowledge and face the pain that may have contributed to addiction. Understand that healing requires confronting and processing these emotions.

Character Building: Recognize that how you respond to challenges in recovery defines your character. Use setbacks as opportunities for growth and resilience-building.

Choosing Joy: Each morning, consciously choose joy and positivity. Understand that your mindset can greatly influence the quality of your recovery journey.

Embracing Growth: Embrace personal growth by taking chances and being willing to make mistakes. Understand that failure is a stepping stone to courage and self-improvement.

Rising from Pain: Embrace the opportunity to rise from the pain and trauma of addiction. Treasure life as a precious gift and a source of renewed purpose.

Embracing Humanity: Embrace your humanity, acknowledging that recovery is a journey filled with ups and downs. Seek support, understanding, and empathy as you navigate this path.

Self-Reflection Questions

> Have I recognized the presence of hate or pain in my life that may have contributed to my addiction, and how am I addressing these emotions in my recovery?

> How have my responses to challenges and setbacks in recovery shaped my character and resilience?

> Do I consciously choose joy and positivity each morning to set a positive tone for my recovery journey?

> How am I embracing personal growth by taking chances and being willing to make mistakes in my recovery?

Have I embraced the opportunity to rise from the pain and trauma of addiction, and how do I treasure life as a precious gift?

In what ways am I embracing my humanity and seeking support and understanding as I navigate the challenges and opportunities of addiction recovery?

The journey of addiction recovery is marked by various stages, each presenting its unique challenges and opportunities for growth. Recognizing and addressing hate or pain, building character through resilience, choosing positivity, embracing personal growth, and rising from pain are essential elements of this transformative process. Ultimately, recovery is about embracing one's humanity and treasuring life as a precious gift. By navigating the challenges and seizing the opportunities at each stage, individuals can embark on a path of healing, self-discovery, and long-lasting recovery.

Common Experiences and Emotions During Each Stage of Addiction Recovery

Addiction recovery is a journey filled with a spectrum of emotions and experiences that evolve as individuals progress through various stages. In this book, we will explore the common experiences and emotions encountered during each stage of addiction recovery. Drawing inspiration from the statement, "You need to go through some stuff to really appreciate life and understand what it means to persevere, overcome, and have faith," we will discuss the challenges, triumphs, and personal growth that accompany each stage of recovery.

Understanding the Stages of Addiction Recovery

Initial Acknowledgment: The first stage often involves acknowledging the existence of addiction. Emotions during this phase may include denial, fear, guilt, and a sense of hopelessness.

Contemplation and Commitment: In the contemplation stage, individuals weigh the pros and cons of recovery. Emotions may fluctuate between ambivalence, uncertainty, and the desire for change.

Commitment brings determination and hope.

Action: The action stage is characterized by active steps toward recovery. Emotions shift towards determination, optimism, and a sense of empowerment as individuals take control of their lives.

Maintenance: In this stage, emotions may include pride, self-confidence, and contentment as individuals work to maintain their recovery. However, challenges and occasional setbacks can also bring frustration and anxiety.

Reflection and Growth: As individuals reflect on their journey and continue to grow, they experience a sense of self-discovery, resilience, and an appreciation for life's opportunities.

A Journey of Transformation

Common Experiences and Emotions in Each Stage

Initial Acknowledgment: Recognize that feelings of denial and hopelessness are common in the early stages of recovery. Seek support and understanding to help navigate these emotions.

Contemplation and Commitment: Understand that ambivalence and uncertainty are natural during this phase. Focus on the desire for positive change and make a commitment to recovery.

Action: Embrace determination and empowerment as you take action in your recovery. Celebrate each milestone and stay focused on your goals.

Maintenance: Recognize that maintaining recovery can be both rewarding and challenging. Seek support during difficult times and draw strength from your achievements.

Reflection and Growth: Embrace self-discovery and resilience as you reflect on your journey. Appreciate the growth and newfound appreciation for life that recovery brings.

Self-Reflection Questions

Have I acknowledged my addiction and experienced emotions such as denial, fear, or guilt? How can I seek support to navigate these feelings?

Am I currently in the contemplation or commitment stage of recovery? How am I dealing with ambivalence and uncertainty, and what steps can I take to strengthen my commitment to change?

In the action stage, how have determination and empowerment propelled me forward in my recovery journey?

What challenges have I faced during the maintenance stage, and how do I seek support and stay focused on my goals?

As I reflect on my recovery journey, what aspects of self-discovery and resilience have I experienced, and how has my appreciation for life evolved?

Addiction recovery is a multifaceted journey, and individuals encounter a range of emotions and experiences as they progress through its various stages. From the initial acknowledgment of addiction to the contemplation, commitment, action, maintenance, and reflection and growth stages, each phase brings its unique challenges and triumphs. By recognizing the common experiences and emotions during each stage and seeking support when needed, individuals can navigate their recovery journey with resilience, determination, and an ever-deepening appreciation for life and its possibilities.

Strategies for Progressing Through the Cycle of Change in Addiction Recovery

Addiction recovery is often likened to a cycle of change, a journey that involves various stages, challenges, and transformations. In this book, we will explore strategies for progressing through the cycle of change in addiction recovery. Drawing inspiration from the statement, "Hope is not pretending that troubles don't exist. It is the hope that it won't last forever," we will discuss the importance of hope, honesty, self-discovery, and resilience as key strategies to navigate the recovery journey successfully.

Embracing Hope and Honesty

Hope as a Catalyst: Hope is a powerful catalyst in addiction recovery. It's not about denying the existence of troubles but believing in the possibility of healing, growth, and overcoming difficulties.

Honesty as a Foundation: Honesty plays a pivotal role in recovery. It means being truthful about one's desires, needs, feelings, and identity. It is the first step towards self-discovery.

Acknowledging Challenges: Recognize that challenges are part of the recovery journey. Instead of denying them, face them with hope and the belief that they won't last forever.

Self-Discovery and Resilience

Discovering Yourself: As you progress through the cycle of change, take the time to discover and understand yourself better. Reflect on your desires, needs, and who you are as a person in recovery.

Getting Lost to Find Yourself: Understand that it's okay to get lost occasionally. Sometimes, losing your way is a crucial part of finding yourself and discovering your true path in recovery.

Trusting Yourself: Trust in yourself and your abilities. You've already survived significant challenges, and you can trust that you'll overcome whatever comes your way in recovery.

Finding Meaning: Embrace the belief that one day, everything will make sense. Recognize that the worries and uncertainties you face in recovery are temporary, and they will ultimately lead to personal growth and understanding.

Strategies for Progressing Through the Cycle of Change

Cultivate Hope: Cultivate hope as a driving force in your recovery journey. Believe in your capacity to heal, grow, and overcome difficulties.

Embrace Honesty: Be honest with yourself about your desires, needs, feelings, and identity. Honesty is the foundation of self-discovery and personal growth.

A Journey of Transformation

Face Challenges: Acknowledge and face challenges without fear. Understand that they are part of your journey and that you have the resilience to overcome them.

Discover Yourself: Take time to discover who you are in recovery. Reflect on your aspirations, values, and the path you want to follow.

Accept Getting Lost: Accept that getting lost at times is a natural part of the journey. Use these moments as opportunities to find yourself and your true path.

Trust Yourself: Trust in your abilities and the strength you've demonstrated in your recovery journey so far.

Find Meaning: Maintain hope that one day, everything will make sense. Understand that your worries are temporary and will lead to personal growth and understanding.

Self-Reflection Questions

How has hope played a role in my recovery journey, and how can I cultivate it further?

In what ways have I been honest with myself about my desires, needs, feelings, and identity in recovery?

How do I approach and face challenges in my recovery, and how can I strengthen my resilience?

What aspects of self-discovery have I embraced, and how can I continue to learn more about myself in recovery?

How have I navigated moments of feeling lost, and what lessons have I learned from these experiences?

Do I trust myself and my abilities in recovery, and how can I build upon this trust?

How can I maintain hope that everything will eventually make sense, and how can I find meaning in my recovery journey?

Progressing through the cycle of change in addiction recovery requires a combination of strategies, including cultivating hope, embracing honesty, facing challenges, self-discovery, resilience, and trusting oneself. Recognize that hope is not about denying troubles but believing in healing and growth. Honesty is the foundation of self-discovery, and challenges are opportunities for personal growth. Getting lost at times is part of finding your true path, and trusting yourself is essential. Ultimately, believe that everything will make sense, and your worries will lead to a deeper understanding of your recovery journey.

Change as a Catalyst for Personal Growth in Addiction Recovery

Change is a powerful catalyst for personal growth, and in the context of addiction recovery, it takes on an even greater significance. In this book, we will explore how embracing change can lead to personal growth and transformation. Drawing inspiration from the statement, "No one can make you feel inferior without your consent," we will discuss the importance of self-empowerment, forward momentum, the impact of worry, and the value of living in the present.

The Empowerment of Self

Taking Control: Change in addiction recovery begins with taking control of one's life. It involves making conscious decisions and refusing to let external forces dictate one's sense of self-worth.

Resisting Inferiority: Personal growth requires resisting the temptation to feel inferior due to past actions or circumstances. Understand that your worth is not determined by your past but by your commitment to change.

Embracing Self-Empowerment: Embrace self-empowerment as a key factor in recovery. Recognize that you have the capacity to shape your future and overcome addiction.

Forward Momentum and Overcoming Worry

Continuous Progress: Every day, take small steps that move you closer to a better tomorrow. Recognize that progress may be gradual but is nonetheless significant.

Managing Worry: Understand that worry is like rust upon a blade; it erodes your well-being and hinders personal growth. Focus on the present moment and take action to alleviate concerns.

Healthy Work vs. Worry: Distinguish between healthy work and destructive worry. Work is a source of growth and vitality, while worry only serves to impede progress.

Living in the Present

Release the Past: Let go of past regrets and mistakes. Understand that dwelling on the past serves no purpose in your journey of personal growth.

Embrace the Present: Embrace the beauty of the present moment. Make it meaningful and worthwhile through positive actions, choices, and relationships.

The Power of Now: Understand that true success depends on your ability to live in the present. The choices you make today shape your future and contribute to your personal growth.

A Journey of Transformation

Change as a Catalyst for Personal Growth

Taking Control: Take control of your life and recovery journey. Recognize that external factors cannot determine your self-worth.

Resisting Inferiority: Refuse to feel inferior due to past actions or circumstances. Your commitment to change defines your worth.

Embracing Self-Empowerment: Embrace self-empowerment as a driving force in recovery. Understand that you have the capacity to shape your future.

Continuous Progress: Take small steps each day that inch you closer to a better tomorrow. Understand the significance of gradual progress.

Managing Worry: Recognize worry as a hindrance to personal growth. Focus on the present moment and take positive actions to alleviate concerns.

Healthy Work vs. Worry: Distinguish between healthy work and destructive worry. Understand that work is a source of growth, while worry impedes progress.

Release the Past: Let go of past regrets and mistakes. Understand that dwelling on the past serves no purpose in your journey of personal growth.

Embrace the Present: Live in the present, making it beautiful and worthwhile through positive actions and choices.

The Power of Now: Recognize that true success depends on your ability to live in the present and make choices that contribute to your personal growth.

Self-Reflection Questions

> How am I taking control of my life and recovery journey, and where can I further embrace self-empowerment?
>
> Have I let past actions or circumstances make me feel inferior, and how can I redefine my self-worth based on my commitment to change?
>
> What small steps can I take each day to move closer to a better tomorrow in my recovery journey?
>
> How do I manage worry and distinguish between healthy work and destructive worry in my life?

What strategies can I employ to release the past and fully embrace the present moment in my personal growth journey?

How can I continue to focus on living in the present and making choices that contribute to my personal growth and success in recovery?

Recognizing Change as a Driver of Personal Development in Addiction Recovery

Change is a powerful catalyst for personal development, especially in the context of addiction recovery. In this book, we will explore the concept of recognizing change as a driver of personal development. Drawing inspiration from the statement, "Relationships are like glass. Sometimes it's better to leave them broken than try to hurt yourself putting it back together," we will discuss the importance of embracing change, moving forward from closed doors, healing, forgiveness, and the resilience of the human spirit.

Embracing Change

Acceptance of Impermanence: Understand that change is a fundamental aspect of life. Embrace the impermanence of situations, relationships, and emotions, especially in the context of addiction recovery.

Leaving Behind Toxicity: Recognize that sometimes, leaving broken relationships or unhealthy habits behind is the healthiest choice. Embrace the courage to let go and make room for personal development.

Moving Forward from Closed Doors

Recognizing Opportunities: Understand that when one door closes, another opens. Often, we become so fixated on the closed door that we fail to see new opportunities for growth, recovery, and personal development.

Embracing Change: Embrace change as a natural part of life. It brings new experiences, challenges, and lessons that contribute to personal growth.

Healing and Forgiveness

The Healing Process: Acknowledge that time alone does not heal wounds. It is our actions and choices during this time that facilitate the healing process. Healing means regaining control over our lives and not letting past damage dictate our future.

The Power of Forgiveness: Recognize the transformative power of forgiveness. Forgiving oneself or others is not about erasing the past but about creating a new way to remember it—a way that allows for hope, growth, and personal development.

A Journey of Transformation

Resilience of the Human Spirit

Rejection and Redirection: Understand that life often redirects us to something better when we perceive rejection. Embrace these redirections as opportunities for personal development and growth.

The Broken Heart: Recognize the resilience of the human spirit. Despite heartbreak and challenges, the heart remains an instrument that can still work, heal, and experience personal development.

Recognizing Change as a Driver of Personal Development

>Acceptance of Impermanence: How can I better embrace the impermanence of situations and emotions in my recovery journey?

>Leaving Behind Toxicity: Have I recognized and let go of toxic relationships or habits that hinder my personal development in recovery?

>Recognizing Opportunities: Am I open to recognizing new opportunities for growth and recovery when one door closes in my life?

>Embracing Change: How can I actively embrace change as a natural and essential part of my recovery and personal development?

>The Healing Process: What actions am I taking during the passage of time to facilitate the healing process and regain control over my life?

>The Power of Forgiveness: Have I embraced forgiveness as a means to create a new way of remembering my past, one that fosters hope, growth, and personal development?

>Rejection and Redirection: How have I experienced redirection in my life when I thought I was being rejected from something good? How can I embrace these redirections in my recovery journey?

>The Broken Heart: How can I tap into the resilience of my own spirit and continue to grow, heal, and experience personal development despite past heartbreak and challenges?

Recognizing change as a driver of personal development is essential in addiction recovery. By embracing the impermanence of life, leaving behind toxicity, recognizing new opportunities, and actively embracing change, individuals can unlock their potential for growth and healing. Healing and forgiveness play a significant role in this process, allowing for a new way of remembering the past—one that fosters hope, growth, and personal development. The resilience of the human spirit ensures that, even in the face of rejection and challenges, personal development remains a possibility, and the heart continues to work and heal.

The Potential for Self-Discovery and Empowerment through Change in Addiction Recovery

Change is a powerful force that, when embraced, can lead to profound self-discovery and empowerment, especially in the context of addiction recovery. In this book, we will explore how change can be viewed as a gift that guides us on our intended path, the importance of not having everything figured out, the impact of choices on our identity, the courage to face and change what we can, and the strength gained through adversity.

Change as a Gift and Pathway to Self-Discovery

Accepting Loss as a Gift: When we lose something, whether it's a substance, a habit, or a relationship, we can choose to view it as a gift. It sets us on a path toward self-discovery and growth by challenging us to redefine our identity and purpose.

Unveiling Hidden Strengths: Change often reveals hidden strengths and resilience within us. As we navigate the challenges of recovery, we uncover qualities we didn't know we possessed, such as determination, courage, and adaptability.

Embracing Uncertainty and Impact

Moving Forward without All the Answers: We don't have to have our entire journey figured out before taking the first step. Embracing change means accepting uncertainty and being open to new possibilities. Each day presents an opportunity for self-discovery.

Born to Make an Impact: Recognize that every individual is born with the potential to make a positive impact, both on their own life and on the lives of others. Change can empower us to realize this potential and fulfill our purpose.

The Influence of Choices and Facing the Unchangeable

The Impact of Choices: Our identity and current circumstances are shaped by the choices we made in the past. Acknowledging this fact allows us to take responsibility for our recovery journey and make conscious decisions that lead to positive change.

Facing the Unchangeable: While not everything can be changed, nothing can be changed until it is faced. This courage to confront our challenges head-on is an essential step in the journey of recovery and self-discovery.

Strength through Struggles and Adversity

Finding Strength in Struggle: Each struggle we encounter is an opportunity to tap into our inner strength. Overcoming obstacles in recovery builds resilience and empowers us to face future challenges with confidence.

A Journey of Transformation

Our Journey Shapes Us: The experiences and trials we go through in life shape our character and define who we are. By embracing change and the difficulties it brings, we become the resilient, empowered individuals we are meant to be.

The Potential for Self-Discovery and Empowerment

Accepting Loss as a Gift: How can I reframe losses in my life, especially those related to addiction, as gifts that guide me toward self-discovery and empowerment?

Unveiling Hidden Strengths: What hidden strengths have I discovered within myself as I navigate the challenges of recovery? How have they empowered me?

Moving Forward without All the Answers: How comfortable am I with embracing uncertainty and taking each day as an opportunity for self-discovery and growth?

Born to Make an Impact: How can I harness my potential to make a positive impact on my own life and the lives of others through my recovery journey?

The Impact of Choices: What role have my past choices played in shaping my current identity and circumstances? How can I make conscious decisions to foster positive change?

Facing the Unchangeable: What unchangeable aspects of my past or present do I need to face in order to move forward in my recovery and self-discovery journey?

Finding Strength in Struggle: How have the struggles and adversity I've faced in my recovery journey strengthened me and contributed to my personal empowerment?

Our Journey Shapes Us: How do I view the experiences and trials in my life as opportunities for personal growth and character development? What aspects of my journey have shaped the person I am today?

Change, even in the face of addiction recovery, can be a gift that guides us toward self-discovery and empowerment. By accepting loss as a pathway to growth, embracing uncertainty, recognizing the impact of our choices, and finding strength in adversity, we uncover our true potential and become the resilient individuals we are meant to be. Through change, we not only redefine our identity but also discover the capacity to make a positive impact on our own lives and those around us.

Self-Reflection Questions

What are some specific fears or anxieties that I believe may be limiting my progress in addiction recovery, and how can I confront them?

How can I cultivate a stronger sense of self-belief and recognize my own talents, abilities, and self-worth as sources of empowerment in my recovery journey?

What are some significant mistakes or challenges I have faced in the past, and how have I learned from these experiences? How can I continue to use them as opportunities for growth?

What concrete steps can I take to actively embrace change as a learning opportunity in my journey of addiction recovery, and how can I overcome fear to walk down a brighter path toward personal growth and transformation?

Embracing Change as a Learning Opportunity in Addiction Recovery

In the journey of addiction recovery, change is not merely a necessity but also a profound learning opportunity. Life is a continuous process of evolution, where what may seem like a mistake to others can be a pivotal milestone in our personal growth. In this book, we will explore the concept of embracing change as a valuable learning experience. We will discuss how fear can limit our potential, the importance of believing in ourselves, and the transformative power of learning from mistakes and overcoming challenges.

The Limitation of Fear

Fear as a Limiter: Fear has the potential to limit our vision and hinder our progress. It often serves as blinders, preventing us from seeing the opportunities and potential growth just a few steps down the road.

Overcoming Fear: To fully embrace change, it is crucial to confront and overcome our fears. By doing so, we open ourselves up to a world of possibilities and learning experiences.

Belief in Self-Worth

Empowerment through Self-Belief: Believing in our talents, abilities, and self-worth is a powerful source of empowerment. It provides us with the confidence to navigate the challenges that come with change.

Brighter Paths: When we recognize our own value, we can choose to walk down brighter paths that align with our true potential. This shift in perspective can be a catalyst for personal growth and transformation.

Learning from Mistakes and Adversity

Human Nature and Mistakes: It is inherent in our nature as humans to make mistakes. These mistakes, whether they result from betrayal, heartbreak, or misunderstanding, hold valuable lessons for us.

A Journey of Transformation

The Power of Learning: Transforming these experiences into opportunities for learning is what truly makes a difference in our lives. By doing so, we turn fear into freedom and personal growth.

Embracing Change as a Learning Opportunity

Confronting Fear: How can I identify and confront the fears that may be limiting my potential for personal growth and recovery in addiction?

Believing in Self-Worth: In what ways can I cultivate self-belief and recognize my own talents, abilities, and self-worth as sources of empowerment in my recovery journey?

Learning from Mistakes and Adversity: Reflecting on my past experiences, how have I grown and learned from mistakes, betrayals, heartbreaks, or misunderstandings in my life? How can I continue to transform such experiences into opportunities for growth?

Embracing Change: How can I actively embrace change as a learning opportunity in my journey of addiction recovery? What steps can I take to overcome fear and walk down a brighter path towards personal growth and transformation?

Embracing change as a learning opportunity is fundamental to addiction recovery and personal growth. By confronting our fears, believing in our self-worth, and transforming mistakes and adversity into valuable lessons, we harness the power to evolve and transform our lives. The journey becomes a process of continuous learning and self-discovery, allowing us to turn fear into freedom and walk down a brighter path toward a healthier and more fulfilling future.

Cultivating Resilience and Adaptability in Addiction Recovery

In the journey of long-term recovery from addiction, one of the most crucial qualities to develop is resilience—the ability to bounce back from setbacks and adapt to life's challenges. When we encounter hardships, we have two choices: succumb to despair and destructive habits, or harness the challenge to discover our inner strength. In this book, we will explore the importance of resilience and adaptability in addiction recovery. We will discuss how facing difficulties can strengthen our mental fortitude, the significance of accepting the past, confidently navigating the present, and fearlessly embracing the future.

Resilience in the Face of Hardships

Two Ways to Handle Hardships: When life presents us with real hardships, we can choose between two paths. We can either lose hope and spiral into self-destructive habits, or we can utilize these challenges to unearth our inner reservoir of strength.

Strength in Adversity: True strength of character is not measured by how happy we are when times are good, but rather by our ability to find reasons to smile even in situations that bring tears.

Cultivating resilience allows us to develop smiles out of situations that would otherwise make us weep.

Trials and Mental Strength

Trials as Catalysts for Growth: The consequence of facing numerous trials and difficulties in life is the gradual accumulation of mental strength and power. Each challenge we overcome becomes a building block, reinforcing our resilience.

Embracing the Past Without Regrets: Accepting our past without regrets is essential in the process of recovery. Every experience, whether positive or negative, has contributed to shaping our journey and strengthening our resilience.

Navigating the Present with Confidence

Confidence in the Present: To cultivate resilience, we must handle the present with confidence. Believing in our ability to face and conquer the challenges of each day empowers us to persevere in our recovery.

Gratitude for the Present: Gratitude is a powerful tool that enables us to appreciate where we are and what we have in the present moment. It fosters a positive outlook and enhances our resilience.

Fearlessly Embracing the Future

A Fearless Approach to the Future: Fear often holds us back from embracing the unknown. In recovery, it is crucial to approach the future without fear, knowing that our newfound resilience will guide us through whatever lies ahead.

Reflecting on Progress: At the end of each day, it is beneficial to reflect on our progress and experiences. Finding reasons to smile and being grateful for our journey helps reinforce our resilience.

Cultivating Resilience and Adaptability

>Resilience-Building Strategies: What specific strategies can I adopt to build resilience and adaptability in my journey of addiction recovery?

>Accepting the Past: How can I work on accepting my past without regrets, recognizing that it has played a crucial role in shaping my resilience and strength?

>Confidence in the Present: What steps can I take to develop confidence in navigating the challenges of the present moment during my recovery?

A Journey of Transformation

Fearless Approach to the Future: How can I adopt a fearless attitude when facing the uncertainties of the future, knowing that my resilience will guide me through?

Daily Reflection: How can I incorporate daily reflection and gratitude into my routine to reinforce my resilience and maintain a positive outlook on my recovery journey?

Cultivating resilience and adaptability is fundamental to achieving long-term recovery from addiction. By embracing hardships as opportunities for growth, accepting the past without regrets, confidently navigating the present, and fearlessly embracing the future, we strengthen our inner resolve. As we develop the ability to find reasons to smile in the face of adversity, we reinforce our resilience and ensure that our recovery journey is marked by hope, growth, and gratitude.

Self-Reflection Questions

How have I historically responded to hardships and challenges in my addiction recovery journey, and what changes can I make to foster greater resilience and adaptability?

What specific experiences from my past, both positive and negative, have contributed to my current level of resilience and inner strength?

In what ways can I boost my confidence in handling the challenges of the present moment during my recovery?

What steps can I take to approach the future without fear and with the knowledge that my resilience will guide me through whatever lies ahead?

How can I incorporate daily reflection and gratitude practices into my routine to reinforce my resilience and maintain a positive outlook on my recovery journey?

Embracing Change: The Path to Long-Term Recovery from Addiction

Long-term recovery from addiction is a transformative journey that demands embracing change at its core. Success in this journey entails walking a fine line between faith and curiosity, expertise and creativity, bias and openness, experience and epiphany, ambition and passion, and arrogance and conviction. In this book, we will explore the essence of change as it relates to addiction recovery, summarizing key points that can guide individuals on this path. We will emphasize the importance of welcoming change, pursuing one's passion with dedication, enjoying the journey, and holding onto the strength, patience, and passion to change the world.

The Dual Nature of Success

Balancing Act: Success in addiction recovery is akin to a balancing act, requiring a delicate equilibrium between opposing forces. It necessitates navigating the tightrope between blind faith and curiosity, remaining open to new possibilities while staying grounded in the faith that recovery is possible.

Expertise and Creativity: Success demands the integration of expertise and creativity. While expertise draws from experience and knowledge, creativity fuels innovation and problem-solving—both crucial elements in overcoming addiction.

Embracing Change

Change as the Rule: Change is not an exception but the rule in the journey of addiction recovery. Accepting this reality is the first step toward a successful recovery.

Change as a Catalyst: Change is not merely a circumstance to endure; it is a catalyst for growth and transformation. Embracing change propels individuals toward a brighter, addiction-free future.

Follow Your Passion

Passion-Driven Dedication: Pursuing recovery with passion involves hard work and sacrifice. It requires unwavering dedication to the goal of sobriety.

Unlimited Dreams: In recovery, one should never allow others to limit their dreams. Passion fuels ambition, and with ambition comes the power to overcome addiction's grip.

Enjoy the Journey

Daily Improvement: Recovery is a journey, not a destination. It involves striving to get better every day, acknowledging that small improvements accumulate over time.

Preserve Love and Passion: Maintaining a sense of love and passion for the recovery journey keeps individuals motivated and committed to their goal.

Strength, Patience, and Passion

Internal Resources: Every individual possesses the inner strength, patience, and passion required for successful recovery. These resources are the building blocks of resilience.

Reaching for the Stars: Recovery is not just about personal healing; it is about changing the world. Every dream, no matter how big, starts with a dreamer who believes they can make a difference.

Summarizing the Essence of Change

Change as a Constant: Addiction recovery is a dynamic process marked by change as a constant presence. Accepting and embracing this change is essential for success.

A Journey of Transformation

Balancing Opposites: Success involves balancing opposing forces, drawing from both expertise and creativity, and remaining open to new possibilities while having faith in recovery.

Passion-Driven Dedication: Following one's passion with dedication is crucial. Recovery demands hard work, sacrifice, and unwavering ambition.

Enjoying the Journey: Recovery is a lifelong journey of daily improvement. Maintaining love and passion for this journey ensures continued progress.

Inner Resources: Each individual possesses the inner strength, patience, and passion needed for recovery and the potential to change the world.

Long-term recovery from addiction hinges on embracing change and the transformative power it holds. Success in this journey involves balancing opposing forces, pursuing one's passion with dedication, enjoying the journey, and recognizing the inner strength, patience, and passion that fuel change. By understanding these key points, individuals can navigate the path to recovery with faith, curiosity, and unwavering determination.

Self-Reflection Questions

How can I embrace change as a constant presence in my journey of addiction recovery and use it as a catalyst for personal growth?

In what ways can I balance opposing forces, such as expertise and creativity, in my recovery journey to achieve a harmonious and successful outcome?

What is my passion, and how can I channel it with dedication to overcome addiction and achieve my dreams in recovery?

How can I maintain a sense of enjoyment and daily improvement in my recovery journey, ensuring that I stay motivated and committed to my goals?

Reflecting on my inner resources, how can I harness my strength, patience, and passion to not only heal myself but also make a positive impact on the world?

Embracing Change: A Lifelong Journey to Fulfillment

Change is an inevitable and integral part of our lives. Whether we like it or not, it's a constant force that shapes our experiences, challenges our perspectives, and molds our destinies. For someone on the path of long-term recovery from addiction, embracing change is not just an option; it's a necessity. In this book, we'll explore the importance of welcoming change as a fundamental aspect of life, and how it can be harnessed to foster growth, happiness, and fulfillment. We'll delve into the power of attitude, adaptability, and gratitude as tools for navigating the ever-changing landscape of existence.

Control Your Attitude

The Attitude Conundrum: We may not have control over every situation in our lives, but we have complete control over our attitudes and how we react to those situations.

Secret to Happiness: True happiness lies in accepting situations for what they are, rather than what we wish they could be. Embracing this perspective allows us to make the best of any circumstance.

Start Subtracting

Life's Equation: When life's challenges and difficulties begin to accumulate, it's time to start subtracting the unnecessary. Sometimes, simplifying our lives is the key to finding clarity and happiness.

Prioritizing: Reflect on what truly matters and what contributes to your well-being. Eliminating distractions and negativity can create space for positive change and personal growth.

Path vs. Destination

Navigating the Rocky Path: The journey of life often feels like a rocky path, filled with challenges and uncertainties. It's easy to get discouraged, but remember that this path leads to amazing places.

Building Resilience: Disappointments and setbacks are not meant to break us. Instead, they are opportunities for growth and the fortitude to fulfill our unique destinies.

Appreciating Life

The Power of Gratitude: When we truly appreciate life, we recognize the abundance of blessings we have. Gratitude shifts our focus from what we lack to what we have and fosters contentment.
Perspective Shift: Never let your desires blind you to the richness of your current reality. Gratitude opens your eyes to the beauty and value in the present moment.

Change is the thread that weaves through the fabric of our lives, constantly reshaping our experiences and aspirations. Embracing change doesn't mean surrendering to chaos; it means acknowledging that life is dynamic, and our attitudes, adaptability, and gratitude play pivotal roles in our journey. By controlling our attitudes, simplifying our lives, recognizing the importance of the path, and embracing gratitude, we can navigate change as an ally on the road to long-term recovery and fulfillment.

Self-Reflection Questions

> How can I improve my attitude toward challenging situations and practice acceptance rather than resistance?

A Journey of Transformation

> What aspects of my life can I simplify or subtract to create more space for positive change and personal growth?
>
> How do I currently view the journey of life—do I focus more on the path or the destination? How can I build resilience and see setbacks as opportunities for growth?
>
> In what ways can I cultivate a sense of gratitude and shift my perspective to appreciate the richness of my present life, fostering contentment and happiness?
>
> Reflecting on my attitude, adaptability, and gratitude, how can I proactively embrace change as an integral part of my life and recovery journey?

Understanding Change: The Prelude to Becoming a Change Maker

Change is a constant force that molds our lives, and understanding its dynamics is essential not only for personal growth but also for becoming a change maker in our own right. For those seeking long-term recovery from addiction, comprehending the intricacies of change is a crucial step toward breaking free from the shackles of addiction and charting a new course in life. In this book, we will explore how understanding change sets the stage for personal transformation and the potential to inspire change in others.

The Power of Dreams

Dreams as Beacons: Our dreams serve as guiding lights, illuminating the path we wish to tread. They have the potential to shape our future and drive us toward personal fulfillment.

Thoughts and Dreams: Our thoughts and dreams have a profound impact on our lives. When we fill our minds with pure joy and positivity, we become the architects of our own destiny.

Protecting Your Dream

Dream Guardianship: There will always be those who lack the courage to pursue their dreams, and they may attempt to discourage you from pursuing yours. It is vital to protect your dreams from external negativity.

Pursuing Your Dream: Don't let the doubts and limitations of others deter you. If you have a dream, it is your responsibility to chase after it, regardless of the naysayers.

The Pursuit of Dreams

Overcoming Obstacles: The pursuit of dreams is often fraught with challenges and setbacks. It is during these moments that our determination is put to the test.

Relentless Pursuit: When you encounter obstacles, remember that if you want something badly enough, you have the power to overcome any adversity and achieve your goals.

Inspiring Change in Others

Leading by Example: Understanding the transformative power of change allows you to lead by example. As you embark on your journey of recovery and personal growth, you become a beacon of hope for others facing similar struggles.

Empowering Change: By sharing your story and demonstrating the positive impact of change in your life, you have the potential to inspire and empower others to embark on their own journeys of transformation.

Understanding the dynamics of change is the first step toward personal growth and becoming a change maker. Dreams are the driving force behind our aspirations, and protecting them from external discouragement is vital. As we pursue our dreams, we encounter obstacles that test our determination, but with unwavering resolve, we can overcome any challenge. By leading by example and sharing our stories, we can inspire and empower others to embrace change and embark on their own journeys of transformation.

Self-Reflection Questions

What are my most cherished dreams and aspirations, and how can I work toward manifesting them in my life?

How do I currently protect my dreams from external negativity and discouragement? Are there ways I can strengthen my resolve to pursue them?

What challenges have I encountered in my pursuit of personal growth and change, and how have I overcome them? What lessons have I learned from these experiences?

How can I share my journey of recovery and personal growth to inspire and empower others who may be facing similar challenges?

In what ways can I become a change maker in my community or in the lives of those around me, leveraging my understanding of change and the power of dreams to make a positive impact?

Conclusion: Embracing Change on the Path to Long-Term Recovery

Summarizing the Essence of Change in Recovery: Throughout our exploration of change, we have come to understand its complex and dynamic nature. For someone on the path of recovery from addiction, recognizing the multifaceted aspects of change is crucial. We have defined change as an inevitable and continuous process, affecting every facet of life. In the context of recovery, this encompasses everything from personal habits and thought patterns to social interactions and environmental influences.

Encouraging Embrace of Change in Recovery: Embracing change is particularly vital in the journey of recovery. The discussion on the drivers of change, both internal factors like personal growth and self-awareness, and external factors such as societal influences and support systems, highlights the importance of a holistic approach to recovery. Understanding the psychological impact of change sheds light on the emotional challenges one might face. However, by recognizing the natural resistance to change and learning to accept and adapt, individuals in recovery can harness change as a powerful ally. This process involves not just coping strategies but a fundamental transformation in how one views themselves and their journey, seeing change as an opportunity for profound personal growth and healing.

Becoming a Change Maker in Recovery: The journey through recovery is an ongoing cycle of change. By navigating through the stages of this cycle, from pre-contemplation to maintenance, individuals in recovery can actively participate in their transformation. This path isn't just about overcoming addiction; it's about becoming an agent of positive change in one's life. Embracing change as a catalyst for personal development opens avenues for self-discovery, resilience, and empowerment. It involves learning to see challenges not as obstacles but as opportunities for growth, self-reflection, and rebuilding.

In conclusion, for those seeking long-term recovery from addiction, understanding and embracing change is more than a strategy—it's a lifeline. It's about building a new, fulfilling life where change is not feared but welcomed as a sign of progress and personal evolution. The insights and strategies discussed here are not just theoretical concepts; they are practical tools to be used daily. By mastering the art of navigating change, individuals in recovery can forge a path of sustained health, wellness, and personal fulfillment. Change, in this light, is not just a part of recovery; it is the heart of a transformative journey towards a renewed self.

Part II
The Principles of Being a Change Maker

The Principles of Being a Change Maker

Life often presents us with challenges that can break us down, leaving us feeling like we have broken ribs on the inside while appearing perfectly intact on the outside. Addiction is one such challenge, an invisible struggle that can shatter our physical, emotional, and spiritual well-being. Seeking long-term recovery from addiction is a courageous journey, one that requires profound inner transformation and the embracing of principles that can guide us towards becoming change makers in our own lives.

Just as a broken heart can be concealed behind a smile, the pain of addiction can hide behind a facade of normalcy. We may go about our daily lives, pretending that everything is fine, while every breath we take is laced with the agony of our addiction. Often, it's easier to mask our hurt with anger, deflecting our pain onto others rather than facing the raw vulnerability of acknowledging that we are wounded.

In this guide, we will explore the principles of being a change maker in the context of addiction recovery. We will delve into the notion that although we cannot choose to avoid pain in this world, we can select who we allow to hurt us. Recovery is not just about quitting the substance; it is a profound process of healing and personal growth. It's about taking ownership of our happiness and choosing not to be miserable, despite the hardships we've endured. It's about understanding that strength lies not in enduring pain, but in learning to live free from it.

Throughout this journey, we'll reflect on the principles of recovery and personal transformation, delving into self-awareness, resilience, and self-compassion. We'll learn how to navigate the path to recovery with authenticity and grace, ultimately emerging as change makers in our own lives, capable of not just surviving but thriving.

Self-Reflection Questions:

> Have I been using anger as a shield to protect myself from the pain of addiction? How can I start acknowledging and addressing my true feelings and vulnerabilities?

> What are the specific challenges I've faced on my path to recovery, and how have they shaped my character and resilience?

> How can I take ownership of my happiness and choose not to be miserable, even in the face of adversity?

> In what ways have I allowed others to hurt me during my addiction, and how can I begin to set healthier boundaries in my life?

> What does being a "change maker" mean to me in the context of my recovery journey, and how can I start implementing these principles in my life?

A Journey of Transformation

As we explore these principles and engage in self-reflection, we embark on a transformative journey toward long-term recovery from addiction, armed with the tools to mend our broken hearts and lead fulfilling, purpose-driven lives.

The Role of Change Makers in Transforming Lives and the World

Change makers are individuals who dream of success and are determined to turn those dreams into reality. They are the ones who stay awake, relentlessly working towards achieving their goals. In the context of long-term recovery from addiction, becoming a change maker takes on a profound significance. It means not only overcoming the personal challenges of addiction but also actively working to transform one's own life and, in turn, contributing to positive change in the world. This book explores the role of change makers in transforming lives and the world, emphasizing the power of mindset, positivity, and resilience in the journey towards recovery and beyond.

One of the fundamental principles of change making is altering the way we perceive and approach life. As the saying goes, "When you change the way you look at things, the things you look at change." In the context of addiction recovery, this means shifting our perspective from one of hopelessness and despair to one of hope and possibility. It involves recognizing that recovery is not only about quitting a substance but also about fundamentally transforming the way we live our lives. It's about believing in the potential for change and growth, no matter how challenging the circumstances may be.

A critical aspect of becoming a change maker in recovery is mastering the art of self-awareness and self-regulation. We must learn to monitor our thoughts and emotions, understanding that "you must think about what you're thinking about." If our thoughts are negative or self-destructive, it's essential to acknowledge them and consciously choose to focus on more positive and constructive thoughts. By doing so, we can create a mental environment conducive to healing and personal growth.

"Make the present good, and the past will take care of itself" is a powerful reminder that dwelling on past mistakes or regrets can hinder our progress. Change makers in recovery recognize that the past is unchangeable, but they have control over their actions and attitudes in the present. They focus on making each moment count and building a brighter future, free from the shackles of addiction.

Negativity, whether from external sources or our inner doubts, can be a formidable obstacle on the path to recovery. Change makers understand the importance of staying true to themselves and ignoring the negativity that may try to bring them down. They know that "whatever brings you down will eventually make you stronger." Adversity becomes an opportunity for growth, and setbacks are seen as stepping stones toward a better, addiction-free life.

Society often exerts pressure to conform to certain norms and expectations, but change makers in recovery resist this influence. They refuse to let society turn them into someone they're not and instead choose authenticity. They understand that "it's not about saying the right things, it's about doing the right things." Their actions align with their values and aspirations, even when faced with societal pressures.

Ultimately, change makers realize that their thoughts shape their reality, and they actively cultivate positivity and optimism. "Happiness is when what you think, what you say, and what you do are in harmony." By aligning their thoughts, words, and actions with their goals, they create a life filled with purpose and fulfillment.

In the broader context of the world, change makers recognize that their individual actions have the potential to inspire global change. "The difference between what we do and what we are capable of doing would suffice to solve most of the world's problems." By transforming their own lives and sharing their experiences, they contribute to a ripple effect of positive change that extends far beyond themselves.

Self-Reflection Questions:

How can I shift my perspective on addiction recovery from one of hopelessness to one of hope and possibility?

Am I consciously monitoring my thoughts and emotions to maintain a positive and constructive mindset on my journey to recovery?

How can I let go of past mistakes and regrets and focus on making the present moment meaningful and productive?

How do I handle negativity from external sources or within myself, and what strategies can I use to remain resilient and true to my goals?

In what ways have societal expectations influenced my recovery journey, and how can I stay authentic to myself despite external pressures?

How can I align my thoughts, words, and actions to create a life that is in harmony with my values and aspirations in recovery?

Do I believe that my individual actions in recovery can have a positive impact on the world, and how can I contribute to positive change on a broader scale?

As we reflect on these questions, we take steps towards becoming change makers in our own lives and, in doing so, contribute to the transformation of not only ourselves but also the world around us.

A Journey of Transformation

The Significance of Understanding and Embodying Change-Making Principles in Addiction Recovery

Addiction recovery is a journey marked by challenges, but it's also a path towards transformation and healing. To achieve long-term recovery, individuals must not only overcome addiction but also embrace change-making principles that enable personal growth and lasting sobriety. In this book, we will explore the significance of understanding and embodying these principles, emphasizing the power of gratitude, positivity, and support in the recovery journey.

In the midst of addiction, many individuals often try to control every aspect of their lives to meet their plans. However, addiction is a formidable force that can disrupt even the best-laid plans. The first change-making principle to understand is that "what will be will be." There are aspects of life that are beyond our control, and acceptance of this fact is essential in the recovery process. Learning to let go of the need for absolute control can be liberating, allowing individuals to adapt to the ebb and flow of life without succumbing to the chaos of addiction.

Gratitude plays a pivotal role in recovery. It is necessary to cultivate the habit of being grateful for everything that comes our way, whether big or small. "Be willing and mindful to give thanks continuously" is a practice that shifts our focus from dwelling on what's lacking to appreciating what we have. In recovery, acknowledging the progress made, the support received, and the small surprises that the universe brings can bolster our commitment to a substance-free life.

Moreover, it's crucial to recognize that not only the positive but also the challenging experiences have contributed to our advancement. "Remember ALL things have contributed to your advancement that you should include in your gratitude." Even the darkest moments can serve as valuable lessons and catalysts for personal growth. Embracing this principle allows individuals to find meaning in their journey, no matter how difficult it may have been.

"Wake up every day with positive energy and share it with people around you." Positivity is contagious, and in recovery, maintaining a positive outlook can be a lifeline. It not only lifts one's own spirits but also influences those around us. By cultivating positivity, individuals in recovery can create a supportive and encouraging environment that bolsters their resilience.

One of the cornerstones of recovery is the support system that surrounds us. "Be grateful to those that give you support at all times of need." Friends, family, therapists, and fellow recovering individuals provide a network of encouragement and understanding. Embracing change-making principles involves recognizing and appreciating the invaluable support that helps individuals navigate the challenges of recovery.

In daily life, we must understand that it is not happiness that makes us grateful but gratefulness that makes us happy. Gratitude has the power to transform our perspective, allowing us to find joy and contentment in the simplest of moments. By focusing on the positive aspects of our journey, we can find the strength to overcome the hurdles of addiction and move towards a life filled with happiness and purpose.

Self-Reflection Questions:

How do I react when things don't go as planned in my recovery journey, and how can I embrace the idea that "what will be will be"?

What are some of the small surprises in my life that I can be grateful for, and how can I cultivate a habit of continuous gratitude?

How have both positive and challenging experiences contributed to my personal growth and advancement in recovery?

Do I wake up each day with a positive mindset, and how can I share this positivity with those around me to create a supportive environment?

Who are the individuals in my life who provide unwavering support during my times of need, and how can I express my gratitude to them?

How can I shift my perspective to understand that it is gratefulness that makes me happy, and how can I incorporate this principle into my daily life?

As we reflect on these questions and internalize the change-making principles discussed, we empower ourselves to not only overcome addiction but also lead a fulfilling life grounded in gratitude, positivity, and support.

Principle 1: Self-awareness

The First Principle of Self-Awareness in Addiction Recovery

The journey towards long-term recovery from addiction is a complex and deeply personal one. It demands a profound understanding of oneself and the factors that led to addiction in the first place. One of the foundational principles that underpin a successful recovery journey is self-awareness. In this book, we will delve into the significance of self-awareness in addiction recovery, exploring how it helps individuals confront their insecurities, find happiness within, and take responsibility for their success.

In the age of social media and constant comparison, it's easy to fall into the trap of measuring our worth against the seemingly perfect lives of others. As the saying goes, "The reason we struggle with insecurity is because we compare our behind-the-scenes with everyone else's highlight reel." In addiction recovery, this tendency to compare ourselves to others can be particularly detrimental.

Self-awareness enables us to recognize that everyone has their struggles and their hidden challenges. It allows us to focus on our own progress, rather than getting lost in unhelpful comparisons.

True happiness is an internal state of being, and self-awareness is the key to unlocking it. "Happiness will come to you when it comes FROM YOU." Addiction often numbs our emotions, making it challenging to connect with our authentic selves. Through self-awareness, we learn to identify our true desires, values, and sources of joy. As we uncover these aspects of ourselves, we can nurture and cultivate happiness from within, independent of external circumstances.

Taking responsibility for one's success is a fundamental aspect of self-awareness. "Success will be yours when you choose to take responsibility for making it so." In addiction, individuals often deflect responsibility for their actions, blaming external factors or circumstances. Self-awareness invites individuals to acknowledge their role in their addiction and, more importantly, in their recovery. It empowers them to make conscious choices that align with their recovery goals and values.

Living authentically is a core component of self-awareness. It involves shedding the facade of pretense and embracing one's true self. "When we choose to live authentically, we chip away at our internal prisons of pretend and create an opportunity for us to walk out of darkness into freedom." Authenticity in recovery means confronting the underlying issues and traumas that may have led to addiction. It means being honest with oneself and seeking the support needed to heal and grow.

The principle of self-awareness also reminds us of our inherent potential. "Be here for a purpose, and that purpose is to grow into a mountain, not to shrink to a grain of sand." Addiction can make individuals feel small and powerless. Self-awareness helps them realize their capacity for growth,

A Journey of Transformation

resilience, and transformation. It encourages them to aim high, to pursue their goals, and to become the best version of themselves.

Every day is a new opportunity for growth and self-discovery. "Each morning when you open your eyes, think only three things: THANK YOU, THANK YOU, THANK YOU!!!!!!!" Gratitude is a powerful tool in cultivating self-awareness. It reminds us of the gift of each day and motivates us to make the most of it. Self-awareness guides us as we set out to harness the potential of each day, making conscious choices that support our recovery.

Self-Reflection Questions:

>How has the tendency to compare myself to others affected my journey in addiction recovery, and how can I shift my focus to my own progress and growth?

>In what ways has addiction numbed my ability to experience true happiness from within, and how can I use self-awareness to reconnect with my authentic sources of joy?

>What steps can I take to actively take responsibility for my success in recovery and make conscious choices that align with my goals and values?

>How can I begin to live authentically in my recovery journey, and what support do I need to confront underlying issues and traumas?

>What are some concrete actions I can take to grow and harness my potential, rather than feeling small and powerless in my recovery?

>How can I incorporate a practice of gratitude into my daily life to enhance my self-awareness and make the most of each day on my recovery journey?

As we reflect on these questions and embrace the principle of self-awareness, we empower ourselves to navigate the complexities of addiction recovery with a deeper understanding of our true selves, our goals, and our capacity for transformation and growth.

**Exploring the Foundation of
Change Within Oneself in the Journey to Recovery**

Addiction recovery is a deeply personal and transformative journey that often involves a profound process of self-exploration and change. It is in the depths of recovery that individuals confront their vulnerabilities, discover their hidden strengths, and lay the foundation for lasting change within themselves. In this book, we will explore the significance of exploring the foundation of change within oneself, drawing inspiration from the wisdom that sometimes the strongest people are those who love beyond faults, cry in solitude, and face battles in silence.

In the world of addiction, strength often takes on a different meaning. It is not merely the absence of vulnerability but the courage to love beyond all faults. Addiction can lead individuals to hurt themselves and those around them, but beneath the struggle, there is often a deep well of love. Loving oneself, despite the faults and mistakes, is the first step toward change. It's about recognizing that recovery is an act of self-love, a commitment to healing and transformation.

Addiction is a silent battle, one that is often fought behind closed doors. "Crying behind closed doors" symbolizes the private suffering that addiction entails. It's the tears shed in solitude, the pain endured in silence, and the internal battles that nobody knows about. In the pursuit of recovery, acknowledging this private struggle is crucial. It's a recognition that true change begins with an intimate understanding of one's own pain and a commitment to healing it.

Life has a way of introducing us to people who, although we may not initially understand, play a significant role in our journey. Some are there to help us, others to hurt us, and some to leave us. Each encounter serves a purpose. Those who support us in recovery become invaluable allies, providing encouragement, understanding, and empathy. Those who challenge us may force us to confront our vulnerabilities, ultimately strengthening our resolve. Even those who leave us teach us lessons about resilience and the importance of self-reliance.

Recovery is not just about sobriety; it's a process of personal growth and self-discovery. As we navigate the challenges, we gradually become the person we were meant to be. The battles we face, the lessons we learn, and the changes we undergo shape us into stronger, more resilient individuals. It's a transformation that extends beyond breaking free from addiction; it's about finding our true selves and becoming the person we were always meant to become.

Your life is your message to the world, and in the context of addiction recovery, it is essential to ensure that it's an inspiring one. The journey of recovery is not just a personal endeavor; it has the potential to inspire others who may be struggling. By embracing change within ourselves and sharing our stories of growth and transformation, we become beacons of hope for others seeking recovery.

Self-Reflection Questions:

How can I cultivate self-love and acceptance, despite my faults and mistakes, as a foundation for my recovery journey?

In what ways have I experienced the private struggle of addiction, and how can I acknowledge and address the pain and challenges I've faced in silence?

What lessons have I learned from the people life has introduced me to on my recovery journey, both those who have supported me and those who have challenged me?

How has the process of recovery transformed me into a stronger and more resilient individual, and how can I continue to grow into the person I am meant to be?

A Journey of Transformation

> What is the message I want my life to convey to the world, and how can I ensure that it is an inspiring one, particularly for those who may be struggling with addiction?

As we reflect on these questions, we deepen our understanding of the foundation of change within ourselves and empower ourselves to continue on the transformative path of addiction recovery, inspiring not only ourselves but also those who may be seeking their own journeys to healing and growth.

Recognizing Your Strengths and Weaknesses:
A Path to Long-Term Recovery from Addiction

Addiction recovery is a journey marked by self-discovery, growth, and transformation. Central to this process is the recognition of one's strengths and weaknesses, a profound step that paves the way for healing and lasting recovery. In this book, we will explore the importance of acknowledging our strengths and weaknesses in the context of addiction recovery, drawing inspiration from the wisdom that we have the power to refuse to be broken, to grow from disappointments, and to embrace change.

Refusing to be broken, unappreciated, used, or disrespected is a declaration of self-worth. Addiction often leads individuals to engage in self-destructive behaviors and relationships, perpetuating a cycle of harm. Recognizing our strengths means understanding that we have the capacity to set boundaries and protect ourselves. We possess the inner strength to demand respect and refuse to be mistreated.

Disappointments in life are inevitable, but they are not meant to destroy us. Instead, they are opportunities for growth and resilience. Understanding our weaknesses means acknowledging that we may stumble and fall on the path to recovery. But every disappointment, setback, or relapse can be viewed as a chance to learn, adapt, and emerge stronger. It's the recognition that our weaknesses do not define us but are stepping stones toward our destiny.

"Life is too short to spend at war with ourselves." Addiction often creates an internal conflict, where the addicted self battles the true self. Recognizing our strengths means making peace with ourselves, accepting who we are in the present moment. It involves practicing self-acceptance and self-forgiveness, releasing the burdens of shame and guilt that can hinder recovery.

Letting go of the past is a pivotal step in recognizing our strengths. The past may be marred by regrets, traumas, and mistakes, but it does not dictate our future. It is an acknowledgment that our weaknesses do not condemn us to a life of addiction. By embracing change and relinquishing the grip of the past, we open the door to happiness and recovery.

"When we're broken, we need to be reborn." This statement encapsulates the essence of recognizing our strengths and weaknesses. Addiction often leaves individuals feeling shattered and lost. The recognition of our weaknesses is the first step toward rebuilding ourselves. It involves embracing the pain and discomfort of recovery, understanding that healing is a gradual process, and that setbacks are part of the journey.

Life has the capacity to replace loss with unexpected blessings. Recognizing our strengths means having faith that, even in the depths of addiction, we possess the resilience to overcome adversity. We may lose relationships, opportunities, and even a sense of self, but life can replace these losses with new connections, unforeseen possibilities, and a deeper understanding of our own strength.

Self-Reflection Questions:

> How can I practice self-worth and set boundaries to refuse being broken, unappreciated, used, or disrespected in my recovery journey?
>
> What disappointments or setbacks have I encountered in my life and recovery, and how can I view them as opportunities for growth and resilience?
>
> In what ways have I been at war with myself, and how can I practice self-acceptance and forgiveness to make peace within?
>
> What steps can I take to let go of the past and embrace change as a catalyst for happiness and recovery?
>
> How can I embrace the process of being reborn when I feel broken, understanding that setbacks and pain are part of the journey toward healing and transformation?
>
> Do I have faith that life can replace loss with unexpected blessings, and how can I remain open to new connections and possibilities on my recovery path?

As we reflect on these questions and recognize our strengths and weaknesses, we embark on a profound journey of self-discovery and healing, laying the foundation for long-term recovery from addiction and a brighter, more fulfilling future.

Understanding Your Values and Beliefs:
A Path to Long-Term Recovery from Addiction

Addiction recovery is not just about abstaining from substances; it is a profound journey of self-discovery and transformation. Central to this process is the exploration and understanding of one's values and beliefs. In this book, we will explore the significance of recognizing and aligning with our values and beliefs in the context of addiction recovery. Drawing inspiration from the wisdom that every storm passes, every hurt heals, and light follows darkness, we will explore how understanding these core principles can empower individuals on their path to lasting recovery.

"Every time it rains, it stops raining. Every time we hurt, we heal." These simple yet profound truths remind us of the cyclical nature of life. Understanding our values and beliefs involves recognizing that life is not a static, unchanging state. It is a continuous flow of experiences, both positive and negative. Recovery, too, is a journey of ups and downs, and by embracing the ebb and flow of life, we can find solace in knowing that no pain or challenge lasts forever.

"After darkness, there is always light, and we get reminded of this every morning, but still, we choose to believe that the night will last forever." Addiction often traps individuals in a cycle of despair and hopelessness. Recognizing our values and beliefs means understanding that even in the darkest of times, there is the potential for light and healing. It's a reminder that recovery is possible, and that hope should never be abandoned.

"Nothing lasts forever. Not the good or the bad. So we might as well smile while we're here." Understanding our values and beliefs involves acknowledging impermanence. In the throes of addiction, individuals may cling to both the highs and lows, seeking solace in familiarity.
Recovery challenges this notion by emphasizing that change is inevitable. It encourages us to find joy and positivity in the present moment, regardless of past or future uncertainties.

"To wish we were someone else is to waste the person we are." Recovery invites individuals to embrace self-acceptance and authenticity. Understanding our values means recognizing that we have inherent worth, regardless of past mistakes. It is an affirmation that we are unique and valuable just as we are, and that our true selves are worth discovering and nurturing.

"People are going to label us. It's how we overcome those labels that count." Recovery often involves facing stigma and judgment from others. Understanding our values and beliefs means recognizing that external labels do not define us. Instead, it's about focusing on our internal strength and resilience, using these qualities to rise above societal expectations and prejudices.

"It eventually gets better, without any sort of explanation; we just wake up one morning, and we're not as upset anymore." Recovery is marked by gradual, often unexplained, improvements in emotional well-being. Understanding our values and beliefs involves having faith in the process, even when the path forward seems uncertain. It's a reminder that, with time and perseverance, things can improve.

"Sometimes we may not get exactly what we thought we wanted because of hidden blessings we never saw coming." Understanding our values and beliefs means being open to unexpected opportunities and blessings. It's the recognition that recovery may lead us in directions we never anticipated, but these detours can lead to profound growth and fulfillment.

Self-Reflection Questions:

How can I embrace the cyclical nature of life, recognizing that both challenges and joys are transient?

What steps can I take to find hope even in the darkest of times, understanding that recovery is possible?

How can I practice living in the present moment and finding joy in impermanence?

What actions can I take to embrace self-acceptance and authenticity, rather than wishing to be someone else?

How can I focus on my internal strength and resilience, rather than allowing external labels to define me?

How can I maintain faith in the recovery process, even when improvement seems slow or unexplained?

Am I open to unexpected opportunities and blessings on my recovery journey, even if they deviate from my original expectations?

By reflecting on these questions and embracing our values and beliefs, we empower ourselves to navigate the challenges of addiction recovery with authenticity, resilience, and hope, ultimately paving the way for lasting recovery and a brighter future.

Cultivating Mindfulness and Introspection:
A Key to Long-Term Recovery from Addiction

Addiction recovery is a journey of self-transformation, and at its core lies the practice of mindfulness and introspection. In this book, we will explore the significance of cultivating mindfulness and introspection in the context of addiction recovery. Drawing inspiration from the wisdom that a great future doesn't require a great past and that the secret to success lies in our daily routine, we will delve into how mindfulness and introspection empower individuals to appreciate the present, make positive changes, and let go of harmful attachments.

"A great future doesn't require a great past." Addiction often leaves individuals burdened by the weight of their past mistakes and regrets. Cultivating mindfulness involves recognizing that the present moment is a blank canvas upon which a brighter future can be painted. It is an invitation to release the grip of the past and focus on the possibilities of the present and the potential for a better tomorrow.

"Sometimes we don't appreciate what we already have because we're too focused on what we want." Mindfulness encourages individuals to shift their attention from cravings and desires to the abundance of the present moment. It involves appreciating the small joys, the support of loved ones, and the progress made in recovery. By cultivating gratitude and contentment, individuals can find fulfillment in what they already possess.

"We will never change our life until we change something we do daily. The secret to our success or happiness is found in our daily routine." Introspection involves a deep examination of daily habits and routines. It is through self-reflection that individuals can identify patterns of behavior that may be hindering their recovery. By making small, positive changes in their daily routines, they can create a foundation for long-term success and happiness.

"We will not get what we truly deserve if we're too attached to the things we're supposed to let go of." Addiction often involves attachment to substances, people, or behaviors that are harmful. Mindfulness and introspection enable individuals to identify these attachments and work towards letting go. It's about understanding that true freedom and growth come from releasing what no longer serves us.

"Some bridges are meant to be burned because there are certain things in our life we can't afford to go back to." Recovery sometimes requires a decisive break from people, places, and situations that trigger addictive behaviors. Mindfulness and introspection empower individuals to recognize when certain bridges must be burned to protect their well-being and future. It's a commitment to making difficult but necessary choices.

"Don't let anyone drain us of our happiness today. Be drama-free. Rise above the petty stuff." Mindfulness encourages individuals to protect their emotional well-being. It involves recognizing toxic relationships or situations and taking steps to disengage from them. It's a commitment to remaining drama-free and rising above the distractions that can hinder recovery.

Self-Reflection Questions:

How can I shift my focus from my past mistakes to the potential for a brighter future in my recovery journey?

In what ways can I cultivate mindfulness to appreciate the present moment and find contentment in what I already have?

What aspects of my daily routine may be hindering my recovery, and how can I make positive changes to support my success and happiness?

What attachments, whether substances or behaviors, am I holding onto that I need to let go of in order to truly recover and grow?

Are there bridges in my life that need to be burned for the sake of my well-being and future, and how can I make those decisions?

How can I protect my emotional well-being and rise above petty conflicts and distractions in my recovery journey?

As we reflect on these questions and embrace mindfulness and introspection, we empower ourselves to navigate the challenges of addiction recovery with greater awareness, resilience, and the potential for lasting transformation and happiness.

Practices for Self-Reflection:
A Path to Long-Term Recovery from Addiction

Addiction recovery is a transformative journey that requires deep self-awareness and continuous self-reflection. In this book, we will explore the significance of practicing self-reflection in the context of addiction recovery. Drawing inspiration from the wisdom that our life is shaped by our choices, our perception affects our happiness, and light can be found in darkness, we will delve into how self-reflection empowers individuals to make better choices, find contentment in the present, and plant seeds of growth and recovery.

"Your life is the result of the choices you make. If you don't like your life, it's time to start making better choices." Self-reflection is about taking a close look at the decisions and choices that have led to addiction and its consequences. It involves recognizing patterns of behavior, triggers, and the impact of past choices on the present. By acknowledging the power of choice, individuals can begin to make better decisions that align with their recovery goals.

"The reason people find it so hard to be happy is that they always see the past better than it was, the present worse than it is, and the future less resolved than it will be." Addiction often distorts one's perception of reality, leading to feelings of hopelessness and discontent. Self-reflection encourages individuals to reevaluate their perceptions and challenge negative thought patterns. It is a reminder that happiness can be found in appreciating the present moment and having faith in the potential for a brighter future.

"It is during our darkest moments that we must focus to see the light." Self-reflection becomes particularly crucial during challenging times in recovery. It involves searching for the lessons and opportunities for growth within adversity. It's a reminder that even in the darkest moments of addiction, there is the potential for recovery and transformation.

"Don't judge each day by the harvest you reap, but by the seeds that you plant." Recovery is a journey that requires patience and persistence. Self-reflection involves setting realistic expectations and focusing on the daily efforts rather than the immediate outcomes. It's about understanding that each positive choice and action is a seed planted for future growth and recovery.

Self-Reflection Questions:

> What choices have led me to addiction, and how can I start making better choices in my recovery journey?

> How has my perception of the past, present, and future affected my happiness and recovery progress, and how can I work on reevaluating and reshaping these perceptions?

> In what ways can I practice self-reflection during my darkest moments in recovery to find hope and growth within adversity?

A Journey of Transformation

> Am I judging my recovery journey solely by immediate results, or am I focusing on the daily seeds of progress that I am planting?
>
> What are some practical self-reflection techniques or practices I can incorporate into my daily routine to support my recovery?
>
> How can I cultivate patience and persistence in my recovery, understanding that the journey is marked by small, incremental steps?

As we reflect on these questions and practice self-reflection, we empower ourselves to navigate the complexities of addiction recovery with greater clarity, resilience, and the potential for long-term transformation and happiness.

The Power of Knowing Oneself:
A Key to Long-Term Recovery from Addiction

Addiction recovery is a journey that requires a deep understanding of oneself. In this book, we will explore the significance of knowing oneself in the context of addiction recovery. Drawing inspiration from the wisdom that our goals can change our lives, success is rooted in hard work and determination, and age should not limit our aspirations, we will delve into how self-awareness empowers individuals to set meaningful goals, adapt to change, and remain steadfast on the path to lasting recovery.

"Don't let life change your goals, because achieving your goals can change your life." Knowing oneself involves setting clear and meaningful goals in the recovery process. It's about understanding what truly matters and working towards those objectives. Goals provide direction and purpose, serving as a driving force for recovery. By knowing oneself, individuals can align their goals with their values and aspirations.

"There are no secrets to success but working harder than the person next to you, thinking smarter than the person next to you, and wanting it just a little more than the person next to you." Self-awareness includes recognizing one's strengths and areas for improvement. It involves putting in the effort, both mentally and physically, to overcome addiction. Success in recovery requires diligence, intelligence, and a strong desire for change.

"You are never too old to set another goal or to dream a new dream." Knowing oneself means acknowledging that age should not be a limiting factor in setting and achieving goals. Recovery is possible at any stage of life. It's about realizing that it's never too late to dream new dreams and work towards a healthier, happier future.

"Start small, think big, and aim somewhere in between." Setting achievable, incremental goals is essential in recovery. Self-awareness allows individuals to assess their current capabilities and gradually build upon them. It's about finding a balance between realistic steps and ambitious aspirations, creating a sustainable path to recovery.

"You have to want to discover new lands without consenting to lose sight of the shore for very long; always know where your foundation is." Knowing oneself involves understanding one's boundaries and limits. Recovery can be an exploration of new possibilities, but it's crucial to maintain a strong foundation of support and self-awareness. It's about taking risks while ensuring that the core principles of recovery remain intact.

"Learn the rules of the game, and reinvent them if they don't apply." Recovery often requires adapting to changing circumstances and challenges. Self-awareness includes being open to learning and evolving. It's about understanding the rules of recovery and, when necessary, reinventing them to fit individual needs and circumstances.

"Be glad about your past, enjoy the present, and decide your future. No matter what, stick to your principles, but always keep an open mind." Knowing oneself involves reconciling with the past, finding joy in the present, and setting a deliberate course for the future. It's about staying true to one's principles while remaining open to new possibilities and perspectives.

Self-Reflection Questions:

- What are my goals in the recovery journey, and how do they align with my values and aspirations?

- In what ways can I work harder, think smarter, and cultivate a stronger desire for change in my recovery process?

- How can I overcome the belief that age limits my ability to set and achieve new goals in my recovery journey?

- What strategies can I use to set achievable, incremental goals while also dreaming big in my recovery?

- How do I balance the desire to explore new possibilities with the need to maintain a strong foundation and principles in my recovery?

- Am I open to learning, adapting, and reinventing the rules of recovery when necessary, and how can I incorporate this flexibility into my journey?

- How can I find gratitude for my past, joy in the present, and a clear direction for my future while staying true to my principles and remaining open-minded?

By reflecting on these questions and embracing the power of knowing oneself, individuals in recovery can navigate the challenges with greater clarity, determination, and the potential for lasting transformation and success.

Principle 2: Empathy and Compassion

A Path to Long-Term Recovery from Addiction

Empathy and compassion are powerful principles that play a significant role in the journey of long-term recovery from addiction. In this book, we will explore the significance of empathy and compassion in the context of addiction recovery. Drawing inspiration from insightful statements, we will delve into how practicing empathy and compassion can help individuals discover the value of life, define their own path, focus on the present moment, and persevere through challenges on their journey to success.

"A person who dares to waste one hour of time has not discovered the value of life." Empathy and compassion involve recognizing the value of every individual's life, including one's own. In recovery, it's important to understand that each moment is precious. Empathy means extending the same understanding and care to oneself that we would offer to others, realizing that our time and life are worth investing in for the sake of recovery.

"Never be bullied into silence. Never allow yourself to be made a victim. Accept no one's definition of your life; define yourself." Empathy and compassion empower individuals to stand up for themselves and take control of their recovery journey. It's about rejecting the victim mentality often associated with addiction and choosing to define one's life on their terms. Empathy means acknowledging one's struggles and showing oneself the kindness and support needed to heal.

"Believe that life is worth living, and your belief will help create the fact." In addiction recovery, fostering empathy and compassion towards oneself involves believing in the worthiness of life despite past mistakes. It is the belief that recovery is not just possible but also worthwhile. This belief can be a driving force in creating a meaningful, sober life.

"Don't dwell in the past, don't dream of the future, concentrate the mind on the present moment." Empathy and compassion extend to the present moment. It is about being fully present and embracing the here and now, both in our own lives and in our interactions with others. By focusing on the present, we can cultivate empathy for our own struggles and those of others, leading to a deeper understanding of the human experience.

"A life spent making mistakes is not only more honorable but more useful than a life spent doing nothing." Empathy and compassion recognize the universality of human imperfections. In recovery, it's crucial to extend understanding and compassion to oneself for past mistakes. This perspective acknowledges that mistakes are an essential part of growth and transformation.

"Life is what happens while you are busy making other plans." Empathy and compassion remind us that life is unpredictable, and recovery may not always follow a linear path. It's about embracing the journey with all its ups and downs, understanding that challenges are opportunities for growth and empathy.

A Journey of Transformation

Self-Reflection Questions:

How can I practice empathy and compassion towards myself, recognizing the value of my own life in my recovery journey?

In what ways can I stand up for myself, reject the victim mentality, and define my own path to recovery?

How can I cultivate the belief that life is worth living in the face of addiction and past mistakes, and how can this belief support my recovery?

What strategies can I employ to stay present and focus on the here and now in my recovery journey, both for myself and in my interactions with others?

How can I embrace the idea that making mistakes is an honorable and useful part of life, fostering empathy and compassion for myself and others?

How can I navigate the unpredictable nature of recovery with empathy and compassion, understanding that challenges are opportunities for growth and learning?

By reflecting on these questions and embracing empathy and compassion, individuals in recovery can foster a deeper sense of self-worth, navigate the challenges of addiction with resilience, and ultimately pave the way for long-term success and fulfillment.

The Importance of Empathy in Driving Positive Change:
A Key to Long-Term Recovery from Addiction

Empathy is a powerful force that can drive positive change in the journey of long-term recovery from addiction. In this book, we will explore the significance of empathy in the context of addiction recovery. Drawing inspiration from motivational statements, we will delve into how embracing empathy can empower individuals to start their recovery journey, face challenges with resilience, trust in the timing of their progress, and find strength in the present moment.

"Start now. Start where you are. Start with fear. Start with pain. Start with doubt. Start with handshakes. Start with voice trembling, but start. Start and don't stop." Empathy is the starting point of recovery, both for oneself and in relation to others. It's about understanding that recovery often begins in a place of vulnerability, fear, and doubt. Embracing empathy means accepting these emotions as part of the journey and starting the process of healing without hesitation.

"Let's start with where we are, with what we have. Let's just start." Empathy encourages individuals to meet themselves and others where they are in the recovery journey. It's about accepting one's current state, regardless of past mistakes, and taking the first step toward positive change. It's also about extending understanding and support to others in their recovery process, acknowledging their unique challenges.

"We'll inevitably face challenges in life. The best defense is believing that we are strong, we will survive, and we will be better for it." Empathy involves recognizing that challenges are a natural part of the recovery process. It's about empathizing with oneself and others when facing adversity and believing in the inherent strength to overcome difficulties. Empathy provides the emotional foundation for resilience.

"Everything we want is coming. Let's just start and let the universe pick the timing and the way. We just need to trust that what we want is coming, and watch how fast it comes." Empathy includes trust in the timing of one's recovery journey. It's about letting go of the need for immediate results and trusting that positive change is on its way. It involves empathizing with oneself, acknowledging the progress made, and allowing patience to guide the process.

"All we need to do is just make it through today. Don't think about tomorrow. Just focus on today." Empathy encourages individuals to focus on the present moment and take recovery one day at a time. It's about understanding that dwelling on past mistakes or worrying about the future can hinder progress. Empathy helps individuals stay grounded in the here and now, where recovery truly happens.

"Never stop trying. Never stop believing. Never give up. Our day will come." Empathy involves extending unwavering support and belief in oneself and others. It's about empathizing with the challenges and setbacks in recovery while maintaining the conviction that change is possible. Empathy provides the emotional strength to persevere through difficulties.

Self-Reflection Questions:

How can I embrace empathy as a starting point in my recovery journey, understanding that it's okay to begin with fear, pain, and doubt?

In what ways can I practice empathy in relation to myself, meeting myself where I am and acknowledging my unique challenges?

How can I cultivate empathy in my interactions with others in their recovery journey, recognizing their individual struggles and strengths?

How can I build resilience by embracing empathy when facing challenges in recovery, believing in my own strength to overcome difficulties?

What strategies can I employ to trust in the timing of my recovery and let go of the need for immediate results, fostering patience and self-compassion?

How can I practice staying present in the moment, focusing on the challenges and progress of today without dwelling on the past or worrying about the future?

> How can I maintain unwavering belief in myself and my ability to achieve positive change in my recovery journey, never giving up on the path to a better future?

By reflecting on these questions and embracing empathy, individuals in recovery can cultivate a deeper sense of understanding, resilience, and trust in the process, ultimately paving the way for long-term success and transformation.

Developing Compassion for Oneself and Others:
A Key to Long-Term Recovery from Addiction

Compassion is a transformative force that holds immense value in the journey of long-term recovery from addiction. In this book, we will explore the significance of developing compassion in the context of addiction recovery. Drawing inspiration from insightful statements, we will delve into how practicing compassion can lead to sincere respect, profound connections, and a clearer, more fulfilling life.

"One of the most sincere forms of respect is actually listening to what another has to say." Compassion begins with active listening and genuine understanding of others. In addiction recovery, it's essential to extend this compassion to oneself and others. By truly listening to the experiences, struggles, and stories of fellow individuals in recovery, we create an environment of respect and support.

"Sometimes it only takes one person to change our life. One to be there for us, to push us, to believe in us. It only takes one." Compassion recognizes the potential for transformation in the smallest acts of kindness and support. It involves being that one person who offers encouragement, pushes for progress, and believes in the capacity for change, both for oneself and others in recovery.

"When we start looking at people's hearts instead of their face, life becomes clear." Compassion encourages individuals to see beyond external appearances and judgments. It's about recognizing the humanity, struggles, and vulnerabilities that lie within each person, including oneself. This shift in perspective leads to a clearer understanding of the interconnectedness of all individuals in their recovery journeys.

"Love people for who they are and not for who we want them to be. That's where the disconnection starts." Compassion entails accepting individuals for who they are, with all their imperfections and struggles. It involves letting go of expectations and judgments, both towards oneself and others. By loving and accepting people as they are, we foster authentic connections and prevent disconnection.

Self-Reflection Questions:

> How can I practice active listening and genuine understanding in my interactions with others in recovery, fostering an environment of respect and support?

In what ways can I be the one person who offers encouragement, pushes for progress, and believes in the capacity for change in the lives of fellow individuals in recovery?

How can I shift my perspective to see beyond external appearances and judgments, recognizing the humanity, struggles, and vulnerabilities within each person, including myself?

What strategies can I employ to love and accept people for who they are, without imposing unrealistic expectations or judgments on them, promoting authentic connections in the process?

How can I extend compassion to myself, acknowledging my own imperfections and struggles while fostering self-acceptance and self-love in my recovery journey?

By reflecting on these questions and embracing compassion, individuals in recovery can create a more empathetic and connected environment, both for themselves and others, ultimately contributing to long-term success, transformation, and fulfillment.

Understanding the Interconnectedness of All Beings:
A Key to Long-Term Recovery from Addiction

Understanding the interconnectedness of all beings is a profound concept that holds great significance in the journey of long-term recovery from addiction. In this book, we will explore the depth of this understanding and its relevance in addiction recovery. Drawing inspiration from inspirational statements, we will delve into how embracing the interconnectedness of all beings can help individuals overcome hurdles, maintain authenticity, adapt to life's challenges, and craft a new, transformative ending to their journey.

"Life's problems wouldn't be called 'hurdles' if there wasn't a way to get over them." The idea of interconnectedness reminds us that we are not alone in our struggles. In addiction recovery, it's important to understand that others have faced similar hurdles and overcome them. This understanding offers hope and inspiration, emphasizing that there is a path to recovery for everyone.

"To be nobody but yourself in a world which is doing its best, day and night, to make you everybody else means to fight the hardest battle which any human being can fight; so never stop fighting." Understanding the interconnectedness of all beings involves recognizing the authenticity and uniqueness of each individual. It's about acknowledging that everyone's journey is distinct, and no one should be pressured to conform to societal expectations. In recovery, staying true to oneself and fighting for one's authenticity is a powerful way to navigate the challenges of addiction.

"Things turn out best for the people who make the best out of the way things turn out." Interconnectedness reminds us that our actions and choices affect not only ourselves but also those around us. In recovery, it's crucial to recognize the ripple effect of our decisions and strive to make the best out of even challenging circumstances. By doing so, we contribute to positive change in our lives and the lives of others.

"Though no one can go back and make a brand new start, anyone can start from now and make a brand new ending." The concept of interconnectedness emphasizes that we are not isolated beings; our actions and choices impact the world around us. In recovery, it's essential to understand that it's never too late to make a fresh start and create a new, transformative ending to our story. By embracing interconnectedness, we can find the motivation and support needed to rewrite our narrative.

Self-Reflection Questions:

How can I draw strength and inspiration from the interconnectedness of all beings, knowing that others have overcome similar hurdles in their recovery journeys?

In what ways can I stay true to myself and resist societal pressures to conform to expectations, recognizing the value of authenticity in recovery?

How can I make the best out of challenging circumstances in my recovery, understanding the impact of my choices on myself and those around me?

What steps can I take to start from where I am now and create a brand new ending to my recovery journey, embracing the interconnectedness that surrounds me?

By reflecting on these questions and embracing the interconnectedness of all beings, individuals in recovery can find inspiration, authenticity, resilience, and the motivation to craft a transformative and lasting ending to their addiction recovery journey.

Practicing Kindness and Empathy in Daily Life:
A Compassionate Path to Long-Term Recovery from Addiction

Practicing kindness and empathy in daily life is a fundamental aspect of the journey toward long-term recovery from addiction. In this book, we will explore the profound impact of cultivating kindness and empathy in the context of addiction recovery. Drawing inspiration from motivational statements, we will delve into how the practice of kindness and empathy can empower individuals to start their recovery journey, face challenges with resilience, trust in the timing of their progress, and ultimately lead to a more fulfilling life.

"Start now. Start where you are. Start with fear. Start with pain. Start with doubt. Start with handshakes. Start with voice trembling, but start. Start and don't stop." The practice of kindness and empathy begins with self-compassion. It involves understanding that recovery often commences from a place of vulnerability, fear, and doubt. Embracing kindness means accepting these emotions as part of the journey and initiating the process of healing without hesitation.

"Let's start with where we are, with what we have. Let's just start." Kindness and empathy encourage individuals to meet themselves and others where they are in the recovery journey. It's about acknowledging one's current state, regardless of past mistakes, and taking the first step toward positive change. It's also about extending understanding and support to others in their recovery process, acknowledging their unique challenges.

"We'll inevitably face challenges in life. The best defense is believing that we are strong, we will survive, and we will be better for it." Kindness and empathy provide the emotional foundation for resilience. It's about recognizing that challenges are a natural part of the recovery process and that believing in one's inner strength is the best defense against adversity. Empathy supports individuals in facing their own challenges while also offering support to others.

"Everything we want is coming. Let's just start and let the universe pick the timing and the way. We just need to trust that what we want is coming, and watch how fast it comes." Kindness and empathy extend to trust in the timing of one's recovery journey. It's about letting go of the need for immediate results and trusting that positive change is on its way. It involves empathizing with oneself, acknowledging the progress made, and allowing patience to guide the process.

"All we need to do is just make it through today. Don't think about tomorrow. Just focus on today." Kindness and empathy encourage individuals to stay present in the moment and take recovery one day at a time. It's about understanding that dwelling on past mistakes or worrying about the future can hinder progress. Empathy helps individuals stay grounded in the here and now, where recovery truly happens.

"Never stop trying. Never stop believing. Never give up. Our day will come." The practice of kindness and empathy involves extending unwavering support and belief in oneself and others. It's about empathizing with the challenges and setbacks in recovery while maintaining the conviction that change is possible. Empathy provides the emotional strength to persevere through difficulties.

Self-Reflection Questions:

How can I embrace the practice of kindness and empathy as a starting point in my recovery journey, understanding that it's okay to begin with fear, pain, and doubt?

In what ways can I practice kindness and empathy in relation to myself, meeting myself where I am and acknowledging my unique challenges in recovery?

How can I cultivate kindness and empathy in my interactions with others in their recovery journey, recognizing their individual struggles and strengths?

How can I build resilience by embracing kindness and empathy when facing challenges in recovery, believing in my own strength to overcome difficulties?

What strategies can I employ to trust in the timing of my recovery and let go of the need for immediate results, fostering patience and self-compassion?

How can I practice staying present in the moment, focusing on the challenges and progress of today without dwelling on the past or worrying about the future?

How can I maintain unwavering belief in myself and my ability to achieve positive change in my recovery journey, never giving up on the path to a better future?

By reflecting on these questions and embracing the practice of kindness and empathy, individuals in recovery can cultivate a deeper sense of understanding, resilience, and trust in the process, ultimately paving the way for long-term success and transformation.

Principle 3: Vision and Purpose

Guiding Principles for Long-Term Recovery from Addiction

Vision and purpose are powerful principles that play a pivotal role in the journey of long-term recovery from addiction. In this book, we will explore the significance of having a clear vision and a sense of purpose in the context of addiction recovery. Drawing inspiration from thought-provoking statements, we will delve into how embracing vision and purpose can help individuals let go of regrets, focus on the present and future, cultivate authenticity, and craft a meaningful narrative of their recovery journey.

"That's the funny thing about time. It is only in looking back that it's easy to connect the dots. To see exactly why everything needed to happen the way that it did. Everything happens kind of the way it's supposed to happen, and we just watch it unfold. And you can't control it." Having a vision and purpose in recovery involves understanding that every experience, even the most challenging ones, contributes to one's growth and transformation. It's about accepting that, in hindsight, the pieces of the puzzle start to make sense, and the journey unfolds as it's meant to.

"Looking back, you can't say, 'I should've...' You didn't, and had you, the outcome would have been different." Vision and purpose encourage individuals to let go of regrets and the "if only" mindset. It's about understanding that dwelling on past actions or decisions can't change the past. Instead, the focus should be on making positive choices in the present and working toward a better future.

"The trouble with 'if only' is that it doesn't change anything. It keeps the person facing the wrong way – backward instead of forward. It wastes time. In the end, if you let it become a habit, it can become a real roadblock – an excuse for not trying anymore." Having a clear vision and purpose shifts the focus forward, encouraging individuals to learn from the past without dwelling on it. It's about using past experiences as lessons to inform and motivate present actions.

"Authenticity is everything! You have to wake up every day and look in the mirror, and you want to be proud of the person who's looking back at you. And you can only do that if you're being honest with yourself and being a person of high character." Vision and purpose guide individuals to live authentically. It's about aligning one's actions with their values and principles, leading to a sense of pride and self-worth. Authenticity becomes the foundation for a purpose-driven life.

"You have an opportunity every single day to write that story of your life." Having a vision and purpose in recovery empowers individuals to take control of their narrative. It's about recognizing that each day presents a chance to make choices that contribute to the story they want to tell. Vision and purpose become the guiding lights in crafting a meaningful and purposeful recovery journey.

A Journey of Transformation

Self-Reflection Questions:

How can I use the concept of connecting the dots in my recovery journey, recognizing that every experience contributes to my growth and transformation?

In what ways can I let go of regrets and the "if only" mindset, focusing on positive choices in the present and a better future?

How can I shift my focus from dwelling on the past to using past experiences as valuable lessons to inform and motivate my present actions in recovery?

What steps can I take to live authentically, aligning my actions with my values and principles, and fostering a sense of pride and self-worth?

How can I view each day as an opportunity to write the story of my life in recovery, guided by a clear vision and a sense of purpose?

By reflecting on these questions and embracing vision and purpose, individuals in recovery can navigate their journey with clarity, resilience, and a strong sense of direction, ultimately leading to long-term success and fulfillment.

Defining a Clear Vision for Change:
A Path to Long-Term Recovery from Addiction

A clear vision for change is a crucial element in the journey of long-term recovery from addiction. In this book, we will explore the significance of defining a clear vision for change in the context of addiction recovery. Drawing inspiration from insightful statements, we will delve into how having a vision can lead to self-discovery, courage, growth, and the pursuit of a brighter future.

"There is nothing outside of yourself that can ever enable you to get better, stronger, richer, quicker, or smarter. Everything is within. Everything exists inside of you. Seek nothing outside of yourself." Defining a clear vision for change involves recognizing that the power for transformation resides within oneself. It's about realizing that change starts from within and that external factors can only support, but not replace, inner resolve and determination.

"No matter how many mistakes you make or how slow you progress, you are still way ahead of everyone who isn't trying." Having a clear vision for change means understanding that mistakes and setbacks are part of the journey. It's about having the resilience to keep moving forward, even when progress is slow. A vision reminds individuals that the effort they put into recovery is always a step ahead of those who do not try.

"Most of the things worth doing in the world had been declared impossible before they were done. The greatest mistake we make is living in constant fear that we will make one." A clear vision for change encourages individuals to embrace the seemingly impossible. It's about pushing boundaries, overcoming self-doubt, and taking bold steps toward recovery. A vision inspires individuals to let go of the fear of making mistakes and to believe in their capacity to achieve the seemingly unachievable.

"Your past was never a mistake if you learned from it. It takes courage to grow up and become who you really are." Having a vision involves learning from the past and using it as a stepping stone for growth. It's about recognizing that one's history, even if marked by mistakes, can be a valuable source of wisdom and resilience. A vision inspires the courage to embrace personal growth and authenticity.

"The past is behind, learn from it. The future is ahead, prepare for it. The present is here, live it." A clear vision for change guides individuals to adopt a balanced perspective on time. It's about learning from the past, preparing for a brighter future, and fully living in the present moment. A vision encourages individuals to make the most of each day in their recovery journey.

"Good things come to those who believe, better things come to those who are patient, and the best things come to those who don't give up and work for it." Having a clear vision involves belief, patience, and determination. It's about understanding that recovery is a journey, not a destination, and that the best outcomes come to those who persistently work toward their vision of change.

Self-Reflection Questions:

How can I tap into my inner resources and recognize that change starts from within, defining a clear vision for my recovery journey?

In what ways can I embrace the inevitability of mistakes and setbacks in recovery, understanding that they are valuable learning experiences that keep me ahead of those who do not try?

How can I challenge preconceived limitations and fears, aligning my vision with the belief that achieving the seemingly impossible is within my reach?

What strategies can I employ to learn from my past without dwelling on it, embracing personal growth and authenticity in my recovery?

How can I balance my focus on the past, present, and future, making the most of each day in my recovery journey guided by my vision?

How can I maintain belief, patience, and determination as I work toward my vision of change, understanding that good things come to those who persistently strive for them?

By reflecting on these questions and defining a clear vision for change, individuals in recovery can empower themselves to pursue a purposeful and transformative journey, leading to long-term success and fulfillment.

A Journey of Transformation

Creating a Vivid Mental Picture of Desired Outcomes:
The Key to Long-Term Recovery from Addiction

Creating a vivid mental picture of desired outcomes is a vital component of the journey towards long-term recovery from addiction. In this book, we will explore the significance of visualizing one's desired outcomes in the context of addiction recovery. Drawing inspiration from thought-provoking statements, we will delve into how the power of mental imagery can help individuals overcome life's challenges, embrace their authentic selves, adapt to circumstances, and craft a new and hopeful ending to their recovery journey.

"Life's problems wouldn't be called 'hurdles' if there wasn't a way to get over them." Creating a vivid mental picture of desired outcomes begins with the understanding that challenges are not insurmountable obstacles but rather hurdles to be overcome. It involves visualizing oneself successfully navigating these hurdles in the journey to recovery.

"To be nobody but yourself in a world which is doing its best, day and night, to make you everybody else means to fight the hardest battle which any human being can fight; so never stop fighting." The power of mental imagery encourages individuals to visualize themselves as their authentic selves, free from the chains of addiction. It involves fighting the battle to maintain one's true identity in a world that often pressures conformity.

"Things turn out best for the people who make the best out of the way things turn out." Visualizing desired outcomes in recovery means actively choosing to see the positive aspects of one's circumstances, even when they seem challenging. It involves creating a mental image of a brighter future and focusing on the potential for growth and transformation.

"Though no one can go back and make a brand new start, anyone can start from now and make a brand new ending." The power of mental imagery empowers individuals to let go of regrets about the past and visualize a new beginning. It involves creating a clear and inspiring mental picture of the ending they want for their recovery journey.

Self-Reflection Questions:

How can I use the power of mental imagery to visualize overcoming the hurdles and challenges in my recovery journey?

In what ways can I create a vivid mental picture of my authentic self and maintain my identity in a world that pressures conformity?

How can I shift my perspective to see the positive aspects of my circumstances, even in challenging moments, and visualize a brighter future in recovery?

What steps can I take to let go of regrets about the past and visualize a new and hopeful ending to my recovery journey?

By reflecting on these questions and harnessing the power of mental imagery, individuals in recovery can gain a clearer sense of direction, inner strength, and resilience. This can ultimately lead to long-term success and a fulfilling recovery journey.

Setting Long-Term Goals Aligned with Your Vision:
A Blueprint for Lasting Recovery from Addiction

Setting long-term goals aligned with your vision is an essential step on the path to long-term recovery from addiction. In this book, we will explore the significance of establishing goals that are in harmony with one's vision for recovery. Drawing inspiration from insightful statements, we will delve into how this process allows individuals to connect the dots of their recovery journey, overcome the "if only" mindset, foster authenticity, and craft a story of transformation and resilience.

"That's the funny thing about time. It is only in looking back that it's easy to connect the dots. To see exactly why everything needed to happen the way that it did. Everything happens kind of the way it's supposed to happen, and we just watch it unfold. And you can't control it." Setting long-term goals aligned with your vision starts with recognizing that every step in your recovery journey, even the seemingly insignificant ones, plays a crucial role. It's about understanding that the path to recovery unfolds as it should, and your past experiences, both triumphs and challenges, have contributed to your growth.

"Looking back, you can't say, 'I should've... ' You didn't, and had you, the outcome would have been different." Establishing goals that align with your vision encourages you to release the "if only" mindset. It involves accepting that dwelling on past regrets or wishing for different choices won't change the past. Instead, it's about focusing on what you can do now and in the future to shape your recovery journey.

"The trouble with 'if only' is that it doesn't change anything. It keeps the person facing the wrong way — backward instead of forward. It wastes time. In the end, if you let it become a habit, it can become a real roadblock — an excuse for not trying anymore." Setting long-term goals involves turning your gaze forward, toward your vision for recovery. It means shedding the weight of regrets and excuses and taking active steps to move in the direction of your aspirations.

"Authenticity is everything! You have to wake up every day and look in the mirror, and you want to be proud of the person who's looking back at you. And you can only do that if you're being honest with yourself and being a person of high character." Goals that align with your vision foster authenticity. It's about setting objectives that resonate with your values and principles. Achieving these goals allows you to wake up each day and be proud of the person you've become in your recovery journey.

"You have an opportunity every single day to write that story of your life. You always knew looking back on your tears would bring you laughter, but you never knew looking back on your laughter would make me cry." Setting long-term goals means taking charge of the narrative of your recovery.

A Journey of Transformation

It's about recognizing that every day offers an opportunity to write a story of resilience and transformation. It involves celebrating not only your moments of joy but also your growth through tears.

Self-Reflection Questions:

How can I set long-term goals that align with my vision for recovery, recognizing the importance of each step in my journey, even the challenging ones?

In what ways can I release the "if only" mindset and focus on shaping my recovery journey through proactive steps and choices in the present?

How can I turn my gaze forward, away from regrets and excuses, and actively pursue my vision for recovery?

What strategies can I employ to ensure that my long-term goals are in harmony with my values and principles, fostering authenticity in my recovery journey?

How can I embrace each day as an opportunity to write a story of resilience and transformation, celebrating both moments of joy and growth through challenges?

By reflecting on these questions and setting long-term goals aligned with your vision, individuals in recovery can take meaningful steps toward lasting change and personal fulfillment. Your recovery journey is a story waiting to be written, one that holds the potential for profound transformation and inspiration.

Connecting Personal Purpose with the Greater Good:
A Path to Lasting Recovery from Addiction

Connecting personal purpose with the greater good is a transformative journey that can lead to long-term recovery from addiction. In this book, we will explore the significance of aligning one's personal purpose with a sense of contribution to the larger community. Drawing inspiration from profound statements, we will delve into how this connection empowers individuals to recognize their inner strength, overcome fear, learn from their past, and work toward a future filled with hope and positive change.

"There is nothing outside of yourself that can ever enable you to get better, stronger, richer, quicker, or smarter. Everything is within. Everything exists inside of you. Seek nothing outside of yourself." The process of connecting personal purpose with the greater good begins with an understanding that the capacity for growth and change resides within. It's about recognizing that the journey to recovery starts from within, where the strength to overcome addiction is found.

"No matter how many mistakes you make or how slow you progress, you are still way ahead of everyone who isn't trying." Aligning personal purpose with the greater good means acknowledging that making mistakes is part of the human experience. It involves accepting that progress may be gradual but is still significant. It's about realizing that the willingness to try, even in the face of setbacks, places you ahead of those who do not attempt to change.

"Most of the things worth doing in the world had been declared impossible before they were done. The greatest mistake we make is living in constant fear that we will make one." Connecting personal purpose with the greater good encourages individuals to break free from the fear of failure. It involves recognizing that many remarkable achievements were once deemed impossible. It's about daring to pursue one's purpose, even if it seems challenging or unconventional.

"Your past was never a mistake if you learned from it. It takes courage to grow up and become who you really are. The past is behind; learn from it. The future is ahead; prepare for it. The present is here; live it." This connection allows individuals to view their past, no matter how marred by addiction, as a source of learning and growth. It involves the courage to embrace one's true self and prepare for a future filled with promise. It's about fully experiencing and living in the present moment.

"Good things come to those who believe, better things come to those who are patient, and the best things come to those who don't give up and work for it." Aligning personal purpose with the greater good instills a belief in the possibility of positive change. It involves patience, knowing that transformation takes time. It encourages individuals to persevere and work diligently toward their goals.

Self-Reflection Questions:

>How can I connect my personal purpose with the greater good, recognizing that my inner strength is a key asset in my recovery journey?

>In what ways can I embrace my past mistakes as opportunities for learning and growth, understanding that they do not define my future?

>How can I overcome the fear of pursuing my personal purpose, even if it seems challenging or unconventional, recognizing that many great achievements were once thought impossible?

>What steps can I take to live in the present moment, fully experiencing the here and now, while also preparing for a future filled with hope and positive change?

>How can I cultivate belief in the possibility of good things to come, practice patience in my recovery journey, and remain committed to working diligently toward my goals?

By reflecting on these questions and connecting personal purpose with the greater good, individuals in recovery can embark on a path of profound self-discovery, resilience, and lasting change. This connection serves as a source of inspiration and motivation, enabling individuals to work towards a future that is aligned with their authentic selves and contributes positively to the world.

Identifying Your Life's Purpose:
A Journey to Long-Term Recovery from Addiction

Identifying your life's purpose is a profound and transformative step toward achieving long-term recovery from addiction. In this book, we will explore the significance of discovering one's life purpose and how it can inspire individuals to see the world in a new light, find strength in adversity, and embrace the beauty of life. Drawing wisdom from insightful statements, we will delve into how recognizing one's purpose is the key to unlocking personal growth and fulfillment.

"Today is an opportunity to see something new or see something in a new way." Identifying your life's purpose begins with a commitment to explore the world with fresh eyes. It encourages individuals to seize each day as an opportunity to gain new perspectives and to challenge preconceived notions.

"Seeing is enough to look, but looking is not enough to see. We mostly see what we have learned to expect to see." Recognizing your life's purpose means transcending superficial observations and delving deeper into the essence of existence. It involves moving beyond mere looking to truly seeing the profound meaning and potential in every aspect of life.

"Easily mistaken, it is not about a love for adversity, it is about knowing a strength and a faith so great that adversity, in all its adverse manifestations, hardly even exists." Discovering your life's purpose empowers you to find strength and resilience in the face of adversity. It's about cultivating a profound inner strength and unwavering faith that can diminish the impact of life's challenges.

"I know people can be judgmental and difficult. But if you shut yourself away from the world, you'll never see how beautiful it really is." Embracing your life's purpose involves connecting with the world and its inhabitants. It encourages individuals to look beyond the judgments and difficulties they encounter and to appreciate the inherent beauty and wonder of life.

"Allow yourself to be amazed, awestruck, and completely dumbfounded by life's mysteries and magic. We don't have to fully understand everything in life to feel meaningfully alive." Identifying your life's purpose invites you to surrender to the awe-inspiring mysteries and magic that life offers. It's about acknowledging that not everything needs to be fully understood to experience a deep sense of meaning and aliveness.

"Destinations are end points. Journeys are learnings, paths of possibilities, blossoming... fresh beginnings." Discovering your life's purpose is not about reaching a final destination; it's about embarking on a lifelong journey of self-discovery and growth. It involves recognizing that every step is an opportunity for learning, and each moment is a fresh beginning.

Self-Reflection Questions:

How can I embark on a journey to discover my life's purpose, viewing each day as an opportunity to see the world in a new way?

In what ways can I move beyond superficial observations and truly see the profound meaning and potential in life's experiences?

How can I cultivate inner strength and unwavering faith to face adversity with resilience, knowing that I possess the power to overcome challenges?

What steps can I take to connect with the world, appreciating its beauty despite the judgment and difficulties that may arise?

How can I surrender to life's mysteries and magic, embracing the profound sense of meaning and aliveness they offer, even without full understanding?

What mindset shift can I make to view life as an ongoing journey of self-discovery and growth, with each moment as a fresh beginning?

By reflecting on these questions and embarking on a journey to identify their life's purpose, individuals in recovery can tap into a deep well of inspiration, resilience, and fulfillment. This connection to purpose can serve as a guiding light, leading them toward lasting recovery and a life rich with meaning.

Aligning Your Purpose with Your Change-Making Goals:
A Path to Lasting Recovery from Addiction

Aligning your purpose with your change-making goals is a pivotal step on the journey to long-term recovery from addiction. In this book, we will explore the significance of aligning personal purpose with goals for change and how it can empower individuals to discover their second wind, make the best choices, and manifest their dreams. Drawing inspiration from insightful statements, we will delve into how this alignment creates a path to patience, happiness, and the realization of aspirations.

"Most people never run far enough on their first wind to find out they've got a second." Aligning your purpose with your change-making goals begins with recognizing that your potential for change and growth is not limited to a single effort. It encourages individuals to persevere and discover their second wind, which often carries them further than they ever imagined in their recovery journey.

"We all must try to be the best person we can by making the best choices, and by making the most of the talents we've been given." Identifying your purpose and aligning it with change-making goals involves a commitment to personal growth. It's about striving to be the best version of yourself by consistently making choices that serve your recovery and by leveraging your unique talents and strengths.

"Dreams come in a few sizes too big so we can grow into them." Aligning your purpose with your goals means setting aspirations that challenge and stretch your capabilities. It acknowledges that dreams are often larger than life, but it's through pursuing these ambitious goals that individuals can expand and grow into the individuals they aspire to become.

"Be patient, the oppressive feeling of want pushes your dreams away! Be patient, BE HAPPY, work hard & they will appear!" Patience is a key component of aligning your purpose with change-making goals. It's about understanding that the feeling of impatience can hinder progress. Instead, patience allows you to maintain a sense of contentment and happiness while diligently working toward your goals. This positive mindset, combined with hard work, ultimately brings dreams closer to realization.

Self-Reflection Questions:

> How can I align my personal purpose with my goals for change in my recovery journey, recognizing that I have the potential to discover my second wind and achieve more than I initially thought possible?
>
> In what ways can I consistently make choices that align with my personal growth and recovery, leveraging my unique talents and strengths to become the best version of myself?
>
> How can I embrace dreams that may seem larger than life, understanding that they provide an opportunity for personal growth and expansion?
>
> What strategies can I employ to cultivate patience in my recovery journey, knowing that impatience can hinder progress, while maintaining a sense of happiness and contentment?
>
> How can I combine patience with hard work to bring my change-making goals closer to realization?

By reflecting on these questions and aligning personal purpose with change-making goals, individuals in recovery can unlock their potential, overcome challenges, and ultimately achieve lasting recovery. This alignment serves as a compass, guiding them toward a future filled with fulfillment, personal growth, and the realization of their dreams.

Principle 4: Resilience and Adaptability

Navigating the Path to Lasting Recovery from Addiction

Resilience and adaptability are fundamental principles in the journey to long-term recovery from addiction. In this book, we will explore the significance of these principles and how they empower individuals to appreciate life's little moments, make everyday decisions, and persevere through challenges. Drawing inspiration from insightful statements, we will delve into how resilience and adaptability can lead to transformation, growth, and the realization of dreams.

"It's the little things that make living worthwhile." Resilience and adaptability begin with an appreciation for life's small pleasures. It encourages individuals to find joy in everyday moments, even during the challenging process of recovery. It's about recognizing that these little things collectively create a fulfilling life.

"When it comes down to it, it isn't the major choices we make in life, career, marriage, etc. that count the most. It is the everyday minor decisions that make life work for us." Resilience and adaptability involve making conscious choices, especially the minor ones, that contribute to the overall well-being and success in recovery. It emphasizes the importance of consistent, positive decisions that align with one's goals.

"Enjoy the little things, for one day you may look back and realize they were the big things." Resilience and adaptability encourage individuals to savor the present moment. It's about recognizing that the little joys and accomplishments in recovery have the power to become significant milestones when viewed through the lens of time.

"Don't ever be afraid to try to make things better; you might be surprised at the results." Resilience and adaptability propel individuals to seek improvements, even when faced with adversity. It instills a sense of courage to embrace change and the unknown, understanding that remarkable outcomes can emerge from such endeavors.

"When you get into a tight place and everything goes against you, and it seems as though you could not hang on a minute longer, never give up, for that is just the place and time that the tide will turn." Resilience and adaptability underscore the importance of perseverance during the most challenging moments. It reminds individuals that difficult times often precede breakthroughs and transformation.

"Never let your head hang down. Never give up and sit down. Find another way." Resilience and adaptability inspire individuals to maintain a positive outlook and to continually seek alternatives when faced with obstacles. It's about refusing to accept defeat and having the determination to find new paths.

A Journey of Transformation

"A dream doesn't become reality through magic; it takes sweat, determination, and hard work." Resilience and adaptability emphasize that the realization of dreams and goals requires effort and persistence. It encourages individuals to work diligently toward their aspirations, knowing that the journey may be demanding but ultimately rewarding.

Self-Reflection Questions:

How can I cultivate resilience and adaptability in my recovery journey, starting with an appreciation for life's little pleasures?

In what ways can I make everyday decisions that align with my recovery goals and contribute to my overall well-being?

How can I embrace the present moment and find joy in the small accomplishments and joys in my recovery journey?

What strategies can I employ to overcome fear and actively seek improvements in my life and recovery, even in the face of adversity?

How can I maintain perseverance during challenging times, recognizing that they often precede moments of transformation and growth?

What steps can I take to remain determined and find alternative paths when faced with obstacles in my recovery journey?

How can I commit to working diligently toward my dreams and goals, understanding that they require effort and persistence to become a reality?

By reflecting on these questions and embodying the principles of resilience and adaptability, individuals in recovery can navigate their journey with greater strength and determination. These principles serve as a guiding force, leading them toward lasting recovery and the fulfillment of their dreams and aspirations.

Embracing Challenges as Opportunities for Growth:
A Path to Lasting Recovery from Addiction

Embracing challenges as opportunities for growth is a profound principle on the journey to long-term recovery from addiction. In this book, we will explore the significance of this principle and how it empowers individuals to forgive, persevere, and transform adversity into strength. Drawing wisdom from insightful statements, we will delve into the power of forgiveness and determination in facing life's difficulties and emerging as stronger individuals.

"A person that cannot forgive others breaks the bridge over which they must pass themselves; for every person has the need to be forgiven." Embracing challenges begins with the act of forgiveness.

It involves letting go of grudges and resentments, not just toward others but also toward oneself. Forgiveness mends the bridges that allow individuals to move forward in their recovery journey.

"If it were not for the hopes of forgiveness, the heart would break." Forgiveness is not just an act of kindness toward others; it is also a means of self-preservation. Recognizing the power of forgiveness gives individuals hope, preventing their hearts from breaking under the weight of past mistakes and regrets.

"All things are difficult before they are easy, but an invincible determination can accomplish almost anything, and in this lies the great distinction between a great person and a little person." Embracing challenges involves acknowledging that growth often arises from tackling difficult situations. It's about developing an unwavering determination to overcome obstacles and transform adversity into a catalyst for personal greatness.

Self-Reflection Questions:

> How can I embrace challenges in my recovery journey as opportunities for growth, starting with forgiveness toward myself and others?
>
> In what ways can I recognize the transformative power of forgiveness, understanding that it mends bridges and preserves the hope needed to heal?
>
> How can I navigate the difficulty of challenges in my recovery journey, knowing that their resolution often leads to ease and personal growth?
>
> What strategies can I employ to cultivate invincible determination in the face of adversity, understanding that it is a key factor that distinguishes greatness from mediocrity?

By reflecting on these questions and embracing challenges as opportunities for growth, individuals in recovery can navigate their journey with greater resilience and determination. This principle serves as a beacon of hope, leading them toward lasting recovery and personal greatness.

Developing a Growth Mindset:
Overcoming Challenges on the Path to Recovery

Developing a growth mindset is a vital principle for someone seeking long-term recovery from addiction. In this book, we will explore the significance of cultivating a growth mindset and how it empowers individuals to embrace failure as a stepping stone to success, navigate obstacles with resilience, and measure success by their ability to overcome challenges. Drawing inspiration from insightful statements, we will delve into the transformative power of a growth mindset in the recovery journey.

"Don't be afraid to fail. Don't waste energy trying to cover up failure. Learn from your failures and go on to the next challenge." Developing a growth mindset starts with the acceptance that failure is a natural part of the journey to recovery. It encourages individuals to view failures as valuable learning experiences, not as reasons to give up. Failure becomes a stepping stone to the next challenge.

"It's OK to fail. If you're not failing, you're not growing." A growth mindset reframes the perception of failure. It acknowledges that failure is not a setback but a sign of growth and progress. When individuals are not failing, they are likely staying within their comfort zone, inhibiting their potential for personal development.

"If you're trying to achieve, there will be roadblocks. Everybody has had them. But obstacles don't have to stop you. If you run into a wall, don't turn around and give up. Figure out how to climb it, go through it, or work around it." A growth mindset empowers individuals to confront obstacles with determination and creativity. It fosters problem-solving skills and resilience, ensuring that roadblocks do not hinder progress.

"People have learned that success is to be measured not so much by the position that one has reached in life as by the obstacles which they had to overcome while trying to succeed." Developing a growth mindset shifts the focus from external achievements to internal growth. Success is redefined as the ability to overcome challenges, demonstrating resilience and a commitment to personal development.

"Most of the important things in the world have been accomplished by people who have kept on trying when there seemed to be no hope at all." A growth mindset reminds individuals that persistence is a powerful force in overcoming seemingly insurmountable challenges. It encourages them to keep trying, even in the face of adversity, knowing that hope can emerge from the darkest moments.

Self-Reflection Questions:

    How can I cultivate a growth mindset in my recovery journey, beginning with an acceptance of failure as a valuable learning experience?

    In what ways can I reframe my perception of failure, recognizing that it signifies growth and progress rather than defeat?

    How can I approach obstacles in my recovery journey with resilience and creativity, understanding that they are opportunities to develop problem-solving skills?

    What strategies can I employ to measure success by my ability to overcome challenges and demonstrate a commitment to personal growth?

    How can I maintain persistence in my recovery journey, even when hope seems elusive, knowing that it is often the key to achieving remarkable accomplishments?

By reflecting on these questions and developing a growth mindset, individuals in recovery can navigate their journey with greater resilience, adaptability, and determination. This principle serves as a foundation for lasting recovery and personal growth, ensuring that challenges are seen as opportunities rather than setbacks.

Building Resilience in the Face of Adversity:
A Path to Lasting Recovery from Addiction

Building resilience in the face of adversity is a crucial principle for those seeking long-term recovery from addiction. In this book, we will explore the significance of developing resilience and how it empowers individuals to let go of the past, embrace change, protect their spirit, and choose growth over stagnation. Drawing inspiration from insightful statements, we will delve into the transformative power of resilience on the path to recovery.

"If you want to reach out for something new, you must first let go of what's in your hand. If you lost it, it's because you're meant to find something better. Trust, let go, and make room for what's coming." Building resilience begins with the willingness to let go of the past, especially when it involves addictive behaviors. It's about trusting that what lies ahead in recovery holds the promise of something better, and making room for growth by releasing old habits.

"The only way to get over the past is to leave it behind. If you spend your time re-living moments that are gone forever, you might miss the special moments that are yet to come." Resilience involves focusing on the present and the future rather than dwelling on past mistakes. It encourages individuals to learn from the past but not be defined by it, allowing them to fully experience the beauty of the present and the potential of the future.

"A person may break your heart and damage your pride, but never give them the power to break your spirit." Building resilience means safeguarding one's inner strength and spirit. It's about recognizing that external setbacks, including the actions of others, should not diminish one's inner resilience. It empowers individuals to protect their spirit from external influences.

"Everything is either an obstacle to growth or an obstacle to keep you from growing. The good thing is: you get to choose." Resilience allows individuals to perceive challenges as opportunities for growth rather than insurmountable obstacles. It emphasizes the power of choice in determining whether adversity hinders or fuels personal development.

Self-Reflection Questions:

> How can I build resilience in my recovery journey by letting go of addictive behaviors and making room for positive change?

> In what ways can I leave the past behind and focus on the present and future, ensuring that I don't miss the special moments yet to come?

A Journey of Transformation

> How can I protect my spirit and inner strength from external influences, even when faced with heartbreak and pride damage?

> What strategies can I employ to view challenges as opportunities for growth, recognizing my power to choose how I respond to adversity?

By reflecting on these questions and embracing the principle of building resilience, individuals in recovery can navigate their journey with greater strength, adaptability, and determination. This principle serves as a cornerstone for lasting recovery and personal growth, ensuring that adversity is transformed into a catalyst for positive change.

Navigating Change and Uncertainty: Embracing a Path to Lasting Recovery

Navigating change and uncertainty is a fundamental principle for someone seeking long-term recovery from addiction. In this book, we will explore the profound importance of embracing change, letting go of the past, protecting one's spirit, and choosing personal growth in the face of adversity and uncertainty. Drawing inspiration from insightful statements, we will delve into the transformative power of navigating change and uncertainty on the path to recovery.

"If you want to reach out for something new, you must first let go of what's in your hand. If you lost it, it's because you're meant to find something better. Trust, let go, and make room for what's coming." Navigating change starts with the act of letting go, especially of addictive behaviors and old patterns. It requires trust in the belief that what lies ahead in recovery holds the promise of something better. Letting go creates space for personal growth and transformation.

"The only way to get over the past is to leave it behind. If you spend your time re-living moments that are gone forever, you might miss the special moments that are yet to come." Embracing change means leaving the past behind. It involves shifting focus from past mistakes to the possibilities of the present and the future. By doing so, individuals can fully experience the richness of life and the potential for positive change.

"A person may break your heart and damage your pride, but never give them the power to break your spirit." Navigating change and uncertainty requires protecting one's inner strength and spirit. It acknowledges that external setbacks, such as heartbreak or damage to one's pride, should not have the power to extinguish one's inner resilience. Protecting one's spirit is vital for maintaining emotional well-being in times of uncertainty.

"Everything is either an obstacle to growth or an obstacle to keep you from growing. The good thing is: you get to choose." Navigating change empowers individuals to perceive obstacles as opportunities for growth rather than insurmountable barriers. It underscores the power of choice in determining how one responds to adversity and uncertainty.

Self-Reflection Questions:

>How can I embrace change and uncertainty in my recovery journey by letting go of addictive behaviors and making room for positive transformation?
>
>In what ways can I leave the past behind and fully engage with the present and future, ensuring that I don't miss the special moments yet to come?
>
>How can I safeguard my spirit and inner strength, even when faced with external setbacks or emotional challenges?
>
>What strategies can I employ to view obstacles as opportunities for personal growth, recognizing my power to choose how I respond to change and uncertainty?

By reflecting on these questions and embracing the principle of navigating change and uncertainty, individuals in recovery can navigate their journey with greater resilience, adaptability, and determination. This principle serves as a foundation for lasting recovery and personal growth, ensuring that change and uncertainty are seen as opportunities rather than hindrances.

Strategies for Adapting to Changing Circumstances:
A Roadmap to Lasting Recovery

Strategies for adapting to changing circumstances are essential for someone seeking long-term recovery from addiction. In this book, we will explore the importance of living in the present, setting clear goals, and embracing change as a means of achieving lasting recovery. Drawing inspiration from insightful statements, we will delve into the transformative power of adapting to changing circumstances on the path to recovery.

"One has to live in the present. Whatever is past is gone beyond recall; whatever is future remains beyond one's reach, until it becomes present." Living in the present moment is a cornerstone of adapting to changing circumstances. It emphasizes the significance of focusing on the here and now, as it is the only realm in which individuals can actively make decisions and effect change.

Dwelling on the past or worrying about the future can hinder progress in recovery.

"Remembering the past and giving thought to the future are important, but only to the extent that they help one deal with the present." While acknowledging the past and planning for the future are valuable, their true worth lies in how they enable individuals to navigate the present. Reflecting on past experiences can inform better decision-making, while setting clear goals for the future can provide motivation and direction.

"Everything you want should be yours: the type of work you want; the relationships you need; the social, mental, and aesthetic stimulation that will make you happy and fulfilled; the money you require for the lifestyle that is appropriate to you; and any requirement that you may (or may not)

A Journey of Transformation

have for achievement or service to others. If you don't aim for it all, you'll never get it all. To aim for it requires that you know what you want." Adapting to changing circumstances involves setting clear goals and envisioning a future in recovery that aligns with one's values and aspirations. By knowing what they want and aiming for it, individuals can effectively navigate change and build the life they desire.

Self-Reflection Questions:

How can I focus on living in the present moment, allowing me to make conscious decisions and adapt to changing circumstances in my recovery journey?

In what ways can I leverage my past experiences to better navigate the present and make informed choices that support my recovery goals?

How can I set clear, specific goals for the future that align with my values and aspirations, providing motivation and direction for my recovery journey?

What strategies can I employ to ensure that I aim for all that I want in life, recognizing that adapting to change is essential for achieving lasting recovery?

By reflecting on these questions and embracing the principle of adapting to changing circumstances, individuals in recovery can develop resilience, flexibility, and determination. This principle serves as a guide for navigating life's twists and turns, ensuring that individuals remain on the path to lasting recovery and personal growth.

Learning from Setbacks and Failures: The Stepping Stones to Lasting Recovery

Learning from setbacks and failures is an indispensable aspect of a long-term recovery journey from addiction. In this book, we will explore the significance of living in the present, setting clear goals, and leveraging past experiences to overcome challenges and failures on the path to lasting recovery. Drawing inspiration from insightful statements, we will delve into the transformative power of embracing setbacks and failures as opportunities for growth.

"One has to live in the present. Whatever is past is gone beyond recall; whatever is future remains beyond one's reach, until it becomes present." Living in the present moment is crucial when facing setbacks and failures. It reminds us that we cannot change the past, nor can we control the future until it becomes our present. By focusing on the present, individuals can address the immediate challenges and decisions in their recovery journey.

"Remembering the past and giving thought to the future are important, but only to the extent that they help one deal with the present." While reflecting on the past and planning for the future hold value, their true significance lies in how they aid us in navigating the present. Past experiences, including setbacks and failures, provide valuable lessons that can guide better decision-making and problem-solving in the present.

"Everything you want should be yours: the type of work you want; the relationships you need; the social, mental, and aesthetic stimulation that will make you happy and fulfilled; the money you require for the lifestyle that is appropriate to you; and any requirement that you may (or may not) have for achievement or service to others. If you don't aim for it all, you'll never get it all. To aim for it requires that you know what you want." Learning from setbacks and failures involves setting clear goals and understanding what one truly desires in recovery. It encourages individuals to persevere, even in the face of challenges, and to remain focused on their ultimate vision of a fulfilling, addiction-free life.

Self-Reflection Questions:

How can I cultivate a mindset of living in the present to effectively address setbacks and failures in my recovery journey?

In what ways can I leverage my past experiences, including setbacks and failures, to better navigate and overcome challenges in the present?

How can I set clear and meaningful goals for my recovery, ensuring that I aim for a life that aligns with my values and aspirations?

What strategies can I employ to embrace setbacks and failures as opportunities for personal growth and resilience in my journey towards lasting recovery?

By reflecting on these questions and embracing the principle of learning from setbacks and failures, individuals in recovery can develop greater resilience, adaptability, and determination. This principle serves as a guide for navigating the inevitable obstacles on the path to lasting recovery and personal growth.

Principle 5: Collaboration and Community

Keys to Long-Term Recovery

In the journey of long-term recovery from addiction, Principle 5, Collaboration and Community, plays a pivotal role. This principle emphasizes the importance of building a strong support network and collaborating with others to overcome challenges and maintain a lasting recovery. In this book, we will explore the significance of this principle and its role in achieving sustained recovery. We will draw inspiration from insightful statements that highlight the essence of collaboration, gratitude, and self-improvement in the recovery process.

"If you keep picking a scab, it will bleed and never heal. If you keep dragging the pain of the past up, it will never heal." These words remind us that dwelling on past mistakes and reliving painful memories can hinder our progress. In recovery, it is essential to acknowledge the past but focus on healing and moving forward. Collaboration and community support provide a safe space to share our experiences and find healing.

"Focus on what you need to make your life better. Do not let wants and desires distract you from what really matters." Collaboration and community offer guidance in discerning needs from wants. By connecting with others who have faced similar challenges, individuals in recovery can prioritize their well-being and make informed choices that lead to lasting positive change.

"Be happy. Just because things are not good doesn't mean you can't see the good side of things. Waking up to see another day is a blessing. Don't take it for granted. Make it count and be happy that you're alive." Collaborating with a supportive community helps individuals shift their focus toward gratitude and positivity. Sharing experiences with others who appreciate life's simple blessings fosters a sense of belonging and happiness.

"People spend too much time looking for more, instead of appreciating what they already have. Life makes us no promises - it only offers us opportunities." Collaboration within a recovery community encourages individuals to appreciate the progress they have made. By supporting one another and recognizing each other's achievements, they build resilience and find motivation in shared success stories.

"Now is the time for massive action. Add more value to others than anyone else! Worth is so vital to your happiness. If you don't feel good about YOU, it's hard to feel good about anything else. Don't be afraid to make mistakes, just be afraid of not learning from them." Collaborating with a community can boost self-esteem and self-worth. By actively participating and helping others on their recovery journey, individuals reaffirm their value and find purpose in their actions.

A Journey of Transformation

Self-Reflection Questions:

How can I actively collaborate with others in my recovery community to strengthen my support network?

In what ways can I express gratitude for the simple blessings in life and focus on the good side of things?

How can I balance my desires and needs to ensure I am making choices that contribute to my long-term recovery?

What actions can I take to add more value to others in my recovery community and enhance my sense of self-worth?

By reflecting on these questions and embracing the principle of Collaboration and Community, individuals in recovery can build a strong support network, find inspiration in shared experiences, and cultivate gratitude and self-worth. This principle serves as a guiding light in the journey toward long-term recovery, reminding us that we are not alone and that together we can achieve lasting positive change.

The Power of Collective Action in Long-Term Recovery

In the journey of long-term recovery from addiction, there is immense power in collective action. This power lies in the collective effort of individuals who come together to support each other's recovery, share their experiences, and work towards a common goal of lasting sobriety. This book explores the significance of collective action in the recovery process and how it can inspire individuals to overcome challenges and achieve personal excellence. Alongside these insights, we will include self-reflection questions to help those seeking recovery connect with this principle on a deeper level.

"Our greatest weakness lies in giving up. The most certain way to succeed is always to try just one more time." In recovery, individuals often face setbacks and moments of doubt. However, when they engage in collective action and share their struggles with others who have experienced similar challenges, they find the strength to persevere. Collective action creates an environment where giving up is not an option, and the belief in the possibility of success remains unwavering.

"Believe in yourself! Have faith in your abilities! Without a humble but reasonable confidence in your own powers, you cannot be successful or happy." Collective action fosters a sense of belief and self-confidence in individuals on their recovery journey. When they witness others achieving milestones and overcoming obstacles, it inspires them to have faith in their own abilities. They realize that they are not alone in their struggle and that success is attainable.

"The will to win, the desire to succeed, the urge to reach your full potential... these are the keys that will unlock the door to personal excellence." Collective action amplifies the will to win and the desire for personal growth. When individuals in recovery collaborate and strive together, they tap into a wellspring of motivation and determination. They understand that the path to personal excellence is paved with continuous effort and the support of a community.

"Be miserable. Or motivate yourself. Whatever has to be done, it's always your choice. Don't believe you have to be better than everybody else. Believe you have to be better than you ever thought you could be." Collective action empowers individuals to choose motivation over misery. It reminds them that they have the power to shape their recovery journey. In a supportive community, they can draw inspiration from the progress of others and aspire to reach their full potential.

Self-Reflection Questions:

> How has collective action played a role in my recovery journey so far? Have I found strength in the support of others?
>
> Do I believe in my abilities and have confidence in my potential for success in recovery? How can I cultivate a humble yet reasonable self-confidence?
>
> What are the keys to personal excellence in my recovery? How can I tap into collective action to unlock these doors?
>
> Am I choosing motivation over misery in my recovery journey? How can I harness the power of collective action to stay motivated and strive for the best version of myself?

Collective action is a transformative force in long-term recovery. By engaging with a supportive community and drawing inspiration from shared experiences, individuals can harness the power of collective action to overcome challenges, believe in their potential, and work towards personal excellence in their recovery journey.

Building Partnerships and Collaborations in the Journey of Recovery

The path to long-term recovery from addiction is a deeply transformative and often challenging journey. One of the most profound aspects of this journey is the power of building partnerships and collaborations with others who share similar goals. This book explores the significance of forming these connections and how they can aid in the recovery process. Alongside these insights, self-reflection questions are provided to encourage individuals seeking recovery to engage with this principle on a personal level.

"We are not human beings on a spiritual journey. We are spiritual beings on a human journey." This profound insight reminds us of our shared humanity and spiritual essence. In recovery, forming partnerships and collaborations means connecting with others who understand our struggles and our aspiration for healing. Recognizing our spiritual essence allows us to see the deeper connection that binds us together.

A Journey of Transformation

"Don't argue for other people's weaknesses. Don't argue for your own." Building partnerships and collaborations involves fostering an environment of understanding and support. Instead of dwelling on each other's weaknesses, we should focus on our strengths and potential for growth. By doing so, we create a space where individuals feel empowered to overcome their challenges.

"When you make a mistake, admit it, correct it, and learn from it immediately." In the journey of recovery, making mistakes is inevitable. However, when we collaborate with others, we create a safe space where admitting our mistakes is encouraged. This transparency allows us to learn and grow together, reinforcing our commitment to sobriety.

"While we are free to choose our actions, we are not free to choose the consequences of our actions." Partnerships and collaborations in recovery provide us with a support system that helps us navigate the consequences of our past actions. Together, we can confront these consequences and work towards a brighter future.

"Sometimes things have to go very wrong before they can be right." Recovery often begins with acknowledging that things have gone wrong in our lives. Building partnerships and collaborations involves connecting with others who have experienced similar hardships. This shared understanding can be a source of strength as we work towards making things right.

"Life has knocked us down a few times. It showed us things that we never wanted to see. We experienced many sadness and failures. But one thing is for sure, We always get up!" In collaboration with others, we find the resilience to rise after being knocked down by addiction. Our collective determination becomes a driving force for our recovery.

Self-Reflection Questions:

How have partnerships and collaborations played a role in my recovery journey? Have I been able to find support and understanding from others who share my goals?

Am I open to admitting my mistakes and learning from them in my recovery? How can I foster an environment that encourages this in my partnerships?

Have I recognized the consequences of my past actions and worked collaboratively to address them in my recovery journey?

How has the shared understanding of challenges and hardships in my partnerships helped me stay resilient and determined in my recovery?

Building partnerships and collaborations in the journey of recovery is not just about shared goals; it's about creating a space where individuals can admit their mistakes, learn from them, and support each other in the pursuit of a better future. By reflecting on these principles, individuals can find deeper meaning in their recovery journey and cultivate relationships that strengthen their commitment to sobriety.

Fostering a Sense of Community and Belonging in the Journey of Recovery

The path to long-term recovery from addiction is a journey that often feels like an uphill climb. Yet, with each new day, we find new strength and new thoughts that inspire us to keep moving forward. One of the essential elements of this journey is the sense of community and belonging that can provide immense support and motivation. This book explores the importance of fostering such a sense of community and offers self-reflection questions to guide individuals in their recovery journey.

"Always continue the climb." Recovery is a challenging process, often filled with setbacks and obstacles. But it is crucial to remember that every step forward, no matter how small, brings us closer to our goals. In a community of like-minded individuals, we can find the encouragement and motivation to persevere, even when the journey seems difficult.

"It is possible for you to do whatever you choose, if you first get to know who you are and are willing to work with a power that is greater than ourselves to do it." Knowing oneself is a fundamental aspect of recovery. It is only when we understand our strengths and weaknesses that we can effectively work towards change. Moreover, seeking support from a higher power or a supportive community can be a source of inspiration and guidance.

"Always do your best. What you plant now, you will harvest later." Building a sense of community involves contributing positively to the lives of others in recovery. By giving our best effort, we not only support our own growth but also sow the seeds of positivity and support within the community. This fosters a sense of belonging and unity.

"Be miserable, or be motivated. Whatever has to be done, it's always your choice." In recovery, we are faced with a choice: we can dwell on the misery of our past struggles or find motivation in the hope of a better future. A supportive community can help us make the positive choice, reminding us that we are not alone in our journey.

Self-Reflection Questions:

>How has being part of a recovery community or support group impacted my journey towards sobriety? Have I found strength and motivation from the sense of belonging within this community?

>What have I learned about myself on this journey, and how has it influenced my commitment to recovery? Have I sought guidance or inspiration from a higher power or a supportive community?

>How have I contributed to my recovery community or support group? In what ways have I planted seeds of positivity and support for others?

> When faced with challenges or setbacks, have I been able to find motivation and support within my recovery community? How can I continue to make the positive choice in my journey?

Fostering a sense of community and belonging in the journey of recovery is not just about receiving support but also about giving back and contributing positively to the lives of others. By reflecting on these principles, individuals can nurture a supportive environment that helps them overcome challenges and remain committed to their recovery goals.

Creating a Ripple Effect of Change in the Journey of Recovery

In the pursuit of long-term recovery from addiction, we often encounter moments of reflection and self-realization. These moments can be pivotal in creating a ripple effect of change, not only in our own lives but also in the lives of those around us. This book explores the concept of creating positive change and offers self-reflection questions to guide individuals on their recovery journey.

"Each morning when you open your eyes, you say to yourself: I, not events, have the power to make me happy or unhappy today. I can choose which it shall be." Recovery teaches us that we have the power to shape our emotional well-being. By choosing happiness and focusing on the present moment, we can set the stage for positive change.

"Yesterday is dead, and tomorrow hasn't arrived yet. I have just one day, today, and I'm going to be happy in it." The concept of "one day at a time" is a cornerstone of recovery. Embracing the present and making the most of each day is crucial. By being mindful and living in the moment, we can create a ripple effect of positivity.

"Each day when we wake up, we have twenty-four brand-new hours to live. What a precious gift! We have the capacity to live in a way that these twenty-four hours will bring peace, joy, and happiness to ourselves and others." Recovery not only benefits us but also those around us. By choosing to live each day in a way that brings positivity and happiness, we inspire others to do the same.

"For every minute you are angry, you lose sixty seconds of happiness." Negative emotions like anger and resentment can hinder our progress in recovery. Recognizing the importance of managing these emotions and choosing happiness instead can have a profound impact on our well-being and those we interact with.

"Trust yourself. Create the kind of self that you will be happy to live with all your life. Make the most of yourself by fanning the tiny, inner sparks of possibility into flames of achievement." Recovery is not just about overcoming addiction but also about personal growth and self-improvement. By nurturing our inner potential and striving for achievement, we can inspire change in ourselves and others.

"A bad attitude is like a flat tire; you can't get very far until you change it." Attitude plays a significant role in recovery. A positive attitude can fuel our progress, while a negative one can hinder it. Changing our attitude can be the first step toward creating a ripple effect of change in our lives.

Self-Reflection Questions:

How has my attitude and outlook on life changed since I started my recovery journey? Have I been able to choose happiness and mindfulness over negative emotions?

In what ways have I inspired positive change in the lives of those around me during my recovery? How do I contribute to a sense of peace, joy, and happiness for others?

What inner sparks of possibility have I identified within myself, and how can I fan them into flames of achievement in my recovery journey?

Have I recognized the importance of a positive attitude in my recovery? How can I continue to change my attitude for the better?

Creating a ripple effect of change in the journey of recovery is not only about personal growth but also about positively impacting the lives of others. By reflecting on these principles, individuals can foster an environment of positivity, inspire change, and continue their path to lasting recovery.

How Individual Efforts Contribute to a Larger Impact in the Journey of Recovery

For individuals seeking long-term recovery from addiction, the path to healing is often paved with individual efforts that, collectively, contribute to a larger impact. In this book, we explore the significance of personal commitment and self-improvement in creating a positive ripple effect within oneself and the recovery community. Additionally, we provide self-reflection questions to aid those on this transformative journey.

"There are two things to aim at in life; first to get what you want, and after that to enjoy it. Only the wisest of mankind has achieved the second." Recovery is not solely about overcoming addiction; it's also about relishing the newfound freedom and joy in life. Wise individuals understand that recovery is not the end but a means to a happier, more fulfilling life.

"Some people give up on their hard work when they have almost reached the goal; while others, on the contrary, obtain a victory by exerting, at the last moment, more vigorous efforts than before." The journey of recovery often involves facing obstacles and setbacks. Those who persevere and intensify their efforts when faced with challenges are more likely to achieve lasting sobriety.

"What seems nasty, painful, and evil can become a source of beauty, joy, and strength if faced with an open mind." Recovery may involve confronting past mistakes, pain, and regrets. By approaching

A Journey of Transformation

these experiences with an open mind and seeking growth from them, individuals can transform their past suffering into sources of strength and resilience.

"Every moment is a golden one for a person who has the vision to recognize it as such. It is not enough to take steps which may someday lead to a goal; each step must be itself a goal and a step likewise." Recovery is not a linear process; it's a collection of moments, each valuable in its own right. By appreciating each step and treating it as a goal, individuals can make the most of their journey.

Self-Reflection Questions:

> How has my journey in recovery evolved from focusing solely on overcoming addiction to also embracing a happier and more fulfilling life?
>
> When faced with obstacles or setbacks in my recovery, have I tended to give up or redouble my efforts? How can I cultivate resilience and determination to achieve my goals?
>
> Can I recall moments in my recovery when I faced something unpleasant or painful and later found beauty, joy, or strength in those experiences? How can I apply this perspective to my ongoing journey?
>
> Do I recognize the value of each moment in my recovery, and am I treating each step as a goal in itself? How can I continue to find purpose and meaning in the small, everyday victories of my journey?

As individuals work on their recovery, their individual efforts ripple outward, creating a larger impact not only in their own lives but also within the recovery community. Recognizing the wisdom in seeking both personal fulfillment and collective progress can inspire continued growth on this transformative path.

Inspiring Change Makers:
The Power of Dreams in the Journey to Recovery

For those seeking long-term recovery from addiction, inspiring and mobilizing others to become change makers can be a powerful force of transformation. In this book, we explore the significance of dreaming big, nurturing passion, and inspiring others to create positive change. Additionally, we provide self-reflection questions to help individuals harness their dreams for personal growth and community impact.

"A person never gets old until regrets take the place of dreams." Dreams are the essence of our vitality and growth. In the context of recovery, it is essential to replace the regrets of the past with dreams for a brighter future.

"Dream no small dreams for they have no power to move the hearts of people." Small dreams lack the capacity to inspire and mobilize others. In recovery, it's crucial to dream big, as it not only transforms one's own life but also motivates and empowers others to strive for positive change.

"There are some people who live in a dream world, and there are some who face reality; and then there are those who turn one into the other." In recovery, individuals have the unique opportunity to transition from the dream world of addiction to facing the reality of sobriety and eventually turning their dreams into reality.

"Every great dream begins with a dreamer. Always remember, you have within you the strength, the patience, and the passion to reach for the stars to change the world." Every individual in recovery is a potential change maker. By nurturing their inner dreamer and recognizing their potential to make a difference, they can inspire others to do the same.

"Never limit yourself because of others' limited imagination; never limit others because of your own limited imagination." The power of dreaming big extends to transcending limitations, both self-imposed and external. In recovery, individuals can challenge these limitations and encourage others to do the same.

"Never give up on a dream just because of the time it will take to accomplish it. The time will pass anyway. The only thing that will stop you from fulfilling your dreams is you." The journey to recovery may be long and challenging, but the time spent on it is an investment in a brighter future. Recognizing this can inspire perseverance and motivate others to embark on their own journeys.

"The future belongs to those who believe in the beauty of their dreams, so dream as if you'll live forever, live as if you'll die today." The beauty of recovery lies in the realization of dreams and the belief that a better future is attainable. Inspiring others to adopt this mindset can create a community of change makers committed to personal growth and positive impact.

Self-Reflection Questions:

What dreams have I set aside or neglected in my journey to recovery? How can I revive and pursue these dreams to inspire my own transformation?

Have I ever witnessed the power of dreaming big in my recovery journey or in the lives of others? How did it inspire positive change?

In what ways have I limited myself or others due to limited imagination or self-doubt? How can I break free from these constraints and encourage others to do the same?

How can I nurture my inner dreamer and inspire others to believe in the beauty of their dreams in the context of recovery and personal growth?

A Journey of Transformation

Dreams have the potential to ignite personal transformation and mobilize individuals to create a ripple effect of change in their lives and communities. By embracing the power of dreams and fostering a sense of passion, individuals can inspire others to join them on the path of recovery and positive transformation.

Principle 6: Authenticity and Integrity

The Path to Long-Term Recovery from Addiction

Addiction is a relentless adversary, one that often leaves individuals feeling powerless and trapped in a never-ending cycle of self-destruction. However, recovery is possible, and it begins with embracing the sixth principle of Authenticity and Integrity. This principle encourages us to welcome each morning with a smile, view each day as a gift, and become self-starters in the pursuit of our recovery. It reminds us that we were not born to fail and that despite the world's suffering, we can overcome our addiction. Furthermore, it urges us not to limit our dreams and to make excellence a habit. In this book, we will explore how embracing this principle can be a beacon of hope for those seeking long-term recovery from addiction.

Embracing Each Morning with a Smile

To welcome every morning with a smile is to acknowledge that each new day is a fresh opportunity for change and growth. Addiction often buries individuals in darkness, but by starting the day with a smile, we can foster a positive mindset that sets the tone for the entire day. This simple act reminds us that we have the power to shape our destiny and that recovery is within our reach.

Viewing Each Day as a Gift

The idea of viewing each day as a gift from our Creator reinforces the concept of gratitude in recovery. Gratitude helps us appreciate the second chance we have been given, making us less likely to squander it on destructive behaviors. By recognizing the preciousness of each day, we are more motivated to seize it and make the most of our recovery journey.

Becoming a Self-Starter

One of the key elements of recovery is taking responsibility for our actions and decisions. Being a self-starter means taking the initiative to move forward in our recovery without external prodding. This proactive approach empowers us to take control of our lives and work towards lasting change. The first hour of the day can set the tone for success, and by being a self-starter, we can ensure that our day begins on a positive note.

Understanding that Failure Is Not Our Destiny

The belief that we were not born to fail is a crucial component of authentic recovery. Addiction often erodes our self-esteem and makes us doubt our worthiness. However, this principle reminds us that failure is not our destiny. We have the potential to overcome addiction and lead fulfilling lives. Embracing this mindset can be a driving force in our journey towards recovery.

A Journey of Transformation

Overcoming Suffering and Temptation

Life is filled with suffering and temptation, but that does not mean we are destined to succumb to them. Instead, we can draw strength from the knowledge that countless individuals have overcome adversity and addiction. By facing our suffering head-on and resisting temptation, we prove to ourselves and others that we are capable of change and growth.

Dreaming Without Limits

The principle of not limiting our dreams encourages us to envision a life beyond addiction. Recovery is not just about quitting drugs or alcohol; it is about rediscovering our passions and purpose in life. By dreaming without limits, we expand our horizons and open ourselves to new possibilities.

Making Excellence a Habit

Excellence is not an occasional achievement but a habit that can be cultivated over time. In recovery, excellence translates into consistently making healthy choices and striving for personal growth. It means refusing to settle for mediocrity and instead aiming for the best version of ourselves.

Resisting the Pull of Mediocrity

Mediocrity often tries to pull us down to its level, but we must resist this gravitational force. By refusing to trade our superiority for inferiority, we maintain our integrity and authenticity in recovery. We choose to rise above the temptations that threaten our progress.

Self-Reflection Questions

> How can I incorporate the practice of welcoming each morning with a smile into my daily routine to foster a positive mindset in my recovery journey?

> What specific steps can I take to view each day as a precious gift and practice gratitude in my recovery?

> In what ways can I become a self-starter in my recovery, taking proactive steps to move forward without external prompting?

> How can I remind myself daily that I was not born to fail and that recovery is within my reach?

> What strategies can I employ to overcome suffering and temptation, knowing that countless others have achieved this in their own recovery journeys?

What dreams and aspirations do I have for my life beyond addiction, and how can I start pursuing them without limitations?

How can I make excellence a habit in my recovery, ensuring that I consistently make healthy choices and strive for personal growth?

How do I plan to resist the pull of mediocrity and maintain my integrity and authenticity in my recovery journey?

Embracing Principle 6: Authenticity and Integrity is a powerful step towards achieving long-term recovery from addiction. By welcoming each day with a smile, viewing each day as a gift, and adopting a proactive, excellence-driven mindset, individuals can transform their lives and break free from the cycle of addiction. Self-reflection on these principles can further empower individuals on their journey to lasting recovery.

The Role of Authenticity in Leading by Example –
A Path to Long-Term Recovery from Addiction

Recovery from addiction is a journey that demands resilience, determination, and the unwavering commitment to change. One vital aspect of this journey is the role of authenticity in leading by example. The principle of stepping out every day with faith, love, kindness, understanding, and hope reinforces the idea that our actions and attitudes can inspire positive change in ourselves and others. It encourages us to embrace our role as the author of our lives, to live our passions, and to pursue success actively. In this book, we will explore how authenticity, when combined with these principles, can be a guiding light for those seeking long-term recovery from addiction.

Stepping Out with Faith, Love, Kindness, Understanding, and Hope

The act of stepping out each day with faith, love, kindness, understanding, and hope is a powerful way to cultivate authenticity. These qualities not only reflect our true selves but also set a positive example for others in our recovery community. By embodying these values, we create an environment of support and encouragement, reinforcing the idea that recovery is possible and worth pursuing.

Being a Blessing Every Day

When we adopt the practice of living authentically and radiating positivity, we become a source of blessings for those around us. In recovery, it's essential to recognize the interdependence of individuals striving for a common goal. By leading with authenticity and exemplifying the principles of hope and understanding, we can inspire others to follow our lead and embark on their path to recovery.

A Journey of Transformation

Writing Our Own Magnificent Story

Embracing the idea that we are the authors of our lives empowers us to take control of our recovery narrative. Addiction can be a dark chapter in our story, but it does not define the entirety of our lives. Every day presents an opportunity to write a new page filled with hope, progress, and transformation. By living authentically, we ensure that each page reflects our true selves and our commitment to recovery.

Living and Loving Our Passions

Recovery is not merely about abstaining from substance use; it's about rediscovering our passions and living a life filled with purpose. Authenticity plays a vital role in this process, as it encourages us to be true to ourselves and engage in activities that bring us joy and fulfillment. When we live and love our passions, success naturally follows as a byproduct of our authenticity.

Dreaming and Achieving Success

The pursuit of success is a common aspiration for individuals in recovery. Authenticity reminds us that success is not a distant dream but a tangible goal within our reach. By staying awake to achieve our dreams and by changing the way we perceive challenges and setbacks, we can unlock our full potential and thrive in recovery.

Monitoring Our Thoughts and Emotions

Authenticity requires us to be honest with ourselves, even about our thoughts and emotions. We must actively monitor our mental and emotional states and refuse to dwell on negative or destructive thoughts. By focusing on the present moment and maintaining a positive mindset, we can break free from the chains of the past and build a brighter future.

Self-Reflection Questions

How can I cultivate authenticity in my daily life to lead by example for others in recovery?

In what ways can I step out every day with faith, love, kindness, understanding, and hope to create a more supportive and encouraging recovery community?

How can I embrace the idea that I am the author of my life and actively write a new page in my recovery story each day?

What are my passions, and how can I infuse my life with them to enhance my sense of purpose and fulfillment in recovery?

How can I shift my perspective on success and actively work towards achieving my dreams in recovery?

> What negative or destructive thoughts and emotions do I need to monitor and address to maintain a positive mindset and build a brighter future in recovery?
>
> How can I ensure that my authenticity is consistently reflected in my actions and attitudes, both in my personal life and within my recovery community?

Authenticity is a cornerstone of successful long-term recovery from addiction. By embodying qualities such as faith, love, kindness, understanding, and hope, and by actively pursuing our passions and success, we not only transform our own lives but also inspire and support others on their recovery journeys. Self-reflection on these principles can help individuals strengthen their commitment to authenticity and positive change.

Staying True to Your Values and Principles – A Path to Long-Term Recovery from Addiction

Recovery from addiction is a journey filled with challenges, self-discovery, and personal growth. Staying true to your values and principles is a crucial component of this journey. The statement, "As we grow up, we learn that even the one person that wasn't supposed to ever let us down, probably will," reminds us that life is unpredictable, and we will face moments of heartbreak, mistakes, and regret. However, it also encourages us to embrace life to the fullest, cherish meaningful moments, and prioritize authentic connections. In this book, we will explore the importance of staying true to our values and principles in the context of long-term recovery from addiction.

Learning from Life's Disappointments

Addiction often leads individuals to compromise their values and principles, causing harm to themselves and others. In recovery, it is essential to acknowledge past mistakes and heartbreaks as opportunities for growth. By learning from these experiences, we can reinforce our commitment to living in accordance with our values and principles, ensuring a more fulfilling and authentic life.

Taking Responsibility for Our Actions

Recovery involves taking responsibility for our past actions and making amends where necessary. Staying true to our values and principles means acknowledging the hurt we may have caused and taking proactive steps to make things right. This process of amends and accountability fosters personal growth and strengthens our commitment to a more authentic and compassionate life.

Embracing Authentic Relationships

Authenticity in recovery extends to our relationships with others. We must acknowledge that we will face conflicts and complexities in our interactions with friends, family, and loved ones. Staying true to our values means addressing these issues honestly and constructively, rather than avoiding them. Authentic relationships are built on open communication, understanding, and forgiveness.

A Journey of Transformation

Living in the Present Moment

The statement reminds us of the fleeting nature of life and the importance of living in the present moment. Addiction often traps individuals in regrets about the past or anxieties about the future. In recovery, we must learn to let go of these negative emotions and fully embrace the here and now. Staying true to our values means choosing to be present, finding joy in small moments, and appreciating the beauty of life.

Expressing Love and Gratitude

Recovery is an opportunity to express love and gratitude to those who have supported us on our journey. It encourages us to tell people what they mean to us and to appreciate their presence in our lives. By living in alignment with our values and principles, we can strengthen our connections and create a support network that promotes long-term recovery.

Self-Reflection Questions

> What values and principles are most important to me in my recovery journey, and how can I stay true to them in the face of challenges?

> How have past disappointments and mistakes shaped my commitment to a more authentic life in recovery?

> In what ways can I take responsibility for my past actions and make amends where necessary to promote personal growth and authenticity?

> How can I foster authentic relationships by addressing conflicts and complexities in a constructive and honest manner?

> What steps can I take to live in the present moment, letting go of past regrets and future anxieties?

> How can I express love and gratitude to those who have supported me in my recovery journey and strengthen my support network?

> What meaningful actions can I take today to fully embrace life, cherish the present, and live authentically?

Staying true to your values and principles is a vital aspect of long-term recovery from addiction. It involves learning from life's disappointments, taking responsibility for your actions, embracing authentic relationships, living in the present moment, and expressing love and gratitude. Self-reflection on these principles can help individuals navigate their recovery journey with authenticity and purpose.

Honoring Your Word and Commitments –
A Foundation for Long-Term Recovery from Addiction

Long-term recovery from addiction is a journey filled with both challenges and triumphs. One of the cornerstones of this journey is the principle of honoring your word and commitments. The provided wisdom reminds us that any change, no matter how positive, comes with its share of discomfort and drawbacks. Optimism, hope, and confidence are essential ingredients for success in recovery. It encourages us to persevere in our search for a better life and to continuously seek understanding in the world around us. In this book, we will explore how honoring our word and commitments can serve as a solid foundation for achieving lasting recovery.

Embracing Change with Optimism

Recovery represents a significant change in one's life. It requires letting go of addictive behaviors and adopting new, healthier habits. This transformation can be uncomfortable and challenging, but optimism is the driving force that helps us navigate these difficulties. Optimism is the belief that change is possible, and it leads to achievement by keeping us motivated and resilient during tough times.

The Power of Hope and Confidence

Hope and confidence are like guiding stars on the path to recovery. Hope gives us the courage to begin the journey, while confidence sustains us as we progress. Without these qualities, the weight of addiction may feel insurmountable. They remind us that recovery is within our reach, and we have the capacity to overcome adversity.

The Unsettled Quest for Meaning

The statement encourages us not to settle in our pursuit of meaning and happiness. In recovery, settling can manifest as complacency or returning to old habits. Honoring our commitments to sobriety and personal growth means recognizing that the journey never truly ends. Like any great endeavor in life, it continually evolves and improves as the years go by.

Seeking Understanding in the World

Understanding the world, culture, and people around us can provide valuable insights into our own lives. Recovery is not just about abstaining from substances; it's about gaining a deeper understanding of ourselves and our place in the world. By looking deeply into the world and the people in it, we can gain perspective, empathy, and wisdom, which are essential for long-term recovery.

Self-Reflection Questions

> How can I embrace change with optimism in my recovery journey, recognizing that discomfort and drawbacks are part of the process?

> In what ways can I nurture and strengthen my hope and confidence to stay motivated and resilient in my recovery?

> What steps can I take to avoid settling in my quest for meaning and happiness in recovery, and how can I keep the journey evolving and improving?

> How can I actively seek understanding in the world, culture, and people around me to gain deeper insights into my own life and recovery?

> Are there specific commitments I need to honor in my recovery, and how can I ensure I stay true to them?

> How has optimism played a role in my recovery journey so far, and how can I cultivate it further?

> What strategies can I use to foster hope and confidence when facing challenges in recovery?

Honoring your word and commitments is a fundamental aspect of achieving long-term recovery from addiction. It involves embracing change with optimism, relying on the power of hope and confidence, avoiding complacency, and continually seeking understanding in the world. Self-reflection on these principles can empower individuals on their journey towards lasting recovery.

The Trust Factor in Change-Making – Navigating Long-Term Recovery from Addiction

Long-term recovery from addiction is a transformative journey filled with both highs and lows. Trusting in the process and in oneself is vital to navigate this path successfully. The provided wisdom reminds us that even a happy life is not devoid of darkness and that the keys to patience are acceptance and faith. It encourages us to accept the ups and downs of life, be patient in our recovery, and trust in our ability to effect change. In this book, we will explore the importance of the trust factor in making lasting changes during the recovery journey.

Embracing Life's Dualities

Life is a tapestry of experiences that includes both joy and sorrow. Recovery is no exception, as it often involves moments of triumph and setbacks. Embracing these dualities, rather than resisting them, allows us to appreciate the full spectrum of human experience. By acknowledging the inevitability of both light and darkness, we can approach our recovery journey with a sense of balance and equanimity.

The Keys to Patience

Patience is an invaluable quality in the process of long-term recovery. It allows us to endure the challenges and uncertainties that come our way. Acceptance and faith are the keys to patience. Accepting the reality of our addiction and the need for change is the first step. Faith, not only in ourselves but also in the path we have chosen, empowers us to persevere through difficult times and setbacks.

Nurturing Great Dreams

The statement encourages us to dream big and to believe in our ability to make a positive impact on the world. Recovery is a journey of self-discovery and transformation. It begins with the dream of a healthier, happier life and the belief that change is possible. Every great dream, whether it's personal or societal, begins with a dreamer who has the strength, patience, and passion to pursue it.

Trusting in Oneself and the Journey

Trust is a foundational element of recovery. It involves trusting in oneself, one's support system, and the process of change. Believing in our capacity to overcome addiction and to live a fulfilling life is crucial. Additionally, having trust in the chosen recovery path and the professionals guiding us can bolster our commitment to long-term change.

Self-Reflection Questions

> How do I currently navigate the dualities of life, including the highs and lows of my recovery journey?
>
> What role does acceptance play in my ability to practice patience in recovery, and how can I cultivate greater acceptance?
>
> In what ways does faith in myself and my chosen path fuel my patience and resilience during challenging times in recovery?
>
> What great dreams do I have for my life and my recovery journey, and how can I nurture them with strength, patience, and passion?
>
> How can I build and maintain trust in myself and my recovery process, and what steps can I take to foster trust in my support network?

A Journey of Transformation

> What strategies can I implement to embrace the dualities of life more fully, recognizing that they are an inherent part of the human experience?
>
> How can I apply the wisdom of acceptance and faith to enhance my ability to navigate the challenges of recovery with patience and serenity?

The trust factor is a cornerstone of making lasting changes during the recovery journey. By embracing life's dualities, practicing patience through acceptance and faith, nurturing great dreams, and trusting in oneself and the journey, individuals can pave the way for successful and long-term recovery from addiction. Self-reflection on these principles can empower individuals to navigate their recovery journey with greater trust and resilience.

Building Trust Through Integrity –
A Foundation for Long-Term Recovery from Addiction

Long-term recovery from addiction is a journey of transformation, self-discovery, and personal growth. One essential element of this journey is the building of trust with others through integrity. The provided wisdom reminds us that our current circumstances do not determine our potential, and that each individual possesses creative potential capable of changing the world. It also underscores the importance of addressing the poverty of being unwanted and uncared for, beginning within our own homes. In this book, we will explore the significance of building trust through integrity in the context of long-term recovery from addiction.

Starting with Integrity

Integrity is the cornerstone of trust-building. It means aligning our actions and decisions with our values and principles, even when faced with challenges or temptations. In recovery, it's vital to be honest with ourselves and others about our past actions and the journey ahead. By starting with integrity, we demonstrate our commitment to change and gain the trust of those around us.

Recognizing Creative Potential

The statement reminds us that everyone possesses creative potential. Recovery is an opportunity to tap into this potential and channel it toward positive change. Whether through self-expression, artistic endeavors, or community involvement, individuals in recovery can harness their creativity to make a difference in their own lives and the lives of others. Trust naturally follows when others witness our dedication to personal growth and contributing to the world.

Addressing the Poverty of Neglect

The concept of poverty extends beyond material deprivation. The poverty of being unwanted, unloved, and uncared for is a profound form of suffering. In recovery, it is essential to recognize the impact of addiction on our relationships and address the emotional and psychological wounds it may have caused. Building trust with others involves mending these relationships through love, care, and genuine connection.

Exploring the Dichotomy of Success and Failure

The statement suggests that success lacks a singular explanation, while failure can be attributed to various factors. In recovery, individuals often grapple with feelings of failure and inadequacy due to their past struggles with addiction. Building trust through integrity involves embracing a growth mindset and understanding that recovery is a journey with ups and downs. By consistently demonstrating integrity in our actions, we pave the way for success in the long run.

Self-Reflection Questions

> How can I start building trust with others through integrity in my recovery journey, beginning with honesty and a commitment to change?

> What creative potential do I possess, and how can I express and utilize it to contribute positively to my life and the world around me?

> In what ways can I address the emotional and relational wounds caused by addiction, and how can I rebuild trust with loved ones through love, care, and connection?

> How do I view success and failure in my recovery, and how can I shift my perspective to embrace a growth mindset and acknowledge my progress?

> Are there specific actions or behaviors from my past that I need to address with honesty and integrity to rebuild trust with others?

> What steps can I take to nurture my creative potential and use it as a tool for personal growth and healing in recovery?

> How can I apply the concept of integrity to my daily life, ensuring that my actions align with my values and principles?

Building trust through integrity is a fundamental aspect of long-term recovery from addiction. It involves starting with honesty, recognizing creative potential, addressing emotional wounds, and understanding the dichotomy of success and failure. Self-reflection on these principles can empower individuals to navigate their recovery journey with authenticity and trustworthiness.

The Ripple Effect of Trust in Communities – Fostering Long-Term Recovery from Addiction

Long-term recovery from addiction is a journey that not only transforms individuals but also has a profound impact on the communities they belong to. Trust plays a pivotal role in this process. The

A Journey of Transformation

provided wisdom encourages us to embrace tough times as opportunities for growth and resilience. It underscores the importance of letting go of past pain, committing to self-improvement, and acknowledging the challenges we face. In this book, we will explore how trust within communities can have a ripple effect on fostering lasting recovery from addiction.

Building Resilience Through Trials

Addiction often leads individuals to experience profound challenges and hardships. However, these trials can serve as the catalyst for personal growth and resilience. Tough times test our resolve and determination, shaping us into stronger, more resilient individuals. In the context of recovery, trust within the community involves supporting one another through these trials, recognizing that growth can emerge from adversity.

The Role of Trust in Tough Times

When going through tough times, trust within the community becomes a vital source of support. Trusting that others have faced similar challenges and overcome them can provide hope and motivation. It fosters a sense of belonging and reassures individuals that they are not alone in their journey towards recovery. The community's trust in each member's ability to heal and grow can be a powerful motivator.

Learning from the Past

The past is a teacher, offering valuable lessons that can guide individuals on their path to recovery. Trust within the community involves acknowledging past mistakes and pain while also embracing the potential for change and growth. This trust in the transformative power of learning from the past encourages individuals to let go of regrets and move forward with a renewed sense of purpose.

Committing to Self-Improvement

Every day presents an opportunity to commit to self-improvement. Recovery is a journey of personal growth, and trust within the community plays a significant role in this process. By fostering a supportive environment that values self-improvement, individuals can be inspired to strive for a better future. Trusting in one's own capacity for change is essential in this endeavor.

Kindness and Self-Compassion

Trust within the community also encompasses kindness and self-compassion. It involves treating oneself with the same kindness and understanding that we extend to others. Recovery can be challenging, and individuals must trust that they deserve self-compassion and support. By fostering a culture of self-kindness and self-trust within the community, individuals can experience greater emotional well-being and resilience.

Acknowledging and Celebrating Success

Success in recovery should not be understated or overlooked. Trust within the community involves acknowledging and celebrating the achievements and milestones of each member. By doing so, individuals gain a sense of accomplishment and motivation to continue their journey. Trust in the community's recognition of these successes can fuel further growth and commitment to recovery.

The Power of Prayer and Connection

Finally, the statement reminds us of the power of prayer and connection. Trust within the community involves supporting one another spiritually and emotionally. Prayer and connection can provide a sense of solace and purpose, reinforcing the trust that individuals have in each other and in their collective ability to overcome addiction.

Self-Reflection Questions

How has trust within my community played a role in my recovery journey, and in what ways has it contributed to my growth and resilience?

How can I foster a greater sense of trust within my recovery community, particularly during tough times when support is needed most?

What lessons have I learned from my past that have influenced my commitment to recovery and self-improvement?

How do I practice self-kindness and self-compassion in my journey, and how can I foster these qualities within my recovery community?

Are there successes or milestones in my recovery that I have not acknowledged or celebrated, and how can I make a conscious effort to do so?

How do prayer and connection with others in my community contribute to my sense of trust and well-being in my recovery journey?

Trust within communities plays a pivotal role in fostering long-term recovery from addiction. It involves building resilience through trials, trusting in each other's ability to overcome challenges, learning from the past, committing to self-improvement, practicing kindness and self-compassion, celebrating success, and embracing the power of prayer and connection. Self-reflection on these principles can empower individuals and communities to thrive on the path to lasting recovery.

Principle 7: Patience and Persistence

Navigating the Present to Secure the Future

Long-term recovery from addiction is a journey marked by challenges, self-discovery, and transformation. Principle 7, emphasizing patience and persistence, reminds us to focus on the present and trust that the future will unfold as it should. The wisdom provided encourages us to let go of past mistakes and stay true to our beliefs, even when they diverge from the norm. It advocates for living life authentically and embracing the courage to pursue what aligns with our desires and values. In this book, we will explore the significance of patience and persistence in achieving lasting recovery from addiction.

Embracing the Present Moment

The present moment is a precious gift that often goes overlooked in the whirlwind of daily life. Patience and persistence in recovery begin with an appreciation for the present. By grounding ourselves in the here and now, we can make conscious choices that lead us toward a future in alignment with our recovery goals.

Releasing the Burden of Past Mistakes

Recovery is a process that requires us to confront past mistakes and failures. Dwelling on these past errors can hinder progress and breed feelings of guilt and shame. Patience and persistence encourage us to release this burden, recognizing that we cannot change the past but have the power to shape our present and future.

Believing in Our Convictions

There are moments in life when we must trust our own judgment, even when it differs from societal norms. Recovery often requires us to make choices that prioritize our well-being over conformity. Patience and persistence empower us to remain steadfast in our beliefs and decisions, even when faced with resistance or criticism from others.

Having the Courage to Act

Courage is a fundamental element of both patience and persistence. It takes courage to let go of past regrets, believe in our convictions, and make choices aligned with our true selves. In recovery, we must find the strength to take action, even in the face of uncertainty and doubt.

Living Authentically

Life is too short to live inauthentically or to follow paths that do not resonate with our desires and values. Patience and persistence urge us to take control of our lives and pursue what genuinely

A Journey of Transformation

matters to us. Recovery provides an opportunity to live authentically and in alignment with our goals.

Self-Reflection Questions

How do I currently navigate the present moment in my recovery journey, and how can I cultivate greater mindfulness and presence?

What past mistakes and failures continue to burden me, and how can I practice patience and persistence in letting go of them?

In what areas of my recovery journey do my convictions differ from societal norms, and how can I find the courage to trust and act on my beliefs?

What steps can I take to build the courage required to make choices that align with my recovery goals and values, even in the face of uncertainty or opposition?

In what ways can I live more authentically in my recovery, and what changes can I make to ensure that my actions and choices align with my true self?

How can I maintain a focus on the present and trust that the future will unfold as it should, while still actively working towards my long-term recovery goals?

What aspects of my life do I need to reevaluate to ensure that I am not doing things I don't want to do or pursuing a career that doesn't align with my true aspirations and values?

Patience and persistence are essential principles in achieving lasting recovery from addiction. They encourage us to embrace the present, release the burden of past mistakes, believe in our convictions, find the courage to act, and live authentically. Self-reflection on these principles can empower individuals on their journey toward long-term recovery and personal growth.

Understanding the Time Required for Meaningful Change in Long-Term Recovery

Long-term recovery from addiction is a journey that requires time, effort, and perseverance. Principle 8 emphasizes the importance of understanding the duration it takes for meaningful change to occur. The provided wisdom reminds us that it is often in our darkest moments that we find the motivation to transform our lives. It encourages us to confront fear, gain strength from our experiences, and work diligently for our freedom from addiction. Moreover, it highlights the need to stand tall and resolute, refusing to allow others to take advantage of us. In this book, we will explore the significance of comprehending the time required for meaningful change in the context of long-term recovery from addiction.

Finding Light in Dark Moments

Recovery can be an arduous journey, and there will be moments when it feels as if we are in the darkest of times. However, it is precisely during these moments of adversity that we can find the motivation and determination to change. These challenges can serve as a catalyst for transformation, pushing us to seek the light of recovery even more fervently.

Strengthening Through Courage

Confronting addiction and pursuing recovery requires immense courage. Each experience in which we face our fears and work through our challenges adds to our strength, confidence, and resilience. In the face of addiction, it is through these experiences that we learn to believe in our ability to overcome adversity and achieve meaningful change.

Embracing Continuous Struggle

Meaningful change is not automatic; it demands persistent effort and commitment. Change is not a process that rolls in effortlessly; it necessitates continuous struggle and determination. Long-term recovery from addiction requires individuals to maintain their resolve and persistently work towards their freedom from the grip of addiction.

Taking Control of Our Lives

The statement reminds us that no one can ride us unless our backs are bent. In the context of recovery, this emphasizes the importance of taking control of our lives and refusing to allow addiction or external influences to dictate our actions. By standing tall and resolute in our recovery journey, we become the change we wish to see in ourselves and in the world.

Self-Reflection Questions

How have my darkest moments in addiction influenced my motivation to pursue meaningful change and recovery?

In what ways have I gained strength, courage, and confidence through confronting my fears and experiences in recovery?

What aspects of my recovery journey have required continuous struggle and persistence, and how have these challenges contributed to my growth and transformation?

How can I take more control of my life in recovery and refuse to allow addiction or external influences to dictate my actions and choices?

What does it mean for me to "be the change I wish to see in the world," and how can I apply this principle to my recovery journey?

A Journey of Transformation

Understanding the time required for meaningful change is a crucial aspect of long-term recovery from addiction. It involves finding light in dark moments, strengthening through courage, embracing continuous struggle, and taking control of our lives. Self-reflection on these principles can empower individuals to navigate their recovery journey with resilience, determination, and a steadfast commitment to transformation.

The Art of Perseverance: Overcoming Obstacles in Long-Term Recovery

Long-term recovery from addiction is a path marked by obstacles, challenges, and moments of self-discovery. Principle 9 underscores the importance of perseverance in the face of these hurdles. The provided wisdom reminds us that the pain we experience today can become the strength we rely on tomorrow. It encourages us to view challenges as opportunities for growth, to believe in our inner resilience, and to maintain our focus on our goals. In this book, we will explore the significance of the art of perseverance in overcoming obstacles on the journey to long-term recovery from addiction.

Turning Pain into Strength

Addiction often brings profound pain and suffering, but this pain can serve as a catalyst for personal growth and change. By enduring and working through the difficulties encountered in recovery, individuals can transform their pain into inner strength. This newfound strength becomes a valuable asset in the ongoing journey towards sobriety.

Opportunities for Growth

Challenges and obstacles are not roadblocks but rather opportunities for growth. They test our determination, resilience, and commitment to recovery. Instead of fearing these difficulties, we can embrace them as chances to learn, evolve, and become more resilient individuals on the path to lasting recovery.

Seeing Purpose in Pain

The statement suggests that no pain comes without purpose. In recovery, it is essential to remind ourselves that the challenges we face are not arbitrary but serve a meaningful role in our journey. They can teach us valuable lessons, help us confront our weaknesses, and lead us to a more profound understanding of ourselves.

Believing in Inner Resilience

Amidst adversity, it is crucial to believe in our inner resilience. Each person possesses a well of strength and determination that can overcome even the most formidable obstacles. Trusting in this inner power is essential in maintaining the perseverance needed for long-term recovery.

Staying Focused on Goals

Obstacles can be distractions that divert us from our recovery goals. The statement emphasizes the importance of keeping our eyes firmly fixed on our objectives. By staying focused on the path ahead and not allowing obstacles to deter us, we increase our chances of achieving lasting sobriety.

Self-Reflection Questions

> How have I experienced pain and challenges in my recovery journey, and in what ways have I turned this pain into personal strength?

> Can I identify specific moments in my recovery where obstacles led to significant personal growth and positive change?

> How can I shift my perspective to see purpose in the challenges and obstacles I face in my recovery?

> Do I believe in my inner resilience, and how can I nurture and trust this inner strength to persevere through difficult times?

> What strategies can I implement to stay focused on my recovery goals and not allow obstacles to deter my progress?

> How can I use the wisdom of this principle to inspire and motivate myself when faced with challenges in my recovery journey?

> What are my long-term recovery goals, and how can I maintain my commitment to achieving them despite the obstacles that may arise?

The art of perseverance is a crucial component of long-term recovery from addiction. It involves transforming pain into strength, embracing opportunities for growth, finding purpose in challenges, believing in inner resilience, and staying focused on recovery goals. Self-reflection on these principles empowers individuals to navigate their recovery journey with resilience and determination, ensuring a higher likelihood of achieving lasting sobriety.

Strategies for Sustaining Commitment to Your Recovery Goals

Long-term recovery from addiction is a transformative journey that demands unwavering commitment and resilience. Principle 10 emphasizes the strategies needed to stay steadfast in pursuing recovery goals. The provided wisdom underscores the idea that pain can be a precursor to strength, that challenges offer opportunities for growth, and that obstacles are distractions from our goals. It encourages us to maintain our focus, believe in our inner capabilities, and set ourselves on fire with determination. In this book, we will explore essential strategies for staying committed to long-term recovery goals.

A Journey of Transformation

Turning Pain into Strength

The pain experienced in addiction and recovery can be an incredible source of motivation. Instead of succumbing to despair, individuals in recovery can use this pain as a driving force to strengthen their resolve. By acknowledging the pain and understanding its potential to fuel growth, one can transform it into a catalyst for positive change.

Embracing Challenges as Opportunities

Challenges are an inherent part of the recovery journey. Rather than viewing them as insurmountable obstacles, it is essential to see them as opportunities for personal growth and development. Challenges test our commitment and provide valuable lessons that contribute to our resilience and determination.

Finding Purpose in Pain

Understanding that pain serves a purpose in our lives is vital for sustaining commitment. Every challenge and pain experienced in recovery can be seen as a step toward a healthier, more fulfilling life. By recognizing the lessons and growth opportunities inherent in pain, we can find purpose in our journey.

Believing in Inner Capabilities

Belief in oneself is a cornerstone of commitment. It is crucial to recognize the inherent strength and resilience within us. Believing that we possess the power to overcome any obstacle or challenge that arises on the path to recovery strengthens our determination to stay committed.

Maintaining Focus on Recovery Goals

Distractions and obstacles can deter individuals from their recovery goals. Maintaining a laser focus on these goals is essential. Regularly reminding oneself of the objectives and the reasons for pursuing recovery can help rekindle motivation and keep commitment alive.

Setting a Fire of Determination

Success in recovery is not passive; it requires setting oneself on fire with determination. It involves igniting a passion for change and actively pursuing it. Determination serves as a driving force that propels individuals forward, even when faced with difficulties.

Self-Reflection Questions

> How has pain influenced my motivation and commitment to recovery, and how can I harness this pain to strengthen my resolve?

Can I identify specific challenges in my recovery journey that have led to personal growth and positive change, and how can I embrace them as opportunities?

How can I find purpose in the pain and challenges I have faced in recovery, recognizing their role in my journey toward a healthier life?

Do I truly believe in my inner capabilities and resilience, and how can I nurture this belief to sustain commitment to recovery?

What strategies can I implement to maintain my focus on recovery goals, even in the face of distractions and obstacles?

How can I ignite a fire of determination within myself to actively pursue my recovery goals and overcome challenges with unwavering commitment?

What are my long-term recovery goals, and how can I regularly remind myself of their importance in my life to stay committed?

Staying committed to long-term recovery goals requires a combination of strategies that embrace pain, recognize challenges as opportunities, find purpose in adversity, believe in inner capabilities, maintain focus, and set a fire of determination. Self-reflection on these principles empowers individuals to navigate their recovery journey with resilience, unwavering commitment, and the determination to achieve lasting sobriety.

Celebrating Small Victories: A Path to Long-Term Recovery from Addiction

Long-term recovery from addiction is a journey filled with challenges and triumphs. Principle 11 emphasizes the importance of celebrating small victories along the way. The provided wisdom encourages us to maturely accept challenges to our opinions and beliefs and to face our responsibilities head-on. It also underscores the significance of not allowing negativity to consume us and of embracing the precious gift of each day. In this book, we will explore the significance of celebrating small victories in the context of long-term recovery from addiction.

Maturity in Accepting Challenges

Maturity entails the ability to have our opinions and beliefs challenged without feeling personally attacked. In the context of recovery, this means being open to new perspectives, feedback, and support. Celebrating small victories requires a willingness to grow and adapt as we encounter challenges that test our commitment to recovery.

Accepting Responsibility

Dodging responsibilities in life often leads to negative consequences. Recovery demands that we take ownership of our actions and choices. Recognizing the consequences of dodging

A Journey of Transformation

responsibilities can motivate us to face them head-on and take positive steps toward lasting sobriety.

Resisting Negativity

Negative influences and people can hinder our recovery progress. It is essential not to allow negative individuals to turn us into one of them. Celebrating small victories involves actively resisting negativity and surrounding ourselves with positive and supportive influences that uplift our spirits.

Embracing Life's Shortness

Life is precious and short, and each day is a gift. In recovery, it is vital to acknowledge this and make the most of every moment. Celebrating small victories reminds us to cherish the progress we have made, regardless of its size, and to appreciate the gift of life in each new day.

Learning from Experiences

Every day presents an opportunity to learn and grow. Life's ups and downs offer valuable experiences that contribute to our personal development. Celebrating small victories encourages us to view even challenging days as opportunities for growth and improvement, fostering a mindset of continuous progress.

Persevering Through Tough Times

Recovery can be challenging, and some days may seem insurmountable due to stress or obstacles. The statement encourages us to hang in there, never give up, and be proud of ourselves. Celebrating small victories, even during tough times, is a reminder of our resilience and the progress we have made in our journey.

Self-Reflection Questions

> How do I typically respond when my opinions and beliefs are challenged, and how can I maturely accept differing perspectives to foster personal growth?

> In what areas of my life have I been dodging responsibilities, and how can I take ownership of my actions and choices to create positive change?

> What strategies can I employ to resist negative influences and people, ensuring that they do not hinder my recovery progress?

> How can I better embrace the precious gift of each day and make the most of every moment in my recovery journey?

Can I identify specific experiences in my recovery that have contributed to my personal growth and development, and how have I learned from them?

How do I persevere through tough times in my recovery, and what strategies can I use to maintain my resilience and determination?

Celebrating small victories along the journey of long-term recovery from addiction is essential for fostering resilience, maintaining a positive mindset, and acknowledging personal growth. Self-reflection on these principles empowers individuals to navigate their recovery journey with maturity, responsibility, and an appreciation for the gift of each new day.

Principle 8: Innovation and Creativity

Embracing Innovation and Creativity in Long-Term Recovery

Long-term recovery from addiction is a journey marked by personal growth, self-discovery, and transformation. Principle 12 emphasizes the importance of innovation and creativity in this journey. The provided wisdom encourages us to embrace our life experiences, whether positive or negative, as they shape our identity. It reminds us that our experiences, including our mistakes, contribute to our uniqueness. Moreover, it encourages us to believe in ourselves as we move forward. In this book, we will explore the significance of innovation and creativity in the context of long-term recovery from addiction.

Embracing Life Experiences

Our experiences, both good and bad, play a significant role in shaping our identity. In recovery, it is crucial to embrace these experiences as part of our personal journey. Innovation and creativity come into play when we reflect on our past, learn from our experiences, and find innovative ways to navigate our recovery path.

Learning from Mistakes

Mistakes are an inevitable part of life, and they can be particularly pronounced in the context of addiction and recovery. Innovation and creativity involve learning from our mistakes and using these experiences to fuel personal growth and transformation. They encourage us to find new approaches to old problems and seek innovative solutions to overcome obstacles.

Understanding Our Uniqueness

Every individual's journey to recovery is unique, shaped by their personal experiences and challenges. Innovation and creativity empower us to embrace our uniqueness and celebrate our individuality. It is through these qualities that we can build a recovery plan that is tailored to our specific needs and aspirations.

Believing in Ourselves

Belief in oneself is a fundamental aspect of recovery. The statement reminds us that if we could believe in Santa Claus for eight years, we can certainly believe in ourselves for a mere five seconds. This self-belief is essential as it fuels our creativity and innovative thinking, allowing us to set and achieve ambitious recovery goals.

Avoiding Self-Doubt

Self-doubt can be a significant barrier to recovery progress. Innovation and creativity encourage us to avoid second-guessing ourselves and to have confidence in our abilities and potential. By embracing our experiences and believing in ourselves, we can overcome self-doubt and continue moving forward in recovery.

Self-Reflection Questions

How have my life experiences, both positive and negative, shaped my identity and influenced my recovery journey?

What mistakes have I made in my recovery, and how can I use innovation and creativity to learn from them and grow as a result?

In what ways can I embrace my uniqueness and celebrate my individuality in my recovery journey?

How can I foster self-belief and confidence in my abilities to achieve my recovery goals?

What strategies can I employ to avoid self-doubt and continue moving forward in my recovery with innovation and creativity?

Innovation and creativity play a crucial role in long-term recovery from addiction. They involve embracing life experiences, learning from mistakes, celebrating uniqueness, believing in oneself, and avoiding self-doubt. Self-reflection on these principles empowers individuals to navigate their recovery journey with resilience, determination, and the creativity to overcome challenges and achieve lasting sobriety.

Embracing Innovation: A Catalyst for Long-Term Recovery

Long-term recovery from addiction is a transformative journey that requires the courage to embrace innovation as a catalyst for change. Principle 13 underscores the significance of welcoming complex challenges as opportunities for growth and progress. The provided wisdom encourages us to recognize the value of time and the importance of aligning our actions with our true selves. Furthermore, it emphasizes that greatness is within reach for those who believe in themselves and are willing to make the necessary sacrifices. In this book, we will explore the importance of embracing innovation as a driving force for change in the context of long-term recovery from addiction.

Turning Challenges into Opportunities

Complex problems and challenges are not to be avoided but embraced as powerful opportunities for growth and transformation. In recovery, it is essential to confront these issues head-on, as they often hold the keys to personal progress and lasting change. Innovation thrives in the face of adversity, and it is through creative problem-solving that individuals can find novel solutions to addiction-related challenges.

Recognizing the Value of Time

Time is a precious resource, and every day that is spent drifting away from recovery goals represents a missed opportunity. Embracing innovation involves understanding that time is limited and that wasting it delays progress. Recovering individuals must make the most of each day, actively seeking innovative approaches to address their challenges and stay on the path to sobriety.

Authentic Expression of the Self

Success in any endeavor, including recovery, depends on the extent to which it aligns with one's true self. Embracing innovation means finding recovery strategies and approaches that resonate with one's individual needs, values, and aspirations. By authentically expressing themselves in the recovery journey, individuals are more likely to achieve lasting change.

Belief in Personal Greatness

Belief in oneself is a fundamental element of embracing innovation. A person can achieve greatness if they have the courage, determination, dedication, and competitive drive to pursue their goals. Recovery often requires sacrifices, but those who are willing to pay the price for meaningful change can unlock their potential and achieve lasting sobriety.

Self-Reflection Questions

> How do I typically approach complex challenges in my recovery journey, and how can I welcome them as opportunities for growth and innovation?
>
> Do I recognize the value of time in my recovery, and how can I make the most of each day to actively seek innovative solutions to addiction-related challenges?
>
> In what ways can I ensure that my recovery journey aligns with my true self, values, and aspirations, fostering authenticity and a greater chance of success?
>
> How can I cultivate belief in myself and my potential for greatness as I navigate the challenges of recovery?
>
> What sacrifices am I willing to make to achieve lasting change in my recovery, and how can I stay committed to the journey despite the difficulties that may arise?

Embracing innovation as a catalyst for change is a vital aspect of long-term recovery from addiction. It involves turning challenges into opportunities, recognizing the value of time, seeking

A Journey of Transformation

authenticity, and believing in one's potential for greatness. Self-reflection on these principles empowers individuals to approach their recovery journey with creativity, resilience, and the determination to achieve lasting sobriety.

Encouraging Creative Thinking and Problem-Solving on the Road to Long-Term Recovery

Long-term recovery from addiction is a journey that demands creative thinking and effective problem-solving skills. Principle 14 underscores the importance of letting go of the past, embracing happiness, and focusing on positive actions. The provided wisdom emphasizes the value of kindness, gratitude, and the significance of giving back. It reminds us that life is a precious gift, and that our past experiences will ultimately reveal their purpose. In this book, we will explore the importance of encouraging creative thinking and problem-solving in the context of long-term recovery from addiction.

Letting Go of the Past

The past can be a heavy burden, especially in the context of addiction. Recovery necessitates letting go of the desire for revenge and choosing to live happily ever after. This choice signifies that the past has not defeated us and that we are ready to move forward with optimism and hope. Creative thinking comes into play when we explore innovative ways to release the grip of the past and focus on a brighter future.

Counting Our Blessings

Gratitude is a powerful tool in the recovery journey. By counting our blessings and appreciating the positive aspects of our lives, we can shift our perspective towards a more optimistic outlook. Creative thinking encourages us to find new ways to practice gratitude and incorporate it into our daily routine.

Giving Back and Helping Others

Recovery is not only about personal growth but also about giving back to others who may be struggling. Kindness and helping others can be incredibly rewarding and fulfilling. Creative problem-solving skills allow us to find unique ways to contribute to the well-being of those around us. When we help others, we reinforce our commitment to a happy and meaningful life.

Appreciating the Gift of Life

Life is a precious gift, and every day we are alive is an opportunity to make the most of it. Creative thinking involves seeking out new experiences, setting meaningful goals, and appreciating the journey of recovery. By valuing our own lives and the lives of our loved ones, we find the motivation to stay on the path of sobriety.

Understanding the Purpose of Challenges

While it may be challenging to understand the reasons for our past experiences, the statement reminds us that eventually, their purpose will be revealed. Creative thinking allows us to reflect on our past struggles and extract valuable lessons from them. By doing so, we can use these lessons to inform our recovery journey and become stronger as a result.

Self-Reflection Questions

> How do I currently handle past grievances and the desire for revenge, and how can I use creative thinking to let go and focus on my happiness in recovery?

> Do I practice gratitude regularly, and what creative ways can I explore to incorporate gratitude into my daily life to enhance my recovery journey?

> In what ways can I give back to others and help those who may be struggling with addiction, using creative problem-solving skills to make a positive impact?

> How can I better appreciate the gift of life and ensure that I make the most of each day in my recovery journey?

> What past experiences have shaped my recovery, and how can I use creative thinking to understand their purpose and derive valuable lessons from them?

Encouraging creative thinking and effective problem-solving are essential aspects of long-term recovery from addiction. It involves letting go of the past, practicing gratitude, giving back, appreciating life, and seeking the lessons in past challenges. Self-reflection on these principles empowers individuals to approach their recovery journey with resilience, creativity, and the determination to achieve lasting sobriety.

Nurturing Your Creative Mindset on the Path to Long-Term Recovery

Long-term recovery from addiction is a journey that demands a creative mindset and the ability to transform challenges into opportunities. Principle 15 emphasizes the importance of letting go of perfect expectations, viewing problems as blessings in disguise, and embracing change as a means of evolution. The provided wisdom reminds us that clinging to the past and negative emotions can hinder our progress, and it encourages us to find strength in perseverance. In this book, we will explore the significance of nurturing a creative mindset in the context of long-term recovery from addiction.

Letting Go of Perfect Expectations

Often, we set unrealistic expectations that lead to disappointment. Recovery is no exception, as we may envision an idealized version of what it should be. Nurturing a creative mindset involves

A Journey of Transformation

acknowledging that perfection is unattainable and being open to embracing the imperfect reality of the recovery journey. By doing so, we free ourselves from the burden of unmet expectations.

Viewing Problems as Blessings in Disguise

Challenges and setbacks are inevitable in recovery, but they can also serve as catalysts for growth. Nurturing a creative mindset means reframing problems as opportunities for personal development. By approaching difficulties with a positive and open attitude, we can extract valuable lessons and transform adversity into progress.

Embracing Change and Evolution

Change is a fundamental aspect of recovery. Nurturing a creative mindset entails recognizing the importance of change as a catalyst for personal evolution. By letting go of what was and embracing new ways of thinking and behaving, we pave the way for personal growth and lasting recovery.

Releasing Negative Emotions

Holding onto negative emotions, such as anger, hurt, or pain, can be detrimental to the recovery journey. Nurturing a creative mindset involves acknowledging these emotions and finding healthy ways to release them. By letting go of emotional baggage, we create space for love, positivity, and personal growth.

Perseverance and Real Strength

Recovery is not without its challenges, but real strength is demonstrated by the determination to keep pushing forward, regardless of the circumstances. Nurturing a creative mindset means understanding that giving up is the easy way out. True strength is found in the resilience to face adversity head-on and continue the journey to lasting sobriety.

Self-Reflection Questions

> How do I currently approach perfect expectations in my recovery journey, and how can I nurture a creative mindset by embracing imperfection?

> Do I tend to view problems in my recovery as insurmountable obstacles or as opportunities for growth, and how can I shift my mindset to see them as blessings in disguise?

> In what ways can I better embrace change and evolution in my recovery, letting go of what was to create space for personal growth?

> Am I holding onto negative emotions that may be hindering my recovery journey, and what strategies can I employ to release them and make room for love and positivity?

> What does perseverance mean to me in the context of recovery, and how can I nurture a creative mindset that embraces challenges with determination and resilience?

Nurturing a creative mindset is a vital aspect of long-term recovery from addiction. It involves letting go of perfect expectations, viewing problems as opportunities, embracing change and evolution, releasing negative emotions, and demonstrating true strength through perseverance. Self-reflection on these principles empowers individuals to approach their recovery journey with creativity, resilience, and the determination to achieve lasting sobriety.

Applying Creative Solutions to Societal Challenges on the Path to Long-Term Recovery

Long-term recovery from addiction is not just a personal journey; it is also an opportunity to contribute to society by applying creative solutions to address challenges. Principle 16 emphasizes the importance of leveraging past experiences as valuable lessons, experimenting in the present to achieve expectations, and embracing adversity as a source of growth. The provided wisdom encourages us to take action, trust the process, and appreciate the blessings in our lives. In this book, we will explore the significance of applying creative solutions to societal challenges in the context of long-term recovery from addiction.

Leveraging Past Experiences

Our past experiences, including the challenges and mistakes we've faced, can serve as valuable lessons that inform our actions in the present and future. Nurturing a creative mindset in recovery means applying the knowledge gained from past experiences to approach societal challenges creatively. It involves understanding that our personal journey can contribute to finding innovative solutions for broader societal issues related to addiction and recovery.

Experimenting in the Present

The present is an opportunity for experimentation and action. Nurturing a creative mindset involves actively seeking out and implementing creative solutions to societal challenges related to addiction. By experimenting with new approaches and interventions, individuals in recovery can contribute to the betterment of their communities and society as a whole.

Embracing Adversity as a Source of Growth

Adversity often holds valuable lessons and opportunities for growth. In the context of societal challenges related to addiction, embracing adversity means recognizing that obstacles can be stepping stones to creative problem-solving. It involves focusing on the lessons learned from adversity and using them to inform innovative solutions that address addiction and its impact on society.

A Journey of Transformation

Taking Action and Trusting the Process

The statement encourages us to take action and trust the process one day at a time. Nurturing a creative mindset involves actively engaging in initiatives and projects aimed at addressing addiction-related societal challenges. It means believing that change is possible and that our efforts, combined with trust in the process, can lead to meaningful solutions.

Appreciating Blessings and Positivity

It is essential to maintain a positive outlook and appreciate the blessings in our lives. Nurturing a creative mindset in recovery involves recognizing the positive aspects of life and using them as sources of inspiration and motivation to address societal challenges creatively. By focusing on the positive, individuals in recovery can harness their energy to make a positive impact on the world around them.

Self-Reflection Questions

> How have my past experiences in addiction and recovery shaped my perspective on societal challenges related to addiction, and how can I leverage these experiences to find creative solutions?
>
> In what ways am I currently experimenting with creative solutions to address addiction-related societal challenges, and how can I expand my efforts in this regard?
>
> How can I embrace adversity as a source of growth and innovation when facing societal challenges related to addiction?
>
> What actions can I take today to contribute to addressing addiction-related societal challenges, and how can I trust the process of creating meaningful change?
>
> How do I currently maintain a positive outlook in recovery, and how can I use positivity and gratitude as motivators to address societal challenges creatively?

Applying creative solutions to societal challenges related to addiction is a meaningful way to contribute to the betterment of society while in long-term recovery. It involves leveraging past experiences, experimenting in the present, embracing adversity, taking action, and maintaining a positive outlook. Self-reflection on these principles empowers individuals to approach their recovery journey with creativity, resilience, and the determination to make a positive impact on society.

Principle 9: Mindful Action

Practicing Mindful Action on the Journey to Long-Term Recovery

Long-term recovery from addiction is a transformative journey that requires mindful action and a proactive approach. Principle 9 emphasizes the importance of mindfulness, acknowledging that life's adversities are an inevitable part of the journey. The provided wisdom reminds us that our reactions to adversity can shape our path, turning stumbling blocks into stepping stones. It highlights that constructive growth often arises from challenging circumstances and encourages us to embrace difficulties as opportunities for personal development. In this book, we will explore the significance of practicing mindful action in the context of long-term recovery from addiction.

The Awakening of Resilience

Life is a continuous process of self-discovery, and sometimes, a single event can awaken within us a resilience that we never knew existed. Long-term recovery is marked by the slow and deliberate growth of an individual who is emerging from the shadows of addiction. Mindful action involves recognizing the transformative power of adversity and using it as a catalyst for personal development.

Accepting the Inevitability of Adversity

Adversity is an inherent aspect of life, and it cannot be controlled. Mindful action requires acknowledging this fact and embracing adversity with an open heart and mind. By accepting the inevitability of challenges in recovery, individuals can prepare themselves to respond in a constructive and mindful manner.

Choosing How to React

The statement highlights that we can control how we react to adversity. Mindful action involves pausing, reflecting, and choosing a response that aligns with our recovery goals. Instead of succumbing to adversity, individuals in recovery can use mindful practices to navigate challenges, making conscious choices that lead to growth and progress.

Transforming Stumbling Blocks into Stepping Stones

Stumbling blocks, such as setbacks or challenges in recovery, can be transformed into stepping stones when approached with mindfulness. These obstacles become opportunities for learning, self-discovery, and personal growth. Mindful action means viewing difficulties as a chance to strengthen one's resolve and deepen their commitment to long-term recovery.

A Journey of Transformation

Becoming Better, Not Bitter

The difficulties in life are intended to make us better, not bitter. Mindful action entails embracing this perspective and using adversity as a tool for self-improvement. It means choosing to respond to life's challenges in a way that fosters resilience, personal development, and a positive outlook on the recovery journey.

Self-Reflection Questions

>Can I recall a specific event or experience in my recovery journey that awakened resilience or personal growth within me? How did I respond to it?
>
>How do I currently view adversity in my life and recovery? Do I tend to react impulsively, or do I practice mindfulness in my responses?
>
>What are some mindful practices or strategies I can incorporate into my daily life to respond more constructively to challenges in recovery?
>
>Can I identify any stumbling blocks or setbacks in my recovery journey? How can I transform these obstacles into stepping stones for personal growth?
>
>In what ways can I ensure that I am becoming better, not bitter, in response to life's difficulties and adversities?

Practicing mindful action is a fundamental aspect of long-term recovery from addiction. It involves awakening resilience, accepting the inevitability of adversity, choosing mindful responses, transforming stumbling blocks into stepping stones, and embracing personal growth in the face of difficulties. Self-reflection on these principles empowers individuals to approach their recovery journey with mindfulness, resilience, and a commitment to becoming better through adversity.

Striking the Balance Between Intention and Action in Long-Term Recovery

Long-term recovery from addiction is a journey marked by the delicate balance between intention and action. Principle 10 emphasizes the transformative power of patience and perseverance in overcoming difficulties and obstacles. The provided wisdom highlights the importance of adapting to challenges, learning from mistakes, and taking pride in personal progress. It reminds us that in life, we have the choice to be passive observers or active pilots, and it encourages us to bring our own positivity and determination, regardless of external circumstances. In this book, we will explore the significance of striking the balance between intention and action in the context of long-term recovery from addiction.

The Magic of Patience and Perseverance

Patience and perseverance are often underestimated but hold a magical effect when applied in the journey of recovery. Long-term recovery is not always linear, and difficulties and obstacles can seem insurmountable. However, by patiently persisting in our efforts, we can gradually dissolve these challenges and pave the way for sustained sobriety.

Adapting to Difficulties

There are two ways to approach difficulties: altering the difficulties themselves or altering ourselves to meet them. Striking the balance between intention and action in recovery involves a dynamic approach. Sometimes, we may need to adjust our recovery strategies or seek new methods to address evolving challenges. At other times, we may need to work on personal growth and self-improvement to better navigate obstacles.

Learning from Mistakes

A mistake in recovery is not a failure, but an opportunity to learn and grow. Striking the balance between intention and action requires us to embrace our mistakes and view them as valuable lessons. By learning from every step we take, we can refine our recovery journey and make continuous progress toward lasting sobriety.

Accepting the Present

Whatever we did today, in recovery or in life, is the way it was meant to be. Accepting the present and taking pride in our efforts is an important aspect of balanced intention and action. It means recognizing that every day is an opportunity for growth and self-improvement, regardless of past choices or circumstances.

Choosing to Be a Pilot

In life, we have the choice to be either a passenger, passively going along with the flow, or a pilot, actively steering our own course. Striking the balance between intention and action in recovery involves choosing to be the pilot of our journey. It means taking control of our choices, setting meaningful goals, and steering our lives in the direction of sustained sobriety.

Bringing Our Own Sunshine

Regardless of external factors or challenges, we have the power to bring our own sunshine. Maintaining a positive outlook and determination is an essential part of balanced intention and action. By cultivating positivity and resilience, we can overcome obstacles and continue on the path of long-term recovery.

A Journey of Transformation

Self-Reflection Questions

> How do I currently balance my intentions for recovery with my actions? What strategies can I employ to achieve a better balance?
>
> Can I identify a specific difficulty or obstacle in my recovery journey? How can I adapt to this challenge, either by altering it or by altering myself to meet it?
>
> Have I made mistakes in my recovery, and what lessons have I learned from them? How can I apply these lessons to improve my recovery journey?
>
> How do I view and accept the present in my recovery? What steps can I take to maintain a positive outlook and take pride in my efforts?
>
> Am I currently a passive passenger or an active pilot in my recovery journey? How can I take more control and steer my recovery toward long-term sobriety?

Striking the balance between intention and action is crucial in the long-term recovery from addiction. It involves harnessing the magic of patience and perseverance, adapting to difficulties, learning from mistakes, accepting the present, and choosing to be an active pilot of one's recovery journey. Self-reflection on these principles empowers individuals to approach their recovery with intention, resilience, and a commitment to lasting sobriety.

Setting Clear Intentions for Change in the Journey to Long-Term Recovery

Long-term recovery from addiction is a transformative journey that requires setting clear intentions for change. Principle 11 emphasizes the necessity of enduring difficulties to achieve the desired rewards, acknowledging the value of the past as it informs the present, and the importance of taking action to find inspiration. The wisdom provided highlights that inspiration often comes when one is willing to take action and emphasizes that taking action is the key to achieving results. In this book, we will explore the significance of setting clear intentions for change in the context of long-term recovery from addiction.

Enduring Rain for the Rainbow

The metaphorical message of "If you want the rainbow, you have to put up with the rain" reminds us that meaningful change often requires enduring difficulties and challenges. In long-term recovery, it's essential to set clear intentions for change and be prepared to weather the storms of addiction, knowing that brighter days and rewards are on the horizon.

Embracing the Past as a Guide

The past, though it may not always align with the present, is a valuable teacher. Setting clear intentions for change involves acknowledging that our past experiences, both positive and negative, inform our present actions. We can draw inspiration and guidance from the lessons learned and use them as stepping stones toward a better future.

Taking Action to Find Inspiration

Action is the catalyst for inspiration. To set clear intentions for change, one must be willing to take action and seek inspiration actively. The Nike slogan, "Just do it," encapsulates the idea that pushing oneself to take action is the key to achieving desired results. In recovery, setting clear intentions and acting upon them are fundamental to progress.

Reflecting on Past Inspirational Moments

Self-reflection plays a crucial role in setting clear intentions for change. Individuals in recovery can ask themselves questions such as, "How do I get inspired?" and recall past moments of inspiration. Reflecting on the circumstances, activities, and people involved in those moments can help identify sources of motivation and guide the setting of clear intentions for change.

Living the Life of Your Dreams

Setting clear intentions for change often leads to the pursuit of one's dreams. The statement, "The biggest adventure you can take is to live the life of your dreams," underscores the transformative nature of setting and pursuing meaningful intentions. Fear may keep us from taking that leap, but faith can serve as a comforting and motivating force on the journey to recovery.

Self-Reflection Questions

> What specific intentions do I have for my long-term recovery from addiction, and how clear are they in my mind?
>
> How have I endured difficulties and challenges in my recovery journey, and what rewards or positive changes have I experienced as a result?
>
> How do I view my past experiences, both positive and negative, as valuable teachers that inform my present actions in recovery?
>
> What actions have I taken in my recovery journey to actively seek inspiration and motivation, and how have they impacted my progress?
>
> Can I recall moments of past inspiration and identify common factors or sources that motivate me to take action and set clear intentions for change?

Setting clear intentions for change is an essential aspect of long-term recovery from addiction. It involves enduring difficulties, embracing the past as a guide, taking action to find inspiration, reflecting on past inspirational moments, and pursuing the life of one's dreams. Self-reflection on

A Journey of Transformation

these principles empowers individuals to approach their recovery journey with intention, resilience, and the determination to achieve lasting sobriety.

Taking Deliberate and Purposeful Steps on the Path to Long-Term Recovery

Long-term recovery from addiction is a journey that requires taking deliberate and purposeful steps. Principle 12 emphasizes the importance of recognizing life as a constant battle and the need to keep fighting and adjusting to achieve one's goals. The wisdom provided underscores that health, happiness, and success are dependent on the fighting spirit within each person. It reminds us that while life may present challenges, our response to those challenges is what truly matters. In this book, we will explore the significance of taking deliberate and purposeful steps in the context of long-term recovery from addiction.

Recognizing Life as a Continuous Contest

Life is a continuous contest where individuals must keep fighting and adjusting if they hope to survive. In the context of addiction recovery, recognizing this contest means acknowledging that the journey is not always smooth, and challenges may arise. Setting the intention to keep fighting and adjusting is essential to navigate these challenges successfully.

Managing Expectations and Avoiding Disappointment

Expectations play a significant role in recovery. Setting unrealistic expectations can lead to constant disappointment when reality does not align with those expectations. Taking deliberate and purposeful steps involves managing expectations and understanding that recovery is a process that may have setbacks. By doing so, individuals can better cope with disappointment and continue their journey with resilience.

The Role of the Fighting Spirit

Health, happiness, and success are intertwined with the fighting spirit within each person. In long-term recovery, the fighting spirit becomes the driving force that propels individuals forward. It involves the determination to overcome obstacles, stay committed to sobriety, and take proactive steps towards personal growth and well-being.

Responding to Life's Challenges

Life presents both opportunities and challenges. How we respond to these challenges defines our character and determines our progress in recovery. Taking deliberate and purposeful steps means actively addressing the challenges that arise in the journey to sobriety. It involves seeking support, practicing self-care, and continuously adapting one's approach to maintain a healthy and fulfilling life.

The Big Thing: What We Do About It

Ultimately, the big thing in life is not what happens to us but what we do about it when it happens to us. Taking deliberate and purposeful steps is about responding constructively to the circumstances that arise during recovery. It involves making choices that align with the goal of long-term sobriety and well-being.

Self-Reflection Questions

How do I currently view the concept of life as a continuous contest, and how does this perspective influence my approach to recovery?

What expectations do I have for my recovery journey, and how can I manage them to avoid constant disappointment?

How would I describe my fighting spirit in the context of my recovery from addiction, and how does it drive me to take deliberate and purposeful steps?

What challenges have I encountered in recovery, and how have I responded to them? Are there areas where I can improve my approach?

How do I define the "big thing" in my life, and what actions can I take to ensure that I respond proactively to challenges in my recovery journey?

Taking deliberate and purposeful steps is a fundamental aspect of long-term recovery from addiction. It involves recognizing life as a continuous contest, managing expectations, embracing the fighting spirit, responding to challenges constructively, and understanding that the big thing is what we do about life's circumstances. Self-reflection on these principles empowers individuals to approach their recovery journey with intention, resilience, and the determination to achieve lasting sobriety.

The Significance of Reflection in the Journey of Long-Term Recovery

Long-term recovery from addiction is a transformative journey that relies on reflection as a vital tool for change. Principle 13 underscores the importance of embracing the unexpected in life, acknowledging the value of resilience, and simplifying the complexities of existence. It highlights that trying and failing is often more rewarding than living with the regret of never trying. In this book, we will explore the significance of reflection in the context of long-term recovery from addiction.

Embracing the Unplanned Path

Life often unfolds differently from our meticulously crafted plans. In the context of addiction recovery, individuals may envision a straightforward path to sobriety, but unexpected twists and

A Journey of Transformation

turns can occur. Embracing the unplanned path means recognizing that growth and change are not always linear. Reflection helps individuals adapt to unexpected circumstances, learn from them, and continue their journey with resilience.

The Power of Rebuilding

No matter how broken one may feel, the power to rebuild and start anew is ever-present. Reflection plays a pivotal role in this process. It allows individuals to assess their current state, identify areas that need improvement, and create a blueprint for personal growth. Through reflection, individuals can take deliberate steps to rebuild their lives and move forward in their recovery journey.

Simplifying the Complexities of Life

Life can become needlessly complicated when we overanalyze or dwell on trivial matters. Reflection encourages individuals to simplify their perspectives and focus on the essentials. In recovery, this means appreciating the progress made, cherishing the present moment, and enjoying the simple pleasures of life without unnecessary complexity.

Living Authentically

The wisdom that advises not to try changing how people feel about us emphasizes the importance of authenticity. Reflection allows individuals to connect with their true selves and live authentically. Instead of seeking external validation or attempting to control others' perceptions, individuals in recovery can reflect on their values, beliefs, and actions to align them with their authentic selves.

Happiness and Self-Love

The ultimate goal of reflection is to live one's life authentically and find happiness within. The statement suggests that attempting to change how others feel about us is futile; instead, focusing on personal well-being and happiness is paramount. Through self-reflection, individuals can nurture self-love, prioritize their happiness, and lead fulfilling lives in recovery.

Self-Reflection Questions

> How do I currently view unexpected challenges and changes in my recovery journey, and how can I embrace the unplanned path with resilience?

> Can I identify areas in my life that need rebuilding and improvement? How can reflection help me create a plan for personal growth and change?

> What complexities do I tend to introduce into my life that hinder my progress in recovery? How can I simplify my perspective and focus on the essentials?

Am I living authentically in my recovery journey, or do I seek external validation? How can reflection help me connect with my true self and align my actions with my values?

What steps can I take to prioritize my happiness and self-love in recovery? How can I use reflection to ensure that I am living a fulfilling life?

Reflection is a fundamental tool in the journey of long-term recovery from addiction. It involves embracing the unplanned path, harnessing the power of rebuilding, simplifying life's complexities, living authentically, and prioritizing happiness and self-love. Self-reflection on these principles empowers individuals to approach their recovery journey with resilience, authenticity, and the determination to achieve lasting sobriety.

Continuous Evaluation and Adaptation in the Journey to Long-Term Recovery

Long-term recovery from addiction is an ongoing and evolving process that requires continuous evaluation and adaptation. Principle 14 encourages individuals to view life not as a fragile temple but as a resilient forest, where growth and renewal are inherent qualities. It reminds us that life comprises both moments of happiness and times of darkness, and that forgiveness and letting go are powerful tools for personal transformation. In this book, we will explore the importance of continuous evaluation and adaptation in the context of long-term recovery from addiction.

Life as a Resilient Forest

The metaphor of life as a resilient forest illustrates the inherent strength and resilience within each individual. In the context of addiction recovery, it emphasizes that setbacks and challenges should not be viewed as permanent destruction but as opportunities for growth and renewal. Continuous evaluation and adaptation involve recognizing one's capacity for recovery and embracing the journey's ups and downs with resilience.

The Role of Darkness in Growth

Just as stars need darkness to shine, personal growth and transformation often emerge from challenging and dark times. Long-term recovery may involve facing relapses, cravings, or emotional turmoil. Continuous evaluation allows individuals to assess these dark moments, learn from them, and use them as catalysts for personal development. It acknowledges that adversity can lead to resilience and strength.

Letting Go of Grudges and Resentment

Forgiveness and the release of grudges are essential components of the recovery journey. Holding onto anger and resentment can hinder progress and perpetuate negative emotions. Continuous evaluation involves reflecting on past grievances, understanding their impact on one's well-being, and actively choosing forgiveness as a means of healing and moving forward.

A Journey of Transformation

The Art of Letting Go

Letting go extends beyond forgiveness. It encompasses the release of burdens, expectations, and attachments that no longer serve a purpose in one's recovery. Continuous evaluation enables individuals to identify what they can let go of, recognizing that relinquishing these burdens does not equate to losing something of value. Letting go can lighten the load and facilitate personal growth.

Self-Reflection Questions

> How do I currently view the concept of life as a resilient forest, and how does this perspective influence my approach to recovery and personal growth?

> Can I recall moments of personal growth and resilience that emerged from challenging or dark times in my recovery journey? How have these experiences shaped me?

> Are there grudges or resentments from my past that I am holding onto, and how do they impact my well-being and progress in recovery? What steps can I take to embrace forgiveness?

> What burdens, expectations, or attachments am I carrying that no longer serve a purpose in my recovery journey? How can continuous evaluation help me identify and release them?

> How can I use the metaphor of life as a resilient forest to remind myself of my inner strength and capacity for growth as I navigate the challenges of long-term recovery?

Continuous evaluation and adaptation are vital aspects of the journey to long-term recovery from addiction. Embracing life as a resilient forest, acknowledging the role of darkness in growth, letting go of grudges and resentment, and mastering the art of letting go empower individuals to approach their recovery journey with resilience, forgiveness, and the determination to achieve lasting sobriety.

Learning from Experiences and Refining Your Approach in the Journey of Recovery

Long-term recovery from addiction is a transformative journey that involves continuous learning and refinement of one's approach. Principle 15 highlights the importance of embracing challenges, learning from mistakes, and understanding the significance of both success and failure in personal growth. It emphasizes the need to remain resilient in the face of adversity and stresses the value of consistency. In this book, we will explore the significance of learning from experiences and refining one's approach in the context of long-term recovery from addiction.

Embracing Challenges and Mistakes

To grow and learn, individuals in recovery must be willing to embrace challenges and make mistakes. Addiction recovery is not a linear path; it involves setbacks and hurdles. By recognizing that challenges and mistakes are an integral part of the journey, individuals can approach them with openness and the intent to learn and grow.

The Role of Success and Failure

Success and failure are intertwined aspects of any meaningful journey. In recovery, success may involve achieving milestones such as periods of sobriety, personal growth, or mending relationships. Failure, on the other hand, may manifest as relapses or setbacks. Both success and failure offer valuable lessons and insights that individuals can use to refine their approach to recovery.

Consistency as the Key

Consistency is a cornerstone of long-term recovery. It involves maintaining a steady commitment to sobriety, self-care, and personal growth. Consistency ensures that individuals do not become complacent during times of success and remain resilient during moments of challenge. It fosters the development of positive habits and behaviors.

Taking It Day by Day

Life can be overwhelming, especially during the recovery journey. Taking life day by day allows individuals to break down their goals into manageable steps. By focusing on the present moment and having faith that things will improve over time, individuals can reduce feelings of overwhelm and anxiety.

Having Faith in the End

Maintaining faith in the ultimate outcome of recovery is crucial. Believing that everything will eventually be okay provides individuals with hope and motivation to persevere through difficult times. It encourages a positive mindset and reinforces the idea that challenges are temporary.

Self-Reflection Questions

> How do I currently approach challenges and mistakes in my recovery journey, and how can I foster a more open and learning-oriented mindset?

> Can I identify specific instances of success and failure in my recovery? What lessons have I learned from these experiences, and how have they influenced my approach?

In what ways do I practice consistency in my recovery efforts, and where can I improve my commitment to sobriety and personal growth?

How do I manage feelings of overwhelm and anxiety during my recovery journey? What strategies can I implement to take life day by day and reduce stress?

How can I strengthen my faith in the ultimate outcome of my recovery? What practices or beliefs can help me maintain a positive mindset and stay motivated?

Learning from experiences and refining one's approach are essential aspects of long-term recovery from addiction. Embracing challenges, understanding the roles of success and failure, prioritizing consistency, taking life day by day, and maintaining faith in the end empower individuals to navigate their recovery journey with resilience, hope, and the determination to achieve lasting sobriety.

The Principles for Someone Seeking Long-term Recovery From Addiction Can Be Summarized as Follows:

Principle 1: Self-awareness
- Exploring the foundation of change within oneself.
  - Recognizing strengths and weaknesses.
  - Understanding values and beliefs.
- Cultivating mindfulness and introspection.
  - Engaging in practices for self-reflection.
  - Embracing the power of self-knowledge.

Principle 2: Empathy and Compassion
- Recognizing the importance of empathy in driving positive change.
- Developing compassion for oneself and others.
  - Understanding the interconnectedness of all beings.
  - Practicing kindness and empathy in daily life.

Principle 3: Vision and Purpose
- Defining a clear vision for change.
  - Creating a vivid mental picture of desired outcomes.
  - Setting long-term goals aligned with the envisioned change.
- Connecting personal purpose with the greater good.
  - Identifying life's purpose.
  - Aligning personal purpose with change-making goals.

Principle 4: Resilience and Adaptability
- Embracing challenges as opportunities for growth.
  - Developing a growth mindset.
  - Building resilience in the face of adversity.
- Navigating change and uncertainty.
  - Employing strategies for adapting to changing circumstances.
  - Learning from setbacks and failures.

Principle 5: Collaboration and Community
- Harnessing the power of collective action.
  - Building partnerships and collaborations.
  - Fostering a sense of community and belonging.
- Creating a ripple effect of change.
  - Recognizing how individual efforts contribute to a larger impact.
  - Inspiring and mobilizing others to become change makers.

Principle 6: Authenticity and Integrity
- Understanding the role of authenticity in leading by example.

A Journey of Transformation

- - Staying true to values and principles.
  - Honoring word and commitments.
- Recognizing the trust factor in change making.
  - Building trust with others through integrity.
  - Understanding the ripple effect of trust in communities.

Principle 7: Patience and Persistence
- Acknowledging the time required for meaningful change.
- Embracing the art of perseverance in the face of obstacles.
  - Implementing strategies for staying committed to goals.
  - Celebrating small victories along the way.

Principle 8: Innovation and Creativity
- Embracing innovation as a catalyst for change.
- Encouraging creative thinking and problem-solving.
  - Nurturing a creative mindset.
  - Applying creative solutions to societal challenges.

Principle 9: Mindful Action
- Striking a balance between intention and action.
  - Setting clear intentions for change.
  - Taking deliberate and purposeful steps.
- Recognizing the importance of reflection in the change-making process.
  - Engaging in continuous evaluation and adaptation.
  - Learning from experiences and refining one's approach.

These principles collectively provide a comprehensive framework to guide individuals seeking long-term recovery from addiction, emphasizing the significance of self-awareness, empathy, resilience, authenticity, and mindful action in the journey towards lasting positive change.

In conclusion, the principles outlined provide a holistic roadmap for individuals on the path to long-term recovery from addiction. These principles encompass various facets of personal growth and change, offering guidance and insights to navigate the challenging journey of recovery. From self-awareness and empathy to resilience and innovation, each principle plays a crucial role in fostering lasting positive change.

Self-awareness serves as the foundation, enabling individuals to recognize their strengths, weaknesses, values, and beliefs. Cultivating mindfulness and introspection empowers them to embark on a transformative journey by understanding themselves better.

Empathy and compassion emerge as powerful drivers of change, fostering understanding not only for oneself but also for others. Recognizing the interconnectedness of all beings and practicing kindness and empathy in daily life create a nurturing environment for personal growth.

Vision and purpose provide direction and motivation. Defining a clear vision for change and aligning long-term goals with this vision empower individuals to make meaningful strides. Connecting personal purpose with the greater good adds depth and meaning to their efforts.

Resilience and adaptability become essential tools in the face of challenges. Embracing adversity as an opportunity for growth, developing a growth mindset, and learning from setbacks enable individuals to navigate change and uncertainty effectively.

Collaboration and community emphasize the collective power of change. Building partnerships and fostering a sense of belonging contribute to a ripple effect, where individual efforts lead to a larger impact, inspiring and mobilizing others to join the journey.

Authenticity and integrity serve as guiding lights in leadership by example. Staying true to values, honoring commitments, and building trust within communities create a fertile ground for positive change.

Patience and persistence underscore the importance of enduring commitment. Acknowledging the time required for meaningful change and celebrating small victories along the way provide motivation and a sense of accomplishment.

Innovation and creativity become catalysts for transformation, encouraging individuals to think outside the box and apply creative solutions to societal challenges.

Mindful action bridges the gap between intention and reality, urging individuals to set clear intentions and take deliberate steps toward their goals. The importance of reflection in the change-making process ensures continuous evaluation and adaptation, allowing for refinement and growth.

In the journey toward long-term recovery from addiction, these principles collectively offer a comprehensive framework. They emphasize the significance of self-awareness, empathy, resilience, authenticity, and mindful action as integral components of the transformative process. Embracing these principles can guide individuals on a path towards lasting positive change and a brighter, healthier future.

Part III
The Steps of Transformation

The Steps of Transformation

Life is a journey filled with uncertainties, challenges, and unexpected twists and turns. For those on the path to long-term recovery from addiction, this journey can be particularly daunting. It is a test of character, resilience, and the ability to adapt to the unpredictable nature of life. This book explores the steps of transformation that individuals seeking recovery from addiction must take in the face of life's unpredictability and unfairness.

Embracing Life's Unpredictability

Life, by its very nature, is characterized by its unpredictability. No one can predict with certainty what the future holds, and for those in recovery, this uncertainty can be especially daunting. However, it is crucial to recognize that everyone faces challenges and obstacles in life, and addiction recovery is one such challenge that demands courage and resilience.

Step 1: Acceptance of Unfairness The first step in transformation involves accepting the unfairness of life. Bad things happen to good people, and addiction can feel like an unjust burden. Yet, dwelling on the unfairness only prolongs suffering. Acceptance is about acknowledging that life's challenges are not personal punishments but part of the human experience.

> Self-Reflection Question: How can I shift my perspective from seeing addiction as a punishment to viewing it as an opportunity for growth and transformation?

Step 2: Taking Risks Recovery is a journey that requires taking risks. It involves stepping into the unknown and embracing change. Staying within the confines of addiction is the real risk, as it hinders personal growth and well-being. To transform, one must take the risk of pursuing a life free from substances.

> Self-Reflection Question: What risks am I willing to take in my journey towards recovery, and how can I overcome the fear of the unknown?

Step 3: Embracing Change Change is the only constant in life. Transformation in recovery requires embracing change as an opportunity for growth. Change might involve seeking help, adopting new habits, or letting go of toxic relationships. It is through change that true recovery can begin.

> Self-Reflection Question: How can I become more comfortable with change and see it as a catalyst for my personal growth and recovery?

Step 4: Learning from Mistakes In the process of recovery, mistakes are inevitable. However, these mistakes should not be seen as failures but as opportunities for learning and growth. Each stumble on the path to recovery can provide valuable insights and wisdom.

A Journey of Transformation

> Self-Reflection Question: How can I reframe my view of mistakes as valuable experiences that contribute to my personal growth and recovery?

Step 5: Being the Change Waiting for circumstances to change or for someone else to make a difference is futile. True transformation in recovery begins when individuals take responsibility for their own change. We are the architects of our recovery journey, and we must be the change we seek.

> Self-Reflection Question: How can I actively be the change I want to see in my life and in my journey to recovery?

Life's unfairness and unpredictability are inescapable realities, but they do not define us. The journey to long-term recovery from addiction is a testament to our ability to transform and grow despite these challenges. By accepting life's unpredictability, taking risks, embracing change, learning from mistakes, and being the change we seek, we can navigate the uncharted waters of recovery with courage and resilience.

Self-Reflection Questions:

> How can I embrace the unpredictability of life and use it as a source of strength in my recovery journey?

> What specific risks am I willing to take to break free from addiction and transform my life?

> In what ways can I actively embrace change as an opportunity for personal growth and recovery?

> How can I reframe my view of mistakes as valuable learning experiences on my journey to long-term recovery?

> What steps can I take to be the change I want to see in my life and in my path to recovery?

> How can I build resilience and adaptability to better navigate the challenges and uncertainties of life's journey?

Setting the Context for Personal Transformation on the Path to Long-Term Addiction Recovery

The journey towards long-term recovery from addiction is a challenging and transformative process that requires more than just a cessation of substance use. It calls for a profound shift in mindset, attitude, and vision. In the words of Dalai Lama, "In order to carry a positive action, we must develop a positive vision." This book explores how setting a positive context and adopting the right mindset can empower individuals seeking recovery to overcome obstacles, cultivate resilience, and ultimately achieve lasting transformation.

The Power of Positive Vision

A positive vision is the cornerstone of personal transformation. It serves as the driving force that propels individuals toward their goals and sustains them through the trials and tribulations of recovery. To embark on this journey, one must cultivate a vision that encompasses hope, determination, and self-belief.

Step 1: Hard Work and Courage Achieving lasting recovery from addiction is not a passive endeavor; it requires unwavering determination and hard work. One must be willing to confront the challenges head-on, no matter how daunting they may seem. Courage becomes the ally that enables individuals to persevere through the most challenging moments.

> Self-Reflection Question: How can I develop the courage and resilience needed to work tirelessly towards my recovery goals?

Step 2: Belief in Oneself Belief in oneself is the cornerstone of personal transformation. In the face of criticism, doubt, or self-criticism, it is essential to maintain unwavering self-belief. Negative words or actions from others can be turned into sources of motivation and determination.

> Self-Reflection Question: How can I bolster my self-belief and use it to counteract negative influences on my recovery journey?

Step 3: Mindful Communication As we navigate the journey of recovery, the words we use and the way we communicate with ourselves and others play a pivotal role. Mindful communication involves thinking twice before speaking and being aware of the impact our words can have on ourselves and those around us. Words can either inspire success or plant the seeds of failure.

> Self-Reflection Question: How can I improve the way I communicate with myself and others to foster a positive environment that supports my recovery?

Step 4: Forgiveness and Accountability Recognizing that words have lasting effects, it is important to be mindful of what we say and how it can affect others. However, we must also acknowledge our own imperfections and be willing to forgive ourselves when we fall short. Accountability and forgiveness are essential components of personal growth and transformation.

> Self-Reflection Question: How can I strike a balance between holding myself accountable for my actions and practicing self-forgiveness when I make mistakes in my recovery journey?

Setting the context for personal transformation on the path to long-term addiction recovery begins with adopting a positive vision and mindset. It requires hard work, courage, self-belief, mindful communication, and a commitment to accountability and forgiveness. By cultivating these qualities, individuals can empower themselves to overcome the challenges of addiction and forge a path toward lasting transformation and sobriety.

A Journey of Transformation

Self-Reflection Questions:

What is my positive vision for a life free from addiction, and how can I use it as motivation on my journey to recovery?

In what ways can I develop the courage and resilience needed to work diligently towards my recovery goals?

How can I strengthen my self-belief and use it to counteract negativity and criticism in my life?

What steps can I take to improve the way I communicate with myself and others to create a more positive and supportive environment for my recovery?

How do I strike a balance between holding myself accountable for my actions and practicing self-forgiveness when I make mistakes on my journey to recovery?

What strategies can I employ to maintain a positive vision and mindset even in the face of adversity and setbacks in my recovery journey?

Understanding the Steps of Transformation:
A Path to Long-Term Recovery from Addiction

Long-term recovery from addiction is a journey fraught with challenges, obstacles, and moments of self-doubt. However, understanding and embracing the steps of transformation can make all the difference in the success of this journey. As the saying goes, "Enter every day without giving mental recognition to the possibility of doubt or defeat." This book explores the importance of comprehending these transformative steps and how an unwavering determination can distinguish those who achieve lasting recovery from those who falter.

The Power of Positive Focus

One of the key elements in the journey towards long-term recovery is the power of positive focus. This entails concentrating on one's strengths, abilities, and determination rather than dwelling on weaknesses and problems. It is this shift in perspective that can set the stage for transformation.

Step 1: Embrace Daily Commitment Recovery is a daily commitment, and entering each day with a determined mindset is crucial. Recognize that doubt and defeat are possibilities, but by choosing not to give them mental recognition, you empower yourself to face challenges with resilience.

Self-Reflection Question: How can I develop a daily commitment to recovery and avoid succumbing to doubt and defeat?

Step 2: Concentrate on Strengths and Powers Focusing on strengths and powers rather than weaknesses and problems can be a game-changer. Addiction often makes individuals feel powerless, but the truth is that they possess inner strengths that can be harnessed for transformation. Concentrating on these assets can boost confidence and motivation.

> Self-Reflection Question: What are my strengths and powers that I can leverage to overcome addiction, and how can I prioritize them in my recovery journey?

Step 3: Cultivate Invincible Determination Invincible determination is the driving force behind overcoming addiction. It is the unwavering resolve to stay on the path of recovery, even when faced with adversity. This determination distinguishes those who succeed in recovery from those who give in to weakness.

> Self-Reflection Question: How can I nurture and maintain invincible determination throughout my recovery journey, and what strategies can help me stay committed?

Step 4: The Distinction Between Greatness and Weakness The distinction between great individuals and weak ones often lies in their ability to confront and conquer their personal challenges. Addiction recovery offers an opportunity for greatness, as it requires individuals to face their demons and emerge stronger on the other side.

> Self-Reflection Question: How can I use my journey of recovery to build resilience and achieve greatness in my life?

Understanding the steps of transformation is crucial for individuals seeking long-term recovery from addiction. By entering each day with a determined mindset, concentrating on strengths, nurturing invincible determination, and recognizing the potential for greatness within, individuals can overcome the challenges of addiction and achieve lasting transformation.

Self-Reflection Questions:

> How can I maintain a daily commitment to my recovery journey and avoid being derailed by doubt or defeat?

> What are my unique strengths and powers that I can leverage to overcome addiction, and how can I prioritize them in my recovery process?

> How can I cultivate and sustain invincible determination in the face of adversity and setbacks during my recovery journey?

> In what ways can I use my recovery journey to distinguish myself and achieve greatness in my life?

A Journey of Transformation

> How can I shift my perspective to focus more on my strengths and abilities rather than my weaknesses and problems, both in recovery and in life in general?
>
> What strategies can I implement to ensure that I consistently concentrate on my strengths and powers as I work towards long-term recovery?

The Transformative Power of Intentional Change on the Journey to Long-Term Recovery from Addiction

Recovery from addiction is a transformative journey, one that necessitates intentional change, resilience, and gratitude. As the saying goes, "What will be will be. You can't shape everything so that it meets your plans." In this book, we explore the profound impact of intentional change in addiction recovery, emphasizing the importance of gratitude and the positive energy it can bring to both the individual and their support network.

The Role of Intentional Change

Intentional change is at the heart of the recovery process. It begins with a conscious decision to break free from the cycle of addiction and a commitment to transform one's life. This transformation is not solely about abstaining from substances; it also involves a shift in mindset and behavior.

Step 1: Cultivating Gratitude Gratitude is a powerful tool for transformation. Cultivating the habit of being grateful for everything that has come to you, even the challenges and setbacks, can change one's perspective and provide motivation for change.

> Self-Reflection Question: How can I incorporate gratitude into my daily life, and how might it impact my journey towards long-term recovery?

Step 2: Positive Energy Intentional change is fueled by positive energy. Waking up every day with a positive mindset and sharing that energy with others can create a ripple effect of positivity. It not only benefits the individual but also those around them.

> Self-Reflection Question: How can I harness the power of positive energy to fuel my recovery journey and inspire those around me?

Step 3: Gratitude for Support Recovery is seldom achieved in isolation. Being grateful to those who provide support, encouragement, and understanding is essential. Acknowledging the role of others in the recovery process fosters a sense of interconnectedness and reinforces the commitment to change.

> Self-Reflection Question: Who has been instrumental in supporting me during my recovery journey, and how can I express my gratitude to them?

Step 4: The Happiness-Gratitude Connection It is important to recognize that happiness does not necessarily precede gratitude; rather, it is gratitude that makes us happy. When individuals intentionally focus on the positive aspects of their lives and recovery, they experience a profound sense of contentment and fulfillment.

> Self-Reflection Question: How can I shift my perspective to embrace gratitude as a source of happiness and fulfillment on my journey to recovery?

The transformative power of intentional change is a guiding light on the path to long-term recovery from addiction. By cultivating gratitude for all experiences, sharing positive energy, acknowledging and appreciating the support received, and understanding the happiness-gratitude connection, individuals can navigate the complexities of recovery with resilience and hope.

Self-Reflection Questions:

> How can I integrate intentional change into my recovery journey to achieve lasting transformation?

> What specific practices can I adopt to cultivate gratitude for all aspects of my life, including the challenges I face in recovery?

> In what ways can I wake up each day with a positive mindset and share that positive energy with those around me?

> Who are the individuals or support networks that have been instrumental in my recovery, and how can I express my gratitude to them?

> How can I shift my perspective to view gratitude as a source of happiness and contentment in my life, especially in the context of my recovery from addiction?

> What strategies can I implement to maintain a sense of gratitude and positive energy throughout my journey to long-term recovery?

Self-Reflection as the Starting Point

The journey to long-term recovery from addiction is a path filled with challenges, but it begins with a critical foundation: self-reflection. As the saying goes, "Don't let anyone ever break your soul." In this book, we will explore the pivotal role of self-reflection in addiction recovery, highlighting how it can empower individuals to stand firm, surround themselves with supportive people, and cultivate the real strength needed to persevere, even in the face of adversity.

The Power of Self-Reflection

Self-reflection is the starting point of any transformative journey, and recovery from addiction is no exception. It requires individuals to look within themselves, understand their motivations, and make conscious choices to change their lives.

Step 1: Standing on Your Own Two Feet Self-reflection enables individuals to recognize the importance of standing on their own two feet. It encourages them to take ownership of their recovery journey and not be swayed by external pressures or negative influences.

> Self-Reflection Question: How can I strengthen my resolve to stand on my own two feet and take full responsibility for my recovery?

Step 2: Resisting Negative Influences In the pursuit of recovery, there will always be those who wish to see individuals fail. Self-reflection helps individuals identify these negative influences and, most importantly, resist them. It empowers individuals to protect their well-being and maintain their commitment to sobriety.

> Self-Reflection Question: How can I identify and distance myself from individuals or situations that may hinder my recovery progress?

Step 3: Embracing Supportive Relationships Self-reflection guides individuals to identify and value the people who bring positivity and encouragement into their lives. These individuals believe in them and offer unwavering support, fostering an environment where self-belief can flourish.

> Self-Reflection Question: Who are the people in my life who believe in me and support my recovery journey, and how can I nurture these relationships?

Step 4: Cultivating Real Strength Real strength, as the saying suggests, comes from persevering despite challenging circumstances. Self-reflection helps individuals find the inner strength to keep pushing forward, even when recovery becomes difficult.

> Self-Reflection Question: How can I cultivate the inner strength needed to overcome challenges and setbacks in my recovery journey?

A Journey of Transformation

Self-reflection is the cornerstone of long-term recovery from addiction. It empowers individuals to stand their ground, resist negative influences, embrace supportive relationships, and cultivate the real strength required for enduring sobriety. By recognizing the importance of self-reflection, individuals can take the first step toward a transformative journey of recovery.

Self-Reflection Questions:

How can I integrate self-reflection into my daily routine to gain a deeper understanding of my motivations and triggers in relation to addiction?

What steps can I take to strengthen my resolve and stand on my own two feet in my recovery journey?

How can I identify and mitigate the negative influences or triggers that may hinder my progress towards sobriety?

Who are the individuals in my life who believe in me and support my recovery, and how can I express gratitude for their presence?

What strategies can I employ to cultivate and nurture my inner strength, ensuring that I can persevere through challenges and setbacks in my recovery?

In what ways can self-reflection help me maintain a positive mindset and unwavering commitment to my long-term recovery goals?

The Role of Self-Awareness in Initiating Transformation on the Path to Long-Term Recovery from Addiction

Initiating and sustaining long-term recovery from addiction is a profound journey that begins with self-awareness. As the saying goes, "Overthinking is the biggest cause of our unhappiness." In this book, we will explore the pivotal role of self-awareness in addiction recovery, emphasizing the need to stay occupied with positive thoughts, embrace humility, and take even the smallest steps in the right direction. Additionally, we will discuss the importance of remembering one's resilience during challenging times.

The Power of Self-Awareness

Self-awareness is the foundation upon which transformation in addiction recovery is built. It involves recognizing one's thoughts, feelings, behaviors, and their connection to addiction, and it sets the stage for meaningful change.

Step 1: Positive Occupation of the Mind The journey to recovery often involves moments of uncertainty and self-doubt. Self-awareness helps individuals shift their focus away from overthinking and negative thoughts. Keeping one's mind occupied with positive and productive activities can be a powerful antidote to cravings and relapses.

> Self-Reflection Question: How can I redirect my thoughts towards positive activities that support my recovery and well-being?

Step 2: Embracing Humility Self-awareness also entails the ability to acknowledge one's mistakes and accept responsibility. It is the humility to say, "I was wrong," without shame. This declaration signifies growth and an openness to change.

> Self-Reflection Question: How can I cultivate humility and a willingness to admit when I am wrong as part of my recovery journey?

Step 3: Taking Small Steps in the Right Direction Transformation in recovery often begins with small, deliberate steps. These seemingly insignificant actions can have a profound impact over time. Self-awareness enables individuals to identify these steps and appreciate their significance.

> Self-Reflection Question: What are the small steps I can take in the right direction today to advance my recovery journey?

Step 4: Remembering Resilience During challenging days, self-awareness reminds individuals of their inherent resilience. By reflecting on past successes in overcoming adversity, individuals can find the strength to persevere through difficult moments.

> Self-Reflection Question: How can I draw strength from my track record of getting through bad days and use it to navigate current challenges in my recovery?

Self-awareness is the cornerstone of initiating transformation on the path to long-term recovery from addiction. It empowers individuals to redirect their thoughts towards positivity, embrace humility, take small steps in the right direction, and remember their resilience. By fostering self-awareness, individuals can lay the foundation for meaningful change and embark on a journey toward lasting sobriety.

Self-Reflection Questions:

> How can I cultivate self-awareness in my daily life to better understand my thoughts, feelings, and behaviors in relation to addiction?

> What positive activities can I engage in to keep my mind occupied and focused on my recovery goals?

> In what ways can I embrace humility and become more willing to acknowledge my mistakes as opportunities for growth?

A Journey of Transformation

> What small steps can I take today to move in the right direction on my path to long-term recovery from addiction?
>
> How can I draw strength from my past experiences of overcoming challenges and remember my resilience during difficult moments in my recovery journey?
>
> How can self-awareness help me maintain a positive mindset and continue making progress even when faced with setbacks or obstacles in my recovery?

Recognizing the Need for Change:
The Journey to Long-Term Recovery from Addiction

The path to long-term recovery from addiction begins with a critical recognition: the need for change. As the saying goes, "You can motivate by fear, and you can motivate by reward. But both those methods are only temporary. The only lasting thing is self-motivation." In this book, we will delve into the importance of recognizing the necessity for change in addiction recovery, emphasizing self-motivation, resilience, and the guiding light of faith in facing the challenges of recovery.

The Imperative of Self-Motivation

Change in addiction recovery must come from within, driven by self-motivation. External incentives and deterrents may provide temporary impetus, but lasting transformation requires a deep internal desire to embrace a new way of life.

Step 1: Acknowledging the Need for Change Self-awareness is the initial step towards recognizing the need for change. It involves an honest assessment of one's addiction, its consequences, and the impact on oneself and others. This recognition is a crucial catalyst for transformation.

> Self-Reflection Question: What specific aspects of my addiction and its consequences have I recognized as unsustainable and motivating factors for change?

Step 2: Embracing Self-Motivation Self-motivation becomes the driving force behind change. It involves a commitment to sobriety and the determination to navigate the challenges that lie ahead. Unlike external motivators, self-motivation is enduring and resilient.

> Self-Reflection Question: How can I nurture and sustain self-motivation as the driving force behind my recovery journey?

Step 3: Drawing Strength from Faith Faith can play a significant role in recognizing the need for change and sustaining self-motivation. Believing in a higher power, a purpose greater than oneself, can provide comfort and guidance throughout the recovery journey.

Self-Reflection Question: How can I strengthen my faith and use it as a source of strength, comfort, and guidance in my recovery from addiction?

Step 4: Trusting the Journey Recognizing the need for change is the first step, but trust in the journey is equally important. Believing that even in the face of pain, tears, and challenges, one will find strength, comfort, and light, can provide the resilience needed to persevere.

Self-Reflection Question: How can I develop trust in the recovery journey and maintain the conviction that I will find the strength and guidance to overcome obstacles?

Recognizing the need for change is the cornerstone of the journey to long-term recovery from addiction. It requires self-motivation, faith, and the trust that even in the darkest moments, one will find the strength and guidance to persevere. By embracing these principles, individuals can initiate and sustain the transformation needed to overcome addiction.

Self-Reflection Questions:

What specific aspects of my addiction and its consequences have I recognized as unsustainable and motivating factors for change?

How can I nurture and sustain self-motivation as the driving force behind my recovery journey?

In what ways can I strengthen my faith and use it as a source of strength, comfort, and guidance in my recovery from addiction?

How can I develop trust in the recovery journey and maintain the conviction that I will find the strength and guidance to overcome obstacles?

What strategies can I employ to remind myself of the importance of self-motivation and the necessity for change on a daily basis during my recovery journey?

How can I incorporate self-motivation, faith, and trust into my daily routines and practices to reinforce my commitment to long-term recovery from addiction?

Identifying Areas in Need of Transformation:
A Key to Long-Term Recovery from Addiction

Long-term recovery from addiction is a transformative journey that begins with self-awareness and the recognition of areas in one's life that require change. As the saying goes, "Obstacles are those frightful things you see when you take your eyes off your goal." In this book, we will explore the crucial process of identifying areas in need of transformation in addiction recovery, emphasizing the importance of staying true to oneself, pursuing dreams, and persisting in the face of obstacles.

A Journey of Transformation

The Significance of Self-Examination

Self-examination is a pivotal component of addiction recovery. It involves an honest assessment of one's life, habits, and behaviors to identify areas that require transformation. This process can be uncomfortable but is essential for personal growth and lasting sobriety.

Step 1: Be True to Yourself Identifying areas in need of transformation begins with being true to oneself. It requires the courage to confront the realities of addiction and its impact on one's life and relationships. Acknowledging the discrepancy between who one is and who one wants to be is a powerful motivator for change.

> Self-Reflection Question: How can I practice self-honesty and confront the realities of my addiction as a crucial step towards identifying areas in need of transformation?

Step 2: Pursue Your Dreams Addiction often derails individuals from pursuing their dreams and passions. Identifying areas that need transformation may involve rekindling long-forgotten aspirations and setting new goals for a fulfilling life in recovery.

> Self-Reflection Question: What dreams and aspirations have I set aside due to my addiction, and how can I reignite my passion for them in my journey to recovery?

Step 3: Persevere Despite Obstacles Obstacles are inevitable on the path to recovery, but they should not deter individuals from identifying and working on areas in need of transformation. Persistence is key, as success often comes from trying one more time, even when faced with setbacks.

> Self-Reflection Question: How can I cultivate the resilience to persevere in the face of obstacles and continue identifying and addressing areas that require transformation?

Step 4: Shoot for the Moon Identifying areas for transformation should be guided by bold aspirations and high goals. As the saying suggests, "Shoot for the moon. Even if you miss, you'll land among the stars." Aim for significant change and personal growth, knowing that even small steps in the right direction can lead to transformation.

> Self-Reflection Question: What are my loftiest aspirations for transformation in my recovery journey, and how can I take action to achieve them?

Identifying areas in need of transformation is a fundamental step on the path to long-term recovery from addiction. It demands self-honesty, the pursuit of dreams, persistence in the face of obstacles, and setting ambitious goals. By embracing this process, individuals can initiate meaningful change, ultimately leading to lasting sobriety and personal growth.

Self-Reflection Questions:

How can I practice self-honesty and confront the realities of my addiction as a crucial step towards identifying areas in need of transformation?

What dreams and aspirations have I set aside due to my addiction, and how can I reignite my passion for them in my journey to recovery?

In what ways can I cultivate the resilience to persevere in the face of obstacles and continue identifying and addressing areas that require transformation?

What are my loftiest aspirations for transformation in my recovery journey, and how can I take action to achieve them?

How can I ensure that I stay focused on my goals and do not let obstacles or setbacks deter me from identifying and addressing areas in need of transformation?

How can I maintain a sense of hope and optimism in my recovery journey, even when faced with challenges and setbacks in the process of transformation?

Assessing Strengths and Weaknesses:
A Path to Long-Term Recovery from Addiction

The journey to long-term recovery from addiction is a process that begins with a crucial self-assessment: the evaluation of one's strengths and weaknesses. As the saying goes, "People who avoid failure avoid success." In this book, we will delve into the significance of assessing one's strengths and weaknesses in addiction recovery. We will emphasize the importance of embracing both positive and negative experiences, trusting the process, and finding blessings in trials. Additionally, we will discuss the role of faith and resilience in the recovery journey.

The Value of Self-Assessment

Self-assessment is an essential element of addiction recovery. It involves an honest evaluation of one's strengths and weaknesses, providing a roadmap for personal growth, sobriety, and lasting change.

Step 1: Embrace Positive and Negative Experiences Self-assessment requires individuals to embrace both positive and negative experiences. Every setback and every success offers an opportunity to learn and grow. Avoiding failure means avoiding the chance to achieve lasting success in recovery.

Self-Reflection Question: How can I develop a mindset that welcomes both success and failure as valuable learning experiences in my journey to recovery?

A Journey of Transformation

Step 2: Trust the Process Recovery is a process filled with uncertainty and challenges. Trusting the process means believing that even the toughest times can lead to positive outcomes. It requires resilience and the willingness to persevere, even when it feels like everything is falling apart.

> Self-Reflection Question: How can I build trust in the recovery process and remain steadfast in my commitment to sobriety, even in the face of adversity?

Step 3: Find Blessings in Trials Self-assessment also involves recognizing the blessings hidden within trials. It requires opening one's heart to see the silver lining in difficult circumstances. Faith plays a significant role in this process, reminding individuals that, no matter the challenges they face, there is a higher purpose.

> Self-Reflection Question: How can I develop the faith and perspective necessary to find blessings in the trials I encounter on my recovery journey?

Step 4: Keep the Faith and Stay Resilient Recovery is a journey that demands faith and resilience. Believing in the possibility of a brighter future and staying strong in the face of adversity are essential components of long-term recovery.

> Self-Reflection Question: How can I maintain my faith and resilience throughout my recovery journey, knowing that the hardest times often lead to the greatest moments in life?

Assessing strengths and weaknesses is a critical step on the path to long-term recovery from addiction. It involves embracing both success and failure, trusting the process, finding blessings in trials, and maintaining faith and resilience. By recognizing the value of self-assessment, individuals can pave the way for personal growth, sobriety, and a fulfilling life in recovery.

Self-Reflection Questions:

> How can I shift my perspective to embrace both success and failure as valuable learning experiences in my recovery journey?

> What strategies can I implement to build trust in the recovery process and remain steadfast in my commitment to sobriety, even in the face of adversity?

> In what ways can I develop the faith and perspective necessary to find blessings in the trials I encounter on my recovery journey?

> How can I stay strong and resilient throughout my recovery journey, keeping the faith that the hardest times will lead to the greatest moments of my life?

> What specific practices or tools can I incorporate into my daily life to help me maintain my faith and resilience as I work towards long-term recovery from addiction?

How can I remind myself of the value of self-assessment and the importance of recognizing both strengths and weaknesses in my ongoing journey to recovery?

Self-Assessment and Introspection: Harnessing the Power of Words in Long-Term Recovery from Addiction

On the journey to long-term recovery from addiction, self-assessment and introspection are powerful tools that can lead to personal growth and transformation. As the saying goes, "Words are singularly the most powerful force available to humanity." In this book, we will explore the vital role of self-assessment and introspection in addiction recovery. We will emphasize the significance of using words constructively, the impact of effective communication, and the understanding that change begins with the words we choose to use.

The Power of Words

Words possess incredible energy and power. They can uplift, inspire, and heal, or they can wound, harm, and discourage. Recognizing the power of words is essential in the process of self-assessment and introspection.

Step 1: Choose Words Constructively Self-assessment involves examining one's thoughts, feelings, and behaviors. It is essential to choose words of encouragement and self-compassion during this process. Negative self-talk can hinder recovery progress, while constructive words can promote growth and healing.

> Self-Reflection Question: How can I use words of encouragement and self-compassion during self-assessment to foster a positive mindset in my recovery journey?

Step 2: Effective Communication Introspection often leads to insights about oneself and one's addiction. Effective communication of these insights with a therapist, counselor, or support network is critical. Being able to articulate thoughts and feelings is a valuable skill in recovery.

> Self-Reflection Question: How can I enhance my communication skills to better express my thoughts and emotions during introspection, therapy, and support group meetings?

Step 3: Harness the Power of Change The words we use not only shape our self-perception but also influence our actions. Recognizing that words have the power to change one's world means consciously choosing language that reinforces positive behaviors and attitudes in recovery.

> Self-Reflection Question: How can I change my world by changing my words and using language that supports my journey to long-term recovery?

Step 4: The Tongue's Power Over Life and Death The ancient wisdom that "death and life are in the power of the tongue" underscores the profound influence words have on our lives.

A Journey of Transformation

Acknowledging this power can motivate individuals to use words that bring life and vitality to their recovery.

> Self-Reflection Question: How can I be more mindful of the words I use in everyday life and ensure they align with my goals and aspirations for long-term recovery?

Self-assessment and introspection are integral components of long-term recovery from addiction. Recognizing the power of words, using them constructively, and practicing effective communication are essential skills for personal growth and healing. By choosing words that uplift, inspire, and promote positive change, individuals can transform their lives and achieve lasting sobriety.

Self-Reflection Questions:

How can I use words of encouragement and self-compassion during self-assessment to foster a positive mindset in my recovery journey?

In what ways can I enhance my communication skills to better express my thoughts and emotions during introspection, therapy, and support group meetings?

How can I consciously choose language that reinforces positive behaviors and attitudes in my recovery, understanding that words have the power to change my world?

What strategies can I implement to remind myself of the ancient wisdom that "death and life are in the power of the tongue" and ensure that the words I use align with my goals for long-term recovery?

How can I take advantage of every opportunity to practice effective communication and improve my ability to express my thoughts, emotions, and needs in a clear and constructive manner during my recovery journey?

How can I harness the power of words to uplift and inspire not only myself but also those around me, creating a supportive and healing environment on my path to sobriety?

Recognizing Personal Attributes That Influence
Transformation on the Path to Long-Term Recovery from Addiction

In the journey to long-term recovery from addiction, recognizing personal attributes that either support or hinder transformation is essential. As the saying goes, "The bad thing that happens today could be paving the way for the good thing coming tomorrow." In this book, we will explore the importance of identifying personal attributes that impact transformation in addiction recovery. We will emphasize the significance of trusting the process, embracing the journey as a beginner, and the power of commitment in building hope and trust.

The Power of Personal Attributes

Personal attributes play a significant role in shaping the recovery journey. Recognizing these attributes can help individuals understand how they can contribute to or hinder their transformation.

Step 1: Trusting the Process Transformation in addiction recovery is a process that unfolds over time. Trusting this process, even when facing adversity or setbacks, is a crucial personal attribute. It requires faith in the journey and the belief that challenges today can lead to brighter outcomes tomorrow.

> Self-Reflection Question: How can I develop the attribute of trusting the recovery process, even when faced with difficulties or uncertainties?

Step 2: Embracing Beginnerhood Addiction recovery often involves learning new ways of living and coping. Embracing the attribute of being a beginner is essential, as no one starts off being excellent in recovery. It involves humility, a willingness to learn, and the understanding that making mistakes is part of the journey.

> Self-Reflection Question: How can I cultivate the attribute of embracing beginnerhood and approach my recovery journey with humility and a commitment to learning?

Step 3: The Power of Commitment Commitment is a powerful attribute in addiction recovery. When individuals make a commitment to their sobriety and recovery goals, they build hope. Keeping that commitment over time builds trust, both in themselves and in their support networks.

> Self-Reflection Question: How can I strengthen my commitment to my recovery journey and use it as a source of hope and trust-building in my life?

Step 4: Striving for Progress Recognizing that personal attributes can be developed and improved is vital. The saying "GOOD, BETTER, BEST NEVER LET IT REST UNTIL YOUR GOOD IS BETTER AND YOUR BETTER IS THE BEST!!!!!!" emphasizes the importance of striving for progress and continual improvement in recovery.

> Self-Reflection Question: How can I adopt a mindset of continuous improvement and strive for progress in my recovery journey by recognizing and developing my personal attributes?

Identifying personal attributes that either support or hinder transformation is a critical step in long-term recovery from addiction. Trusting the process, embracing beginnerhood, making commitments, and striving for progress are attributes that can positively impact the transformation journey. By recognizing and nurturing these attributes, individuals can pave the way for lasting sobriety and personal growth.

A Journey of Transformation

Self-Reflection Questions:

How can I develop the attribute of trusting the recovery process, even when faced with difficulties or uncertainties?

In what ways can I cultivate the attribute of embracing beginnerhood and approach my recovery journey with humility and a commitment to learning?

How can I strengthen my commitment to my recovery journey and use it as a source of hope and trust-building in my life?

What specific strategies can I employ to adopt a mindset of continuous improvement and strive for progress in my recovery journey by recognizing and developing my personal attributes?

How can I remind myself regularly of the importance of recognizing and nurturing personal attributes that support transformation, ensuring that I remain focused on my long-term recovery goals?

How can I leverage the attributes of trust, commitment, and embracing beginnerhood to create a positive and supportive environment for myself and those around me in my recovery journey?

Setting Clear Goals for Personal Change

In the pursuit of long-term recovery from addiction, setting clear and meaningful goals for personal change is essential. As the saying goes, "We have to hurt in order to know, fall in order to grow, lose in order to gain because most of life's lessons are taught through pain." In this book, we will explore the significance of establishing clear goals in addiction recovery. We will emphasize the transformative power of pain and adversity, the importance of being true to oneself, and the value of cherishing the present moment.

The Transformative Power of Pain

Pain and adversity are powerful catalysts for personal growth and change. Addiction often brings immense pain to individuals and their loved ones. Recognizing the potential for growth within this pain is the first step toward setting clear goals for recovery.

Step 1: Embracing Lessons Through Pain Pain has the unique ability to teach life's most profound lessons. It provides individuals with the opportunity to gain insight into their addiction, its consequences, and the need for change. This understanding becomes the foundation for setting clear goals.

> Self-Reflection Question: How can I embrace the lessons that pain has taught me in my addiction journey and use them as a source of motivation for setting clear goals in recovery?

Step 2: Being True to Oneself Setting clear goals in recovery involves authenticity and self-acceptance. It means letting go of the need to chase the approval of others and instead focusing on being true to oneself. Authentic goals are more likely to be achieved and sustained.

> Self-Reflection Question: How can I ensure that the goals I set for personal change in recovery align with my authentic self and values, rather than seeking external validation?

Step 3: Cherishing the Present Moment Addiction often causes individuals to live in a perpetual cycle of regret about the past and anxiety about the future. Recognizing that yesterday is gone and tomorrow is uncertain highlights the importance of cherishing the present moment. Setting clear goals includes a commitment to making the most of today.

> Self-Reflection Question: How can I cultivate mindfulness and gratitude to fully enjoy and make the most of each present moment in my recovery journey?

Setting clear goals for personal change is a fundamental step on the path to long-term recovery from addiction. Pain and adversity can serve as powerful motivators for growth, as they teach life's most profound lessons. Being true to oneself and embracing authenticity in goal-setting enhances

A Journey of Transformation

the likelihood of success. Finally, cherishing the present moment reminds individuals of the precious gift of life and the opportunity for change that exists in every moment.

Self-Reflection Questions:

How can I embrace the lessons that pain has taught me in my addiction journey and use them as a source of motivation for setting clear goals in recovery?

In what ways can I ensure that the goals I set for personal change in recovery align with my authentic self and values, rather than seeking external validation?

How can I develop mindfulness and gratitude to fully enjoy and make the most of each present moment in my recovery journey?

What strategies can I employ to maintain focus on my clear goals for personal change, even when faced with challenges or setbacks along the way?

How can I integrate the lessons learned from past experiences and the newfound authenticity in my goal-setting to create a meaningful and sustainable recovery journey?

How can I continue to draw strength and motivation from the recognition that every moment holds the potential for transformation and growth in my long-term recovery from addiction?

The Significance of Goal Setting in the Transformation Process:
A Beacon of Hope in Long-Term Recovery from Addiction

In the journey toward long-term recovery from addiction, goal setting stands as a pivotal and transformative process. As the saying goes, "Hatred paralyzes life; love releases it. Hatred confuses life; love harmonizes it. Hatred darkens life; love illuminates it." In this book, we will explore the profound significance of goal setting in addiction recovery. We will emphasize the transformative power of love, the strength of faith and patience, and the importance of character over reputation.

Goal Setting: A Beacon of Hope

Setting clear and meaningful goals is akin to lighting a beacon of hope on the path to recovery. It provides individuals with direction, motivation, and a sense of purpose. Goals not only serve as a roadmap but also as a source of inspiration and transformation.

Step 1: The Transformative Power of Love Love, both for oneself and for the journey of recovery, can be a powerful motivator in setting and achieving goals. Love releases the paralysis of addiction, harmonizes the confusion it brings, and illuminates the darkness that often shrouds life in addiction.

Self-Reflection Question: How can I harness the power of love as a driving force in my goal-setting process, both for my own well-being and the well-being of those around me?

Step 2: The Strength of Faith and Patience Faith and patience are vital attributes on the path to recovery. Believing that "God has perfect timing; never early, never late" provides comfort and assurance. It reminds individuals that recovery is a journey, and transformation takes time.

Self-Reflection Question: How can I cultivate faith and patience as I work toward my recovery goals, trusting that I am on the right path, no matter the challenges I encounter?

Step 3: Character Over Reputation Goal setting in recovery should be rooted in the desire for personal growth and character development. It's about being true to oneself and aligning actions with values. Understanding that character is more important than reputation emphasizes authenticity in the transformation process.

Self-Reflection Question: How can I ensure that the goals I set for myself in recovery are driven by a desire for personal growth and the development of my character, rather than seeking validation or approval from others?

Goal setting is a beacon of hope in the transformation process of addiction recovery. It provides individuals with direction, motivation, and purpose. Love, faith, and patience serve as guiding lights, while character development takes precedence over reputation. By embracing these principles, individuals can embark on a transformative journey toward long-term recovery from addiction.

Self-Reflection Questions:

How can I harness the power of love as a driving force in my goal-setting process, both for my own well-being and the well-being of those around me?

In what ways can I cultivate faith and patience as I work toward my recovery goals, trusting that I am on the right path, no matter the challenges I encounter?

How can I ensure that the goals I set for myself in recovery are driven by a desire for personal growth and the development of my character, rather than seeking validation or approval from others?

What strategies can I employ to maintain focus on my recovery goals and use them as a source of inspiration and motivation throughout my journey to long-term sobriety?

How can I remind myself of the transformative power of love and faith when doubts or challenges arise in my recovery journey?

A Journey of Transformation

> How can I incorporate the principles of love, faith, and character development into my daily life and recovery practices to reinforce my commitment to personal growth and transformation?

Goals as Guiding Lights for Change:
Illuminating the Path to Long-Term Recovery from Addiction

In the quest for long-term recovery from addiction, goals serve as guiding lights that illuminate the path to transformation. As the saying goes, "Life is about breaking our personal limits and outgrowing ourselves to live our best lives." In this book, we will explore the profound significance of setting and pursuing goals in addiction recovery. We will emphasize the value of embracing life's challenges, seeking positivity in each day, and the transformative power of doing something new with great love.

Goals: Beacons of Transformation

Setting and pursuing goals in recovery is akin to turning on a beacon of light in the darkness of addiction. Goals provide individuals with purpose, direction, and a sense of achievement. They act as beacons that guide individuals toward a life of sobriety and personal growth.

Step 1: Embracing Life's Challenges Challenges are an integral part of life's journey, and they take on special significance in addiction recovery. Embracing these challenges is essential, as they make life interesting and meaningful. Overcoming them becomes a testament to one's strength and resilience.

> Self-Reflection Question: How can I embrace life's challenges as opportunities for personal growth and transformation in my recovery journey?

Step 2: Seeking Positivity Each Day Even on the most difficult days, seeking something positive is a valuable practice. It fosters gratitude and resilience. Recognizing the small joys and victories along the way can be a powerful motivator in the pursuit of recovery goals.

> Self-Reflection Question: How can I train my mind to look for and appreciate the positive aspects of each day, no matter how challenging it may be?

Step 3: Doing Something New with Great Love Setting and pursuing recovery goals often requires stepping outside one's comfort zone. The saying, "If you want something you've never had, then you've got to do something you've never done," underscores the importance of embracing change with love and dedication.

> Self-Reflection Question: How can I approach new experiences and challenges in my recovery journey with great love and a commitment to personal growth?

Goals serve as guiding lights for change in the journey to long-term recovery from addiction. They provide purpose, direction, and motivation. Embracing life's challenges, seeking positivity, and approaching change with great love are essential principles that foster transformation. By incorporating these principles, individuals can navigate the path of recovery with determination and resilience.

Self-Reflection Questions:

How can I embrace life's challenges as opportunities for personal growth and transformation in my recovery journey?

In what ways can I train my mind to look for and appreciate the positive aspects of each day, no matter how challenging it may be?

How can I approach new experiences and challenges in my recovery journey with great love and a commitment to personal growth?

What strategies can I employ to set clear and meaningful goals in my recovery, using them as guiding lights to illuminate my path toward long-term sobriety?

How can I remind myself of the value of embracing challenges, seeking positivity, and approaching change with great love as I navigate the ups and downs of my recovery journey?

How can I incorporate the principles of embracing challenges, seeking positivity, and approaching change with love into my daily life and recovery practices to reinforce my commitment to personal growth and transformation?

The Concept of SMART Goals:
A Roadmap to Long-Term Recovery from Addiction

In the pursuit of long-term recovery from addiction, the concept of SMART goals plays a crucial role in providing a clear roadmap for transformation. As the saying goes, "Sometimes beautiful things come into our lives out of nowhere. We can't always understand them, but we have to trust in them." In this book, we will explore the significance of setting SMART goals in addiction recovery. We will emphasize the importance of specificity, measurability, achievability, relevance, and time-bound planning as key principles to guide individuals toward a successful recovery journey.

The Power of SMART Goals

SMART goals are a structured approach to goal setting that enhances the likelihood of success. They provide individuals with a clear, actionable plan and a sense of direction on their path to recovery.

Step 1: Specificity Specificity is the first pillar of SMART goals. It requires individuals to clearly define their objectives. In recovery, specific goals help individuals focus on what they want to achieve, providing clarity and motivation.

> Self-Reflection Question: How can I make my recovery goals more specific and well-defined to ensure I have a clear understanding of what I want to achieve?

Step 2: Measurability Measurability ensures that goals can be tracked and monitored. Setting measurable goals allows individuals to assess their progress, celebrate milestones, and make necessary adjustments in their recovery journey.

> Self-Reflection Question: What metrics or indicators can I use to measure my progress toward achieving my recovery goals, and how can I use this information to stay motivated?

Step 3: Achievability Achievability involves setting goals that are realistic and attainable. While it's essential to aim high, setting achievable goals prevents discouragement and frustration. It's about finding the right balance between ambition and feasibility.

> Self-Reflection Question: How can I ensure that my recovery goals are challenging yet attainable, and how can I maintain a sense of motivation and belief in my ability to achieve them?

Step 4: Relevance Relevance entails setting goals that align with one's values and priorities. In recovery, goals should be relevant to the individual's well-being and sobriety. Ensuring relevance helps maintain focus and commitment.

> Self-Reflection Question: Are my recovery goals aligned with my values and priorities, and how can I ensure that they remain relevant and meaningful throughout my journey?

Step 5: Time-Bound Time-bound goals have a defined timeframe for achievement. Setting deadlines creates a sense of urgency and accountability. It prevents procrastination and encourages consistent effort.

> Self-Reflection Question: How can I establish realistic timelines for my recovery goals, and how can I use deadlines to maintain momentum and commitment in my journey to long-term sobriety?

The concept of SMART goals serves as a powerful tool on the path to long-term recovery from addiction. Specificity, measurability, achievability, relevance, and time-bound planning provide a structured and actionable approach to goal setting. By applying these principles, individuals can enhance their clarity, motivation, and commitment to achieving a successful recovery journey.

Self-Reflection Questions:

How can I make my recovery goals more specific and well-defined to ensure I have a clear understanding of what I want to achieve?

What metrics or indicators can I use to measure my progress toward achieving my recovery goals, and how can I use this information to stay motivated?

How can I ensure that my recovery goals are challenging yet attainable, and how can I maintain a sense of motivation and belief in my ability to achieve them?

Are my recovery goals aligned with my values and priorities, and how can I ensure that they remain relevant and meaningful throughout my journey?

How can I establish realistic timelines for my recovery goals, and how can I use deadlines to maintain momentum and commitment in my journey to long-term sobriety?

How can I apply the principles of SMART goals to my recovery journey and use them as a roadmap to guide me toward a successful and fulfilling life in sobriety?

Prioritizing Transformation Goals:
The Journey to Long-Term Recovery from Addiction

On the path to long-term recovery from addiction, prioritizing transformation goals is a critical step in the journey. As the saying goes, "The difference between who you ARE and who you WANT TO BE is the work you put in." In this book, we will explore the significance of prioritizing transformation goals in addiction recovery. We will emphasize the value of self-worth, time management, and the continuous effort required to create lasting change.

The Power of Prioritization

Prioritizing transformation goals in recovery is akin to placing a spotlight on the most essential aspects of one's journey. It involves identifying what matters most and directing efforts toward meaningful change.

Step 1: Valuing Oneself Recovery often begins with recognizing one's self-worth. Until individuals truly value themselves, they may struggle to allocate their time and effort toward positive change. Self-worth serves as the foundation for setting and prioritizing transformation goals.

Self-Reflection Question: How can I cultivate a sense of self-worth and begin to recognize my intrinsic value as I embark on my journey to long-term recovery?

Step 2: Valuing Time Time is a precious resource that must be managed wisely. Prioritizing transformation goals involves acknowledging the importance of time management. Until individuals value their time, they may not fully commit to the actions required for change.

> Self-Reflection Question: How can I better value and manage my time to ensure that I allocate it toward activities and goals that align with my transformation journey in recovery?

Step 3: Continuous Effort and Raising Standards Transformation is an ongoing process that requires consistent effort. Demanding more from oneself than others expect and raising personal standards are essential components of prioritizing transformation goals. These actions raise the quality of one's life in recovery.

> Self-Reflection Question: How can I set higher standards for myself in recovery and maintain a commitment to continuous effort and growth in my transformation journey?

Prioritizing transformation goals is a pivotal step on the path to long-term recovery from addiction. It involves recognizing one's self-worth, valuing time as a precious resource, and committing to continuous effort and personal growth. By prioritizing these aspects, individuals can create lasting change and become the person they aspire to be in recovery.

Self-Reflection Questions:

> How can I cultivate a sense of self-worth and begin to recognize my intrinsic value as I embark on my journey to long-term recovery?

> What strategies can I implement to better value and manage my time, ensuring that I allocate it toward activities and goals that align with my transformation journey in recovery?

> How can I set higher standards for myself in recovery and maintain a commitment to continuous effort and personal growth in my transformation journey?

> What specific transformation goals are most important for me to prioritize in my recovery journey, and how can I ensure that they align with my values and aspirations?

> How can I remind myself regularly of the significance of prioritizing transformation goals and maintaining a sense of self-worth, time management, and continuous effort as I work toward long-term sobriety?

> How can I apply the principles of prioritization to my recovery journey and use them to guide me toward becoming the person I aspire to be in sobriety?

Identifying High-Impact Areas for Change:
Empowering Long-Term Recovery from Addiction

In the journey to long-term recovery from addiction, the ability to identify high-impact areas for change is a catalyst for transformation. As the saying goes, "Incredible change happens in your life when you decide to take control of what you do have power over instead of craving control over what you don't." In this book, we will explore the significance of recognizing high-impact areas for change in addiction recovery. We will emphasize the importance of focusing on what one can control, managing worry, embracing courage, and converting negatives into positives to foster a successful recovery journey.

The Power of High-Impact Areas

Identifying high-impact areas for change involves recognizing the aspects of one's life that can most significantly influence the recovery process. By directing energy and effort toward these areas, individuals can empower themselves on their journey to sobriety.

Step 1: Focus on What You Can Control Addiction recovery is often accompanied by a desire to regain control over one's life. However, the focus should shift from craving control over external factors to taking control of what one can influence. This shift empowers individuals to make meaningful changes.

> Self-Reflection Question: What aspects of my life can I realistically control, and how can I channel my energy into these areas to facilitate my long-term recovery?

Step 2: Managing Worry and Building Strength Worry is a common obstacle in recovery, as it can deplete one's strength and resilience. Managing worry involves staying present and not allowing it to overshadow the strength and courage required for recovery.

> Self-Reflection Question: How can I shift my mindset to reduce worry and focus on building the strength needed to overcome challenges in my recovery journey?

Step 3: Embracing Courage and Possibilities Courage plays a pivotal role in addiction recovery. It is the catalyst for taking the necessary steps toward change. Embracing courage means dreaming big, believing in possibilities, and persisting in the face of adversity.

> Self-Reflection Question: How can I super-size my courage and abilities, allowing them to guide me through the ups and downs of my recovery journey with determination and resilience?

Step 4: Turning Negatives into Positives Adversity and setbacks are common in life and recovery. However, they also hold the potential to become sources of strength and growth. By converting negatives into positives, individuals gain resilience and motivation.

A Journey of Transformation

> Self-Reflection Question: How can I transform negative situations or experiences in my recovery journey into opportunities for personal growth and empowerment?

Identifying high-impact areas for change is a transformative step in the recovery process from addiction. By focusing on what can be controlled, managing worry, embracing courage, and converting negatives into positives, individuals can empower themselves to create a successful and fulfilling recovery journey.

Self-Reflection Questions:

What aspects of my life can I realistically control, and how can I channel my energy into these areas to facilitate my long-term recovery?

How can I shift my mindset to reduce worry and focus on building the strength needed to overcome challenges in my recovery journey?

In what ways can I super-size my courage and abilities, allowing them to guide me through the ups and downs of my recovery journey with determination and resilience?

How can I develop the mindset and skills to turn negative situations or experiences in my recovery journey into opportunities for personal growth and empowerment?

How can I remind myself regularly of the importance of focusing on high-impact areas for change and embracing courage, while letting go of worry and negativity, as I work toward long-term sobriety?

How can I apply the principles of identifying high-impact areas for change to my recovery journey and use them as a roadmap to guide me toward a successful and fulfilling life in sobriety?

Creating a Roadmap for Achieving Multiple Goals:
Navigating the Journey to Long-Term Recovery from Addiction

In the pursuit of long-term recovery from addiction, creating a roadmap for achieving multiple goals is essential. As the saying goes, "Life isn't about how to survive the storm, but it's about how to dance in the rain." This book will explore the significance of creating a comprehensive plan for achieving multiple goals in addiction recovery. We will emphasize the importance of seizing the present, overcoming fear and self-limiting beliefs, and transforming challenges into opportunities for growth.

The Power of a Comprehensive Roadmap

A comprehensive roadmap for achieving multiple goals in recovery provides individuals with direction, focus, and a sense of purpose. It enables them to navigate the challenges and uncertainties of the recovery journey with confidence and determination.

Step 1: Seizing the Present In addiction recovery, it's crucial to seize the present moment and make the most of the time given. Waiting for the perfect time can be a hindrance. Instead, individuals should focus on taking meaningful actions in the present to advance their goals.

> Self-Reflection Question: How can I make the most of the present moment in my recovery journey, taking actions that align with my goals and aspirations?

Step 2: Overcoming Fear and Self-Limiting Beliefs Fear and self-limiting beliefs can build walls and boundaries in one's mind, impeding progress in recovery. Overcoming these barriers is essential for growth. Successful recovery requires the courage to take big leaps, dream big, and believe in possibilities.

> Self-Reflection Question: What steps can I take to conquer my fears and self-limiting beliefs in my recovery journey, allowing me to pursue my goals with confidence and determination?

Step 3: Transforming Challenges into Opportunities Challenges and setbacks are inevitable in life and recovery. However, they also offer the opportunity to grow and transform. By turning negatives into positives, individuals can gain strength and resilience.

> Self-Reflection Question: How can I shift my perspective to view challenges in my recovery journey as opportunities for personal growth and empowerment?

Creating a roadmap for achieving multiple goals is a pivotal step in the recovery process from addiction. It involves seizing the present, overcoming fear and self-limiting beliefs, and transforming challenges into opportunities. By following this roadmap, individuals can navigate their recovery journey with determination and resilience.

Self-Reflection Questions:

> How can I make the most of the present moment in my recovery journey, taking actions that align with my goals and aspirations?

> What specific fears and self-limiting beliefs are holding me back in my recovery, and how can I work to overcome them and pursue my goals with confidence?

> In what ways can I shift my perspective to view challenges in my recovery journey as opportunities for personal growth and empowerment?

How can I remind myself regularly of the importance of creating a comprehensive roadmap for achieving multiple goals in my recovery journey, and how can I stay committed to this plan over the long term?

How can I apply the principles of seizing the present, conquering fear, and transforming challenges into opportunities to my recovery journey, using them as a guiding framework for success in sobriety?

What strategies can I employ to maintain focus and determination as I work toward achieving multiple goals in my recovery, and how can I celebrate my progress along the way to stay motivated and inspired?

Cultivating a Vision for Transformation

In the pursuit of long-term recovery from addiction, cultivating a vision for transformation is a pivotal step. As the saying goes, "Sometimes we stare so long at the wrong things, we miss out on the RIGHT things standing right in front of us." This book will explore the significance of developing a clear vision for transformation in addiction recovery. We will emphasize the importance of living in the present, embracing change with courage and faith, and understanding that personal transformation can have a ripple effect on the world.

The Power of a Clear Vision

A clear vision for transformation serves as a guiding light on the journey to recovery. It enables individuals to shift their focus from the past or the future to the present moment, where life truly exists.

Step 1: Living in the Present Addiction often leads individuals to dwell on the past or worry about the future, causing them to miss the beauty of the present moment. Cultivating a vision for transformation involves redirecting one's attention to the here and now, where real life unfolds.

> Self-Reflection Question: How can I practice mindfulness and ensure that I fully engage with the present moment in my recovery journey, appreciating the opportunities it offers for transformation?

Step 2: Embracing Change with Courage and Faith Transformation requires change, and change can be daunting. However, having the courage to initiate change and the faith that things will turn out for the best is crucial. It is through these changes that personal growth and recovery occur.

> Self-Reflection Question: How can I summon the courage to make the necessary changes in my life and maintain the faith that these changes will lead me to a better and more fulfilling future in sobriety?

Step 3: Inspiring Positive Change While individual transformation is significant, it can also inspire positive change in others and contribute to making the world a better place. Each person has the potential to spark the brain that will change the world, even in small ways.

> Self-Reflection Question: How can I harness the power of my personal transformation to inspire and positively impact those around me, fostering a ripple effect of change and growth?

Cultivating a vision for transformation is a vital element of the recovery journey from addiction. It involves living in the present, embracing change with courage and faith, and recognizing the potential for personal transformation to inspire positive change in the world. By cultivating this vision, individuals can take meaningful steps toward long-term recovery and a more fulfilling life.

A Journey of Transformation

Self-Reflection Questions:

How can I practice mindfulness and ensure that I fully engage with the present moment in my recovery journey, appreciating the opportunities it offers for transformation?

In what ways can I summon the courage to make the necessary changes in my life and maintain the faith that these changes will lead me to a better and more fulfilling future in sobriety?

How can I actively use my personal transformation as a source of inspiration to positively impact the lives of others and contribute to making the world a better place?

How can I remind myself regularly of the importance of cultivating a vision for transformation in my recovery journey, and how can I stay committed to this vision over the long term?

How can I apply the principles of living in the present, embracing change with courage and faith, and inspiring positive change to my recovery journey, using them as a guiding framework for success in sobriety?

What strategies can I employ to celebrate my progress and achievements as I work toward my vision for transformation, and how can I use these milestones as motivation to continue on my path to long-term recovery?

Envisioning the Desired Future:
Building a Path to Long-Term Recovery from Addiction

In the journey toward long-term recovery from addiction, envisioning the desired future is a powerful force that can propel individuals forward. As the saying goes, "Your chances of success at anything can always be measured by your belief in yourself." This book explores the importance of envisioning a desired future in addiction recovery. We will emphasize the significance of excelling in one's pursuits, fostering a belief in oneself, and understanding the profound impact one can have on the world, one person at a time.

The Power of Envisioning a Desired Future

Envisioning a desired future serves as a beacon of hope and motivation on the path to recovery. It provides individuals with a clear sense of direction and purpose, enabling them to overcome obstacles and reach their goals.

Step 1: Excelling in One's Pursuits Recovery often involves redirecting one's energy and focus toward positive endeavors. When individuals strive to excel in their chosen pursuits, they not only gain a sense of accomplishment but also build self-confidence and self-worth.

Self-Reflection Question: How can I identify and pursue activities or goals that align with my desired future in recovery, and how can I commit to excelling in these pursuits?

Step 2: Belief in Oneself Belief in oneself is the cornerstone of success. It's the unwavering confidence that what one is capable of achieving is attainable. Cultivating self-belief is essential for overcoming the challenges that often accompany addiction recovery.

Self-Reflection Question: How can I nurture and strengthen my belief in myself as I work toward my desired future in recovery, and how can I use this belief as a driving force to stay committed to my goals?

Step 3: Impact on the World, One Person at a Time While one person may not be able to change the entire world, they can certainly change the world of another. The power of personal transformation ripples outward, positively influencing those in one's sphere of influence.

Self-Reflection Question: How can I recognize and appreciate the positive impact I have on the lives of others as I progress in my recovery journey, and how can I continue to inspire and support those around me?

Envisioning the desired future is a critical aspect of the recovery journey from addiction. It involves excelling in one's pursuits, fostering a belief in oneself, and recognizing the potential to positively impact the world, one person at a time. By harnessing the power of these principles, individuals can navigate their path to long-term recovery with purpose and determination.

Self-Reflection Questions:

How can I identify and pursue activities or goals that align with my desired future in recovery, and how can I commit to excelling in these pursuits?

What strategies can I implement to nurture and strengthen my belief in myself as I work toward my desired future in recovery, and how can I use this belief as a driving force to stay committed to my goals?

In what ways can I recognize and appreciate the positive impact I have on the lives of others as I progress in my recovery journey, and how can I continue to inspire and support those around me?

How can I remind myself regularly of the importance of envisioning a desired future and maintaining self-belief in my recovery journey, and how can I stay dedicated to this vision over the long term?

How can I apply the principles of excelling in one's pursuits, fostering self-belief, and positively impacting others to my recovery journey, using them as a roadmap to guide me toward a successful and fulfilling life in sobriety?

A Journey of Transformation

> What strategies can I employ to celebrate my progress and achievements as I work toward my desired future, and how can I use these milestones as motivation to continue on my path to long-term recovery?

Imagining the Ideal Outcomes of Transformation: A Path to Long-Term Recovery from Addiction

In the journey toward long-term recovery from addiction, imagining the ideal outcomes of transformation is a powerful motivator. As the saying goes, "Strength doesn't come from what you can do; it comes from overcoming the things you once thought you couldn't do." This book explores the importance of envisioning and striving for ideal outcomes in addiction recovery. We will emphasize the significance of being authentic, pursuing dreams tirelessly, and embracing trials as opportunities for growth.

The Power of Imagining Ideal Outcomes

Imagining ideal outcomes serves as a source of inspiration and resilience on the path to recovery. It empowers individuals to overcome challenges, embrace their uniqueness, and manifest their dreams.

Step 1: Embracing Authenticity Recovery involves rediscovering one's authentic self, free from the influence of addiction. Being oneself is a powerful affirmation that fosters self-worth and self-acceptance.

> Self-Reflection Question: How can I embrace my authentic self in my recovery journey, acknowledging my strengths and weaknesses, and using them to my advantage?

Step 2: Pursuing Dreams Tirelessly Dreams are the fuel that propels individuals forward in their recovery journey. It's not just about waiting for good things to happen; it's about tirelessly pursuing one's aspirations, even in the face of adversity.

> Self-Reflection Question: What steps can I take to actively pursue my dreams and goals in recovery, and how can I maintain my determination and perseverance throughout this journey?

Step 3: Embracing Trials as Opportunities for Growth Trials and challenges are an integral part of life and recovery. Instead of worrying about hard times, individuals can view them as opportunities for personal growth and resilience-building.

> Self-Reflection Question: How can I shift my perspective to see challenges and setbacks as opportunities for personal growth and development, allowing them to strengthen my resolve in recovery?

Imagining the ideal outcomes of transformation is a crucial aspect of the recovery journey from addiction. It involves embracing authenticity, pursuing dreams tirelessly, and viewing trials as opportunities for growth. By harnessing the power of these principles, individuals can navigate their path to long-term recovery with resilience and purpose.

Self-Reflection Questions:

How can I embrace my authentic self in my recovery journey, acknowledging my strengths and weaknesses, and using them to my advantage?

What strategies can I employ to actively pursue my dreams and goals in recovery, and how can I maintain my determination and perseverance throughout this journey?

In what ways can I shift my perspective to see challenges and setbacks as opportunities for personal growth and development, allowing them to strengthen my resolve in recovery?

How can I remind myself regularly of the importance of imagining ideal outcomes in my recovery journey, and how can I stay committed to striving for these outcomes over the long term?

How can I apply the principles of authenticity, tireless pursuit of dreams, and embracing trials as opportunities to my recovery journey, using them as a roadmap to guide me toward a successful and fulfilling life in sobriety?

What strategies can I employ to celebrate my progress and achievements as I work toward my ideal outcomes, and how can I use these milestones as motivation to continue on my path to long-term recovery?

Creating a Vivid Mental Picture of a Transformed Life:
Navigating the Path to Long-Term Recovery from Addiction

In the journey toward long-term recovery from addiction, creating a vivid mental picture of a transformed life is a powerful motivator. As the saying goes, "Without hope and faith, the best powers of the mind remain dormant." This book delves into the importance of envisioning a life transformed by recovery. We will highlight the significance of hope, faith, and the development of habits that lead to a brighter future.

The Power of a Vivid Mental Picture

A vivid mental picture of a transformed life acts as a guiding light on the path to recovery. It ignites hope, fuels faith, and empowers individuals to take the necessary steps toward change.

A Journey of Transformation

Step 1: Igniting Hope and Faith Hope and faith are the driving forces that propel individuals forward in their recovery journey. They act as the sparks that ignite the fuel within, enabling individuals to move beyond addiction.

> Self-Reflection Question: How can I cultivate and maintain hope and faith in my recovery journey, even during challenging times, and use them as sources of motivation and resilience?

Step 2: Developing Habits of Transformation Hope and faith are not merely feelings; they are habits that drive dreams, goals, and lives. Developing habits of transformation involves consistent and purposeful actions that align with one's vision of a transformed life.

> Self-Reflection Question: What positive habits can I cultivate in my daily life that align with my vision of a transformed life in recovery, and how can I integrate these habits into my routine?

Step 3: Embracing the Journey The path to transformation is not always smooth, and shadows may appear along the way. However, embracing the journey with acceptance of the past, confidence in the present, and fearlessness of the future is essential for progress.

> Self-Reflection Question: How can I maintain a sense of acceptance, confidence, and fearlessness in my recovery journey, knowing that each step forward brings me closer to my transformed life?

Creating a vivid mental picture of a transformed life is a vital element of the recovery journey from addiction. It involves igniting hope and faith, developing habits of transformation, and embracing the journey with acceptance and confidence. By harnessing the power of these principles, individuals can navigate their path to long-term recovery with determination and purpose.

Self-Reflection Questions:

> How can I cultivate and maintain hope and faith in my recovery journey, even during challenging times, and use them as sources of motivation and resilience?

> What specific positive habits can I cultivate in my daily life that align with my vision of a transformed life in recovery, and how can I integrate these habits into my routine?

> In what ways can I maintain a sense of acceptance, confidence, and fearlessness in my recovery journey, knowing that each step forward brings me closer to my transformed life?

> How can I remind myself regularly of the importance of creating a vivid mental picture of a transformed life in my recovery journey, and how can I stay committed to this vision over the long term?

How can I apply the principles of igniting hope and faith, developing transformational habits, and embracing the journey to my recovery journey, using them as a roadmap to guide me toward a successful and fulfilling life in sobriety?

What strategies can I employ to celebrate my progress and achievements as I work toward my transformed life, and how can I use these milestones as motivation to continue on my path to long-term recovery?

Connecting Personal Purpose with Transformation:
A Path to Long-Term Recovery from Addiction

In the journey toward long-term recovery from addiction, connecting personal purpose with transformation is a profound and empowering endeavor. As the saying goes, "Pain will not go away by getting angry or bitter, it will go away when you learn to accept life's challenges with grace and ease." This book explores the significance of aligning one's personal purpose with the transformative process of recovery. We will emphasize the importance of acceptance, mindset change, and perseverance on this transformative journey.

The Power of Connecting Personal Purpose

Connecting personal purpose with transformation provides individuals with a deeper and more meaningful motivation for change. It helps them embrace life's challenges and foster the resilience needed to overcome addiction.

Step 1: Embracing Acceptance Recovery begins with accepting the reality of one's addiction and acknowledging the pain it has caused. Acceptance is not a sign of weakness but rather the first step toward healing and transformation.

> Self-Reflection Question: How can I foster a greater sense of acceptance in my recovery journey, recognizing that it is a key factor in my transformation, and how can I navigate the challenges that arise with grace and ease?

Step 2: Changing Mindset Personal transformation is closely tied to a shift in mindset. Changing oneself and one's life begins with altering the way one thinks and perceives the world. A positive mindset is crucial for long-term recovery.

> Self-Reflection Question: What steps can I take to actively change my mindset in a way that supports my recovery goals, and how can I maintain this positive shift in thinking over time?

Step 3: Cultivating Perseverance Recovery is a journey that takes time, and instant results are rare. Cultivating perseverance is essential for staying committed to the process and not giving up when faced with challenges or setbacks.

A Journey of Transformation

> Self-Reflection Question: How can I develop and strengthen my perseverance in recovery, recognizing that transformation is a gradual process, and how can I stay dedicated to my personal purpose throughout this journey?

Connecting personal purpose with transformation is a vital aspect of the recovery journey from addiction. It involves embracing acceptance, changing mindset, and cultivating perseverance. By harnessing the power of these principles, individuals can navigate their path to long-term recovery with resilience, determination, and a deeper sense of meaning.

Self-Reflection Questions:

> How can I foster a greater sense of acceptance in my recovery journey, recognizing that it is a key factor in my transformation, and how can I navigate the challenges that arise with grace and ease?

> What specific steps can I take to actively change my mindset in a way that supports my recovery goals, and how can I maintain this positive shift in thinking over time?

> In what ways can I develop and strengthen my perseverance in recovery, recognizing that transformation is a gradual process, and how can I stay dedicated to my personal purpose throughout this journey?

> How can I remind myself regularly of the importance of connecting personal purpose with transformation in my recovery journey, and how can I stay committed to this purpose over the long term?

> How can I apply the principles of acceptance, mindset change, and perseverance to my recovery journey, using them as a roadmap to guide me toward a successful and fulfilling life in sobriety?

> What strategies can I employ to celebrate my progress and achievements as I work toward my personal purpose, and how can I use these milestones as motivation to continue on my path to long-term recovery?

Clarifying Core Values and Beliefs:
A Catalyst for Long-Term Recovery from Addiction

In the journey toward long-term recovery from addiction, clarifying core values and beliefs is a fundamental and transformative process. As the saying goes, "Frustration and Love can't exist in the same place at the same time, so get real and start doing what you would rather be doing in life." This book explores the significance of aligning one's core values and beliefs with the transformative journey of recovery. We will emphasize the importance of embracing authenticity, love for life, and the role of anger and frustration in this process.

The Power of Clarifying Core Values

Clarifying core values and beliefs provides individuals with a compass for navigating the challenges of addiction recovery. It allows them to align their actions with their true selves and foster a deep sense of fulfillment.

Step 1: Embracing Authenticity Recovery involves the process of rediscovering one's authentic self. Authenticity is the cornerstone of transformation, as it enables individuals to live in alignment with their core values and beliefs.

> Self-Reflection Question: How can I foster greater authenticity in my recovery journey, and what steps can I take to ensure that I am living in accordance with my true self and values?

Step 2: Cultivating Love for Life Love for life, including all its complexities and challenges, is a driving force for change. It encourages individuals to embrace their entire life journey, even the past experiences that may have contributed to addiction.

> Self-Reflection Question: How can I cultivate a deeper love for life and all its aspects, acknowledging that my entire life, including past experiences, is a part of my journey toward transformation?

Step 3: Managing Anger and Frustration Anger and frustration often arise when individuals are not living authentically or when they are not aligned with their core values and beliefs. Recognizing and addressing these emotions is essential for progress in recovery.

> Self-Reflection Question: How can I better understand and manage my anger and frustration in my recovery journey, recognizing that they may be indicators of areas where I am not living authentically or aligned with my core values?

Clarifying core values and beliefs is a pivotal aspect of the recovery journey from addiction. It involves embracing authenticity, cultivating love for life, and addressing anger and frustration as signals for transformation. By harnessing the power of these principles, individuals can navigate their path to long-term recovery with self-acceptance, fulfillment, and resilience.

Self-Reflection Questions:

> How can I foster greater authenticity in my recovery journey, and what steps can I take to ensure that I am living in accordance with my true self and values?

> What specific actions can I take to cultivate a deeper love for life and all its aspects, acknowledging that my entire life, including past experiences, is a part of my journey toward transformation?

A Journey of Transformation

> In what ways can I better understand and manage my anger and frustration in my recovery journey, recognizing that they may be indicators of areas where I am not living authentically or aligned with my core values?

> How can I remind myself regularly of the importance of clarifying core values and beliefs in my recovery journey, and how can I stay committed to this process over the long term?

> How can I apply the principles of authenticity, love for life, and anger/frustration management to my recovery journey, using them as a roadmap to guide me toward a successful and fulfilling life in sobriety?

> What strategies can I employ to celebrate my progress and achievements as I clarify my core values and beliefs, and how can I use these milestones as motivation to continue on my path to long-term recovery?

Aligning Transformation Goals with Life Purpose: A Journey to Long-Term Recovery from Addiction

In the pursuit of long-term recovery from addiction, aligning transformation goals with one's life purpose is a transformative and empowering endeavor. As the saying goes, "The best feeling in the whole world is watching things finally fall into place after watching them fall apart for so long." This book explores the significance of harmonizing transformation goals with one's life purpose in the recovery process. We will emphasize the importance of self-care, positive relationships, and gratitude on this transformative journey.

The Power of Aligning Goals with Life Purpose

Aligning transformation goals with one's life purpose provides individuals with a sense of direction and fulfillment. It enables them to focus on what truly matters and empowers them to overcome addiction.

Step 1: Prioritizing Self-Care Recovery necessitates prioritizing self-care as a means to align transformation goals with life purpose. Self-care includes not only abstaining from substances but also nurturing physical, emotional, and mental well-being.

> Self-Reflection Question: How can I elevate the practice of self-care in my recovery journey, recognizing that it is essential for aligning my transformation goals with my life purpose?

Step 2: Cultivating Positive Relationships Surrounding oneself with positive, supportive people is crucial for recovery. Building and maintaining healthy relationships can serve as a pillar for transformation and help individuals align their goals with their life purpose.

> Self-Reflection Question: How can I identify and cultivate positive relationships in my life that align with my life purpose and support my recovery journey?

Step 3: Embracing Gratitude Gratitude is a powerful tool that can shift one's perspective and enhance the recovery process. Embracing gratitude for the positive aspects of life, no matter how small, can strengthen the connection between transformation goals and life purpose.

> Self-Reflection Question: How can I incorporate a daily practice of gratitude into my life, recognizing its role in aligning my transformation goals with my life purpose and fostering positivity in my recovery journey?

Aligning transformation goals with one's life purpose is a pivotal aspect of the recovery journey from addiction. It involves prioritizing self-care, cultivating positive relationships, and embracing gratitude. By harnessing the power of these principles, individuals can navigate their path to long-term recovery with clarity, resilience, and a deep sense of purpose.

Self-Reflection Questions:

> How can I elevate the practice of self-care in my recovery journey, recognizing that it is essential for aligning my transformation goals with my life purpose?

> What specific steps can I take to identify and cultivate positive relationships in my life that align with my life purpose and support my recovery journey?

> In what ways can I incorporate a daily practice of gratitude into my life, recognizing its role in aligning my transformation goals with my life purpose and fostering positivity in my recovery journey?

> How can I remind myself regularly of the importance of aligning transformation goals with my life purpose in my recovery journey, and how can I stay committed to this alignment over the long term?

> How can I apply the principles of self-care, positive relationships, and gratitude to my recovery journey, using them as a roadmap to guide me toward a successful and fulfilling life in sobriety?

> What strategies can I employ to celebrate my progress and achievements as I align my transformation goals with my life purpose, and how can I use these milestones as motivation to continue on my path to long-term recovery?

Personal States of Being

In the pursuit of long-term recovery from addiction, understanding and managing one's personal states of being is essential. As the saying goes, "Learn from yesterday, live for today, hope for tomorrow." This book explores the significance of self-awareness, the unpredictability of life, and the power of choice in the recovery process. We will emphasize the importance of embracing the present moment, cultivating lifelong learning, and fostering a positive mindset on this transformative journey.

The Power of Personal States of Being

Understanding and managing personal states of being empowers individuals to navigate the challenges of addiction recovery more effectively. It allows them to take control of their emotional and mental well-being and make choices that support their long-term goals.

Step 1: Embracing Self-Awareness Recovery begins with self-awareness. It involves recognizing and understanding one's emotions, thoughts, and behaviors. Self-awareness is the cornerstone of personal growth and transformation.

> Self-Reflection Question: How can I enhance my self-awareness in my recovery journey, and how can this awareness help me make better choices for my long-term well-being?

Step 2: Embracing the Present Moment Life is unpredictable, and the future is uncertain. Embracing the present moment allows individuals to let go of regrets about the past and anxieties about the future. It encourages them to find joy and contentment in the here and now.

> Self-Reflection Question: What practices can I incorporate into my daily life to embrace the present moment more fully, recognizing that it is the only time in which I can make choices that impact my recovery?

Step 3: Cultivating Lifelong Learning Recovery is an ongoing process that involves continuous learning and growth. Cultivating a mindset of lifelong learning enables individuals to adapt to new challenges and develop the skills needed for long-term recovery.

> Self-Reflection Question: How can I foster a commitment to lifelong learning in my recovery journey, recognizing that personal growth and transformation are lifelong endeavors?

Understanding and managing personal states of being is a vital aspect of the recovery journey from addiction. It involves embracing self-awareness, living in the present moment, and fostering a mindset of lifelong learning. By harnessing the power of these principles, individuals can navigate their path to long-term recovery with resilience, optimism, and a sense of purpose.

A Journey of Transformation

Self-Reflection Questions:

How can I enhance my self-awareness in my recovery journey, and how can this awareness help me make better choices for my long-term well-being?

What practices can I incorporate into my daily life to embrace the present moment more fully, recognizing that it is the only time in which I can make choices that impact my recovery?

In what ways can I foster a commitment to lifelong learning in my recovery journey, recognizing that personal growth and transformation are lifelong endeavors?

How can I remind myself regularly of the importance of understanding and managing my personal states of being in my recovery journey, and how can I stay committed to this process over the long term?

How can I apply the principles of self-awareness, present moment awareness, and lifelong learning to my recovery journey, using them as a roadmap to guide me toward a successful and fulfilling life in sobriety?

What strategies can I employ to celebrate my progress and achievements as I work on understanding and managing my personal states of being, and how can I use these milestones as motivation to continue on my path to long-term recovery?

The Importance of Self-Awareness in Transformation:
A Journey to Long-Term Recovery from Addiction

Self-awareness is a fundamental pillar of transformation and recovery from addiction. As the saying goes, "Use your eyes to see the needs, and use your talents to meet them." This book delves into the significance of self-awareness in the recovery process and explores how it empowers individuals to overcome addiction. We will emphasize the importance of self-reflection, positive thinking, and gratitude on this transformative journey.

The Power of Self-Awareness

Self-awareness is the first step towards lasting transformation. It involves recognizing one's strengths, weaknesses, thoughts, and emotions. Through self-awareness, individuals gain insight into their addictive behaviors and the underlying causes, setting the stage for meaningful change.

Step 1: Self-Reflection Recovery begins with self-reflection. It requires individuals to examine their lives honestly and identify patterns of behavior that contribute to addiction. Self-reflection allows for a deeper understanding of the root causes of addiction, paving the way for effective solutions.

Self-Reflection Question: How can I incorporate regular self-reflection into my recovery journey, recognizing that it is a powerful tool for understanding and addressing the underlying causes of my addiction?

Step 2: Positive Thinking Positive thinking is a catalyst for transformation. It involves shifting one's mindset from negativity to optimism. Embracing positive thinking enables individuals to break free from self-destructive thought patterns and build a foundation for lasting change.

Self-Reflection Question: What strategies can I employ to cultivate positive thinking in my recovery journey, understanding that it is essential for overcoming addiction and embracing a healthier, more fulfilling life?

Step 3: Gratitude Gratitude is a transformative force that can reshape one's perspective on life. It involves appreciating the present moment and recognizing the value of what one has. Gratitude can counteract feelings of emptiness and longing that often drive addiction.

Self-Reflection Question: How can I integrate a daily practice of gratitude into my life, acknowledging its role in fostering self-awareness and helping me appreciate the positive aspects of my journey towards recovery?

Self-awareness is a cornerstone of the recovery journey from addiction. It involves self-reflection, positive thinking, and gratitude. By harnessing the power of these principles, individuals can navigate their path to long-term recovery with clarity, resilience, and a renewed sense of purpose.

Self-Reflection Questions:

How can I incorporate regular self-reflection into my recovery journey, recognizing that it is a powerful tool for understanding and addressing the underlying causes of my addiction?

What strategies can I employ to cultivate positive thinking in my recovery journey, understanding that it is essential for overcoming addiction and embracing a healthier, more fulfilling life?

In what ways can I integrate a daily practice of gratitude into my life, acknowledging its role in fostering self-awareness and helping me appreciate the positive aspects of my journey towards recovery?

How can I remind myself regularly of the importance of self-awareness in my recovery journey, and how can I stay committed to this practice over the long term?

How can I apply the principles of self-reflection, positive thinking, and gratitude to my recovery journey, using them as a roadmap to guide me toward a successful and fulfilling life in sobriety?

A Journey of Transformation

> What strategies can I employ to celebrate my progress and achievements as I cultivate self-awareness, and how can I use these milestones as motivation to continue on my path to long-term recovery?

Exploring Thoughts, Emotions, and Behaviors:
A Path to Long-Term Recovery from Addiction

Exploring one's thoughts, emotions, and behaviors is a crucial aspect of the journey towards long-term recovery from addiction. It is essential to recognize that addiction often stems from a complex interplay of these factors. This book delves into the significance of understanding and managing thoughts, emotions, and behaviors and how they influence the process of recovery. We will emphasize the importance of self-compassion, acceptance, and love in this transformative journey.

The Power of Self-Exploration

Self-exploration is a foundational step towards healing from addiction. It entails delving into one's thoughts, emotions, and behaviors to gain insight into the underlying causes of addiction and pave the way for lasting change.

Step 1: Self-Compassion Recovery begins with self-compassion. It involves acknowledging that everyone, including oneself, is susceptible to making mistakes and facing challenges. Self-compassion fosters self-acceptance and allows individuals to forgive themselves for their past actions and choices.

> Self-Reflection Question: How can I cultivate self-compassion in my recovery journey, understanding that it is a key component of healing and self-forgiveness?

Step 2: Acceptance Acceptance is the doorway to transformation. It involves embracing one's past, acknowledging the consequences of addiction, and recognizing that change is possible. Acceptance paves the way for personal growth and recovery.

> Self-Reflection Question: How can I practice acceptance in my recovery journey, understanding that it is essential to let go of the past and move forward towards a healthier future?

Step 3: Love and Connection Love and connection are powerful healers. Building supportive relationships and seeking connection with others who understand the challenges of addiction can provide invaluable support on the path to recovery. Love, both self-love and love from others, can be a driving force for positive change.

> Self-Reflection Question: How can I foster love and connection in my recovery journey, recognizing that they are vital sources of strength and motivation?

Exploring thoughts, emotions, and behaviors is a transformative process that can guide individuals towards long-term recovery from addiction. It involves cultivating self-compassion, practicing acceptance, and fostering love and connection. By embracing these principles, individuals can embark on a journey of healing, self-discovery, and lasting positive change.

Self-Reflection Questions:

How can I cultivate self-compassion in my recovery journey, understanding that it is a key component of healing and self-forgiveness?

What strategies can I employ to practice acceptance in my recovery journey, recognizing that it is essential to let go of the past and move forward towards a healthier future?

In what ways can I foster love and connection in my recovery journey, acknowledging that they are vital sources of strength and motivation?

How can I remind myself regularly of the importance of exploring my thoughts, emotions, and behaviors in my recovery journey, and how can I stay committed to this process over the long term?

How can I apply the principles of self-compassion, acceptance, and love and connection to my recovery journey, using them as a roadmap to guide me toward a successful and fulfilling life in sobriety?

What strategies can I employ to celebrate my progress and achievements as I explore my thoughts, emotions, and behaviors, and how can I use these milestones as motivation to continue on my path to long-term recovery?

Recognizing Patterns that Facilitate or Impede Progress:
A Path to Long-Term Recovery from Addiction

Recognizing and understanding the patterns that either facilitate or impede progress is a crucial aspect of the journey towards long-term recovery from addiction. Just as all the water in the world cannot sink a ship unless it gets inside of it, external challenges cannot defeat an individual unless they allow them to infiltrate their mind. This book explores the significance of recognizing and managing these patterns and their influence on the recovery process. We will emphasize the importance of focusing on potential, hope, and unfulfilled dreams in this transformative journey.

The Power of Self-Awareness

Self-awareness is a foundational step towards healing from addiction. It involves recognizing and analyzing patterns of thoughts, emotions, and behaviors that either contribute to progress or hinder it.

A Journey of Transformation

Step 1: Focus on Potential Recovery begins with recognizing one's potential. It involves acknowledging that despite past mistakes and challenges, there is still untapped potential within every individual. Focusing on one's potential can serve as a powerful motivator for change.

> Self-Reflection Question: How can I shift my focus towards my potential in my recovery journey, understanding that it is a driving force for positive change and growth?

Step 2: Embrace Hope Hope is a beacon of light in the darkest moments. Embracing hope involves believing in the possibility of recovery and a brighter future. Hope can counteract feelings of frustration and anxiety that often accompany addiction.

> Self-Reflection Question: How can I nurture hope in my recovery journey, recognizing that it is essential for maintaining a positive outlook and resilience in the face of challenges?

Step 3: Unfulfilled Dreams Exploring unfulfilled dreams is a transformative process. It involves identifying aspirations and goals that have been overshadowed by addiction. Reconnecting with these dreams can provide a sense of purpose and direction.

> Self-Reflection Question: How can I reconnect with my unfulfilled dreams in my recovery journey, understanding that they can serve as a driving force for personal growth and fulfillment?

Recognizing patterns that either facilitate or impede progress is a transformative process that can guide individuals towards long-term recovery from addiction. It involves focusing on potential, embracing hope, and exploring unfulfilled dreams. By recognizing and managing these patterns, individuals can embark on a journey of self-discovery, healing, and lasting positive change.

Self-Reflection Questions:

> How can I shift my focus towards my potential in my recovery journey, understanding that it is a driving force for positive change and growth?

> What strategies can I employ to nurture hope in my recovery journey, recognizing that it is essential for maintaining a positive outlook and resilience in the face of challenges?

> In what ways can I reconnect with my unfulfilled dreams in my recovery journey, understanding that they can serve as a driving force for personal growth and fulfillment?

> How can I remind myself regularly of the importance of recognizing and managing patterns that facilitate or impede progress in my recovery journey, and how can I stay committed to this process over the long term?

How can I apply the principles of focusing on potential, embracing hope, and exploring unfulfilled dreams to my recovery journey, using them as a roadmap to guide me toward a successful and fulfilling life in sobriety?

What strategies can I employ to celebrate my progress and achievements as I recognize and manage patterns in my recovery journey, and how can I use these milestones as motivation to continue on my path to long-term recovery?

Fostering a Growth Mindset:
A Path to Long-Term Recovery from Addiction

Fostering a growth mindset is a crucial aspect of the journey towards long-term recovery from addiction. Believing that you can be better than you ever thought possible is a powerful mindset shift that can lead to personal growth, resilience, and lasting change. This book explores the significance of fostering a growth mindset and its impact on the recovery process. We will emphasize the importance of self-belief, determination, and confidence in this transformative journey.

The Power of a Growth Mindset

A growth mindset is the belief that abilities and intelligence can be developed through dedication and hard work. Embracing this mindset is fundamental to overcoming addiction and achieving long-term recovery.

Step 1: Self-Belief Recovery begins with believing in oneself. It involves acknowledging that you have the potential to be better, to grow, and to overcome addiction. Self-belief serves as the foundation for positive change.

> Self-Reflection Question: How can I cultivate self-belief in my recovery journey, understanding that it is the starting point for personal growth and transformation?

Step 2: Determination Determination is the driving force behind recovery. It involves the will to win, the desire to succeed, and the commitment to reach your full potential. Determination propels individuals to persevere in the face of challenges.

> Self-Reflection Question: How can I nurture determination in my recovery journey, recognizing that it is the fuel that keeps me moving forward even when faced with obstacles?

Step 3: Confidence Confidence is the key to personal excellence. It involves having a humble but reasonable belief in your own powers and abilities. Confidence empowers individuals to take risks, make positive changes, and face adversity with resilience.

A Journey of Transformation

> Self-Reflection Question: How can I boost my confidence in my recovery journey, understanding that it is essential for success and happiness in sobriety?

Fostering a growth mindset is a transformative process that can guide individuals towards long-term recovery from addiction. It involves cultivating self-belief, nurturing determination, and boosting confidence. By embracing a growth mindset, individuals can embark on a journey of self-discovery, healing, and lasting positive change.

Self-Reflection Questions:

How can I cultivate self-belief in my recovery journey, understanding that it is the starting point for personal growth and transformation?

What strategies can I employ to nurture determination in my recovery journey, recognizing that it is the fuel that keeps me moving forward even when faced with obstacles?

In what ways can I boost my confidence in my recovery journey, understanding that it is essential for success and happiness in sobriety?

How can I remind myself regularly of the importance of fostering a growth mindset in my recovery journey, and how can I stay committed to this mindset over the long term?

How can I apply the principles of self-belief, determination, and confidence to my recovery journey, using them as a roadmap to guide me toward a successful and fulfilling life in sobriety?

What strategies can I employ to celebrate my progress and achievements as I foster a growth mindset in my recovery journey, and how can I use these milestones as motivation to continue on my path to long-term recovery?

Embracing Challenges and Setbacks as Opportunities for Growth:
A Path to Long-Term Recovery from Addiction

Embracing challenges and setbacks as opportunities for growth is a pivotal aspect of the journey towards long-term recovery from addiction. Life often teaches us that we don't truly appreciate what we have until it's gone. Similarly, we may not realize what we've been missing until new opportunities arrive. This book explores the significance of embracing adversity and setbacks as catalysts for personal growth and transformation. We will highlight the importance of letting go of the past, staying focused on the future, and learning from both successes and mistakes in this transformative journey.

The Power of Embracing Challenges

Embracing challenges and setbacks as opportunities for growth is a mindset shift that can lead to profound personal development.

Step 1: Letting Go of the Past Recovery requires letting go of the past, particularly the mistakes and regrets that may have led to addiction. Holding onto past pain and negativity can hinder progress.

> Self-Reflection Question: How can I release the grip of my past in my recovery journey, understanding that it is essential for moving forward and embracing new opportunities?

Step 2: Staying Focused on the Future Recovery is about looking ahead with hope and determination. The future holds countless opportunities for change, personal development, and a better life.

> Self-Reflection Question: How can I maintain focus on the future in my recovery journey, recognizing that it is where I can create the life I desire free from addiction?

Step 3: Learning and Growth Challenges and setbacks offer valuable lessons. Embracing them as opportunities for learning and growth allows individuals to develop resilience and adaptability.

> Self-Reflection Question: How can I extract lessons and growth from challenges and setbacks in my recovery journey, understanding that they can lead to personal development and lasting change?

Embracing challenges and setbacks as opportunities for growth is a transformative process that can guide individuals towards long-term recovery from addiction. It involves letting go of the past, staying focused on the future, and extracting lessons from adversity. By embracing these principles, individuals can embark on a journey of self-discovery, healing, and lasting positive change.

Self-Reflection Questions:

> How can I release the grip of my past in my recovery journey, understanding that it is essential for moving forward and embracing new opportunities?

> What strategies can I employ to maintain focus on the future in my recovery journey, recognizing that it is where I can create the life I desire free from addiction?

> In what ways can I extract lessons and growth from challenges and setbacks in my recovery journey, understanding that they can lead to personal development and lasting change?

A Journey of Transformation

> How can I remind myself regularly of the importance of embracing challenges and setbacks as opportunities for growth in my recovery journey, and how can I stay committed to this mindset over the long term?

> How can I apply the principles of letting go of the past, staying focused on the future, and learning from adversity to my recovery journey, using them as a roadmap to guide me toward a successful and fulfilling life in sobriety?

> What strategies can I employ to celebrate my progress and achievements as I embrace challenges and setbacks as opportunities for growth in my recovery journey, and how can I use these milestones as motivation to continue on my path to long-term recovery?

Cultivating Belief in One's Capacity to Change and Evolve: A Key to Long-Term Recovery from Addiction

Cultivating belief in one's capacity to change and evolve is a fundamental aspect of the journey towards long-term recovery from addiction. The path to sobriety can be daunting, filled with challenges and setbacks. However, maintaining faith in one's ability to change and grow is essential for overcoming these obstacles. This book explores the significance of self-belief in the recovery process and provides guidance on how to cultivate and sustain it.

The Power of Self-Belief

Belief in oneself is a powerful force that can lead to lasting transformation and recovery.

Step 1: Overcoming Defeat Being defeated is often a temporary condition. It's essential to recognize that setbacks and relapses are part of the recovery journey. What matters is the determination to get back up and continue moving forward.

> Self-Reflection Question: How can I shift my perspective from seeing defeat as permanent to viewing it as a temporary setback in my recovery journey?

Step 2: Valuing Self-Worth Understanding that one's value is inherent, regardless of past actions or mistakes, is crucial. Recognizing your worth as a human being can provide the foundation for self-belief.

> Self-Reflection Question: How can I remind myself regularly that my value comes from simply being, rather than what I do or have done?

Step 3: Pursuing Personal Growth Success in recovery means having the courage to become the person you believe you were meant to be. This involves self-discovery, personal development, and embracing the potential for positive change.

Self-Reflection Question: How can I nurture the belief that I have the determination and will to become the person I envision in my recovery journey?

Cultivating belief in one's capacity to change and evolve is a cornerstone of long-term recovery from addiction. It involves shifting one's perspective on defeat, recognizing intrinsic self-worth, and actively pursuing personal growth. By embracing these principles, individuals can build a solid foundation for sustained recovery and personal transformation.

Self-Reflection Questions:

How can I shift my perspective from seeing defeat as permanent to viewing it as a temporary setback in my recovery journey?

What strategies can I employ to remind myself regularly that my value comes from simply being, rather than what I do or have done?

In what ways can I nurture the belief that I have the determination and will to become the person I envision in my recovery journey?

How can I actively pursue personal growth and development in my recovery journey, and how can I use these experiences to reinforce my belief in my capacity to change and evolve?

What steps can I take to build a support system that encourages and reinforces my belief in my ability to overcome addiction and achieve lasting recovery?

How can I celebrate my successes and milestones along the path to recovery, using these moments as evidence of my capacity for change and evolution?

How can I ensure that I maintain a positive and self-affirming inner dialogue throughout my recovery journey, and what practices can I adopt to reinforce my self-belief regularly?

Energy, Vibration, and Frequency

In the journey towards long-term recovery from addiction, understanding the concepts of energy, vibration, and frequency can have a profound impact on one's path to healing. This book explores the importance of being fully present in the moment, the ability to make adjustments for a better future, and the idea that it's never too late for a new beginning in life.

The Power of Presence

Most people are never fully present in the now because they unconsciously believe that the next moment must be more important. However, by constantly focusing on the future or dwelling on the past, they miss out on the richness of life, which unfolds in the present.

Step 1: Embracing the Now Recovery requires being fully engaged in the present moment. Acknowledging that every moment is an opportunity for change and growth can be transformative.

> Self-Reflection Question: How can I become more mindful and present in my daily life, especially during challenging moments in my recovery journey?

Step 2: Making Adjustments While you cannot change the past, you can make adjustments in your present to shape a better future. Recovery is about learning from past mistakes and actively working towards a healthier, more fulfilling life.

> Self-Reflection Question: What specific adjustments can I make in my current lifestyle, habits, or thought patterns to improve my chances of achieving long-term recovery?

Step 3: Never Settling In recovery, it's crucial never to settle for less than what you deserve. This applies to all aspects of life, including your career, relationships, dreams, and love. Embrace the belief that you are worthy of a life filled with joy and purpose.

> Self-Reflection Question: How can I overcome any limiting beliefs or fears that may be preventing me from pursuing the life, career, dreams, and love that I truly deserve?

Step 4: New Beginnings One of the most empowering aspects of life is the opportunity for new beginnings. No matter where you are in your recovery journey, it's never too late to make positive changes, set new goals, and embark on a path of personal transformation.

> Self-Reflection Question: What new beginnings can I envision for my life, and how can I take the first steps towards realizing them in my recovery journey?

Understanding the principles of energy, vibration, and frequency can be a catalyst for personal transformation in the recovery process. By embracing the present moment, making necessary

A Journey of Transformation

adjustments, refusing to settle for less, and embracing the concept of new beginnings, individuals can navigate their journey towards long-term recovery with optimism and purpose.

Self-Reflection Questions:

How can I become more mindful and present in my daily life, especially during challenging moments in my recovery journey?

What specific adjustments can I make in my current lifestyle, habits, or thought patterns to improve my chances of achieving long-term recovery?

What limiting beliefs or fears may be holding me back from pursuing the life, career, dreams, and love that I truly deserve, and how can I overcome them?

What new beginnings can I envision for my life, and how can I take the first steps towards realizing them in my recovery journey?

How can I remind myself regularly that the present moment is the most valuable time for personal growth and transformation, and what practices can I adopt to stay grounded in the now?

In what ways can I actively engage with the concept of energy, vibration, and frequency in my recovery journey, using these principles to enhance my overall well-being and success in maintaining sobriety?

How can I celebrate the progress I've made in my recovery journey and use this as a source of motivation and positive energy moving forward?

Understanding the Concept of Energy and Vibration in the Journey to Recovery

In the pursuit of long-term recovery from addiction, it is essential to comprehend the concept of energy and vibration. This book explores the significance of never giving up on one's aspirations, the importance of commitment, and the role of personal control in the recovery journey.

The Power of Persistence

Step 1: Never Give Up One of the most critical aspects of recovery is the unwavering commitment to achieving what you truly desire. The journey towards sobriety can be challenging, and setbacks may occur, but it is essential to never give up on the goal of a healthier, addiction-free life.

Self-Reflection Question: What strategies can I implement to maintain my determination and motivation, even when faced with obstacles or setbacks in my recovery journey?

Step 2: Commitment vs. Interest Commitment goes beyond mere interest. It requires dedication, focus, and a willingness to take consistent action towards recovery. Being committed means fully embracing the recovery process and making it a top priority.

> Self-Reflection Question: How can I transition from being interested in recovery to being fully committed, and what changes can I make in my approach to solidify my commitment?

Step 3: Control Over Your Future Recovery is a journey where you are in control of your destiny. No external factors or other people can determine your success in maintaining sobriety. Recognizing your personal agency and the power to shape your future is crucial.

> Self-Reflection Question: In what ways can I exercise greater control over my recovery journey, and how can I become more proactive in creating the future I desire?

Step 4: Pursuing Unrealistic Dreams No dream is truly unrealistic if you are willing to put in the effort and determination to make it come true. Recovery opens the door to countless possibilities, and it is essential to believe in your potential to achieve your goals.

> Self-Reflection Question: What dreams or aspirations have I set aside due to addiction, and how can I reintegrate them into my life as motivating forces for positive change in my recovery?

Understanding the concept of energy and vibration can be a source of strength and inspiration in the journey towards long-term recovery. By embracing the power of persistence, making a commitment beyond mere interest, recognizing personal control, and pursuing even seemingly unrealistic dreams, individuals can embark on a path of transformation and sobriety with confidence and determination.

Self-Reflection Questions:

> What strategies can I implement to maintain my determination and motivation, even when faced with obstacles or setbacks in my recovery journey?

> How can I transition from being interested in recovery to being fully committed, and what changes can I make in my approach to solidify my commitment?

> In what ways can I exercise greater control over my recovery journey, and how can I become more proactive in creating the future I desire?

> What dreams or aspirations have I set aside due to addiction, and how can I reintegrate them into my life as motivating forces for positive change in my recovery?

> How can I cultivate a mindset of never giving up on my aspirations and goals in the face of adversity or challenges related to my addiction recovery?

A Journey of Transformation

> How can I remind myself regularly that I have control over my future and that my commitment to recovery is the driving force behind my progress?
>
> Are there specific tools or practices, such as mindfulness or visualization, that I can incorporate into my daily routine to align my energy and vibration with my recovery goals and aspirations?

The Connection Between Personal Energy and Outcomes in Addiction Recovery

Addiction is a complex and challenging condition that can have devastating effects on an individual's life. Seeking long-term recovery from addiction is a courageous journey that demands commitment, perseverance, and a deep understanding of oneself. One often-overlooked aspect of this recovery process is the profound connection between personal energy and outcomes. This book explores the significance of personal energy and its impact on the recovery journey, emphasizing the importance of maintaining a positive mindset, self-belief, and the ability to learn from mistakes.

The Power of Personal Energy

Personal energy, often described as the mental and emotional state of an individual, plays a pivotal role in addiction recovery. It encompasses one's attitude, motivation, and overall outlook on life. In the pursuit of long-term recovery, maintaining a positive and resilient personal energy is crucial. It is the driving force behind the decisions and actions taken during the recovery process.

Understanding the Link Between Energy and Outcomes

To comprehend the connection between personal energy and outcomes, one must acknowledge that addiction recovery is a holistic process. It involves addressing not only the physical aspects of addiction but also the psychological and emotional components. When an individual approaches recovery with a positive and determined mindset, they are more likely to achieve positive outcomes.

Believing in the Possibility of Recovery

The statement, "To accomplish great things, we must not only act, but also dream; not only plan, but also believe," holds significant relevance in addiction recovery. Belief in oneself and the possibility of long-term recovery is a driving force that can fuel the journey. It is essential to have faith in one's ability to overcome addiction and lead a fulfilling life in sobriety.

The Role of Mindset in Recovery

A positive mindset can be a powerful tool in overcoming addiction. It enables individuals to face challenges with resilience and adaptability. When individuals approach recovery with a growth mindset, they view setbacks as opportunities for learning and growth rather than as insurmountable obstacles. This mindset shift can significantly impact the outcomes of their recovery journey.

The Importance of Effective Communication

The statement, "The greatest mistake we make in our lives is we listen halfway, understand a quarter of the way, think zero, and react double," highlights the importance of effective communication in recovery. Open and honest communication with oneself and with support networks is essential for progress. Misunderstandings and miscommunications can hinder recovery efforts, emphasizing the need for clarity and empathy in interactions.

Learning from Mistakes

Recovery is not a linear path, and setbacks are a part of the journey. It is crucial to approach mistakes with a constructive attitude, as they offer opportunities for growth. By acknowledging and learning from their mistakes, individuals can refine their recovery strategies and build resilience.

In the pursuit of long-term recovery from addiction, the connection between personal energy and outcomes cannot be underestimated. Maintaining a positive mindset, self-belief, effective communication, and the ability to learn from mistakes are key factors that influence the recovery journey's success. Recovery is not solely about eliminating addiction; it is about reclaiming one's life, finding purpose, and realizing one's full potential. By understanding the significance of personal energy and its impact on outcomes, individuals on the path to recovery can increase their chances of achieving lasting sobriety and a brighter future.

Self-Reflection Questions:

How do I currently perceive my personal energy and mindset in my addiction recovery journey?

Do I believe in my ability to achieve long-term recovery, and if not, what steps can I take to cultivate self-belief?

Am I open to learning from my mistakes and setbacks in recovery, or do I tend to react negatively to them?

How can I improve my communication with myself and with my support network to enhance my recovery experience?

What steps can I take to maintain a positive and resilient personal energy throughout my recovery journey?

A Journey of Transformation

Raising Vibrational Frequency through Positivity and Alignment in Addiction Recovery

Recovery from addiction is a challenging journey that requires profound inner transformation. Beyond the physical aspects of overcoming substance dependency, it involves healing on emotional, mental, and spiritual levels. One often-overlooked but crucial element of this transformation is the concept of raising one's vibrational frequency through positivity and alignment. This book delves into the significance of this approach in the context of addiction recovery, highlighting the importance of truth, self-acceptance, and inner guidance.

The Power of Truth and Authenticity

The adage, "Hurting someone with the truth is better than making them happy with a lie," carries a profound message for individuals seeking long-term recovery from addiction. Honesty, both with oneself and with others, is an essential foundation for healing. Admitting the reality of addiction and its impact is a courageous step toward recovery. It is through truth and authenticity that individuals can shed the layers of denial and self-deception that often accompany addiction.

Negativity and Its Detrimental Effects

Negativity, whether self-inflicted or coming from external sources, can be a significant barrier to recovery. It is essential to recognize that not everyone will support or understand the journey to sobriety. The statement, "Don't let anyone bring you down. Be yourself and ignore the negativity," underscores the importance of maintaining a positive outlook and staying true to one's path, even in the face of criticism or doubt.

The Strength in Letting Go

Addiction often involves clinging to destructive patterns, relationships, or substances. However, true strength lies in knowing when to let go. The act of giving up in the context of addiction recovery does not signify weakness but rather an acknowledgment of one's own well-being. The statement, "Giving up doesn't always mean you're weak, sometimes it means you are strong and smart enough to let go and move on," reflects the wisdom of choosing recovery over continued suffering.

Embracing Change and Transformation

Recovery is a journey of profound transformation, and it requires individuals to let go of the past and embrace change. When an individual finally releases the grip of addiction and the baggage of their history, they open themselves up to the possibility of something better. Recovery is not merely about abstaining from substances; it is about discovering a new way of living and finding fulfillment in healthier pursuits.

Seeking Answers Within

External advice and opinions have their place, but true wisdom and guidance come from within. The statement, "Stop looking for the answers from strangers. The answers to your life are within you and you only," underscores the importance of self-awareness and introspection in addiction recovery. Each individual's path to sobriety is unique, and the answers lie within their own hearts and minds.

The Power of Self-Reflection

To tap into the inner wisdom and guidance, one must learn to ask the right questions and listen to their inner voice. Self-reflection is a powerful tool in raising one's vibrational frequency and aligning with their true self. It allows individuals to explore their values, desires, and goals, paving the way for a more purposeful and fulfilling life in recovery.

In the pursuit of long-term recovery from addiction, the concept of raising one's vibrational frequency through positivity and alignment is paramount. Honesty, authenticity, and the strength to let go of negativity and destructive patterns are vital components of this transformative journey. Recovery is a process of self-discovery and inner guidance, where the answers to a fulfilling life in sobriety are found within. By embracing truth, self-acceptance, and self-reflection, individuals can raise their vibrational frequency and align with their true selves, leading to a more fulfilling and sustainable recovery.

Self-Reflection Questions:

How do I currently view the concept of truth and authenticity in my addiction recovery journey? Is there room for improvement in being more honest with myself and others?

How do I handle negativity and criticism from others regarding my recovery journey? Do I let it affect my progress, and if so, how can I better ignore negativity?

Have I recognized the strength in letting go of destructive patterns or relationships in my life as part of my recovery process?

How can I embrace change and transformation as a positive force in my recovery journey, rather than resisting it?

Am I actively seeking answers and guidance from within myself through self-reflection and introspection? What can I do to improve my ability to listen to my inner voice and align with my true self?

A Journey of Transformation

Practicing Mindfulness and Meditation in the Journey of Addiction Recovery

Recovery from addiction is a deeply personal and transformative journey that often involves addressing not only the physical aspects of addiction but also the emotional and mental dimensions. One powerful and holistic approach to addiction recovery is the practice of mindfulness and meditation. This book explores the significance of incorporating mindfulness and meditation into the recovery process, emphasizing the role of choice, positive thinking, and resilience in shaping one's destiny.

The Power of Choice and Mindfulness

The statement, "Destiny is not a matter of chance; but a matter of choice. It is not a thing to be waited for, It is a thing to be achieved," underscores the importance of personal agency in shaping one's life. Mindfulness is about being fully present in the moment and making conscious choices. In the context of addiction recovery, it involves making the choice to heal, to seek help, and to transform one's life.

Aligning Thoughts with Desires

Our thoughts have a profound impact on our actions and outcomes. The destiny we create is closely tied to the thoughts we habitually entertain. When our thoughts align with our desires for a healthier, addiction-free life, we move closer to achieving that destiny. Practicing mindfulness can help individuals become aware of their thought patterns and make positive changes.

Taking Responsibility for Our Fate

It is common for people to blame external factors like nature and fate for their circumstances, but the statement suggests that our fate is largely a reflection of our character, passions, mistakes, and weaknesses. In addiction recovery, taking responsibility for one's actions and choices is a crucial step toward lasting change. Mindfulness encourages individuals to confront their past and present, allowing for personal growth and accountability.

Embracing the Present and Loved Ones

Addiction often leads individuals to neglect the present moment and the people who care about them. Mindfulness teaches us to adapt to the life we have been given and truly appreciate the present. Loving and cherishing the people who surround us, even in the face of our past mistakes, can be a powerful motivator for recovery.

The Power of Positive Thinking

The phrase, "Positive anything is better than negative thinking," highlights the importance of maintaining a positive mindset in addiction recovery. Positive thinking can be a source of motivation, resilience, and hope. It counteracts the negativity that often accompanies addiction and empowers individuals to believe in their capacity for change.

Resilience and Perseverance

Success in addiction recovery is closely linked to action and resilience. The statement, "Success seems to be connected with action. Successful people keep moving. They make mistakes but don't quit," emphasizes that recovery is not a linear path. Mistakes and setbacks are part of the journey, but they should not deter individuals from pursuing their goals. Mindfulness and meditation provide tools for coping with challenges and bouncing back from setbacks.

Practicing mindfulness and meditation in the journey of addiction recovery is a powerful and transformative approach. It empowers individuals to make conscious choices, align their thoughts with their desires, take responsibility for their fate, and embrace the present moment and loved ones. Positive thinking and resilience are essential elements that can help individuals persevere in their recovery journey. By incorporating these practices, individuals can take active steps towards achieving their destiny of a healthier, addiction-free life.

Self-Reflection Questions:

How mindful am I in my addiction recovery journey? Do I consciously make choices that align with my desire for a better, addiction-free life?

What habitual thought patterns do I recognize in myself, and how do they impact my recovery efforts? How can I cultivate more positive thoughts that support my goals?

Do I take full responsibility for my actions and choices in the context of addiction recovery, or do I tend to blame external factors?

How can I better embrace the present moment and express love and gratitude toward the people who support me in my recovery?

What steps can I take to maintain a positive mindset and practice resilience when faced with challenges and setbacks in my recovery journey?

Techniques for Centering Oneself and Managing Energy in Addiction Recovery

Recovery from addiction is a challenging and transformative journey that demands a holistic approach. Beyond addressing the physical aspects of addiction, it is crucial to manage one's emotional and mental well-being. This book explores the significance of centering oneself and managing energy as essential techniques in addiction recovery, emphasizing self-worth, facing challenges, self-compassion, and the power of prayer.

A Journey of Transformation

Self-Worth and Personal Growth

Every day presents an opportunity for personal growth and self-improvement. The statement, "Every single day, you should wake up and commit yourself to becoming a better person," emphasizes the importance of self-commitment in addiction recovery. It is essential not to let external judgments define one's self-worth. Recovery is a journey of self-discovery and self-improvement, and individuals should focus on their progress and personal growth.

Facing Challenges and Avoiding Denial

Ignoring problems and challenges does not make them disappear; instead, it postpones the inevitable and often makes them more daunting. The statement, "Ignoring things won't make them go away. It only makes it harder to face them when they finally come around," underscores the importance of confronting issues in addiction recovery. It is crucial to acknowledge the challenges and obstacles on the path to recovery and address them with resilience and determination.

Self-Compassion and Acknowledging Difficulty

Addiction recovery can be an arduous journey, and it is essential to be kind to oneself throughout the process. The statement, "Be kind to yourself. Stop telling yourself that whatever you are struggling with 'should' be easy. If something is hard for you, it is hard for you. Acknowledge these things," highlights the importance of self-compassion. It is okay to acknowledge that recovery is difficult and to treat oneself with the same kindness and understanding given to others.

Embracing Happiness and Celebrating Success

Life is fleeting, and happiness should not be postponed. The statement, "Life passes by so fast. Whatever makes you happy, that's what you should do," encourages individuals in recovery to pursue happiness and engage in activities that bring joy. Additionally, celebrating achievements, no matter how small, is an essential aspect of boosting one's self-esteem and motivation during recovery. When you finish something challenging, be proud of yourself.

The Power of Prayer and Spirituality

Spirituality and prayer can be powerful sources of strength and support in addiction recovery. The statement, "Never underestimate the power of prayer, because it may have been a prayer once that saved you," underscores the importance of spirituality as a grounding force. For many individuals, prayer provides a sense of connection, purpose, and guidance in their recovery journey.

Centering oneself and managing energy are essential techniques that can significantly enhance the quality of life in addiction recovery. These techniques emphasize self-worth, the importance of facing challenges, self-compassion, the pursuit of happiness, and the power of spirituality and prayer. By incorporating these practices into their daily lives, individuals can find greater resilience, self-acceptance, and motivation to overcome the challenges of addiction recovery.

Self-Reflection Questions:

How do I view my self-worth in the context of my addiction recovery journey? Do I let external judgments define my sense of value, or do I focus on self-improvement and personal growth?

Am I proactive in facing challenges and addressing obstacles in my recovery, or do I tend to avoid or postpone them?

How can I cultivate greater self-compassion and kindness toward myself as I navigate the difficulties of addiction recovery?

What activities bring me happiness and fulfillment in my recovery journey, and am I making time for them in my life?

Do I incorporate spirituality or prayer into my recovery process? How has it contributed to my sense of purpose and strength on this journey?

Harnessing the Power of Focused Intention in Addiction Recovery

Recovery from addiction is a profound transformation that requires a combination of inner strength, determination, and the power of focused intention. This book explores the significance of harnessing the power of focused intention in addiction recovery, emphasizing the importance of non-judgment, overcoming the past, embracing the present, and maintaining a positive mindset.

Non-Judgment and Embracing Hearts

The statement, "Do not judge people by the scriptures of their faith or the scars from their past, embrace them by the content of their hearts," underscores the value of compassion and empathy in addiction recovery. Judgment and stigmatization can be barriers to healing, both for oneself and for others. Embracing people for who they are at their core, rather than dwelling on their past mistakes, is essential for fostering a supportive and non-judgmental recovery environment.

Letting Go of the Past

The past can be a weight that hinders progress in the present. The statement, "No one can control what happened in the past. It's gone and it's over. Don't allow the past to hinder us from getting to the place in life where we want to be," highlights the importance of letting go of the past in addiction recovery. Forgiving oneself and focusing on the present moment can free individuals from the shackles of regret and guilt, allowing them to move forward.

A Journey of Transformation

Embracing the Present Moment

Life is a collection of moments, and each one is unique. The statement, "Life becomes more meaningful when we realize the simple fact that we'll never get the same moment twice," encourages individuals to be present and fully engage in their recovery journey. By embracing the present moment, individuals can find meaning and purpose in their daily lives, which can be a powerful motivator for recovery.

The Futility of Worrying About the Future

Worrying about the future can be a significant source of anxiety and stress. The statement, "Worrying about the future is tempting but useless. Do the best we can with what's right in front of us, and the future will fall into place," reminds individuals that the future is shaped by the actions they take in the present. Focused intention on the tasks at hand and making the best of the current moment can pave the way for a brighter future.

Maintaining a Positive Mindset

A positive mindset is a vital asset in addiction recovery. The statement, "Stay strong, be positive. We all struggle sometimes... and that's okay. Overthinking is the biggest cause of our unhappiness. Keep ourselves occupied. Keep our mind off things that don't help us. Think positive," emphasizes the importance of maintaining a positive and constructive outlook. Positive thinking can boost resilience and provide the motivation needed to overcome the challenges of addiction recovery.

Harnessing the power of focused intention in addiction recovery is a transformative and empowering approach. It involves embracing non-judgment, letting go of the past, embracing the present moment, and maintaining a positive mindset. By incorporating these practices into their recovery journey, individuals can find greater peace, purpose, and motivation on the path to long-term recovery.

Self-Reflection Questions:

> How do I perceive judgment and stigmatization in the context of my addiction recovery journey, both from myself and from others?

> Am I holding onto past mistakes and regrets that are hindering my progress in the present? How can I work on letting go of the past?

> Do I actively embrace and engage in the present moment, finding meaning and purpose in my daily life?

> How much of my mental energy is spent worrying about the future? What steps can I take to focus on the present and trust that the future will fall into place?

What strategies do I currently use to maintain a positive mindset in my recovery journey, and how can I further strengthen my resilience through positive thinking?

Manifestation as a Catalyst for Transformation

Recovery from addiction is a journey filled with challenges and triumphs, and it often requires a deep sense of purpose and determination. Manifestation, the process of turning thoughts and intentions into reality, can serve as a powerful catalyst for transformation in addiction recovery. This book explores the significance of manifestation in the context of addiction recovery, emphasizing the value of resilience, hope, and focusing on the journey's transformative moments.

Embracing the Journey

The statement, "Beginnings are usually scary and endings are usually sad, but it's everything in between that makes it all worth living," underscores the idea that recovery is not just about achieving sobriety but also about embracing the entire journey. Manifestation in recovery involves setting intentions and goals for personal growth, healing, and positive change. It is the journey itself, with all its ups and downs, that makes life worth living.

Finding Strength and Comfort

Addiction recovery is often accompanied by moments of pain and sorrow. However, the statement, "The Lord didn't promise days without pain, laughter without sorrow, or sun without rain, but He did promise strength for the day, comfort for the tears, and light for the way," reminds individuals that they are not alone in their struggles. Manifestation can involve seeking strength, comfort, and guidance from a higher power or from within, leading to greater resilience and inner peace.

Discovering Inner Resilience

Sometimes, the strength required for recovery only becomes apparent when it becomes the only choice. The statement, "You never know how strong you are until being strong is the only choice you have," emphasizes the hidden reservoirs of strength that individuals can tap into during their recovery journey. Manifestation involves believing in one's ability to overcome challenges and make positive changes, even in the face of adversity.

Living for Tomorrow's Potential

Addiction often leaves individuals dwelling on the past and its losses. However, the statement, "Live for what tomorrow has to bring not for what yesterday has taken away," encourages individuals to focus on the potential and opportunities of the future. Manifestation in recovery involves setting intentions for a brighter and healthier tomorrow, allowing individuals to move forward with hope and purpose.

A Journey of Transformation

The Role of Hope and Faith

Hope and faith are integral components of manifestation in addiction recovery. The statement, "If God brings you to it, He will bring you through it," reflects the belief that there is a guiding force, whether it be a higher power or one's inner strength, that can lead individuals through the challenges of recovery. Manifestation involves nurturing hope and faith in the possibility of transformation.

Manifestation is a powerful catalyst for transformation in addiction recovery, allowing individuals to set intentions for personal growth, resilience, and positive change. It involves embracing the entire journey, finding strength and comfort in difficult moments, discovering inner resilience, living for the potential of tomorrow, and nurturing hope and faith. By incorporating manifestation into their recovery journey, individuals can create a path to lasting transformation and a life filled with purpose and fulfillment.

Self-Reflection Questions:

How do I currently perceive my recovery journey, and am I focusing on the entire journey or just the end goal of sobriety?

How do I seek strength and comfort during difficult moments in my recovery, and how can I incorporate manifestation into this process?

Have I discovered hidden reservoirs of strength within myself during my recovery journey? How can I further tap into this inner resilience?

Am I living in the present and focusing on the potential of tomorrow, or do I dwell on the losses of the past?

How does hope and faith play a role in my recovery journey, and how can I nurture these beliefs to support my transformation?

How Thoughts, Beliefs, and Actions Shape Reality in Addiction Recovery

Recovery from addiction is a journey that not only involves overcoming physical dependency but also reshaping one's thoughts, beliefs, and actions to create a brighter and healthier future. This book explores the profound influence of thoughts, beliefs, and actions in shaping the reality of addiction recovery, emphasizing the importance of positivity, self-starting, living in the present, and trusting the journey.

The Power of Positivity and Attitude

The journey to recovery can be daunting, but the statement, "Don't expect to achieve your best while you expect the worst," reminds individuals of the transformative power of positivity and a positive attitude. Believing in the possibility of change and adopting a more positive outlook can pave the way for progress and growth in recovery. Great things are indeed possible when one approaches recovery with optimism.

Welcoming Each Day with Gratitude

Each new day in recovery is an opportunity for growth and transformation. The statement, "Welcome every morning with a smile. Look on the new day as another special gift from your Creator, another golden opportunity to complete what you were unable to finish yesterday," highlights the importance of starting each day with gratitude and enthusiasm. This positive mindset can set the tone for a day filled with purpose and achievement.

Becoming a Self-Starter

Initiating positive actions and maintaining momentum are critical in addiction recovery. The statement, "Be a self-starter. Let your first hour set the theme of success and positive action that is certain to echo through your entire day," emphasizes the importance of taking the initiative to make each day productive. By starting the day with intention and positive action, individuals can cultivate a pattern of success in recovery.

Living in the Present Moment

Worrying about the future can be counterproductive in addiction recovery. The statement, "Worrying about the future is tempting but useless. Do the best you can with what's right in front of you, and the future will fall into place," underscores the significance of living in the present moment and making the most of the opportunities at hand. By focusing on the present, individuals can build a foundation for a brighter future.

Trusting the Journey of Recovery

The belief that one was not born to fail is a powerful mindset for addiction recovery. Trusting in the journey of recovery and one's own ability to overcome challenges is a fundamental element of success. By maintaining faith in the process, individuals can navigate the ups and downs of recovery with resilience and determination.

In addiction recovery, thoughts, beliefs, and actions play a pivotal role in shaping one's reality. Positivity and a positive attitude can bring about transformation, while welcoming each day with gratitude can set the stage for success. Being a self-starter and living in the present moment are essential for building a strong foundation for recovery. Finally, trusting the journey and believing in one's own potential are crucial elements that can lead to long-term sobriety and a fulfilling life.

A Journey of Transformation

Self-Reflection Questions:

How do I perceive the role of positivity and attitude in my recovery journey? Am I fostering a positive mindset to support my progress?

Do I start each day with gratitude and enthusiasm, seeing it as an opportunity for growth and achievement in my recovery?

Am I actively taking the initiative and making positive actions to set a productive tone for my day in recovery?

How much of my mental energy is spent worrying about the future, and how can I redirect that energy toward living in the present moment?

Do I trust in the journey of recovery and believe in my own potential for success? How can I cultivate greater faith in the process?

The Role of Mindset in Achieving Transformation
Goals in Addiction Recovery

Recovery from addiction is a transformative journey that requires not only physical changes but also a profound shift in mindset. This book explores the pivotal role of mindset in achieving transformation goals in addiction recovery, emphasizing the importance of happiness from within, the power of choice, setting positive intentions, and cherishing the uniqueness of each moment.

Happiness from Within

The statement, "So many people have so little but still find a way to be happy. It just goes to show that happiness comes from within you, not material things or people," highlights the fundamental truth that happiness is an internal state of being. In addiction recovery, individuals often seek fulfillment and happiness through sobriety and personal growth. A positive mindset starts with the recognition that true happiness arises from within, not external sources.

Chasing vs. Choosing Happiness

The choice between chasing and choosing happiness is a critical aspect of mindset in recovery. The statement, "You can CHASE happiness or you can CHOOSE happiness... it all depends on how much time you want to save!" underscores that happiness is not an elusive goal to chase after but a conscious choice to be made in every moment. A positive mindset in recovery involves actively choosing happiness, even in the face of challenges.

Setting Positive Intentions

Intentions are powerful drivers of behavior and outcomes. The statement, "Try to find the place in your mind where you have already decided how good today will be, how good this year will be, how good your life will be," encourages individuals to set positive intentions for their recovery journey. By consciously deciding to make each day and each year better and more enjoyable, individuals can create a mindset conducive to transformation and growth.

Cherishing Unique Moments

Every moment in life is unique and irreplaceable. The statement, "Life becomes more meaningful when you realize the simple fact that you'll never get the same moment twice," reminds individuals to cherish the present moment. In addiction recovery, this means recognizing the opportunities for growth and transformation that each moment presents. A positive mindset involves embracing the uniqueness of each day in the journey toward long-term recovery.

The role of mindset in achieving transformation goals in addiction recovery cannot be overstated. A positive mindset involves understanding that happiness comes from within, actively choosing happiness, setting positive intentions, and cherishing the uniqueness of each moment. By cultivating a mindset that supports personal growth and transformation, individuals can navigate the challenges of addiction recovery with resilience and hope.

Self-Reflection Questions:

How do I currently perceive happiness in the context of my addiction recovery journey? Do I recognize that it comes from within, or do I seek it externally?

Am I actively choosing happiness in my recovery journey, even in the face of challenges and setbacks? How can I strengthen my ability to make this choice?

Have I set positive intentions for my recovery, both for the present and the future? How can I ensure that these intentions guide my actions?

Do I appreciate the uniqueness of each moment in my recovery journey, recognizing the opportunities for growth and transformation? How can I better embrace the present moment?

How can I cultivate and maintain a positive mindset that supports my long-term recovery goals and personal growth?

A Journey of Transformation

Using Visualization and Affirmations in the Journey of Addiction Recovery

Recovery from addiction is a deeply personal and transformative journey that requires a multifaceted approach. Visualization and affirmations are powerful tools that can play a significant role in this process. This book explores the importance of using visualization and affirmations in addiction recovery, highlighting the significance of understanding, patience, embracing adversity, resilience, and the power of kindness.

Listening with the Intent to Understand

The statement, "Most people do not listen with the intent to understand; they listen with the intent to reply," underscores the importance of empathetic communication in addiction recovery. Visualization and affirmations are not just about self-reflection but also about understanding others and the impact of one's actions on them. By listening and empathizing with others, individuals can build stronger connections and support networks in their recovery.

Being the Best Self

In addiction recovery, it is crucial to strive to be the best version of oneself. Visualization and affirmations can help individuals set intentions for personal growth and transformation. The statement, "Be yourself, but be your best self," encourages individuals to embrace their authentic selves while continuously working towards self-improvement.

Patience and Embracing Change

Patience is a virtue that is particularly important in addiction recovery. The statement, "Be patient. Things will change for the better," reminds individuals that recovery is a process, and positive change takes time. Visualization and affirmations can help individuals maintain a patient and positive mindset as they navigate the challenges of recovery.

Embracing Understanding and Adversity

Addiction recovery often involves confronting personal struggles and adversity. The statement, "The day we let go of fear and instead embrace understanding is the day we begin to live," emphasizes the transformative power of understanding and acceptance. Visualization and affirmations can support individuals in letting go of fear and embracing the difficulties of their journey, knowing that growth arises from adversity.

Resilience and Strength

Resilience is a key attribute that individuals develop on their path to recovery. The statement, "Greatness comes not when things go always good for us, but greatness comes when we're really tested, when we take some knocks, some disappointments, when sadness comes," highlights the strength that can emerge from facing adversity. Visualization and affirmations can help individuals tap into their inner resilience and find the motivation to persevere.

Focusing on Positives and Practicing Kindness

Positivity and kindness are essential elements of a successful recovery journey. The statement, "Focus on the positives, and soon the negatives will disappear," encourages individuals to shift their focus toward the good in their lives. Additionally, the statement, "Everyone we meet is fighting a battle we know nothing about. Be kind," underscores the importance of compassion and empathy in recovery. Visualization and affirmations can promote a positive and kind outlook on life and interactions with others.

Finding What Is Truly Important

Addiction recovery often prompts individuals to reevaluate their priorities. The statement, "Always ask ourselves what is really important, and then have the wisdom and courage to build our life around our answer," encourages individuals to align their actions and choices with their values and what truly matters to them. Visualization and affirmations can help individuals clarify their goals and stay committed to their recovery journey.

Using visualization and affirmations is a powerful approach in addiction recovery. It involves understanding others, striving to be one's best self, practicing patience, embracing adversity, nurturing resilience, focusing on positivity, showing kindness, and aligning one's life with what is truly important. By incorporating these practices into their recovery journey, individuals can find greater strength, purpose, and transformation on the path to long-term recovery.

Self-Reflection Questions:

> How well do I listen to others in my recovery journey, and am I genuinely seeking to understand their perspectives and challenges?
>
> How do I currently envision and affirm my best self in the context of addiction recovery, and what intentions have I set for my personal growth?
>
> Am I practicing patience in my recovery and embracing the changes that come with it?
>
> How can I use visualization and affirmations to let go of fear and better understand and embrace the adversities in my recovery journey?
>
> In what ways do I focus on the positives and practice kindness in my interactions with others? How can I further develop these qualities?

A Journey of Transformation

Visualizing Goals as Already Achieved:
A Powerful Tool in Addiction Recovery

Recovery from addiction is a journey marked by transformation, growth, and healing. One effective strategy in this journey is visualizing goals as already achieved. This book explores the profound impact of visualization in addiction recovery, emphasizing the importance of removing unnecessary problems, directing positivity toward the good, finding purpose in trials, and maintaining unwavering faith.

Deleting Unnecessary Problems

The statement, "When you delete the unnecessary problems from your life, good things will start happening for you and it won't be a coincidence," highlights the significance of decluttering one's life, both internally and externally. Visualization in addiction recovery involves identifying and eliminating detrimental factors, such as negative influences, enabling behaviors, and self-destructive habits. By clearing the path of unnecessary problems, individuals create space for positive change and growth.

Directing Positivity Toward the Good

In addiction recovery, it is essential to focus on the positive aspects of life. The statement, "Find something good within your life and give every ounce of positivity you have towards it, then watch how your life changes," emphasizes the transformative power of positive thinking and intention. Visualization encourages individuals to identify sources of positivity and direct their energy and attention toward these aspects, fostering an environment conducive to recovery.

Turning Mess into a Message

Trials and challenges are an inherent part of the recovery journey. However, these difficulties can be transformed into sources of inspiration and motivation. The statement, "Let your mess be your message. Don't let your trials get you down, but let them inspire someone else," encourages individuals to view their personal struggles as opportunities to inspire others who may be facing similar challenges. Visualization enables individuals to see their past as a stepping stone to a brighter future.

Preserving Faith Amidst Problems

Maintaining faith and hope is paramount in addiction recovery. The statement, "Never let your problems ruin your faith," underscores the importance of resilience and unwavering belief in the possibility of recovery. Visualization involves visualizing one's goals as already achieved, reinforcing the idea that faith and positivity can lead to the desired outcome.

Visualizing goals as already achieved is a potent tool in addiction recovery. It involves removing unnecessary problems, directing positivity toward the good, turning personal trials into sources of inspiration, and preserving unwavering faith. By incorporating these practices into their recovery journey, individuals can harness the power of visualization to manifest their goals and transform their lives.

Self-Reflection Questions:

What unnecessary problems or negative influences are currently present in my life that may hinder my recovery journey, and how can I address or eliminate them?

Do I actively seek out sources of positivity in my life, and how can I redirect my energy and attention toward these aspects to enhance my recovery?

Have I considered how my personal struggles in addiction recovery can serve as sources of inspiration for others facing similar challenges?

How strong is my faith and belief in the possibility of recovery? In what ways can I reinforce and maintain my faith throughout my journey?

How can I use visualization to not only set goals but also to believe in their achievement, ultimately contributing to my long-term recovery?

Creating and Repeating Affirmations:
Empowering Positive Beliefs in Addiction Recovery

Recovery from addiction is a challenging but transformative journey that can be supported by the practice of creating and repeating affirmations. This book explores the vital role of affirmations in addiction recovery, highlighting the importance of eliminating unnecessary problems, focusing on positivity, finding purpose in adversity, and nurturing unshakable faith.

Eliminating Unnecessary Problems

The statement, "When you delete the unnecessary problems from your life, good things will start happening for you, and it won't be a coincidence," underscores the need to declutter one's life for successful recovery. Creating affirmations involves identifying and addressing issues that hinder progress, such as negative influences, unhealthy habits, or self-destructive thought patterns. By affirming the removal of these problems, individuals pave the way for positive change.

Focusing on Positivity

Positivity is a cornerstone of successful addiction recovery. The statement, "Find something good within your life and give every ounce of positivity you have towards it, then watch how your life changes," emphasizes the transformative power of positive thinking and affirmation. Creating and repeating affirmations enables individuals to identify and amplify sources of positivity, fostering an environment conducive to recovery.

A Journey of Transformation

Turning Adversity into Inspiration

Trials and challenges are inherent in the recovery process. However, they can be transformed into sources of inspiration and motivation. The statement, "Let your mess be your message. Don't let your trials get you down, but let them inspire someone else," encourages individuals to view their struggles as opportunities to inspire others facing similar difficulties. Affirmations help individuals affirm their resilience and ability to inspire others through their journey.

Preserving Faith Amidst Problems

Maintaining faith and hope is crucial in addiction recovery. The statement, "Never let your problems ruin your faith," highlights the importance of unwavering belief in the possibility of recovery. Creating and repeating affirmations reinforces the idea that faith and positivity can lead to the desired outcome, even in the face of challenges.

Self-Reflection Questions:

What unnecessary problems or negative influences are currently present in my life that may hinder my recovery journey, and how can I address or eliminate them through affirmations?

Do I actively seek out sources of positivity in my life, and how can I create affirmations that redirect my energy and attention toward these aspects to enhance my recovery?

Have I considered how my personal struggles in addiction recovery can serve as sources of inspiration for others facing similar challenges? How can I create affirmations to reinforce this perspective?

How strong is my faith and belief in the possibility of recovery? How can I use affirmations to maintain and strengthen my faith throughout my journey?

In what ways can I incorporate affirmations into my daily routine to not only set positive beliefs but also to reinforce and manifest my goals in addiction recovery?

Goals and Alignment

Long-term recovery from addiction is a transformative process that requires setting and aligning goals with one's aspirations and values. This book explores the importance of goals and alignment in addiction recovery, emphasizing the power of silent support, facing fears, trusting the journey, setting standards, taking action, embracing dreams, and self-acceptance as essential elements on the path to recovery.

Silent Presence in Storms

The statement, "When people are going through a storm, your silent presence is more powerful than a million empty words," underscores the significance of being there for individuals in recovery. Silent support and understanding can be more meaningful than mere words. In addiction recovery, offering a listening ear and a non-judgmental presence can provide valuable comfort and encouragement.

Facing Fears

Addiction recovery often involves confronting deep-seated fears and uncertainties. The statement, "Maybe the thing you're most scared of is exactly what you should do," encourages individuals to confront their fears head-on. Setting recovery goals may involve stepping out of one's comfort zone and facing uncomfortable truths. By addressing fears and anxieties, individuals can make progress towards their recovery.

Trusting the Journey

Trust is a crucial element of addiction recovery. The statement, "Don't worry. If it's supposed to happen, it will," reminds individuals to trust the process of recovery. Setting goals and aligning them with one's values and aspirations is an act of faith. Believing in the journey and the possibility of lasting recovery is essential for success.

Setting Standards

In addiction recovery, having standards is key to maintaining progress. The statement, "Without standards, you'll settle for anything," emphasizes the importance of setting boundaries and expectations. Goal-setting in recovery involves defining what one will and will not accept, which can help individuals stay on track and avoid relapse triggers.

Taking Action on Dreams

Dreams and aspirations are powerful motivators in recovery. The statement, "Rise up & become what you hope to attract!" encourages individuals to take action to achieve their dreams. Setting

A Journey of Transformation

recovery goals is about aligning one's actions with their aspirations. By working diligently towards their dreams, individuals can create lasting change in their lives.

Embracing Self-Acceptance

Self-acceptance is a cornerstone of addiction recovery. The statement, "Always accept and feel comfortable with your flaws, that way no one can ever use them against you," highlights the importance of embracing one's imperfections and vulnerabilities. Setting goals in recovery involves recognizing one's strengths and weaknesses and working towards self-improvement with self-compassion.

Self-Reflection Questions:

How can I offer silent support and understanding to those in my life who are in recovery from addiction?

What are the fears and uncertainties that I need to face in my own recovery journey? How can I confront them to progress further?

Do I trust the process of recovery and the journey I am on? How can I strengthen my belief in the possibility of lasting recovery?

Have I set clear standards and boundaries for myself in my recovery? How can I ensure that I maintain these standards?

What dreams and aspirations drive my recovery journey, and how can I take action to align my actions with these aspirations?

Am I embracing self-acceptance and self-compassion in my recovery, recognizing that flaws are part of being human? How can I use self-acceptance to support my goals in recovery?

The Importance of Ongoing Goal Refinement in the Journey of Addiction Recovery

Long-term recovery from addiction is a dynamic process that involves setting and refining goals to align with one's values and aspirations. This book explores the significance of ongoing goal refinement in addiction recovery, emphasizing the need to embrace both joy and sorrow, confront fear, adapt to change, discern what is truly beneficial, prioritize meaningful pursuits, take ownership of choices, and embrace the opportunity for a fresh start.

Embracing Joy and Sorrow

The statement, "We can't protect ourselves from sadness without protecting ourselves from happiness," highlights the interconnected nature of joy and sorrow in life. In addiction recovery, individuals may encounter both moments of triumph and setbacks. Ongoing goal refinement involves accepting the full spectrum of emotions and experiences and learning from both the highs and lows of the journey.

Confronting Fear

Fear can be a powerful barrier in addiction recovery. The statement, "We have to decide that we want it more than we are afraid of it," emphasizes the importance of confronting fear head-on. Ongoing goal refinement may require individuals to face their fears and take steps towards their desired future, even when it feels challenging or uncomfortable.

Adapting to Change

Change is a constant in the recovery journey. The statement, "Sometimes good things fall apart so better things can fall together," suggests that setbacks and changes can lead to greater opportunities for growth and transformation. Ongoing goal refinement involves adapting to new circumstances, reassessing priorities, and remaining flexible in the pursuit of recovery goals.

Discerning What Is Truly Beneficial

Not all things that seem good are genuinely beneficial in the context of addiction recovery. The statement, "We have to realize that some things that are good TO us just aren't always good FOR us," underscores the importance of discernment. Ongoing goal refinement requires individuals to evaluate whether their goals align with their recovery and overall well-being.

Prioritizing Meaningful Pursuits

Success in recovery is not solely defined by external achievements. The statement, "Our greatest fear shouldn't be of failure, but of succeeding at things in life that don't really matter," encourages individuals to prioritize meaningful pursuits aligned with their values. Ongoing goal refinement involves setting goals that contribute to a fulfilling and purposeful life in recovery.

Taking Ownership of Choices

Taking responsibility for one's choices and actions is a crucial aspect of addiction recovery. The statement, "We must take responsibility for our own choices and actions, for we learn nothing until we take ownership of our life," highlights the need for self-accountability. Ongoing goal refinement empowers individuals to make conscious choices that support their recovery journey.

Embracing Fresh Starts

Every day is an opportunity for a fresh start in addiction recovery. The statement, "Every day is a NEW beginning, take a deep breath and START AGAIN," reminds individuals that recovery is an ongoing process of growth and renewal. Ongoing goal refinement involves approaching each day

A Journey of Transformation

with a sense of possibility and the determination to continue the journey toward long-term recovery.

Self-Reflection Questions:

How do I handle both moments of joy and setbacks in my recovery journey, and how can I use these experiences to refine my goals?

What fears or obstacles am I currently facing in my recovery, and how can I make a conscious decision to prioritize recovery over fear?

How adaptable am I to change in my recovery journey, and how can I embrace change as an opportunity for growth and refinement?

Are my current goals truly aligned with my recovery and well-being, or do I need to reassess and refine them?

What meaningful pursuits and values are guiding my recovery, and how can I ensure that my goals prioritize what truly matters to me?

Am I taking full ownership of my choices and actions in my recovery journey, and how can I further develop self-accountability?

How can I embrace each new day as an opportunity for a fresh start and use ongoing goal refinement to support my long-term recovery goals?

Regularly Reviewing and Adjusting Objectives in the Journey of Addiction Recovery

Addiction recovery is a complex and evolving process that requires constant adaptation to changing circumstances and personal growth. This book explores the importance of regularly reviewing and adjusting objectives in addiction recovery, emphasizing the value of embracing life as it is, learning from experience, surrendering control, seeking understanding, taking small steps, and seeing situations from a new perspective.

Embracing Life as It Is

The statement, "Happiness is letting go of what you think your life is supposed to look like and celebrating it for everything that it is," reminds us that true happiness is found in accepting and appreciating our lives as they are. In addiction recovery, individuals often have preconceived notions about what their journey should look like. Regularly reviewing and adjusting objectives allows for a more realistic and fulfilling experience of recovery.

Learning from Experience

Experience is a valuable teacher in addiction recovery. The statement, "Sometimes you have to experience what you don't want in life to come to a full understanding of what you do want," highlights the importance of learning from past mistakes and missteps. By regularly reviewing objectives and reflecting on past experiences, individuals can refine their goals and aspirations for recovery.

Surrendering Control

Control can be a double-edged sword in recovery. The statement, "Maybe it's okay that you don't know what's going to happen. Maybe you should stop predicting and controlling and enjoy each moment as it comes," encourages individuals to let go of the need for absolute control. Regularly adjusting objectives requires a degree of flexibility and openness to the unknown, allowing room for growth and unexpected opportunities.

Seeking Understanding

Understanding others and their perspectives is crucial in addiction recovery. The statement, "If you can't change people, understand them better," suggests that empathy and understanding can be more effective than attempting to change others. Regularly reviewing and adjusting objectives involves considering the impact of relationships and interactions on one's recovery journey.

Taking Small Steps

In recovery, progress often comes from taking small steps. The statement, "Sometimes the smallest step in the right direction ends up being the biggest step of your life," reminds individuals that incremental changes can lead to significant growth. Regularly reviewing objectives allows for the identification of small, achievable steps that contribute to long-term recovery.

Seeing Situations Differently

Perspective plays a crucial role in how individuals interpret and respond to situations. The statement, "If you can't change the situation, see it differently," encourages individuals to shift their perspective when faced with challenging circumstances. Regularly adjusting objectives involves adapting to changing situations and finding new ways to navigate them.

Self-Reflection Questions:

> Am I embracing my life in recovery for what it is, or do I find myself constantly comparing it to unrealistic expectations?

> What valuable lessons have I learned from my past experiences in addiction recovery, and how can I use these lessons to refine my objectives?

A Journey of Transformation

> Do I have a tendency to overcontrol and predict my recovery journey, and how can I learn to let go and enjoy the present moment more?
>
> How well do I understand the people and relationships that influence my recovery journey, and how can I improve my empathy and understanding?
>
> What small steps can I take in my recovery that will lead me in the right direction, and how can I regularly adjust my objectives to accommodate these steps?
>
> Am I open to seeing challenging situations from a new perspective, and how can I regularly review and adjust my objectives to better navigate these situations?

Ensuring Alignment with the Transformation Vision in Addiction Recovery

Addiction recovery is a profound and transformative journey that requires individuals to align their actions with a vision of personal growth and positive change. This book explores the importance of ensuring alignment with the transformation vision in addiction recovery, emphasizing the significance of self-awareness, authenticity, gradual progress, taking action, and the continuous pursuit of improvement.

The Beginning of Wisdom: Knowing Yourself

The statement, "Knowing yourself is the beginning of all wisdom," underscores the fundamental importance of self-awareness in addiction recovery. Understanding one's strengths, weaknesses, triggers, and motivations is essential for setting a transformational vision. Regular self-reflection helps individuals gain insights into their recovery journey and guides them towards goals that align with their true selves.

Insisting on Authenticity

Authenticity is a key component of successful recovery. The statement, "Insist on yourself, never imitate," encourages individuals to remain true to their unique identities and values. Aligning with a transformation vision means setting goals that reflect one's genuine desires and aspirations rather than conforming to external expectations or societal norms.

Embracing Gradual Progress

Recovery is a gradual process, and progress may not always be rapid. The statement, "Be not afraid of growing slowly; be afraid only of standing still," emphasizes that consistent and incremental progress is more valuable than stagnation. Ensuring alignment with a transformation vision requires patience and a commitment to continuous growth, even when the pace is slow.

Taking Action with Purpose

Action is the driving force behind transformation in recovery. The statement, "Heaven never helps the man who will not act, but God will always work with those who work," reminds individuals that taking purposeful steps towards their vision is essential. Aligning with a transformation vision means translating goals into concrete actions and actively working towards them.

Pursuing Improvement Every Day

Addiction recovery is an ongoing journey of self-improvement. The statement, "Every day, do something that will inch you closer to a better tomorrow," emphasizes the importance of daily efforts to achieve the transformation vision. Regular self-reflection and adjustment of goals help individuals stay committed to their path of recovery and improvement.

Self-Reflection Questions:

How well do I know myself in the context of my addiction recovery journey? What steps can I take to deepen my self-awareness?

Am I staying true to my authentic self and values in my recovery, or am I conforming to external pressures and expectations?

How comfortable am I with the gradual progress in my recovery, and how can I overcome any fears of standing still?

Are my goals in recovery translated into actionable steps, and am I consistently working towards them with purpose?

What daily actions can I take to inch closer to my vision of a better tomorrow in my recovery journey?

How can I ensure that my goals and actions in recovery are continuously aligned with my transformation vision, allowing me to grow and progress effectively?

Setting Intentions and Taking Inspired Actions in Addiction Recovery

The journey of addiction recovery is a path of healing, growth, and transformation. To navigate this challenging journey successfully, individuals must set intentions and take inspired actions that align with their values and aspirations. This book explores the importance of setting intentions and taking inspired actions in addiction recovery, emphasizing the value of perseverance, small acts of kindness, and the profound impact that even the smallest gestures can have on the recovery journey.

A Journey of Transformation

Perseverance in the Face of Challenges

Addiction recovery is often marked by ups and downs, but perseverance is key to long-term success. The statement, "One of the things I learned the hard way was that it doesn't pay to get discouraged," highlights the need to stay resilient and determined, even in the face of setbacks. Setting intentions involves committing to the recovery journey and persistently working toward a healthier, addiction-free life.

Small Acts with Great Love

Recovery is not solely about grand gestures but also about small acts of kindness and compassion. Mother Teresa's statement, "In this life we cannot always do great things, but we can do small things with great love," underscores the transformative power of small acts. Setting intentions for recovery includes showing kindness to oneself and others, embracing self-compassion, and fostering an environment of love and support.

The Power of Action in the Face of Inaction

In addiction recovery, there may be moments when inaction or indifference from others can be disheartening. However, as the statement suggests, "The world is a dangerous place, not because of those who do evil, but because of those who look on and do nothing." Setting intentions involves taking inspired actions that promote healing and positive change, not only for oneself but also for the recovery community as a whole.

The Profound Impact of Small Gestures

Small acts of kindness and care have the potential to make a significant difference in the recovery journey. The statement, "Too often we underestimate the power of a touch, a smile, a kind word, a listening ear, an honest compliment, or the smallest act of caring, all of which have the potential to turn a life around," highlights the ripple effect of such gestures. Setting intentions for recovery includes recognizing the power of these small acts in one's own life and in the lives of others in recovery.

Belief in Purpose and Contribution

Believing in one's ability to make a positive impact in the world is crucial in recovery. The statement, "Believe, when you are most unhappy, that there is something for you to do in the world. So long as you can sweeten another's pain, life is not in vain," encourages individuals to find purpose and fulfillment in helping others. Setting intentions for recovery means actively seeking opportunities to support and uplift those in need.

Self-Reflection Questions:

How do I handle discouragement and setbacks in my recovery journey, and what steps can I take to persevere and stay committed to my intentions?

How can I incorporate small acts of kindness and compassion into my daily life, both for myself and for others in recovery?

What inspired actions can I take to contribute positively to the recovery community, and how can I combat indifference and inaction?

Have I recognized the profound impact that small gestures of care and support can have on my own recovery journey and the journeys of others?

How can I find meaning and purpose in my recovery by seeking opportunities to sweeten the pain of others and make a positive difference in their lives?

Developing a Habit of Setting Daily Intentions in Addiction Recovery

Addiction recovery is a journey of healing, self-discovery, and transformation. One powerful tool for navigating this path is the daily practice of setting intentions. This book explores the importance of developing a habit of setting daily intentions in addiction recovery, emphasizing the value of resilience, embracing change, acknowledging emotions, and maintaining positivity, patience, and faith throughout the journey.

Resilience in Picking Up the Pieces

Life often presents us with challenges that can leave us feeling broken. However, as the statement suggests, "We all at certain times in our lives find ourselves broken. True strength is found in picking up the pieces." Developing a habit of setting daily intentions requires resilience. It involves recognizing that, despite past struggles, we have the inner strength to piece our lives back together, one intention at a time.

Embracing Change for Growth

Change is an essential part of personal growth and recovery. The statement, "You cannot grow unless you are willing to change. You will never improve yourself if you cling to what used to be," underscores the necessity of embracing change. Setting daily intentions involves a commitment to personal growth and a willingness to let go of old habits and beliefs that no longer serve us.

Acknowledging a Range of Emotions

Addiction recovery is a journey filled with a wide range of emotions. The statement encourages us to "allow space for all the feelings our heart holds" and not to hide from ourselves. Developing a

A Journey of Transformation

habit of setting daily intentions requires self-compassion and self-awareness. It involves acknowledging both the challenging and beautiful emotions that come with the recovery process.

Embracing the Wholeness of Self

Recovery is about embracing the wholeness of self, both the good and the challenging aspects. As the statement states, "It's okay to be yourself, all of yourself, not just the good." Setting daily intentions involves self-acceptance and authenticity. It means setting intentions that align with our true selves and recognizing that personal growth can occur in even the most unlikely of circumstances.

The Power of Spoken Words

Communication is vital in addiction recovery, and sometimes the most important words are the ones left unspoken. The statement, "Sometimes the words we leave unspoken are the most important ones that should have been said," highlights the importance of open and honest communication. Setting daily intentions can include expressing our feelings and needs to others, fostering healthier relationships in recovery.

Choosing Positivity in Adversity

Adversity is an inevitable part of life, but our response to it is within our control. As the statement advises, "Never let a bad situation bring out the worst in you. Choose to stay positive and be strong." Setting daily intentions involves maintaining a positive mindset and choosing resilience over negativity, even in the face of challenges.

Patience and Faith in Timing

Patience and faith play a significant role in addiction recovery. The statement reminds us that "God has perfect timing; never early, never late." Developing a habit of setting daily intentions requires patience in the face of uncertainty and faith that, with time and perseverance, positive changes will occur.

Self-Reflection Questions:

> How can I develop a daily practice of setting intentions that align with my recovery goals and aspirations?
>
> In what ways have I shown resilience in my recovery journey, and how can I apply this strength to setting daily intentions?
>
> What changes have I been resistant to in my life, and how can I embrace change as a catalyst for personal growth in my daily intentions?

Am I acknowledging and processing the full range of emotions I experience in recovery, and how can I incorporate emotional awareness into my daily intentions?

How can I practice self-acceptance and embrace my whole self, including both the challenging and beautiful aspects, in my daily intention-setting?

Are there important words or feelings I've left unspoken in my recovery journey that need to be expressed in my daily intentions and communication with others?

How can I cultivate a daily practice of positivity and maintain faith and patience in the timing of my recovery journey through setting intentions?

Celebrating Successes Along the Way

Addiction recovery is a challenging journey filled with ups and downs, but it is also a path of personal growth and transformation. To navigate this journey successfully, it is essential to recognize and celebrate the successes along the way. This book explores the importance of celebrating successes in addiction recovery, emphasizing the joy of watching life fall into place, surrounding oneself with positivity, appreciating the present moment, and fostering gratitude for the smallest blessings.

The Joy of Watching Life Fall into Place

One of the most rewarding aspects of addiction recovery is witnessing the positive changes that gradually unfold. The statement, "The best feeling in the whole world is watching things finally fall into place after watching them fall apart for so long," highlights the sense of accomplishment and fulfillment that comes with seeing one's life gradually improve. Celebrating successes involves recognizing the progress made and taking pride in the steps taken toward recovery.

Surrounding Oneself with Positivity

In addiction recovery, the people we surround ourselves with can significantly impact our journey. The statement encourages us to "give ourselves permission to cut negative people from our life, and surround ourselves with people who bring out the best in us." Celebrating successes requires cultivating a supportive network of individuals who understand and celebrate our achievements, both big and small. These positive influences can help sustain motivation and provide encouragement on the path to recovery.

Embracing the Present Moment

It's easy to get caught up in the past or worry about the future, but addiction recovery emphasizes the importance of living in the present. The statement urges us not to wait until it's too late to appreciate the precious experiences of life. Celebrating successes means recognizing the beauty and significance of the present moment, acknowledging how far we've come, and finding joy in the process of recovery itself.

Practicing Gratitude

Gratitude is a powerful tool in addiction recovery. Even in challenging times, there is always something to be grateful for. The statement suggests that, before falling asleep, we reflect on at least one good thing that happened today. Cultivating gratitude and celebrating successes can enhance our overall well-being and provide a sense of positivity and hope, even in the face of adversity.

A Journey of Transformation

Self-Reflection Questions:

How do I currently acknowledge and celebrate the successes, no matter how small, in my addiction recovery journey?

Who are the people in my life who bring out the best in me and support my recovery goals, and how can I nurture these relationships?

In what ways can I cultivate a greater appreciation for the present moment and find joy in the process of recovery itself?

What strategies can I employ to practice gratitude regularly and celebrate the blessings, no matter how minor, in my life?

How does celebrating successes contribute to my motivation and overall well-being in addiction recovery?

Acknowledging and Celebrating Achievements in the Journey of Addiction Recovery

The path to addiction recovery is marked by its challenges and triumphs, often accompanied by personal growth and transformation. In this journey, it is crucial to acknowledge and celebrate achievements, no matter how small or seemingly insignificant. This book explores the significance of acknowledging and celebrating achievements in addiction recovery, emphasizing the lessons learned from life's ups and downs, the value of living in the present, and the importance of expressing love, gratitude, and joy.

Learning from Life's Ups and Downs

Life is filled with both joy and disappointment, as the statement aptly reminds us: "As we grow up, we learn that even the one person that wasn't supposed to ever let us down, probably will." In addiction recovery, acknowledging achievements involves recognizing that setbacks and hardships are a natural part of the journey. It is through these experiences that we learn, grow, and gain resilience, ultimately appreciating our achievements even more.

Embracing Life's Imperfections

Addiction recovery may involve complex emotions, including heartbreak and difficult interpersonal experiences. The statement encourages us to "forgive freely, and love like you've never been hurt." Celebrating achievements means embracing life's imperfections and understanding that each experience, even the painful ones, contributes to our personal growth. It involves finding strength and compassion in forgiving oneself and others.

Living Life to the Fullest

Addiction recovery teaches us the preciousness of life and the importance of living it to the fullest. We are urged to "live life to the fullest, tell someone what they mean to you and tell someone off, speak out, dance in the pouring rain, hold someone's hand, comfort a friend, fall asleep watching the sun come up, stay up late, be a flirt, and smile until your face hurts." Acknowledging and celebrating achievements involve actively participating in life's moments and appreciating the simple pleasures.

Seizing the Present Moment

In recovery, the concept of "one day at a time" reminds us to embrace the present moment. We are reminded that "every second you spend angry or upset is a second of happiness you can never get back." Celebrating achievements means recognizing that life is too short to dwell on negativity or missed opportunities. It involves seizing the present moment, finding happiness in the now, and focusing on the positive aspects of our journey.

Self-Reflection Questions:

How do I currently acknowledge and celebrate my achievements, no matter how small or significant, in my addiction recovery journey?

What lessons have I learned from life's ups and downs, including setbacks and hardships, and how have they contributed to my personal growth in recovery?

In what ways can I practice forgiveness and embrace life's imperfections, finding strength and compassion in both my achievements and challenges?

How do I currently live life to the fullest and seize the present moment in my recovery journey, and how can I enhance this aspect of my life?

What strategies can I employ to focus on the positive aspects of my journey, finding happiness in the now and celebrating my achievements in the moment?

Recognizing Both Small and Significant Achievements in Addiction Recovery

The journey of addiction recovery is filled with challenges, setbacks, and triumphs, both big and small. It is crucial to recognize and celebrate all achievements, no matter how minor they may seem. This book explores the importance of acknowledging both small and significant accomplishments in addiction recovery, emphasizing the power of hope, self-discovery, the role of dreams, perseverance in adversity, and the innate strength and passion within each individual.

A Journey of Transformation

The Power of Hope

Hope is a driving force in addiction recovery. As the statement suggests, "If you do not hope, you will not find what is beyond your hopes." Recognizing achievements, whether small or significant, begins with the hope of a better future. Hope gives us the motivation and belief that change is possible, allowing us to see the progress we've made and appreciate even the smallest steps toward recovery.

Finding Happiness Within

Happiness is often sought externally, but true contentment is discovered within oneself. The statement wisely advises, "It is not easy to find happiness in ourselves, but it's not possible to find it elsewhere." In addiction recovery, acknowledging achievements involves recognizing the inner strength and resilience that contribute to personal growth and happiness. It means understanding that self-discovery and self-worth are crucial aspects of the journey.

The Role of Dreams

Dreams play a significant role in shaping our recovery journey. "No one has ever achieved anything from the smallest to the greatest unless the dream was dreamed first." Acknowledging both small and significant achievements involves recognizing that every great accomplishment, no matter its size, began as a dream. Dreams give us direction and purpose, motivating us to take the necessary steps toward recovery.

Perseverance in Adversity

Addiction recovery is not without its challenges and moments of adversity. The statement encourages us to "never give up then, for that is just the place and time that the tide will turn." Recognizing and celebrating achievements means persisting through difficult times and understanding that adversity can lead to growth. It involves acknowledging the progress made even in the face of setbacks.

Inner Strength and Passion

Each individual possesses inner strength and passion that can propel them forward in recovery. "Always remember, you have within you the strength, the patience, and the passion to reach for the stars to change the world." Recognizing both small and significant achievements involves tapping into this inner reservoir of strength and passion, using it to overcome challenges and create positive change in one's life and the lives of others.

Self-Reflection Questions:

How do I currently acknowledge and celebrate my achievements, both small and significant, in my addiction recovery journey?

How has hope played a role in my recovery, and how can I use it to continue recognizing and celebrating my progress?

In what ways can I find happiness within myself and appreciate the inner strength and resilience that contribute to my recovery journey?

How do my dreams and aspirations shape my recovery journey, and how can I use them as a source of motivation to acknowledge and celebrate achievements?

What strategies can I employ to persevere through adversity and understand that setbacks are part of the journey toward recovery?

How can I tap into my inner strength and passion to continue making positive changes in my life and the lives of those around me, recognizing and celebrating achievements along the way?

The Path to Long-Term Recovery from Addiction:
Embracing Gratitude, Kindness, and Wisdom

Addiction is a relentless battle that often leaves individuals feeling isolated, damaged, and filled with pain. However, amidst the turmoil and despair, there is a profound opportunity for transformation. Recovery from addiction is a journey of healing, self-discovery, and resilience. It is a path where individuals can turn their mistakes into valuable lessons, their fears into hope, and their pain into wisdom. In this book, we will explore the importance of expressing gratitude for progress made in addiction recovery and how the loneliest, saddest, and most damaged individuals can harness their experiences to become beacons of kindness and wisdom.

Gratitude for Progress in Recovery

One of the fundamental steps towards achieving long-term recovery from addiction is to express gratitude for the progress made. Acknowledging how far you have come, despite the challenges, setbacks, and relapses that may have occurred, is essential for maintaining motivation and staying on course. Gratitude can be a powerful tool for individuals seeking recovery, as it helps shift the focus from dwelling on past mistakes to appreciating the present moment and the potential for a brighter future.

Gratitude allows individuals to recognize the support and love they receive from friends, family, and support groups. It fosters a sense of belonging and connection, which are often lacking during the depths of addiction. When you express gratitude for the people who have stood by you through thick and thin, you build stronger relationships and find solace in knowing that you are not alone in your journey towards recovery.

A Journey of Transformation

The Loneliest People and the Kindest Hearts

The phrase, "The loneliest people can be the kindest," holds a profound truth for individuals in recovery. Addiction can be an isolating experience, where individuals often distance themselves from loved ones and feel disconnected from the world. However, this loneliness can cultivate empathy and kindness. Those who have experienced the depths of despair and isolation are often the ones who extend a helping hand to others facing similar struggles.

In recovery, individuals have the opportunity to channel their loneliness into acts of compassion and support for others. By sharing their own stories of addiction and recovery, they offer hope to those still trapped in the throes of addiction. This kindness not only benefits others but also contributes to their own healing and sense of purpose.

The Saddest People and the Brightest Smiles

"The saddest people sometimes smile the brightest" reflects the idea that individuals in recovery may carry the weight of their past mistakes and regrets, yet they often wear a smile that radiates hope and resilience. This apparent contradiction can be explained by the newfound joy and inner peace that come with sobriety.

Recovery is not just about abstaining from substances; it is also about rediscovering the joys of life, finding fulfillment in healthy relationships, and learning to love oneself. When individuals experience this transformation, their smiles become genuine expressions of happiness. They smile because they have overcome adversity and found a way to live a life filled with purpose and meaning.

The Most Damaged People and Wisdom

Addiction often inflicts profound damage on individuals, both physically and emotionally. However, this damage can serve as a source of wisdom and strength. The struggles and challenges faced in recovery become valuable life lessons that shape one's character and perspective.

Those who have weathered the storm of addiction gain insights into the complexities of human nature, the power of resilience, and the importance of self-compassion. Their wisdom can be a guiding light for others on the path to recovery, offering valuable advice, encouragement, and support.

In the journey towards long-term recovery from addiction, expressing gratitude for progress made is a pivotal step. It not only fosters a positive mindset but also strengthens the bonds of connection and support. Moreover, the loneliest, saddest, and most damaged individuals have the potential to be the kindest and wisest, offering hope and empathy to others in need.

Self-Reflection Questions:

How can I express gratitude for the progress I've made in my own recovery journey?

In what ways can I use my experiences of loneliness and pain to show kindness and empathy towards others facing addiction?

How can I cultivate genuine happiness and a brighter smile through my recovery efforts?

What lessons have I learned from my struggles with addiction, and how can I use them to offer wisdom and support to those who are still suffering?

How can I maintain faith in myself and stay strong in the face of challenges, knowing that today is the tomorrow I once worried about yesterday?

In embracing these questions and the themes of gratitude, kindness, and wisdom, individuals on the path to recovery can find the strength and purpose needed to build a brighter and more fulfilling future.

Sharing Successes in Addiction Recovery:
Finding Strength and Resilience

Addiction recovery is a challenging journey that demands unwavering determination and resilience. It is a path filled with both triumphs and setbacks, but it's crucial to acknowledge and celebrate the successes along the way. Sharing these successes not only reinforces one's commitment to recovery but also inspires others to stand up for themselves and believe in their own capacity to overcome addiction. In this book, we will explore the importance of sharing successes with others during the recovery process and the strength that arises when we refuse to let anyone break our soul.

The Power of Sharing Successes

Sharing successes in addiction recovery serves several essential purposes. First and foremost, it allows individuals to take stock of their progress and acknowledge their accomplishments, no matter how small they may seem. Often, in the throes of addiction, individuals focus on their failures and shortcomings. Sharing successes shifts the focus towards the positive aspects of recovery, boosting self-esteem and motivation.

Moreover, when we share our successes with others, we become a source of inspiration and hope for those still struggling with addiction. Our achievements can serve as proof that recovery is possible and that change is attainable. This encouragement can be a lifeline for someone teetering on the edge of hopelessness, providing them with the belief that they too can stand on their own two feet and begin their journey towards recovery.

A Journey of Transformation

Resilience in the Face of Adversity

The journey to recovery is rarely a straight path; it often involves relapses, external challenges, and moments of doubt. However, it's crucial to remember that there are those who may wish to see us fail, but we must never give them the satisfaction. This determination not to be defeated by external negativity is a testament to our resilience.

When we share our successes, we demonstrate to ourselves and others that we are strong enough to withstand adversity and overcome obstacles. It reinforces the idea that recovery is a personal journey, and the opinions or doubts of others should not deter us from our path. By holding our heads high, smiling, and standing our ground, we not only protect our own recovery but also become a symbol of strength for those around us.

The Impact of Positive Relationships

In the process of recovery, we often encounter people who believe in us so much that we start to believe in ourselves too. These individuals are the ones who see the sun where we once saw clouds. They love us for simply being ourselves and provide unwavering support through our darkest moments. They are the once-in-a-lifetime kind of people who have an immeasurable impact on our recovery journey.

The positive relationships formed during recovery are invaluable sources of strength and encouragement. They remind us that we are not alone in our struggle, and they bolster our resolve to keep pushing forward. These connections serve as a reminder that we are deserving of love and support, even when we may doubt our worth.

In addiction recovery, sharing successes is a powerful tool that reinforces commitment, inspires others, and builds resilience. It allows individuals to celebrate their progress, share hope with those in need, and stand up for themselves in the face of adversity. Surrounding ourselves with people who believe in us and love us unconditionally empowers us to keep pushing forward, no matter the circumstances.

Self-Reflection Questions:

> How can I celebrate and share my successes in addiction recovery to inspire others on their journey?

> What strategies can I employ to protect my own recovery from those who may wish to see me fail?

> Who are the people in my life who believe in me and support me unconditionally, and how can I nurture those relationships?

How can I continue to stand on my own two feet and stand up for myself in the face of adversity?

What does real strength mean to me, and how can I continue to push forward, regardless of the circumstances?

By reflecting on these questions, individuals in addiction recovery can find renewed determination, resilience, and the strength to continue their journey towards lasting sobriety and well-being.

Inspiring and Motivating Others in Addiction Recovery: Embracing Positivity and Self-Forgiveness

Addiction recovery is not only a personal journey but also an opportunity to inspire and motivate those around you. By sharing your story, your successes, and your newfound positivity, you can become a source of hope and encouragement for others who are struggling with addiction. In this book, we will explore the importance of inspiring and motivating those around you in the context of long-term recovery. We will also delve into the significance of focusing on the present moment, practicing self-forgiveness, and staying positive throughout the journey.

Inspiring and Motivating Others

One of the most profound ways to make a lasting impact in addiction recovery is to inspire and motivate those who are walking a similar path. Your journey from addiction to recovery is a testament to the strength of the human spirit and the possibility of transformation. By openly sharing your experiences and the lessons you've learned, you can offer a beacon of hope to others who may be struggling with their own addiction issues.

When you inspire and motivate others, you create a ripple effect of positivity and encouragement. Your words and actions can help individuals regain faith in their ability to overcome addiction and build a better future. By providing support and guidance, you become a lifeline for those who may be feeling lost or hopeless.

Embracing the Present and Self-Forgiveness

The statement, "Every second you spend dwelling on the past is a second of your present that you are missing," underscores the importance of living in the present moment. Addiction often involves regrets, guilt, and shame stemming from past mistakes. However, constantly dwelling on these negative emotions can hinder your progress in recovery.

To inspire and motivate others effectively, it's essential to show them that you have learned from your past mistakes and have forgiven yourself for not knowing better. Self-forgiveness is a vital step in the recovery process. It allows you to let go of the burden of guilt and shame, freeing you to focus on the present and the future.

Staying Positive and Looking Forward

Recovery is a journey filled with both successes and setbacks. It's crucial to remember that just because one thing doesn't go right doesn't mean your life is ruined. Staying positive is a powerful mindset that can help you navigate the challenges of recovery with resilience and determination.

Taking pride in how far you've come is a testament to your strength and commitment to change. Having faith in how far you can go is the driving force behind your continued progress. By looking forward with hope, rather than dwelling on regret, you maintain a positive outlook that inspires not only yourself but also those around you.

In addiction recovery, inspiring and motivating those around you is a powerful way to contribute to the healing process, both for yourself and others. By sharing your journey, practicing self-forgiveness, and staying positive, you become a beacon of hope and encouragement. Remember that every second you spend dwelling on the past is a second of your present that you are missing. Instead, embrace the present moment, learn from your mistakes, and look
forward with hope.

Self-Reflection Questions:

How can I share my addiction recovery journey with others to inspire and motivate them?

What steps can I take to practice self-forgiveness and let go of the burden of past mistakes?

How can I maintain a positive outlook and stay focused on the present and the future in my recovery journey?

What specific actions can I take to provide support and encouragement to those who may be struggling with addiction?

What does it mean to me to look forward with hope and not backward with regret in the context of my recovery journey?

By exploring these questions, individuals in addiction recovery can cultivate a sense of purpose and become a source of inspiration for others, ultimately contributing to their own long-term well-being and the well-being of those they touch with their journey.

Building a Supportive Network in Addiction Recovery:
Finding Strength and Resilience

Addiction recovery is a journey that is often most successful when undertaken with the support of like-minded individuals who understand the challenges and triumphs that come with it. Building a network of people who share similar goals and experiences can be a powerful asset in achieving long-term recovery. In this book, we will explore the significance of creating a supportive network of like-minded individuals and the impact it can have on one's recovery journey. Additionally, we will discuss the importance of letting go of unnecessary stress, staying positive, and taking proactive steps toward personal growth.

Building a Supportive Network

Addiction recovery can be a lonely and arduous journey. It is during these times that having a supportive network of like-minded individuals becomes invaluable. These individuals can include peers in recovery, support groups, therapists, or mentors who have walked a similar path. They provide understanding, empathy, and encouragement when faced with challenges.

A supportive network offers a safe space to share experiences, struggles, and successes without judgment. It fosters a sense of belonging and reduces feelings of isolation, which are often triggers for relapse. Additionally, these connections provide motivation and accountability, reinforcing one's commitment to recovery.

Letting Go of Unneeded Stress

The statement, "Life becomes easier when you let go of the unneeded stress," highlights the importance of managing stress during the recovery process. Addiction recovery itself is a demanding journey, and adding unnecessary stressors can hinder progress. Stress can trigger cravings and jeopardize sobriety.

Building a supportive network can be a significant source of stress relief. It allows individuals to share their burdens, seek advice, and receive emotional support. Moreover, the understanding and empathy of like-minded individuals can help individuals reframe their perspective on stressors, making them more manageable.

Staying Positive and Focused

Staying positive and maintaining a focused mindset are vital aspects of addiction recovery. Hard times are inevitable in life, but they can also serve as opportunities for personal growth and resilience. Overthinking, as the book mentions, can be a major source of unhappiness and can hinder progress.

A supportive network can provide a positive and growth-oriented environment. Surrounding oneself with individuals who emphasize positivity and personal development can be uplifting and motivating. Together, you can explore strategies for maintaining a positive outlook and managing the challenges that arise during recovery.

Self-Reflection Questions

> How can I build and expand my supportive network of like-minded individuals in my recovery journey?

What sources of unneeded stress can I identify in my life, and how can I let go of them to improve my well-being?

How can I foster a positive mindset and resilience in the face of life's challenges?

Are there specific activities or practices that help me stay occupied and keep my mind off negative thoughts?

In what ways can I actively work on loving myself, knowing my worth, and accepting growth in my life?

By considering these self-reflection questions, individuals in addiction recovery can proactively work on strengthening their support system, managing stress, and embracing a positive outlook. Building a supportive network of like-minded individuals can be a cornerstone of a successful long-term recovery journey, helping individuals navigate the ups and downs of life with resilience and hope.

Turning Change into a Lifestyle

Long-term recovery from addiction is a journey that involves profound change, self-discovery, and the transformation of one's lifestyle. To successfully navigate this path, individuals must learn to live life one day at a time, prioritize self-care, and embrace a positive outlook. This book explores the concept of turning change into a lifestyle in the context of addiction recovery. It highlights the importance of letting go of the past, maintaining faith, and finding strength in resilience. Additionally, it emphasizes the value of being open to unexpected joys and opportunities.

Living One Day at a Time

Recovery is a process that requires patience and a commitment to taking each day as it comes. "Live life one day at a time" is a powerful reminder to stay present in the moment and not be overwhelmed by the weight of the past or the uncertainty of the future. Focusing on the here and now allows individuals to make gradual, sustainable changes and avoid becoming overwhelmed.

Furthermore, laughter is an invaluable tool in recovery. It lightens the spirit, reduces stress, and brings joy to life. When we choose to laugh, even in the face of challenges, we reinforce our resilience and create a positive atmosphere that supports our recovery journey.

Letting Go of the Past

To truly embrace change and make it a lifestyle, it is essential to let go of the things that hurt us in our past. Carrying the baggage of past mistakes, regrets, and resentments can hinder personal growth and hinder the recovery process. As the saying goes, "They don't deserve any room in our future."

Letting go of the past is an act of self-compassion and forgiveness. It is about acknowledging that while we cannot change our past actions, we can shape our future by making healthier choices and cultivating a positive mindset.

Faith and Resilience

Recovery often presents challenges and moments of uncertainty. "Faith is moving forward even when things don't make sense" underscores the importance of trust and resilience in the face of adversity. Believing in the process of recovery and having faith that, in hindsight, everything will become clear can provide the strength needed to overcome obstacles.

The journey of recovery is a testament to one's inner strength and resilience. The battles fought in silence and the victories won behind closed doors showcase the true measure of one's character.

A Journey of Transformation

Embracing the Unexpected

As we navigate the path of recovery, we may discover that the best things in life are often found when we are not actively seeking them. By remaining open to unexpected joys, opportunities, and connections, we enrich our lives and reinforce the idea that positive change can be an ongoing and fulfilling part of our lifestyle.

Self-Reflection Questions

How can I implement the practice of living one day at a time in my recovery journey?

In what ways can I incorporate more laughter and joy into my life as a means of reducing stress and enhancing my well-being?

What steps can I take to let go of the past and make room for personal growth and positive change in my future?

How can I strengthen my faith and resilience to navigate the challenges of recovery with determination and hope?

Am I open to unexpected joys, opportunities, and connections that may enrich my life and contribute to my ongoing recovery journey?

By reflecting on these questions, individuals in addiction recovery can actively embrace change as a lifestyle, prioritize self-care, and maintain a positive outlook. Turning change into a lifestyle not only supports long-term recovery but also fosters a fulfilling and purpose-driven life.

Embracing Transformation as a Lifelong Journey in Addiction Recovery

Recovery from addiction is not merely about abstaining from substances; it is a profound journey of personal transformation. To achieve long-term recovery, individuals must embrace this transformation as a lifelong process. This book explores the concept of continuous transformation in addiction recovery and the importance of patience, meaning, commitment, and humility in this journey. It underscores the idea that life should be allowed to flow naturally, and recovery should be approached with unwavering commitment and a positive attitude.

Embracing Lifelong Transformation

Recovery from addiction is not a destination; it is a continuous, lifelong journey. This journey entails personal growth, self-discovery, and the development of resilience and coping strategies. The idea that "we must let life flow naturally" reminds us to accept the ebbs and flows of our recovery journey. Instead of pushing for change or expecting immediate results, we must be patient and allow things to unfold at their own pace.

Patience is Key

"Life's secret is patience," and in the context of addiction recovery, patience is indeed a vital virtue. Recovery often involves setbacks and relapses, but it is through these challenges that we learn, grow, and develop the resilience needed to maintain sobriety in the long run. Patience allows us to stay committed to the process, even when progress seems slow or elusive.

Finding Meaning and Building Attitude

The meaning of life is often defined by the sense of purpose and fulfillment we derive from our actions and experiences. In addiction recovery, giving life meaning can be synonymous with finding purpose in staying clean and sober. Two key aspects that define us in this journey are our patience when we have nothing and our attitude when we have everything.

When we commit to recovery, we are building hope for a brighter future, one free from the grips of addiction. This commitment fuels our determination and guides our actions. When we keep this commitment, we build trust in ourselves and our ability to overcome challenges.

Humility and Perspective

To truly embrace transformation, we must approach recovery with humility. Climbing mountains, whether they are physical or metaphorical, is not about seeking attention or recognition. It is about gaining a broader perspective and seeing the world in a new light. Recovery is a journey of self-discovery and growth, where we learn to let go of ego and embrace humility as a source of strength.

Self-Reflection Questions

How can I cultivate patience in my recovery journey and embrace the idea of letting life flow naturally?

What gives meaning to my life in the context of addiction recovery, and how can I use this sense of purpose to stay committed to sobriety?

How can I maintain a positive attitude even when faced with challenges and setbacks in my recovery?

What specific commitments can I make to myself in support of my recovery, and how can I ensure that I keep these commitments to build trust in my journey?

In what ways can I approach recovery with humility and a desire to gain a broader perspective, rather than seeking attention or recognition?

A Journey of Transformation

By reflecting on these questions, individuals in addiction recovery can actively embrace transformation as a lifelong journey. This approach fosters resilience, personal growth, and a deep sense of meaning and purpose in the ongoing process of recovery.

Recognizing Ongoing Personal Growth in the Journey of Addiction Recovery

Addiction recovery is a transformative journey that extends beyond mere abstinence from substances. It is a path of continuous personal growth and self-discovery. In the quest for long-term recovery, individuals must recognize that personal growth is an ongoing process. This book explores the concept of ongoing personal growth in addiction recovery, highlighting the importance of time, responsibility for happiness, embracing the unknown, and maintaining a sense of humor in the face of challenges.

Time: A Precious Commodity

Time is a precious and irreplaceable resource. The saying, "Every time we get upset at something, ask ourselves if we were to die tomorrow, was it worth wasting our time being angry?" serves as a poignant reminder of the value of time. In addiction recovery, every moment is an opportunity for growth and positive change. When we waste time dwelling on anger or negativity, we miss out on the chance to invest in our well-being and personal development.

Personal Responsibility for Happiness

Personal growth in addiction recovery is closely tied to the recognition that we are responsible for our own happiness. Relying on others to make us happy often leads to disappointment. To achieve lasting happiness, we must cultivate it from within. This involves self-awareness, self-acceptance, and the willingness to seek joy in the simple moments of life.

Embracing the Unknown

Recovery often involves facing the unknown, as individuals grapple with life without the crutch of addiction. "We can't be in such a rush to figure everything out. We need to embrace the unknown and let our life surprise us." This wisdom encourages individuals to relinquish the need for absolute control and allow room for unexpected, positive experiences and personal growth.

Letting Go and Finding Greater Things

Sometimes, personal growth requires letting go of things or habits that no longer serve us. Addiction recovery often involves relinquishing substances and the associated lifestyle. This process can be challenging, as individuals may initially perceive these things as too great to let go. However, personal growth and greater opportunities often follow once we release what holds us back.

Maintaining a Sense of Humor

Life is filled with challenges, and addiction recovery is no exception. It's essential not to take life too seriously. "Sometimes we just have to laugh at our problems knowing it's not the end of everything." Humor can be a coping mechanism and a source of resilience. It allows individuals to maintain perspective and keep a positive outlook, even in the face of adversity.

Self-Reflection Questions

> How can I better prioritize and make the most of my time in the context of my recovery journey?

> In what ways can I take greater personal responsibility for my happiness and well-being?

> How can I become more comfortable with embracing the unknown and allowing life to surprise me in my recovery journey?

> What aspects of my life or habits do I need to let go of to facilitate personal growth and positive change?

> How can I incorporate humor and a light-hearted perspective into my approach to life, particularly when facing challenges in my recovery?

By reflecting on these questions, individuals in addiction recovery can acknowledge and embrace the ongoing nature of personal growth. Recognizing that recovery is a continuous journey allows individuals to invest their time wisely, take responsibility for their happiness, welcome the unknown, and find greater fulfillment and resilience in their pursuit of long-term recovery.

Committing to Continuous Self-Improvement in the Journey of Addiction Recovery

Addiction recovery is not only about breaking free from the shackles of substance abuse; it is a profound journey of self-improvement and personal growth. To achieve long-term recovery, individuals must commit to continuous self-improvement, nurturing their inner selves and discovering their true worth. This book delves into the concept of continuous self-improvement in the context of addiction recovery, emphasizing the difference between price and value, the complexities of societal pressures, and the importance of resilience and self-identity.

Differentiating Price from Value

In today's world, it's all too common for people to focus on the price of things rather than their intrinsic value. This narrow perspective can be applied to addiction recovery as well, where individuals may become fixated on the sacrifices they must make or the difficulties they face.

A Journey of Transformation

However, the true value lies in the journey itself, in the personal growth, resilience, and newfound sense of self that recovery brings.

Recovery teaches us that the price of addiction is steep, often costing us our health, relationships, and well-being. But the value of recovery is immeasurable, as it restores our sense of purpose, self-worth, and the possibility of a fulfilling life.

Societal Complexity and Self-Identity

Modern society can complicate our existence, leading us to forget our true selves and become preoccupied with external expectations and material pursuits. In the context of addiction recovery, societal pressures can exacerbate the challenges individuals face. However, the path to recovery demands that we shed these societal layers and rediscover our authentic selves.

Committing to continuous self-improvement involves aligning our actions with our core values and beliefs, regardless of external pressures. It requires us to cultivate self-awareness and the courage to defy societal norms when they conflict with our well-being.

Resilience and Adaptability

The analogy of boiling water illustrates the importance of resilience and adaptability in addiction recovery. Some individuals may be like potatoes, softening in the face of adversity, while others are like eggs, hardening in response to life's challenges. The key is to recognize that it's not the circumstances themselves that define us, but rather what we are made of internally.

Recovery necessitates inner strength and the ability to adapt to changing circumstances. It is about discovering the resilience within ourselves to overcome obstacles, maintain our commitment to self-improvement, and emerge stronger in the process.

Self-Reflection Questions

> What is the true value I find in my addiction recovery journey, and how can I keep this perspective in mind when facing challenges?

> How has societal complexity influenced my self-identity, and in what ways can I reclaim my authentic self in the journey of self-improvement?

> What sacrifices am I willing to make for my recovery, and how can I ensure that they serve as stepping stones to a more fulfilling life?

> How can I cultivate resilience and adaptability to face the uncertainties and challenges that may arise in my recovery journey?

> When I reflect on the statement, "It's about what you're made of, not the circumstances," how does this perspective shape my approach to addiction recovery and personal growth?

By reflecting on these questions, individuals in addiction recovery can reaffirm their commitment to continuous self-improvement. Recognizing the value of their journey, defying societal pressures, and cultivating resilience and self-identity are pivotal steps toward long-term recovery and personal fulfillment.

Establishing Daily Rituals and Habits:
The Foundations of Long-Term Recovery

Long-term recovery from addiction is a transformative journey that requires commitment, structure, and the establishment of daily rituals and habits. In the pursuit of sobriety, individuals must build a solid foundation that encompasses love, compassion, faith, and the determination to create positive change. This book explores the importance of establishing daily rituals and habits in addiction recovery, with a focus on nurturing relationships, fostering compassion, maintaining faith, and overcoming obstacles to build a meaningful life.

The Power of Love, Compassion, and Faith

Love, compassion, and faith are essential pillars of a successful recovery journey. Love is not merely a feeling but an active choice to accept someone's differences, weaknesses, and shortcomings, including our own. In recovery, this love extends to oneself and others, promoting empathy and understanding.

Compassion is the capacity to forgive and refuse to take advantage of another's vulnerability. It involves showing kindness and understanding to those who have hurt us, recognizing that everyone has their struggles.

Faith is the belief in the potential for positive change, both in ourselves and in others. It is the expectation of the best from ourselves and those around us. In the context of recovery, faith drives the commitment to overcome addiction and rebuild a fulfilling life.

The Significance of Daily Rituals and Habits

Establishing daily rituals and habits is a practical way to incorporate love, compassion, and faith into one's recovery journey. These rituals create structure and consistency, offering a sense of stability in times of uncertainty. They serve as daily reminders of the commitment to self-improvement and sobriety.

Nurturing Relationships: Building Bridges, Not Walls

Recovery involves repairing relationships that may have been damaged by addiction. It requires the willingness to extend love, compassion, and faith to oneself and to others. Daily rituals and

A Journey of Transformation

habits can be used to nurture these relationships, whether through regular communication, acts of kindness, or shared moments of reflection and growth.

Overcoming Obstacles: Building Something Great

In the journey of recovery, there will always be obstacles and challenges, often represented as stones in one's path. The response to these obstacles defines the recovery process. Individuals have the power to choose whether to build walls or bridges.

Building walls entails allowing obstacles to become insurmountable barriers, hindering progress and personal growth. In contrast, building bridges represents the resilience to overcome challenges, using them as opportunities for growth and positive change.

Self-Reflection Questions

> How can I incorporate daily rituals and habits into my recovery journey to nurture love, compassion, and faith in myself and my relationships with others?

> What concrete steps can I take to practice love and empathy towards myself and those around me, especially in challenging situations?

> How can I foster compassion and forgiveness as part of my daily routine, both towards others and myself?

> What strategies can I employ to maintain faith and belief in my ability to achieve long-term recovery, even in the face of obstacles?

> When I encounter obstacles in my recovery journey, how can I shift my perspective to view them as opportunities for personal growth and transformation?

By reflecting on these questions, individuals in addiction recovery can establish daily rituals and habits that strengthen their foundation for long-term sobriety. Embracing love, compassion, and faith and choosing to build bridges over obstacles empowers individuals to create meaningful and lasting change in their lives.

Incorporating Positive Practices into Daily Life:
A Blueprint for Long-Term Recovery

Long-term recovery from addiction is not just about abstaining from substances; it is a holistic transformation that requires the incorporation of positive practices into daily life. These practices encompass self-awareness, empathy, resilience, and a commitment to personal growth. This book explores the importance of incorporating positive practices into the daily routine of addiction recovery. It emphasizes the significance of active listening, being one's best self, patience, embracing understanding, resilience, kindness, prioritization, and perspective.

The Power of Active Listening and Understanding

Active listening is a practice that allows us to connect with others on a deeper level. Often, people listen with the intent to reply rather than to understand. In addiction recovery, the ability to listen and understand the experiences, challenges, and emotions of oneself and others is invaluable. It fosters empathy, strengthens relationships, and promotes personal growth.

Being Your Best Self

The journey of recovery is an opportunity to not only be yourself but to be your best self. It involves self-improvement, growth, and the pursuit of a fulfilling life. This commitment to self-betterment can be incorporated into daily life through intentional actions and habits that align with one's values and goals.

Patience and Resilience

Recovery is a process that unfolds over time, and it requires patience and resilience. Incorporating patience into daily life allows individuals to weather the ups and downs without becoming discouraged. It reminds us that things will change for the better with time and effort. Resilience, on the other hand, empowers individuals to bounce back from setbacks and disappointments, emerging stronger and more determined.

Embracing Understanding and Kindness

The day we let go of fear and instead embrace understanding is the day we truly begin to live. In the context of addiction recovery, understanding oneself and the underlying causes of addiction is essential for lasting change. Furthermore, kindness, both towards oneself and others, creates a nurturing and supportive environment that fosters recovery and personal growth.

Prioritizing Positivity and Perspective

Incorporating positive practices into daily life means focusing on the positives and allowing the negatives to gradually fade away. This shift in perspective is a powerful tool for recovery. By embracing a positive outlook, individuals can overcome challenges and setbacks with resilience and determination.

Self-Reflection Questions

> How can I actively practice active listening and understanding in my daily interactions with myself and others in my recovery journey?

> What specific actions can I take to be my best self and align my daily habits with my values and goals?

A Journey of Transformation

> How can I incorporate patience and resilience into my daily routine to navigate the challenges of recovery effectively?
>
> In what ways can I cultivate kindness and empathy, both towards myself and those I encounter in my recovery journey?
>
> When faced with adversity, how can I shift my perspective to prioritize positivity and maintain focus on my goals and values?

By reflecting on these questions, individuals in addiction recovery can actively incorporate positive practices into their daily lives. This approach not only supports long-term recovery but also fosters personal growth, resilience, and a fulfilling life centered around what truly matters.

Making Transformation a Daily Routine: A Roadmap to Long-Term Recovery

Long-term recovery from addiction is a transformative journey that requires consistent effort and the integration of transformation into daily routines. This process involves self-reflection, taking responsibility for one's choices and actions, and embracing the courage to live authentically. In this book, we will explore the importance of making transformation an integral part of daily life in addiction recovery. It emphasizes self-assessment, self-ownership, breaking free from external control, living in the present, and having faith in the future.

The Mirror of Self-Reflection

True transformation begins with self-reflection. We must look at ourselves in the mirror and ask the fundamental question: "Are we truly happy?" If the answer is not an immediate "yes," then it is a sign that change is needed. Self-reflection allows us to gain insight into our thoughts, emotions, and behaviors, serving as a compass for the transformative journey ahead.

Taking Ownership of Choices and Actions

To achieve long-term recovery, it is essential to take responsibility for our own choices and actions. Ownership of our life is the first step toward growth and transformation. It empowers us to break free from the patterns of addiction and external control, placing us in the driver's seat of our recovery journey.

Breaking Free from External Control

Addiction often leads individuals to seek approval or control from external sources, which can hinder personal growth and self-discovery. Breaking free from this cycle is essential for transformation. It involves letting go of the fear of displeasing others and taking control of our destiny.

Living in the Present

Focusing on the present moment is a key aspect of making transformation a daily routine. Dwelling on the fear of the future or past regrets can consume our lives and impede progress. By living in the now, we can fully engage with the present and make the right choices for our recovery journey.

Having Faith in the Future

Although living in the present is crucial, having faith in the future is equally important. Trusting that the right things will fall into place, even when the path is uncertain, provides hope and motivation. Faith in the future reinforces our commitment to transformation as an ongoing process.

Self-Reflection Questions

> How can I incorporate regular self-reflection into my daily routine to assess my happiness and progress in my recovery journey?
>
> What steps can I take to take ownership of my choices and actions and actively shape the direction of my life?
>
> In what ways can I break free from external control and prioritize my own well-being and recovery goals?
>
> How can I practice living in the present and fully engage with the current moment to enhance my daily routines?
>
> What strategies can I implement to strengthen my faith in the future, even when faced with uncertainty in my recovery journey?

By reflecting on these questions, individuals in addiction recovery can actively make transformation an integral part of their daily routines. This approach fosters personal growth, empowerment, and the courage to live authentically, ultimately supporting long-term recovery and a fulfilling life.

Prioritizing Self-Care and Well-being

Long-term recovery from addiction is a journey that requires dedication, resilience, and a deep commitment to self-care and well-being. While the pursuit of personal goals and dreams is important, it should never come at the expense of one's health and recovery. In this book, we will explore the significance of prioritizing self-care and well-being in the context of addiction recovery. It emphasizes the importance of supporting others, having faith and belief in oneself, overcoming obstacles, and remaining confident in the face of adversity.

Supporting Others through Self-Care

Prioritizing self-care and well-being is not a selfish act; it is a means to support others on their journey as well. By taking care of ourselves, we set an example for our family, friends, and loved ones. We motivate them to prioritize their own well-being and inspire them to achieve their goals.

Having Faith and Belief in Oneself

Recovery from addiction demands unwavering faith and belief in oneself. It is about understanding that one has the potential for change and personal growth. This belief in oneself serves as a powerful motivator to persevere through the challenges of recovery, no matter how daunting they may seem.

Overcoming Obstacles with Determination

Obstacles and setbacks are an inevitable part of any journey, including addiction recovery. However, they should never deter us from our path. As the saying goes, "If you run into a wall, don't turn around and give up. Figure out how to climb it, go through it, or work around it." Recovery is a testament to human resilience, and every obstacle is an opportunity to learn, adapt, and grow.

Never Giving Up and Maintaining Confidence

The journey of recovery may present tough times and difficulties, but these challenges should not be viewed as insurmountable roadblocks. Instead, they should serve as the catalyst for greater determination. It is essential to maintain unwavering confidence in oneself and the recovery process. Difficulties are not barriers but stepping stones towards personal growth and achievement.

Self-Reflection Questions

> How can I prioritize self-care and well-being in my daily life to support my own recovery journey and set a positive example for others?

A Journey of Transformation

> What strategies can I implement to strengthen my faith and belief in myself as I navigate the challenges of addiction recovery?
>
> In what ways can I view obstacles and setbacks as opportunities for personal growth and resilience, rather than as insurmountable roadblocks?
>
> How can I maintain confidence in my ability to achieve my objectives, even during tough times and moments of doubt?
>
> What does self-care mean to me, and how can I incorporate self-care practices into my daily routine to enhance my overall well-being and recovery journey?

By reflecting on these questions, individuals in addiction recovery can actively prioritize self-care and well-being as the foundation of their long-term recovery. This approach not only supports personal growth but also inspires others and reinforces the belief that all things are possible for those who persevere and maintain faith in themselves.

Focusing on Physical, Emotional, and Mental Well-being:
A Holistic Approach to Long-Term Recovery

Long-term recovery from addiction is a multifaceted journey that extends beyond the cessation of substance use. It necessitates a comprehensive focus on physical, emotional, and mental well-being. This book explores the importance of this holistic approach to addiction recovery, emphasizing effective communication, the essence of freedom, the courage to conquer fear, resilience in the face of setbacks, and the pursuit of one's fullest potential.

Effective Communication: Speaking to the Heart and the Head

A successful recovery journey often involves connecting with others on a profound level. Effective communication is the bridge that allows us to reach people both intellectually and emotionally. It is about speaking in a language that resonates with their hearts and minds. By fostering understanding and empathy, we create a supportive environment conducive to long-term recovery.

The Essence of Freedom

To achieve long-term recovery is to embrace freedom in its truest sense. It is not merely the absence of physical chains but living in a way that respects and enhances the freedom of others. Freedom in recovery means liberation from the clutches of addiction, enabling individuals to lead fulfilling lives and make choices that align with their well-being.

The Courage to Conquer Fear

Fear often stands as a formidable obstacle on the path to recovery. However, courage is not the absence of fear; it is the triumph over it. Those who succeed in long-term recovery are not devoid of fear but possess the bravery to confront and conquer it. This courage empowers individuals to face triggers, cravings, and challenges head-on.

Resilience and the Will to Rise

Success in recovery should not be measured solely by one's achievements but by their ability to rise after each fall. Setbacks are an inevitable part of any journey, including addiction recovery. True resilience lies in the determination to get back up, learn from the experience, and continue the pursuit of sobriety.

The Pursuit of One's Fullest Potential

Recovery is not about settling for a life less than what one is capable of living. It is about striving for one's fullest potential. By embracing the journey of long-term recovery and committing to holistic well-being, individuals can unlock their inner strength and realize their capabilities, leading to a life of fulfillment and purpose.

Self-Reflection Questions

> How can I enhance my communication skills to better connect with others on an intellectual and emotional level, supporting their recovery journey?

> In what ways can I view freedom in the context of recovery and strive to live in a manner that respects and enhances the freedom of others?

> What strategies can I employ to summon the courage to confront and conquer fear on my path to long-term recovery?

> How can I cultivate resilience and the determination to bounce back from setbacks, recognizing that they are part of the recovery journey?

> What steps can I take to pursue my fullest potential in recovery and refuse to settle for a life that is less than what I am capable of living?

By reflecting on these questions, individuals in addiction recovery can embrace a holistic approach to well-being and establish a foundation for long-term recovery that encompasses physical, emotional, and mental aspects. This approach fosters resilience, courage, and the realization of one's potential for a fulfilling and purposeful life in recovery.

A Journey of Transformation

Practices for Self-Care and Stress Management: Illuminating the Path to Long-Term Recovery

Long-term recovery from addiction is a journey filled with challenges, and the importance of self-care and stress management cannot be overstated. This book explores the significance of practicing self-care and effective stress management in addiction recovery. It emphasizes the enduring qualities of hope, faith, and love as essential tools to navigate the stormy seas of recovery, highlighting their role in overcoming adversity and finding the light at the end of the tunnel.

The Resilience of Hope

In the darkest of times, hope is a beacon that guides us through the storm. It reminds us that every storm runs out of rain and that every night turns into day. Hope fuels our determination to persevere, even when recovery feels treacherous. Through the practice of self-care, we can nurture and strengthen our hope, enabling us to weather the most challenging moments.

The Power of Faith

Faith is a steadfast belief that the difficulties we face in recovery will ultimately subside. It is the unwavering trust that, despite the present hardships, there is light at the end of the tunnel. As we engage in practices for self-care and stress management, we reinforce our faith in the recovery process and our own ability to overcome addiction.

The Triumph of Love

Love is the greatest of these virtues, as it sustains us through the most trying times. It is the unwavering love for ourselves and the desire to reclaim our lives that keeps us going. On the journey of long-term recovery, we encounter pain, but the love for the life we are rebuilding is the splendid prize that awaits us at the finish line.

Practices for Self-Care and Stress Management

Self-care and stress management are essential components of the recovery journey. These practices can take various forms, including physical exercise, mindfulness meditation, therapy, support groups, and healthy lifestyle choices. By incorporating these practices into daily life, individuals in recovery can manage stress, build resilience, and nurture their hope, faith, and love.

Self-Reflection Questions

> What specific self-care practices can I incorporate into my daily routine to nurture my hope, faith, and love during my recovery journey?

> How can I strengthen my belief in the eventual subsiding of challenges and the presence of light at the end of the tunnel through faith and trust in the recovery process?

In what ways can I cultivate love for myself and my journey, understanding that it is the driving force behind my recovery?

What strategies for stress management can I employ to navigate the stormy moments in my recovery journey more effectively?

When faced with adversity and challenges, how can I remind myself that every storm runs out of rain and every night turns into day?

By reflecting on these questions, individuals in addiction recovery can actively incorporate self-care and stress management practices into their lives. Embracing hope, faith, and love as guiding principles allows them to persevere through adversity, ultimately reaching the splendid prize of long-term recovery and a brighter future.

Maintaining Overall Health during Transformation:
The Power of Positive Thinking in Long-Term Recovery

Long-term recovery from addiction is a transformative journey that requires a holistic approach to health, encompassing physical, emotional, and mental well-being. This book delves into the importance of maintaining overall health during the process of recovery and highlights the transformative power of positive thinking. By embracing positivity, individuals can overcome adversity, replace negative thoughts with positive ones, and achieve lasting success in their recovery journey.

The Resilience of the Human Spirit

In the face of addiction and its challenges, individuals may suffer defeats, but they are not defeated. The resilience of the human spirit shines through as individuals rise stronger and wiser after each trial. Maintaining overall health during transformation involves recognizing that setbacks are not the end but opportunities for growth.

The Power of Positive Thinking

Positive thinking is a potent tool that can dramatically impact the recovery journey. When negative thoughts are replaced with positive ones, the trajectory of recovery changes. Positive thinking fosters optimism, hope, and a belief in one's ability to overcome addiction and achieve lasting change.

Developing a Positive Vision

To carry out positive actions, individuals must cultivate a positive vision for their future. This vision serves as a roadmap, guiding them toward their recovery goals and fostering a sense of purpose. By envisioning a life free from addiction, individuals are more likely to take positive steps to achieve it.

A Journey of Transformation

The Positive Push

Positive thinking acts as a powerful push in the journey of recovery. It is akin to a smile, a world of optimism, and a message that says, "You can do it" when faced with adversity. Positivity provides the motivation to persevere through tough times and offers a beacon of hope even in the darkest moments.

Self-Reflection Questions

How can I embrace positivity and replace negative thoughts with positive ones in my daily life to enhance my overall well-being during my recovery journey?

What specific actions can I take to develop a positive vision for my future, focusing on the life I aspire to live free from addiction?

In what ways can I leverage the power of positive thinking to motivate myself to take positive actions and stay committed to my recovery goals?

How can I maintain overall health, encompassing physical, emotional, and mental well-being, as an integral part of my transformation during recovery?

When facing challenges and setbacks, how can I remind myself that I have the resilience to rise stronger and wiser, ultimately achieving lasting success in my recovery journey?

By reflecting on these questions, individuals in addiction recovery can actively incorporate positive thinking and overall health maintenance into their transformation process. Positivity serves as a guiding light, motivating them to persevere, overcome obstacles, and find the strength to achieve a life free from addiction.

Seeking Ongoing Personal Growth:
Navigating the Storms of Addiction Recovery

The journey of long-term recovery from addiction is akin to navigating through stormy seas, often filled with challenges and hardships. To navigate these turbulent waters successfully, individuals must seek ongoing personal growth. This book delves into the significance of personal growth in addiction recovery, emphasizing the enduring qualities of faith, hope, and love as the keys to survival and transformation. It underscores the idea that every storm eventually subsides, leading to a brighter future.

The Resilience of the Human Spirit

Addiction recovery is a journey filled with ups and downs, much like the unpredictability of a storm. However, the human spirit is remarkably resilient. Just as every storm eventually runs out of rain, individuals in recovery can overcome adversity and emerge stronger. Personal growth is the foundation upon which resilience is built.

The Power of Faith

Faith is a beacon of light that guides individuals through the darkest moments of their recovery journey. It is the unwavering belief that despite the challenges and setbacks, there is always hope for a brighter future. By fostering faith in themselves and the recovery process, individuals gain the strength to persevere.

The Endurance of Hope

Hope is the driving force that propels individuals forward in their recovery. It is the belief that every night turns into day and that there is light at the end of the tunnel. Hope is the fuel that sustains individuals during the most challenging phases of recovery, inspiring them to keep moving forward.

The Triumph of Love

Love is the most potent force in addiction recovery. It serves as the motivation to endure the pain and difficulties of the journey. Love for oneself, for life, and for the desire to be free from addiction is the splendid prize that awaits at the finish line, making the arduous journey worthwhile.

Self-Reflection Questions

> How can I nurture personal growth in my recovery journey by embracing the enduring qualities of faith, hope, and love?
>
> What specific actions can I take to strengthen my faith in myself and the recovery process, especially during challenging times?
>
> In what ways can I maintain hope as a driving force in my recovery, even when facing setbacks and obstacles?
>
> How can I harness the power of love as motivation to endure the pain and difficulties of my recovery journey and ultimately achieve lasting success?
>
> When confronted with the storms of life, how can I remind myself that every storm runs out of rain, leading to a brighter future?

By reflecting on these questions, individuals in addiction recovery can actively seek ongoing personal growth. Embracing faith, hope, and love as guiding principles enables them to navigate the storms of addiction, emerge stronger, and ultimately achieve a fulfilling life in recovery.

A Journey of Transformation

Lifelong Learning and Self-Improvement: The Journey to Long-Term Recovery

The path to long-term recovery from addiction is a transformative journey that extends far beyond abstinence. It requires individuals to embark on a lifelong quest for learning and self-improvement. This book explores the significance of lifelong learning and self-improvement in addiction recovery, emphasizing the resilience of individuals who persevere when hope seems lost. It also highlights the importance of expanding the dimensions of life by gaining wisdom through pain, betrayal, disappointment, and experience.

Perseverance in the Face of Despair

Many of the world's most significant achievements have been realized by individuals who refused to give up, even when there appeared to be no hope. In addiction recovery, there may be moments of despair and doubt, but it is through perseverance that individuals continue to strive for betterment. Lifelong learning and self-improvement require the determination to overcome setbacks and keep moving forward.

Expanding the Dimensions of Life

Life is not solely about its length but also about its width and depth. Addiction recovery offers an opportunity to broaden one's horizons and delve into personal growth. By actively seeking knowledge, skills, and self-improvement, individuals can expand the dimensions of their life, embracing a fuller and more meaningful existence.

Gaining Wisdom Through Adversity

Pain, betrayal, disappointment, and experience are the crucibles that forge wisdom. In addiction recovery, individuals often face these challenges, which, although painful, contribute to personal growth and resilience. Each trial becomes an opportunity to grow stronger, wiser, and more skilled in navigating the complexities of life.

Avoiding Complacency

One of the essential aspects of lifelong learning and self-improvement is the determination never to take the best parts of life for granted. By acknowledging and appreciating the hardships endured during recovery, individuals cultivate gratitude and a renewed commitment to their journey of self-improvement.

Self-Reflection Questions

> How can I maintain perseverance and resilience in my addiction recovery journey, even when faced with moments of despair and hopelessness?

What steps can I take to actively seek lifelong learning and self-improvement as an ongoing process in my recovery?

In what ways can I expand the dimensions of my life, focusing not only on its length but also on its width and depth, to lead a more fulfilling existence?

How can I leverage the challenges of pain, betrayal, disappointment, and experience as opportunities to gain wisdom and personal growth during my recovery?

What strategies can I implement to avoid complacency and ensure that I never take the best parts of life for granted, maintaining gratitude and commitment to my journey of self-improvement?

By reflecting on these questions, individuals in addiction recovery can actively embrace the principles of lifelong learning and self-improvement. These principles serve as the foundation for continued personal growth, resilience, and a fulfilling life in recovery.

Setting New Goals for the Evolving Self:
The Journey to Long-Term Recovery

Long-term recovery from addiction is a journey of transformation and self-discovery. It is a process of breaking down, rebuilding, and evolving into a stronger version of oneself. This book explores the importance of setting new goals for the evolving self in addiction recovery, highlighting the resilience that emerges from facing personal challenges. It emphasizes the significance of focusing on what is truly important, learning from both positive and negative experiences, and embracing the journey towards personal growth and self-realization.

Resilience Through Adversity

The process of recovery often brings individuals to their breaking point. It is during these challenging moments that one discovers their inner strength and resilience. When broken down, individuals have the opportunity to rebuild themselves, emerging stronger, more resilient, and better equipped to face life's challenges.

Learning from Life's Lessons

Life is akin to a camera, capturing both the good times and the negatives. The mistakes and setbacks experienced during addiction and recovery serve as valuable lessons. By reflecting on these experiences, individuals can learn, grow, and make the necessary changes to create a healthier and more fulfilling life.

A Journey of Transformation

Appreciating Life's Blessings

In the pursuit of long-term recovery, it is essential to fix mistakes by focusing on positivity. Smiling, dreaming big, laughing, and recognizing one's blessings are powerful tools for personal transformation. They provide individuals with the strength and motivation to continue on their journey towards recovery and self-improvement.

Unlocking One's Potential

Many individuals live their lives in chains, unaware of the potential for change within them. Setting new goals and pursuing dreams is the key to unlocking this potential. Every great dream begins with a dreamer, and individuals in recovery possess the strength, patience, and passion needed to reach for the stars and make a positive impact on the world.

Self-Reflection Questions

> How can I harness the resilience that emerges from facing personal challenges in my addiction recovery journey to become a stronger version of myself?

> What strategies can I employ to focus on what truly matters in life and learn from both positive and negative experiences?

> In what ways can I actively practice gratitude and positivity as I fix mistakes and continue my journey of recovery and self-improvement?

> How can I unlock my full potential by setting new goals, pursuing dreams, and confidently moving in the direction of a life I have imagined in sobriety?

> What steps can I take to ensure that I embrace the evolving self and view the journey of recovery as an opportunity for personal growth and self-realization?

By reflecting on these questions, individuals in addiction recovery can actively set new goals for their evolving selves. This process of self-discovery and transformation serves as a foundation for long-term recovery and a life filled with purpose, resilience, and positivity.

Summarizing the Key Steps of Transformation:
A Guide to Long-Term Recovery

Long-term recovery from addiction is a transformative journey that requires dedication, resilience, and a commitment to self-improvement. This book summarizes the key steps of transformation in addiction recovery, emphasizing the power and potential individuals possess to change their lives. It underscores the importance of overcoming fear, embracing personal growth, and taking ownership of one's life to create a brighter future.

Unleashing Inner Strength

Individuals in addiction recovery should never underestimate their own strength. Each person is born with a unique purpose and possesses the power to achieve it. In recovery, tapping into this inner strength is essential. It is the driving force that empowers individuals to overcome addiction, face challenges, and work toward lasting change.

Confronting Fear

Change can be intimidating, but what's even scarier is allowing fear to hinder personal growth and progress. In long-term recovery, individuals must confront their fears head-on. By acknowledging and addressing the fears that hold them back, they can break free from the chains of addiction and embrace positive transformation.

Embracing Progress

Recovery is a journey filled with ups and downs, and making mistakes is a natural part of the process. Progress may be slow, but it is essential to remember that every step forward is a significant achievement. Even when faced with setbacks, individuals in recovery are still ahead of those who are not making an effort.

Taking Ownership of Life

Life is neither inherently good nor bad; it is a gift, and individuals have the power to shape it. Long-term recovery involves taking ownership of one's life and making it the best it can be. By actively working toward a life free from addiction, individuals can create a brighter and more fulfilling future.

Self-Reflection Questions

- How can I tap into my inner strength to fuel my journey of transformation in long-term recovery?

- What specific fears or obstacles do I need to confront and overcome to achieve personal growth and progress in recovery?

- In what ways can I embrace the idea that making mistakes and progressing slowly is still a significant achievement in my recovery journey?

- How can I take active ownership of my life and work toward creating a future that is both fulfilling and free from addiction?

- What steps can I take to remind myself daily that I possess the power to shape my life and make it the best it can be in long-term recovery?

A Journey of Transformation

By reflecting on these questions, individuals in addiction recovery can summarize the key steps of transformation and actively work toward long-term recovery and self-improvement. It is through self-discovery, resilience, and the willingness to confront fear that individuals can unlock their potential and create a brighter future.

In conclusion, the journey of personal transformation is a profound and life-altering process that demands commitment, self-awareness, and deliberate action. In Part III, we have explored the key steps that serve as the foundation for this transformative journey.

Setting the context for transformation, understanding the importance of the transformation process, and recognizing the power of intentional change are crucial initial steps. Self-reflection, as the starting point, requires us to delve deep into our own thoughts, emotions, and behaviors, identifying areas that require change and understanding our strengths and weaknesses.

Setting clear and SMART goals for personal change provides us with a roadmap for the transformation ahead. Cultivating a vision that aligns with our life purpose fuels our motivation and determination. Being mindful of our personal states of being, fostering a growth mindset, and managing our energy and vibration become essential tools in our transformation toolkit.

Understanding the principles of manifestation, utilizing visualization and affirmations, and aligning our goals with our vision propel us forward. Regularly reviewing and refining our goals, setting intentions, and taking inspired actions keep us on track and adaptable.

Celebrating our successes along the way not only acknowledges our progress but also inspires those around us. Embracing transformation as a lifelong journey and integrating positive rituals and habits into our daily routines help make change a sustainable part of our lives.

Prioritizing self-care and well-being ensures we stay physically, emotionally, and mentally resilient throughout our transformation. Finally, the commitment to ongoing personal growth and setting new goals for our evolving self completes the cycle of transformation.

In the end, personal transformation is not a destination but a continuous journey of self-discovery and growth. By following these key steps and embracing transformation as a way of life, we unlock our full potential and create a future that aligns with our deepest aspirations.

May your journey of personal transformation be filled with fulfillment, purpose, and a profound sense of self-realization.

Part IV
How and Why We Change

How and Why We Change

Change is an inevitable and often challenging part of our lives. It is a concept that transcends personal, societal, and cultural boundaries. For someone seeking long-term recovery from addiction, the process of change takes on profound significance. This book explores the intricate dynamics of change and self-acceptance in the context of addiction recovery. It delves into the idea that we are often too much or too little for others, emphasizes the importance of embracing our authentic selves, and highlights the transformative power of acknowledging our needs. Throughout this journey, individuals discover the wisdom in doing what they believe is right rather than conforming to external expectations.

Embracing Authenticity

"You will always be too much of something for someone: too big, too loud, too soft, too edgy." These words resonate deeply with anyone in recovery. Addiction often emerges as a means to cope with the pressures and expectations of society, leading individuals to suppress their authentic selves. In the pursuit of acceptance and belonging, they may become someone they are not, ultimately leading them down a path of self-destruction.

Recovery, however, is a journey of rediscovery. It entails unearthing the true self buried beneath layers of addiction. This process requires courage and vulnerability. It means acknowledging that, yes, you may be too much or too little for some people, but that's perfectly okay. Embracing your authenticity is not a sign of weakness; it is a testament to your strength.

Apologizing and Self-Reflection

"Apologize for mistakes. Apologize for unintentionally hurting someone. Don't apologize for being who you are." This piece of advice is invaluable in the context of addiction recovery. Addiction often leaves a trail of destruction, hurting not only the individual but also those around them. Recognizing and taking responsibility for one's mistakes is an essential step towards healing and rebuilding trust with loved ones.

However, there is a crucial distinction between apologizing for actions rooted in addiction and apologizing for one's inherent nature. You should never apologize for being true to yourself. Self-acceptance is a cornerstone of recovery, and it involves embracing both the flaws and strengths that make you unique.

Acknowledging Needs and Vulnerability

"Sometimes we have to lose our way to find out what we really want, because we often ignore our needs until we are lost." Addiction can be seen as a misguided attempt to fulfill unmet needs. Individuals may turn to substances to numb emotional pain, escape reality, or seek connection. In the process, they often neglect their authentic needs, leading to further despair.

A Journey of Transformation

Recovery demands a profound shift in perspective. It involves acknowledging that it's okay to have needs, and it's crucial to address them in healthy ways. This process requires vulnerability, a willingness to ask for help, and a commitment to self-care. It means recognizing that your needs are valid, and ignoring them can be more damaging than any external harm.

The Power of Self-Determination

"Do what you think is right, not what people think is right. In the end, it's you who goes through it, not them." This piece of advice encapsulates the essence of recovery. The journey to sobriety is deeply personal, and the path to lasting change is paved with self-determination and self-empowerment. While external support and guidance are essential, the ultimate decision to change and the strength to persevere must come from within.

Self-Reflection Questions:

> How do you perceive your own authenticity, and have you ever felt the need to suppress it in the past?

> Can you identify any past actions or behaviors related to addiction that require apologies and amends? How do you plan to make them right?

> What are some of your unmet needs that you may have ignored or numbed through addiction? How can you address these needs in healthier ways?

> How much of your recovery journey do you feel is driven by external expectations or societal pressures, as opposed to your own genuine desire for change?

> What steps can you take to strengthen your self-determination and ensure that your recovery journey aligns with your true self?

The path to long-term recovery from addiction is a profound journey of self-discovery, self-acceptance, and personal transformation. It is a process that requires embracing your authentic self, apologizing for mistakes while valuing your inherent worth, acknowledging your needs, and finding the strength within to determine your own path to recovery. Remember that change is not always easy, but it is worth it, for it leads to a life that is authentic, fulfilling, and free from the chains of addiction.

The Mechanisms and Motivations of Personal Change:
A Guide to Long-Term Recovery from Addiction

Change is an intrinsic part of the human experience, and its exploration within the context of addiction recovery is both fascinating and essential. Personal change involves a complex interplay of emotions, motivations, and actions. It requires trust in one's feelings, taking chances, and a deep understanding of the journey ahead. In this book, we delve into the mechanisms and motivations behind personal change, emphasizing the importance of living in the present, embracing both the ups and downs of life, and learning from past experiences. We also explore the idea that, through adversity, some individuals are not defeated but are instead forged into stronger versions of themselves.

The Dynamics of Personal Change

"Life is about trusting your feelings and taking chances, losing and finding happiness, appreciating the memories, learning from the past, and realizing people change." These words encapsulate the essence of personal change. Addiction can be a result of suppressed feelings, a fear of taking chances, and an attempt to escape pain or unhappiness. Recovery, on the other hand, is a journey of rediscovering these emotions, confronting pain, and learning to cope with it in healthier ways.

Trusting your feelings is a fundamental aspect of recovery. It involves acknowledging and validating your emotions, even the uncomfortable ones. Addiction often thrives in the shadows of repressed feelings, so embracing them is a crucial step toward healing.

Learning from the past is equally essential. It's an opportunity to reflect on mistakes and gather wisdom from previous experiences. In recovery, past actions can serve as a powerful reminder of the consequences of addiction, motivating individuals to stay on the path of sobriety.

The Importance of Living in the Present

"Some people are lost in the fire. Some people are built from it." This statement highlights the transformative power of adversity. Addiction can feel like being consumed by a relentless fire, but it also provides an opportunity for rebirth. The flames of addiction can forge inner strength and resilience, ultimately leading to personal growth.

Living in the present is a central theme in addiction recovery. Focusing on the 24 hours in front of you allows individuals to break down the daunting journey into manageable steps. It prevents the overwhelming anxiety that can come from contemplating long-term sobriety and instead encourages a day-by-day approach.

Forgiveness and Self-Compassion

"Don't think about what can happen in a month. Don't think about what can happen in a year. Just focus on the 24 hours in front of you and do what you can to get closer to where you want to be. Today you will do your best. If you have a good day, you will be proud of yourself. If you have a bad day, you will not dwell on it, you will forgive yourself, you will put it behind you and you will continue to move forward."

Recovery is a journey with ups and downs, and setbacks are a natural part of the process. The ability to forgive oneself and move forward is a testament to resilience. Self-compassion is a

A Journey of Transformation

powerful motivator, as it allows individuals to acknowledge their humanity and continue striving for their goals without dwelling on past mistakes.

Learning to Trust the Journey

"Learn to trust the journey, even when you do not understand it." This final piece of advice encapsulates the overarching theme of addiction recovery. Trusting the process, even when it seems unclear, is a profound act of faith in oneself. It involves embracing the uncertainty and acknowledging that change is not always linear or predictable.

Self-Reflection Questions:

How comfortable are you with trusting and expressing your feelings, especially the difficult ones, in your journey of recovery?

What have you learned from your past experiences with addiction, and how have these lessons shaped your commitment to recovery?

How do you typically deal with setbacks in your recovery journey, and can you identify ways to enhance self-compassion and forgiveness?

In what ways can you incorporate the practice of living in the present and focusing on daily progress into your recovery strategy?

What aspects of your recovery journey do you find challenging to trust, and how can you work on developing greater faith in the process?

Personal change within the context of addiction recovery is a complex and transformative journey. It involves trusting one's emotions, embracing the present, learning from past experiences, and having the resilience to move forward despite setbacks. By understanding the mechanisms and motivations behind personal change, individuals can navigate the path to long-term recovery with greater clarity, self-compassion, and trust in their journey.

Setting the Stage for Understanding the Intricacies of Change:
A Guide to Long-Term Recovery from Addiction

Change is a fundamental aspect of life, and for someone seeking long-term recovery from addiction, it takes on profound significance. Understanding the complexities of change is essential in this journey, as it involves breaking free from the shackles of addiction and embracing a life of sobriety. This book explores the intricacies of change, drawing inspiration from powerful statements that offer insights into the transformative process. It emphasizes the importance of taking risks, pursuing dreams, and actively working on creating the life one desires. Furthermore, it underscores the significance of self-reflection and learning from one's experiences and interactions with others.

Navigating the Waters of Change

"You don't drown by falling into a river, but by staying submerged in it." Addiction often feels like a river that threatens to engulf and drown those who fall into it. However, the key to recovery lies in the determination to rise above the currents of addiction. To achieve lasting change, one must learn to swim against the tide and eventually find solid ground.

The Desire for Change

"When you really desire something, all the universe can conspire to help you realize your dream." Recovery from addiction begins with a burning desire for change. This desire becomes the driving force that propels individuals forward, and it is what allows the universe, in its own mysterious way, to align circumstances, opportunities, and support systems to aid in the realization of that dream.

Confronting Fear

"Tell your heart that the fear of suffering is worse than the suffering itself. And no heart should ever suffer when it goes in search of its dream." Fear is a powerful obstacle on the path to recovery. It often paralyzes individuals, preventing them from taking the necessary steps toward change. However, acknowledging that the fear of suffering is often more painful than the suffering itself can provide the courage needed to confront addiction head-on.

The Importance of Taking Risks

"You have to take risks. You will only understand the miracle of life fully when you allow the unexpected to happen." Recovery is inherently risky. It involves stepping out of one's comfort zone and embracing the unknown. Change rarely happens without some degree of uncertainty and vulnerability. It is through taking these risks that individuals can fully grasp the beauty and unpredictability of life.

Actively Creating Your Life

"If you don't make the time to work on creating the life you want, you're eventually going to be forced to spend a LOT of time dealing with a life you DON'T want." Recovery is not a passive process. It requires individuals to actively engage in shaping their future. Focusing on building a life in alignment with one's values and aspirations is a powerful motivator for change.

Seeking and Recognizing Signs

"You can ask the universe for all the signs you want, but ultimately, we see what we want to see when we're ready to see it." Recovery often involves seeking signs of progress and positive change. However, these signs may not always be apparent until individuals are truly ready to embrace them. It requires patience and self-awareness to recognize and appreciate the signs of personal growth and transformation.

A Journey of Transformation

Self-Reflection Questions:

What is your deepest desire when it comes to your recovery journey, and how can you nurture and sustain this desire?

What fears or anxieties have held you back in the past, and how can you work on addressing and overcoming them in your pursuit of change?

In what ways have you actively taken risks or embraced uncertainty as part of your recovery journey, and how have these experiences shaped your growth?

How can you become more proactive in creating the life you want in sobriety, focusing on your values and aspirations?

Reflect on recent experiences where you sought signs of progress in your recovery. What did you learn from these moments, and how did they impact your journey?

Understanding the intricacies of change is essential for those seeking long-term recovery from addiction. It involves the desire for transformation, the courage to confront fear, the willingness to take risks, and the active creation of a life aligned with one's aspirations. By reflecting on these aspects and drawing inspiration from the wisdom of the statements mentioned, individuals can navigate the challenging but rewarding path to lasting recovery.

The Significance of Self-Awareness in the Change Process:
A Key to Long-Term Recovery from Addiction

Self-awareness is a critical component of the change process, particularly for individuals seeking long-term recovery from addiction. This book explores the profound significance of self-awareness in the journey to sobriety, drawing inspiration from poignant statements that emphasize the importance of perspective, attitude, and delayed gratification. It highlights the idea that self-awareness allows individuals to navigate the challenges of addiction recovery with resilience, wisdom, and the ability to differentiate between what they want and what they truly need.

The Silent Teacher: Self-Awareness in Difficult Times

"When you are going through difficulty and wonder where GOD is, remember that the teacher is always quiet during the test." Addiction and the path to recovery are often likened to tests of character and resilience. In moments of hardship, it can be tempting to question the presence of guidance or divine intervention. However, it is precisely during these times that self-awareness becomes the silent teacher, offering insights and lessons that are instrumental in the journey to sobriety.

Understanding and Accepting the Self

"Instead of obsessing over the things you can't change, focus on what you CAN: Your attitude, mindset, and energy." Self-awareness begins with understanding and accepting the self, flaws and all. Obsessing over past mistakes or things beyond one's control can be counterproductive, leading to negative emotions that may trigger relapse. Focusing on what can be changed—the attitude, mindset, and energy—empowers individuals to make meaningful transformations in their lives.

The Difference Between Want and Need

"What you want and what you need aren't always the same. Be willing to delay short-term gratification for long-term greatness." Addiction often revolves around immediate gratification, while the true needs of the individual are sidelined. Self-awareness allows individuals to discern between their wants and their needs. It enables them to prioritize long-term recovery and personal growth over short-term pleasure.

Self-Awareness: A Key to Resilience

Self-awareness is not just about recognizing one's strengths and weaknesses; it is also about acknowledging personal triggers, patterns, and emotional responses. This knowledge equips individuals with the tools to better navigate the challenges of recovery. It enables them to identify potential relapse triggers and develop coping strategies to maintain their sobriety.

Self-Reflection Questions:

> How well do you understand and accept yourself, including your past mistakes and vulnerabilities, in your journey to recovery?
>
> Can you identify instances in which self-awareness has played a role in helping you navigate difficult moments or cravings during your recovery process?
>
> Reflect on situations where you have prioritized short-term gratification over long-term goals. How might increased self-awareness help you make different choices in the future?
>
> In what ways have you used self-awareness to recognize and address triggers or patterns that could potentially lead to relapse? How can you continue to enhance this skill?
>
> Consider the balance between what you want and what you need in your life. How can self-awareness guide you in making choices that prioritize your long-term well-being?

Self-awareness is a profound and invaluable tool in the journey to long-term recovery from addiction. It empowers individuals to embrace the lessons in difficult times, focus on what they can change, and discern between their wants and needs. With self-awareness as their guide, individuals can navigate the path of recovery with resilience, wisdom, and the confidence to build a better, sober future.

The Intrinsic Motivations for Change

The journey towards long-term recovery from addiction is marked by transformative change, driven by intrinsic motivations. This book delves into the powerful messages of inspirational statements to explore the intrinsic motivations that fuel the process of recovery. It emphasizes the importance of recognizing one's desires, conquering the fear of suffering, taking risks, and actively working towards creating a fulfilling life. Furthermore, it underscores the role of self-reflection in understanding and empathizing with others, recognizing that the lessons learned from self-improvement can extend to fostering empathy and support for fellow individuals in recovery.

Recognizing Desires as Catalysts for Change

"When you really desire something, all the universe can conspire to help you realize your dream." In the context of addiction recovery, this statement highlights the significance of recognizing one's desire for a sober and fulfilling life. The intrinsic motivation to break free from addiction becomes a catalyst for change. This desire becomes a driving force that propels individuals to seek help, engage in treatment, and commit to a life of sobriety.

Conquering the Fear of Suffering

"Tell your heart that the fear of suffering is worse than the suffering itself. And no heart should ever suffer when it goes in search of its dream." Fear often holds individuals back from pursuing recovery, as they anticipate the pain and discomfort associated with withdrawal and change. However, conquering this fear is a vital step. It involves understanding that the suffering endured during recovery is a necessary part of the journey towards a healthier, more fulfilling life.

Taking Risks and Embracing the Unexpected

"You have to take risks. You will only understand the miracle of life fully when you allow the unexpected to happen." Recovery from addiction is inherently risky. It involves stepping out of one's comfort zone, facing uncertainties, and embracing change. By taking calculated risks and being open to the unexpected, individuals can discover the beauty of life beyond addiction.

Active Creation of a Fulfilling Life

"If you don't make the time to work on creating the life you want, you're eventually going to be forced to spend a LOT of time dealing with a life you DON'T want." Intrinsic motivations drive individuals to actively work towards creating a life aligned with their values and aspirations. Recovery is not passive; it requires dedication and effort. By investing time and energy into building a fulfilling life, individuals are less likely to revert to the destructive patterns of addiction.

A Journey of Transformation

Persistence in Pursuit of Goals

"If you really want something, really work hard, take advantage of opportunities, and never give up, you will find a way." Recovery is a journey filled with challenges, setbacks, and moments of doubt. Intrinsic motivations provide the perseverance needed to overcome these obstacles. Individuals who truly desire sobriety are more likely to persist in their efforts, taking advantage of opportunities and never giving up on their journey towards recovery.

Empathy and Self-Reflection

"Take a good look at yourself before you criticize another, for what you see wrong in them will also be a lesson for you." Self-reflection plays a significant role in addiction recovery. Recognizing one's flaws and challenges allows individuals to empathize with others who are on similar journeys. By understanding one's own struggles and growth, individuals can extend compassion and support to those who face similar challenges in their pursuit of recovery.

Self-Reflection Questions:

> What intrinsic motivations drive your desire for long-term recovery from addiction, and how can you nurture and sustain these motivations throughout your journey?

> Reflect on instances where fear of suffering has hindered your progress in recovery. How can you work on conquering this fear and embracing the discomfort as part of the healing process?

> Consider the risks you have taken or are willing to take in your recovery journey. How have these risks influenced your understanding of life beyond addiction?

> In what ways are you actively working to create a life that aligns with your values and aspirations in sobriety?

> How can self-reflection on your own experiences and challenges foster empathy and support for others in recovery, allowing you to share the lessons you have learned?

Intrinsic motivations are the driving force behind meaningful change in the journey to long-term recovery from addiction. By recognizing desires, conquering fear, taking risks, actively creating a fulfilling life, persisting in pursuit of goals, and fostering empathy through self-reflection, individuals can navigate the path of recovery with resilience and determination, ultimately finding freedom from the chains of addiction.

Internal Drivers of Personal Change: Empowering Long-Term Recovery from Addiction

Personal change, especially when seeking long-term recovery from addiction, is often driven by internal forces and motivations. This book explores the profound influence of these internal drivers in the context of addiction recovery. Drawing inspiration from motivational statements, it highlights the importance of self-reliance, resilience, and surrounding oneself with supportive individuals. It also emphasizes the value of self-belief and the power of unwavering determination when facing the challenges of addiction recovery.

The Resilience to Stand Strong

"Don't let anyone ever break our soul. We have to stand on our own two feet and stand up for ourselves." Recovery from addiction often involves moments of vulnerability and external pressures. However, it is the internal resilience that empowers individuals to stand strong, defend their sobriety, and protect their inner selves from external influences that could lead to relapse.

Maintaining Self-Respect and Dignity

"There are those that would give anything to see us fail, but we must never give them the satisfaction. Hold our head up high, smile, and stand our own ground." Internal drivers push individuals to maintain their self-respect and dignity, even in the face of adversity. The desire to prove wrong those who doubt their ability to recover fuels a strong commitment to sobriety. It compels individuals to hold their heads high, withstanding external pressures and standing firm in their journey to long-term recovery.

The Power of Supportive Relationships

"The best kind of people are the ones that come into our life and make us see the sun where we once saw clouds. The people that believe in us so much we start to believe in us too. The people that love us, simply for us being us. The once in a lifetime kind of people." Internal drivers include the recognition of the transformative power of supportive relationships. Those who offer unwavering belief and love bolster individuals' self-esteem, making it easier for them to believe in their own potential for recovery.

The Unyielding Commitment to Persevere

"We can always take the easy way out and give up, but real strength comes when we decide to keep pushing no matter what the circumstances are." Long-term recovery from addiction is a challenging journey with numerous hurdles and temptations. Internal drivers motivate individuals to persevere through adversity, demonstrating real strength by refusing to succumb to the easy way out.

A Journey of Transformation

Self-Reflection Questions:

> Reflect on the internal drivers that motivate your journey to long-term recovery from addiction. How do these drivers manifest in your daily life and actions?
>
> Consider instances where you have demonstrated resilience in standing up for your sobriety and maintaining self-respect in challenging situations. How can you continue to harness this inner strength?
>
> Reflect on the impact of supportive relationships in your recovery journey. How have these relationships influenced your self-belief and commitment to change?
>
> Think about moments when you've faced adversity and decided to keep pushing forward. What strategies and internal motivations have helped you persevere, and how can you cultivate more of them?
>
> How can you further develop and nurture the internal drivers that empower your long-term recovery? Are there specific practices or mindsets that can strengthen your resolve?

Personal change in the context of addiction recovery is often driven by powerful internal motivations. These internal drivers include resilience, self-respect, the transformative impact of supportive relationships, and an unwavering commitment to persevere. By recognizing and nurturing these internal forces, individuals can navigate the challenges of addiction recovery with greater determination, ultimately achieving long-term sobriety and personal transformation.

The Desire for Personal Growth and Self-Improvement:
Fueling Long-Term Recovery from Addiction

The journey towards long-term recovery from addiction is intrinsically tied to the desire for personal growth and self-improvement. This book explores the profound significance of this desire in the context of addiction recovery. Drawing inspiration from motivational statements, it highlights the importance of perseverance, seizing opportunities, and overcoming fear. It emphasizes that by nurturing a genuine desire for personal growth and relentlessly pursuing self-improvement, individuals can navigate the challenging path of recovery with determination and ultimately achieve lasting sobriety.

The Path to Opportunity through Effort

"Opportunity follows struggle. It follows effort. It follows hard work. It doesn't come before." In the journey to recovery, it's crucial to understand that opportunities for personal growth and positive change often arise as a result of hard work and persistent effort. By actively engaging in the recovery process and putting in the effort, individuals create the conditions for transformative opportunities to emerge.

The Pursuit of Goals through Determination

"If you really want something, and really work hard, and take advantage of opportunities, and never give up, you will find a way." The genuine desire for personal growth fuels determination. It drives individuals to set meaningful goals and relentlessly pursue them. This unwavering commitment to self-improvement becomes a powerful force that propels individuals forward on their journey to recovery.

The Cost of Neglecting Self-Improvement

"If you don't make the time to work on creating the life you want, you're eventually going to be forced to spend a LOT of time dealing with a life you DON'T want." Neglecting self-improvement and personal growth can lead to a life marked by dissatisfaction and unfulfillment. Addiction often thrives in the absence of a sense of purpose and meaning. By investing time and effort into creating a better life, individuals can reduce the risk of relapse and increase their chances of sustained recovery.

Overcoming Fear to Achieve Dreams

"Remember, the greatest failure is not to try. Fear kills more dreams than failure ever will." Fear can be a formidable obstacle on the path to recovery. It can paralyze individuals, preventing them from taking the necessary steps towards change. The desire for personal growth and self-improvement serves as a powerful motivator to confront and overcome these fears, enabling individuals to move forward with determination.

Self-Reflection Questions:

Reflect on the genuine desire for personal growth and self-improvement that drives your journey to long-term recovery from addiction. How does this desire manifest in your actions and choices?

Consider instances where your persistent effort and hard work have created opportunities for positive change in your recovery journey. How can you continue to nurture this effort?

Reflect on the goals you've set for yourself in recovery. How does your determination to achieve these goals contribute to your sense of purpose and motivation?

Think about moments when fear has held you back from taking necessary steps in your recovery. How can you harness your desire for personal growth to overcome these fears and continue moving forward?

How can you maintain and cultivate the genuine desire for personal growth and self-improvement as a driving force in your long-term recovery? Are there specific practices or mindsets that can help you stay motivated?

A Journey of Transformation

The desire for personal growth and self-improvement is a powerful catalyst for change in the journey to long-term recovery from addiction. By embracing this desire, individuals can persevere through struggles, seize opportunities, overcome fear, and ultimately achieve a life of sobriety and fulfillment. Through self-reflection and unwavering determination, individuals can harness this desire as a driving force on their path to lasting recovery.

The Pursuit of Happiness and Fulfillment:
A Guiding Light in Long-Term Recovery from Addiction

The journey to long-term recovery from addiction is often driven by the pursuit of happiness and fulfillment. This book explores the profound significance of this pursuit in the context of addiction recovery. Drawing inspiration from motivational statements, it highlights the importance of faith, resilience, emotional control, adaptability, and the ability to find joy even in challenging times. It emphasizes that by seeking happiness and fulfillment, individuals can navigate the path of recovery with hope, positivity, and a renewed sense of purpose.

Faith in the Face of Uncertainty

"When you have come to the edge of all the light that you know and are about to drop off into the darkness of the unknown, faith is knowing one of two things will happen: There will be something solid to stand on, or you will be taught to fly." In recovery, faith serves as a guiding light, illuminating the path forward. It's the belief that, even in the face of uncertainty and fear, there is hope for a brighter future. The pursuit of happiness and fulfillment is intimately connected to this faith, as individuals strive to find solace and meaning in their lives.

Resilience in the Face of Defeat

"Treat defeat as a temporary roadblock. Always stay in control of your emotions and never allow them to influence you in a negative way." Recovery is not without its setbacks and challenges. However, the pursuit of happiness and fulfillment fuels resilience. It enables individuals to view defeat as a temporary obstacle and to maintain emotional control in the face of adversity. This emotional resilience becomes a vital tool in sustaining long-term recovery.

Adaptability and Adjustments

"If something in your life is not going according to plan, make the necessary adjustments to put yourself back on track." The pursuit of happiness and fulfillment requires adaptability. Addiction recovery is a journey of growth and transformation, and individuals must be willing to make adjustments and changes when necessary. This adaptability ensures that individuals remain on the path to recovery, even when faced with unexpected challenges.

Finding Joy in the Midst of Pain

"Life isn't always sunshine and butterflies. Sometimes you got to learn to smile through the pain because, in the end, it's not going to matter how many breaths you have taken, but how many moments have taken your breath away." The pursuit of happiness and fulfillment acknowledges that life can be challenging. However, it encourages individuals to find joy and beauty in the midst of pain. By focusing on the moments that take their breath away, individuals can cultivate positivity and resilience, even in the face of addiction and recovery.

Self-Reflection Questions:

Reflect on the role of faith in your recovery journey. How does your belief in a brighter future contribute to your pursuit of happiness and fulfillment?

Consider instances where you've encountered defeat or setbacks in recovery. How has your pursuit of happiness helped you stay resilient and emotionally in control?

\Reflect on your adaptability in recovery. In what ways have you made necessary adjustments to stay on track towards happiness and fulfillment?

Think about moments in your recovery journey when you found joy despite challenging circumstances. How can you continue to cultivate positivity and resilience in your pursuit of happiness?

How can you make the pursuit of happiness and fulfillment a central focus in your long-term recovery plan? Are there specific practices or mindsets that can help you sustain a sense of purpose and hope?

The pursuit of happiness and fulfillment serves as a guiding light in the journey to long-term recovery from addiction. It encompasses faith, resilience, adaptability, and the ability to find joy even in challenging times. By emphasizing this pursuit, individuals can navigate the path of recovery with positivity, hope, and a renewed sense of purpose, ultimately achieving lasting happiness and fulfillment in their lives. Through self-reflection and unwavering determination, individuals can harness this pursuit as a driving force on their path to lasting recovery.

Understanding the Role of Intrinsic Motivations in Sustaining Change:
A Roadmap to Long-Term Recovery from Addiction

Long-term recovery from addiction is not a destination but a continuous journey, and intrinsic motivations play a pivotal role in sustaining change throughout this process. This book explores the profound significance of intrinsic motivations in addiction recovery, drawing inspiration from motivational statements. It highlights the importance of faith, self-awareness, gratitude, and the power of taking the first step. It emphasizes that by understanding and nurturing intrinsic

A Journey of Transformation

motivations, individuals can embark on a path of lasting transformation, ultimately achieving sustained recovery from addiction.

The Courage to Move Forward

"This is not the time to shrink back in fear. Move forward in faith." Intrinsic motivations often begin with the courage to move forward despite the challenges and uncertainties of recovery. This inner strength, driven by a deep desire for change, enables individuals to overcome the fear that might otherwise hinder their progress.

Recognizing and Nurturing Your Gifts

"Get up every morning knowing you are gifted. Don't let fear intimidate you." Intrinsic motivations involve recognizing and nurturing one's own gifts and potential. By understanding their intrinsic worth and value, individuals can counteract the negative self-perceptions often associated with addiction. This self-awareness becomes a powerful tool in sustaining change.

Gratitude for Life's Lessons

"Appreciate every day that you're alive because somewhere in the world others are struggling to survive. Life does not always give you what you want, but if you look closely, you will see that it gives what you need for growth." Gratitude is a core intrinsic motivation in recovery. It involves appreciating the gift of life and recognizing that even challenges and setbacks hold valuable lessons for personal growth. This perspective shift fosters resilience and sustains individuals on their recovery journey.

The Value of Taking the First Step

"Everything begins with the resolve to take the first step. From that action, wisdom arises, and change begins. Without action, nothing changes." The intrinsic motivation to change often begins with the resolve to take the first step towards recovery. This initial action is the spark that ignites the transformation process. By recognizing the value of that first step, individuals can harness their intrinsic motivations to initiate and sustain change.

Self-Reflection Questions:

> Reflect on the intrinsic motivations that drive your desire for long-term recovery from addiction. How do these motivations influence your daily actions and choices?
>
> Consider moments when you've faced fear and had the courage to move forward in faith. How can you continue to nurture and harness this inner strength in your recovery journey?
>
> Reflect on your self-awareness and the recognition of your own gifts and potential. How does this self-awareness contribute to your sense of worth and value in recovery?

Think about the role of gratitude in your recovery journey. How can you cultivate a deeper sense of gratitude for life's lessons, both the challenges and the opportunities for growth?

How can you maintain and nurture your intrinsic motivations as a driving force in your long-term recovery plan? Are there specific practices or mindsets that can help you sustain your commitment to change?

Intrinsic motivations are a fundamental force in sustaining change in the journey to long-term recovery from addiction. They encompass courage, self-awareness, gratitude, and the power of taking the first step. By understanding and nurturing these intrinsic motivations, individuals can embark on a path of lasting transformation, ultimately achieving sustained recovery and a fulfilling life in sobriety. Through self-reflection and unwavering determination, individuals can harness their intrinsic motivations as a driving force on their path to lasting recovery.

The Importance of Aligning Change with One's Values and Beliefs:
A Guide to Long-Term Recovery from Addiction

Long-term recovery from addiction is a transformative journey that is deeply rooted in aligning change with one's values and beliefs. This book delves into the profound significance of this alignment in addiction recovery, drawing inspiration from inspirational statements. It emphasizes the importance of trust, embracing change, living in the present, self-compassion, and learning from life's experiences. By recognizing and nurturing this alignment, individuals can navigate the path of recovery with authenticity, purpose, and sustained commitment to change.

Trusting Feelings and Embracing Change

"Life is about trusting our feelings, taking chances, losing, finding happiness, appreciating the memories, learning from the past, and realizing people change." The journey to recovery begins with the trust in one's feelings and the recognition that change is not only possible but necessary. Aligning change with one's values and beliefs involves a deep understanding of the transformative potential of recovery.
Living in the Present

"Don't think about what can happen in a month. Don't think about what can happen in a year. Just focus on the 24 hours in front of us and do what we can to get closer to where we want to be." Alignment with one's values and beliefs requires a commitment to living in the present moment. It involves setting daily intentions and taking small steps toward personal growth, without being overwhelmed by distant future goals.

Self-Compassion and Forgiveness

"Today we will do our best. If we have a good day, we will be proud of ourselves. If we have a bad day, we will not dwell on it, we will forgive ourselves, we will put it behind us, and we will continue to move forward." Self-compassion is an integral aspect of aligning change with one's values and

A Journey of Transformation

beliefs. In recovery, there will be good days and bad days. Self-forgiveness and the ability to move forward with kindness and understanding are crucial to maintaining the alignment with one's values and beliefs.

Learning from Life's Experiences

"Learn to trust the journey, even when we do not understand it." Recovery is a journey filled with challenges, setbacks, and moments of uncertainty. Aligning change with one's values and beliefs involves a willingness to learn from every experience, even when the path is unclear. Trusting the journey, even in moments of doubt, is key to sustaining change.

Self-Reflection Questions:

> Reflect on the alignment between your values and beliefs and your journey to long-term recovery from addiction. How do your core values and beliefs guide your actions and decisions in recovery?

> Consider moments when you've trusted your feelings and embraced change in your recovery journey. How has this alignment contributed to your personal growth and transformation?

> Reflect on your ability to live in the present and focus on the 24 hours in front of you. How can you continue to nurture this mindfulness and set daily intentions in your recovery?

> Think about instances when self-compassion and forgiveness played a role in your recovery. How can you further cultivate these qualities to maintain your alignment with your values and beliefs?

> How can you deepen your trust in the journey of recovery, even when you don't fully understand it? Are there specific practices or mindsets that can help you maintain this trust and alignment?

Aligning change with one's values and beliefs is fundamental in the journey to long-term recovery from addiction. It involves trust, embracing the present, self-compassion, and a commitment to learning from life's experiences. By recognizing and nurturing this alignment, individuals can navigate the path of recovery with authenticity and purpose, ultimately achieving lasting change and a life in sobriety that resonates with their deepest values and beliefs. Through self-reflection and unwavering determination, individuals can harness this alignment as a guiding force on their path to lasting recovery.

Finding Purpose and Meaning in Transformation:
A Path to Long-Term Recovery from Addiction

The journey to long-term recovery from addiction is a profound transformation, and it becomes all the more meaningful when individuals find purpose and meaning within this process. This book explores the deep significance of discovering purpose and meaning in addiction recovery, drawing inspiration from insightful statements. It underscores the importance of embracing change, dealing with pain, and valuing meaningful connections. By recognizing the transformative potential of their journey and finding purpose within it, individuals can navigate the path of recovery with newfound motivation and fulfillment.

Embracing Life's Surprises

"Life is always full of surprises. You never know who we are going to meet that will change our life forever." Recovery is a journey filled with unexpected twists and turns. The process of finding purpose and meaning begins with embracing these surprises and recognizing that every encounter, every experience, has the potential to transform our lives.

Overcoming the Fear of Change

"Don't let the concept of change scare you as much as the prospect of remaining unhappy." Change is often met with resistance and fear. However, finding purpose and meaning in transformation requires individuals to prioritize their well-being over the fear of the unknown. It involves recognizing that the status quo, marked by addiction and unhappiness, is no longer acceptable.

Dealing with Pain and Resilience

"Everyone deals with pain differently." In the journey to recovery, pain is a constant companion. Finding purpose and meaning means acknowledging this pain and learning to deal with it in healthy ways. It requires resilience and the willingness to confront one's own struggles, recognizing that pain can be a catalyst for growth.

Valuing Meaningful Connections

"Don't come into someone's life when you have no intentions of staying. Tools are meant to be used, not hearts." Recovery often involves building and nurturing meaningful connections with others who share similar experiences. Finding purpose and meaning means valuing these connections and realizing that genuine support and empathy can be transformative.

Letting Go and Moving Forward

"We can't change what has already happened, so let's not waste our time thinking about it. Let's try and move on, let go, and get over it." Finding purpose and meaning in transformation requires

A Journey of Transformation

individuals to let go of the past and focus on the present and future. It involves a commitment to moving forward and making the most of the opportunities that lie ahead.

Learning from Unexpected Teachers

"Sometimes the most valuable lessons come from people who didn't intend to give them." Finding purpose and meaning involves being open to learning from unexpected sources. It means recognizing that valuable lessons can emerge from unexpected teachers, even in the midst of addiction recovery.

Self-Reflection Questions:

> Reflect on the surprises you have encountered in your recovery journey. How have these unexpected experiences impacted your life, and how can you continue to embrace them?
>
> Consider the fear of change and the prospect of remaining unhappy. How can you shift your perspective to prioritize your well-being and transformation over the fear of the unknown?
>
> Reflect on how you deal with pain in your recovery. What strategies or coping mechanisms have helped you develop resilience and find meaning within your journey?
>
> Think about the meaningful connections you've built in recovery. How can you continue to value and nurture these connections as sources of support and transformation?
>
> How can you let go of the past and focus on moving forward in your recovery journey? Are there specific practices or mindsets that can help you fully embrace the present and future?
>
> Consider the lessons you have learned from unexpected sources in your recovery. How can you remain open to new insights and wisdom from unexpected teachers along the way?

Finding purpose and meaning in transformation is a powerful catalyst in the journey to long-term recovery from addiction. It involves embracing life's surprises, overcoming the fear of change, dealing with pain, valuing meaningful connections, letting go of the past, and learning from unexpected teachers. By recognizing the transformative potential of their journey and finding purpose within it, individuals can navigate the path of recovery with newfound motivation, resilience, and fulfillment. Through self-reflection and unwavering determination, individuals can continue to harness purpose and meaning as guiding forces on their path to lasting recovery.

The Extrinsic Factors Influencing Change

In the pursuit of long-term recovery from addiction, individuals are often influenced and supported by extrinsic factors that play a pivotal role in their transformation. This book explores the profound significance of extrinsic factors in the context of addiction recovery, drawing inspiration from motivational statements. It underscores the importance of hope, honesty, self-discovery, trust, resilience, and the ultimate realization that life's challenges can be overcome. By recognizing and harnessing these extrinsic influences, individuals can navigate the path of recovery with determination, growth, and a renewed sense of purpose.

The Power of Hope

"Hope is not pretending that troubles don't exist. It is the hope that it won't last forever. That hurts will be healed and difficulties overcome. That we will be led out of the darkness and into the sunshine." Extrinsic factors often begin with the power of hope. Hope serves as a beacon of light in the darkest moments of addiction, offering the belief that change and recovery are possible. It encourages individuals to persevere, even when faced with seemingly insurmountable challenges.

The Honesty of Self-Discovery

"We find out that growing up means being honest. About what we want. What we need. What we feel. Who we are." Honesty, often instilled through external support systems, becomes a powerful force in recovery. Extrinsic influences encourage individuals to be honest about their desires, needs, emotions, and identity. This self-discovery is a cornerstone of personal growth and transformation.

Navigating through Getting Lost

"It's okay to get lost every once in a while. Sometimes getting lost is how we find ourselves. Trust ourselves." Extrinsic factors provide guidance and support during times of confusion and uncertainty. They reassure individuals that it's okay to get lost in the journey because, often, it is through these experiences that they discover their true selves and learn to trust their own capabilities.

The Resilience to Survive

"We've survived a lot, and we'll survive whatever is coming." Extrinsic factors remind individuals of their resilience. They offer a sense of strength and determination that has carried them through past challenges. This reminder reinforces the belief that, no matter what obstacles arise in recovery, they have the resilience to overcome them.

A Journey of Transformation

Realizing the Ultimate Sense

"Smile because one day it'll all make sense, and then we'll realize our worries were for no reason." Extrinsic influences provide encouragement and reassurance that, in the end, the challenges faced in recovery will lead to a greater understanding and sense of purpose. The realization that worries were unfounded becomes a source of motivation and positivity.

Self-Reflection Questions:

Reflect on the extrinsic factors that have influenced your recovery journey. How have these external influences played a role in your transformation and growth?

Consider the role of hope in your recovery. How has hope served as a guiding light during challenging times, and how can you continue to nurture and harness this sense of optimism?

Reflect on the honesty and self-discovery that have been encouraged by external support systems. How has this honesty contributed to your personal growth and understanding of yourself?

Think about moments when you got lost in your journey to recovery. How did external influences provide you with guidance and reassurance during those times of uncertainty?

Reflect on your resilience and the challenges you've overcome. How can you continue to draw strength from your past experiences to face future obstacles in recovery?

How can you maintain a sense of positivity and trust in the journey of recovery, even when faced with uncertainty and challenges? Are there specific practices or mindsets that can help you do so?

Extrinsic factors play a vital role in influencing and supporting change in the journey to long-term recovery from addiction. These external influences encompass hope, honesty, self-discovery, trust, resilience, and the ultimate realization that life's challenges can be overcome. By recognizing and harnessing these extrinsic influences, individuals can navigate the path of recovery with determination, growth, and a renewed sense of purpose. Through self-reflection and unwavering determination, individuals can continue to embrace the transformative power of these extrinsic factors on their path to lasting recovery.

External Catalysts for Change:
The Persistent Fight for Long-Term Recovery from Addiction

In the arduous journey toward long-term recovery from addiction, external catalysts often serve as a powerful driving force for transformation. This book explores the profound significance of external catalysts in the context of addiction recovery, drawing inspiration from motivational statements. It emphasizes the importance of resilience, determination, and the unwavering commitment to keep fighting for a life of health, happiness, and success. By recognizing and harnessing these external influences, individuals can navigate the path of recovery with renewed vigor, purpose, and a steadfast commitment to change.

The Fight for Survival

"One of the most difficult things everyone has to learn is that for your entire life you must 'KEEP FIGHTING' and adjusting if you hope to survive." The fight for survival is a fundamental external catalyst in addiction recovery. It underscores the necessity of resilience and adaptation to overcome the challenges posed by addiction. Acknowledging this ongoing struggle is a crucial step in the journey to recovery.

The Pursuit of Desires and Achievements

"No matter who you are or what your position, you must keep fighting for whatever it is you desire to achieve." External catalysts drive individuals to pursue their deepest desires and aspirations. These external factors often motivate individuals to persistently fight for their goals, including sobriety and a fulfilling life free from addiction.

Managing Expectations and Disappointment

"If someone is not aware of this contest and expects otherwise, then constant disappointment occurs." External influences also guide individuals in managing their expectations. Understanding that the path to recovery is marked by challenges and setbacks helps individuals avoid constant disappointment and stay focused on their ultimate goals.

The Fighting Spirit

"People who fall sometimes do not realize that the simple answer to everyday achievement is to keep fighting. Health, happiness, and success depend upon the fighting spirit of each person." External catalysts reinforce the importance of maintaining a fighting spirit. This spirit becomes a source of strength and determination in the pursuit of health, happiness, and success in recovery.

The Power of Action

"The big thing is not what happens to us in life but what we do about what happens to us." External influences remind individuals that their actions and responses to life's challenges are paramount. It's not solely about what happens but about the proactive steps taken to overcome adversity and achieve lasting recovery.

A Journey of Transformation

Self-Reflection Questions:

Reflect on the external catalysts that have influenced your recovery journey. How have external factors, such as the pursuit of desires and the fight for survival, motivated your transformation and growth?

Consider the role of expectations in your recovery. How can managing your expectations and understanding the ongoing contest for recovery help you avoid constant disappointment?

Reflect on your fighting spirit and determination. How can you continue to nurture and harness this spirit as a driving force in your recovery journey?

Think about the actions you have taken to overcome challenges in your recovery. How can you maintain a proactive approach to address the obstacles and setbacks that may arise?

How can you continue to embrace external catalysts for change and remain committed to the persistent fight for a life of health, happiness, and success in recovery? Are there specific practices or mindsets that can help you do so?

External catalysts play a crucial role in guiding and supporting change in the journey to long-term recovery from addiction. These external influences encompass resilience, determination, and the unwavering commitment to keep fighting for a life of health, happiness, and success. By recognizing and harnessing these external influences, individuals can navigate the path of recovery with renewed vigor, purpose, and a steadfast commitment to change. Through self-reflection and unwavering determination, individuals can continue to embrace the transformative power of external catalysts on their path to lasting recovery.

Life Events and Transitions:
Letting Go and Moving Forward in Long-Term Addiction Recovery

Long-term recovery from addiction is a journey filled with life events and transitions that require individuals to confront their past, embrace change, and move forward. This book delves into the profound significance of life events and transitions in addiction recovery, drawing inspiration from motivational statements. It underscores the importance of letting go of the past, accepting the things we cannot change, and finding the courage to forge ahead. By recognizing and navigating these transformative moments, individuals can continue their journey to lasting recovery with determination, growth, and a sense of renewal.

The Need to Leave the Past Behind

"If you want to fly in the sky, you need to leave the earth. If you want to move forward, you need to let go of the past that drags you down." One of the fundamental aspects of addiction recovery is the necessity to leave the past behind. The past, often marked by addiction and its consequences, can weigh individuals down. Letting go of this burden becomes an essential step in moving forward toward recovery.

The Imperative of Moving Forward

"The only thing a person can ever really do is keep moving forward. Take that big leap forward without hesitation, without once looking back." Addiction recovery is a journey of progress and growth. Moving forward becomes a conscious choice, a big leap that requires determination and courage. This transition marks a significant step towards lasting recovery.

Acceptance of the Unchangeable

"There are things that we don't want to happen but have to accept, things we don't want to know but have to learn, and people we can't live without but have to let go." Life events and transitions often necessitate acceptance of the unchangeable. In recovery, individuals must learn to accept the past, even if it includes painful events, and let go of attachments that may hinder their progress.

Embracing the Future

"Simply forget the past and forge toward the future. One of the happiest moments in life is when you find the courage to let go of what you cannot change." Embracing the future becomes a source of joy and renewal. It involves the courage to release the grip of the past and look ahead to a life filled with possibilities and purpose.

The Struggle of Growth and Letting Go

"Anything you can't control is teaching you how to let go. You only struggle because you're ready to grow but aren't willing to let go." Life events often present challenges that test an individual's ability to let go. These struggles are opportunities for growth, and the willingness to let go of control becomes a valuable lesson in recovery.

The Wisdom of Moving On

"Why let go of yesterday? Because yesterday has already let go of you." Ultimately, the decision to move forward is grounded in the wisdom of recognizing that yesterday's past has already released its hold on us. Letting go is an act of self-compassion and empowerment.

Self-Reflection Questions:

> Reflect on the past events and transitions that have shaped your addiction recovery journey. How have these moments influenced your path to lasting recovery?

> Consider the significance of letting go of the past in your recovery. How has releasing the burden of past mistakes and regrets allowed you to move forward with greater determination?
>
> Reflect on your ability to accept things you cannot change. How can you continue to practice acceptance and let go of attachments that may hinder your progress in recovery?
>
> Think about your commitment to embracing the future. How does this outlook contribute to your sense of joy and renewal in recovery, and how can you maintain this perspective?
>
> Reflect on moments of struggle in your recovery journey. How can you embrace the lessons they offer and be more willing to let go of control when necessary?
>
> How can you continue to harness the wisdom of moving on and recognizing that yesterday's past has already released its hold on you? Are there specific practices or mindsets that can help you maintain this outlook?

Life events and transitions are integral components of the journey to long-term recovery from addiction. These moments necessitate letting go of the past, accepting the unchangeable, and finding the courage to move forward. By recognizing and navigating these transformative events, individuals can continue their path to lasting recovery with determination, growth, and a sense of renewal. Through self-reflection and unwavering determination, individuals can continue to embrace the transformative power of life events and transitions on their path to a brighter future.

Social and Environmental Influences:
Embracing Change on the Path to Long-Term Recovery from Addiction

Long-term recovery from addiction is a transformative journey often shaped by social and environmental influences. This book delves into the profound significance of these external factors in addiction recovery, drawing inspiration from motivational statements. It underscores the importance of acceptance, self-empowerment, and the desire for success in the face of fear. Additionally, it highlights the wisdom gained from past mistakes and the importance of seizing opportunities when they arise. By recognizing and embracing these social and environmental influences, individuals can navigate the path of recovery with resilience, growth, and a renewed sense of purpose.

Accepting the Unchangeable

"The past cannot be changed, forgotten, edited, or erased; it can only be accepted. Keep moving forward." One of the fundamental aspects of addiction recovery is the acceptance of the past. Acknowledging that the past cannot be altered is a pivotal step in the journey toward lasting recovery. By embracing acceptance, individuals can move forward without being hindered by past regrets or mistakes.

Transforming Weaknesses into Strengths

"We create our own weaknesses and strengths. Our limitations begin in our mind where we can always replace negative with positive." Social and environmental influences can play a crucial role in reshaping individuals' perceptions of themselves. They encourage the transformation of perceived weaknesses into strengths by fostering a positive mindset. Self-empowerment becomes a valuable tool in the recovery journey.

Desiring Success Over Fearing Failure

"In order to succeed, your desire for success should be greater than your fear of failure." Social and environmental influences can inspire individuals to prioritize their desire for success over the fear of failure. This shift in perspective empowers individuals to take meaningful steps toward their recovery goals, despite the inherent challenges.

Learning from Mistakes and Pain

"In life, we have made a lot of mistakes and have felt a lot of pain, but mistakes make us wiser and pain makes us stronger. Don't regret the things you've done. Regret the things you didn't do when you had the chance." Social and environmental influences encourage individuals to view their past mistakes as valuable lessons and their experiences of pain as sources of strength. Regret is redirected toward missed opportunities rather than actions taken.

Faith in Divine Guidance

"You are exactly where you need to be though. Be faithful, for God is always working to bring what you need most into your life." Social and environmental influences can also foster faith and spiritual growth in recovery. Individuals are encouraged to trust that they are on the right path and that divine guidance is continuously leading them toward what they need most.

The Secret of Success: Taking Action

"The secret of success: stop wishing, start doing." Ultimately, social and environmental influences inspire individuals to take action. Success in recovery is not achieved through mere wishes but through concrete steps and persistent effort.

Self-Reflection Questions:

> Reflect on the social and environmental influences that have shaped your recovery journey. How have these external factors influenced your perspective on the past and your ability to move forward?

A Journey of Transformation

> Consider your journey of transforming weaknesses into strengths. How has self-empowerment and a positive mindset contributed to your growth in recovery, and how can you continue to foster these qualities?
>
> Reflect on your desire for success and your fear of failure in recovery. How can you ensure that your desire for success remains greater than your fear of failure in the face of challenges?
>
> Think about the wisdom you've gained from past mistakes and pain. How can you continue to embrace these experiences as valuable lessons and sources of strength in your journey?
>
> Reflect on your faith and spiritual growth in recovery. How can you continue to trust that you are on the right path and that divine guidance is leading you toward what you need most?
>
> How can you maintain the commitment to taking action in your recovery journey? Are there specific practices or mindsets that can help you stop wishing and start doing on your path to lasting recovery?

Social and environmental influences are integral components of the journey to long-term recovery from addiction. These external factors encompass acceptance, self-empowerment, the desire for success, the wisdom gained from past experiences, faith, and the commitment to taking action. By recognizing and embracing these social and environmental influences, individuals can navigate the path of recovery with resilience, growth, and a renewed sense of purpose. Through self-reflection and unwavering determination, individuals can continue to harness the transformative power of these influences on their path to lasting recovery.

Recognizing the Impact of External Factors on Personal Choices: A Path to Long-Term Recovery from Addiction

In the journey toward long-term recovery from addiction, recognizing the profound influence of external factors on personal choices is pivotal. This book explores the significance of external influences in the context of addiction recovery, drawing inspiration from motivational statements. It emphasizes the importance of resilience, belief in oneself, faith in the journey, and the alignment of actions with aspirations. By acknowledging and understanding these external influences, individuals can make informed choices, navigate the path of recovery with determination, and build a foundation for lasting change.

The Test of Resilience

"When life knocks you down, it's testing you to see whether you have the strength or not to stand back up. Don't give up!" External factors often present challenges and obstacles in the journey to recovery. These challenges serve as tests of resilience, pushing individuals to demonstrate their strength and determination. The choice to stand back up in the face of adversity is a critical one in the recovery process.

Belief in One's Superiority to Circumstance

"All things splendid have been achieved by those who dared BELIEVE that something inside them was superior to circumstance." External factors can either serve as limitations or as catalysts for personal growth. Believing in one's innate potential and resilience can be a powerful force in overcoming the circumstances of addiction. This belief is a driving factor in achieving splendid and transformative outcomes in recovery.

Faith in the Journey

"Have faith in your journey. Everything had to happen exactly as it did to get you where you're at today." Recognizing the impact of external factors involves having faith in the journey itself. Every event, choice, and circumstance has contributed to an individual's current state in recovery. Trusting that the journey is unfolding as it should provides solace and motivation to continue.

Dreams, Actions, and Overcoming Fear

"Let your dreams be bigger than your fears and your actions louder than your words." External factors often shape an individual's aspirations and choices. The desire to overcome addiction and build a better life must be fueled by dreams that outweigh the fears associated with change. Taking bold actions aligned with those dreams becomes a pivotal step in the recovery process.

Self-Reflection Questions:

Reflect on the external factors that have influenced your choices in your recovery journey. How have these external influences tested your resilience and strength in standing back up when life knocked you down?

Consider your belief in your own superiority to circumstance. How has this belief played a role in your ability to achieve splendid outcomes in recovery, and how can you continue to nurture it?

Reflect on your faith in the journey of recovery. How can you continue to trust that every experience, whether positive or challenging, has contributed to your current state in recovery?

Think about the alignment of your dreams with your actions in recovery. How can you ensure that your dreams are bigger than your fears, and how can you continue to take bold actions toward your goals?

A Journey of Transformation

> How can you maintain a deep understanding of the impact of external factors on your choices and decisions in recovery? Are there specific practices or mindsets that can help you make informed and positive choices on your path to lasting recovery?

Recognizing the impact of external factors on personal choices is integral to the journey of long-term recovery from addiction. These external influences encompass resilience, self-belief, faith in the journey, and the alignment of dreams with actions. By acknowledging and understanding these external influences, individuals can make informed and positive choices, navigate the path of recovery with determination, and build a foundation for lasting change. Through self-reflection and unwavering determination, individuals can continue to harness the transformative power of these influences on their path to lasting recovery.

Navigating External Pressures and Expectations:
Embracing Self-Validation on the Path to Long-Term Recovery from Addiction

In the journey towards long-term recovery from addiction, the ability to navigate external pressures and expectations plays a crucial role. This book explores the profound significance of self-validation in the context of addiction recovery, drawing inspiration from motivational statements. It emphasizes the importance of self-awareness, forgiveness, adaptability, and self-filling in the face of external influences. By recognizing and embracing these principles, individuals can fortify their recovery journey, build resilience, and cultivate lasting change.

The Peril of Seeking External Validation

"As long as you look for someone else to validate who you are by seeking their approval, you are setting yourself up for disaster. You have to be whole and complete in yourself. No one can give you that. You have to know who you are – what others say is irrelevant." Addiction recovery can be profoundly affected by external pressures and the need for validation from others. Seeking approval from external sources can lead to disappointment and hinder the recovery process. True validation must come from within, rooted in self-awareness and self-acceptance.

Rebuilding Trust After Mistakes

"It's easy to forgive the mistakes of others, but it's hard to rebuild the trust that has been destroyed." The impact of addiction often extends beyond the individual, affecting relationships and trust. In recovery, rebuilding trust can be challenging, requiring time and effort. This process involves understanding that forgiveness alone may not be enough; one must also actively work towards restoring trust.

Embracing Change and Adaptability

"Never assume that you're stuck with the way things are. Life changes, and so can you. Move on. There's no point of living in the past. Just because it's hard, doesn't mean it's impossible." External pressures and expectations may be rooted in the past, but recovery demands an ability to adapt and embrace change. Recognizing that change is possible, even when it's challenging, can empower individuals to move forward and overcome obstacles.

Self-Filling and Personal Growth

"Only you can fill in what's missing. It's not something another person can do for you." External influences may leave gaps or voids in an individual's life. In recovery, it's essential to recognize that self-filling and personal growth are personal responsibilities. This self-awareness empowers individuals to take charge of their journey and fill in what's missing.

Ignoring Negative Opinions

"Don't worry about what others think. Just focus on yourself and stay positive. Some people are always negative, so don't let it bother you." External pressures often include the opinions and judgments of others. Learning to disregard negative opinions and staying focused on one's own path to recovery is crucial. Negativity from external sources should not deter the commitment to personal growth and change.

Letting Go and Moving Forward

"In the end, you can't always choose what to keep. You can only choose how you let it go." External pressures and expectations may involve holding onto past beliefs or habits. Letting go of what no longer serves the recovery journey is a powerful choice. It involves taking control of one's decisions and choosing how to move forward with purpose.

Self-Reflection Questions:

Reflect on your journey of seeking external validation in your recovery. How has the need for approval from others affected your progress, and how can you work on being whole and complete within yourself?

Consider the process of rebuilding trust after mistakes in your recovery. How have your actions influenced the rebuilding of trust in your relationships, and how can you continue to nurture trust in your life?

Reflect on your ability to embrace change and adapt to new circumstances. How can you remain open to the possibility of change and continue to move forward, even when it's challenging?

Think about self-filling and personal growth in your recovery journey. How can you take responsibility for filling in what's missing in your life and nurturing your personal growth?

A Journey of Transformation

> Reflect on the impact of external opinions and judgments in your recovery. How can you develop resilience in the face of negativity from external sources and stay focused on your path to recovery?

> How can you continue to practice letting go of what no longer serves your recovery journey and choosing how to move forward with purpose? Are there specific practices or mindsets that can help you make this choice?

Navigating external pressures and expectations is a crucial aspect of the journey to long-term recovery from addiction. These external factors encompass self-validation, forgiveness, adaptability, self-filling, ignoring negative opinions, and the choice to let go and move forward. By recognizing and embracing these principles, individuals can fortify their recovery journey, build resilience, and cultivate lasting change. Through self-reflection and unwavering determination, individuals can continue to harness the transformative power of these influences on their path to lasting recovery.

Leveraging External Support Systems for Change: Empowering Long-Term Recovery from Addiction

In the pursuit of long-term recovery from addiction, leveraging external support systems becomes a vital aspect of the journey. This book explores the profound significance of external support in addiction recovery, drawing inspiration from motivational statements. It underscores the importance of resilience, self-belief, self-worth, and individuality in the context of recovery. By recognizing and harnessing external support systems, individuals can fortify their recovery efforts, overcome obstacles, and find empowerment on the path to lasting change.

The Challenge of Walking Away from Battles

"Sometimes the hardest battles to fight are the ones we walk away from." Addiction recovery often involves challenging battles, and the decision to walk away from destructive habits can be the most challenging of all. Recognizing that walking away from addiction is a sign of strength and self-preservation is a critical step in the recovery journey.

Overcoming the Weight of the Past

"We have to remember and remind ourselves that the past cannot hurt us. It's all in our heads. There's no need to look back. What's behind us is smaller than what's in front of us." Addiction recovery necessitates letting go of the past and its associated regrets and guilt. External support systems can provide the encouragement and perspective needed to focus on the future and the possibilities that lie ahead.

Embracing Self-Worth and Uniqueness

"We are worthy. We are somebody. We are great. We are special. You are the only version of 'you' to ever exist in the universe." External support systems often reinforce self-worth and uniqueness. Recognizing one's inherent value and embracing individuality can boost self-esteem and self-belief, essential components of a successful recovery journey.

Self-Validation and Independence

"It takes a strong person to do their own thing and not wait for anybody else to validate their existence." External support systems empower individuals to seek self-validation rather than waiting for external validation. Self-validation fosters independence and confidence in one's ability to make choices that align with their recovery goals.

Facing Opposition on the Path to Recovery

"We will face our greatest opposition when we are closest to achieving our biggest goals and miracles. We have to be sure to do what is right for us as individuals. No one else can or is walking in our shoes." External support systems can provide the strength and encouragement needed to confront opposition on the journey to recovery. The belief that one must do what is right for themselves as individuals can be empowering in the face of challenges.

Self-Reflection Questions:

Reflect on the battles you have walked away from in your recovery journey. How has the decision to walk away empowered your recovery efforts, and how can you continue to find strength in making this choice?

Consider the weight of your past and the role of external support systems in helping you focus on the future. How can you further let go of past regrets and guilt to embrace the possibilities ahead?

Reflect on the self-worth and uniqueness you have cultivated in your recovery journey. How has recognizing your value and individuality contributed to your self-esteem and self-belief, and how can you nurture these qualities further?

Think about your ability to seek self-validation and make independent choices in recovery. How can you continue to rely on your inner strength and confidence rather than waiting for external validation?

Reflect on the opposition you have faced on your path to recovery and the role of external support in overcoming challenges. How can you maintain your belief in doing what is right for yourself as an individual, even in the face of opposition?

> How can you continue to leverage external support systems for empowerment and resilience in your recovery journey? Are there specific practices or mindsets that can help you make the most of these external resources?

Leveraging external support systems is a crucial aspect of the journey to long-term recovery from addiction. These external factors encompass resilience, self-belief, self-worth, individuality, self-validation, and the ability to face opposition. By recognizing and harnessing these external support systems, individuals can fortify their recovery efforts, overcome obstacles, and find empowerment on the path to lasting change. Through self-reflection and unwavering determination, individuals can continue to harness the transformative power of these influences on their path to lasting recovery.

The Science of Behavior Change

The journey to long-term recovery from addiction is marked by numerous challenges, triumphs, and moments of introspection. This book explores the science of behavior change in the context of addiction recovery, drawing inspiration from motivational statements. It emphasizes the significance of resilience, problem-solving, personal growth, persistence, attitude, empathy, and letting go of the past. By understanding the science behind behavior change, individuals can better navigate the complexities of addiction recovery, foster lasting change, and embrace a brighter future.

Facing Each Day with Faith

"The greatest act of faith some days is to simply get up and face another day." Addiction recovery often requires unwavering faith and determination. Recognizing that each day presents an opportunity for progress is the foundation of resilience in the face of addiction's challenges.

From Problem Talk to Solution Thinking

"Stop talking about the problem and start thinking about the solution." In the journey of recovery, individuals must transition from focusing on the problems associated with addiction to seeking viable solutions. The shift in mindset toward solution thinking is pivotal in addressing the root causes of addiction and building a healthier future.

Strength through Struggles and Personal Growth

"Find strength through every struggle because the things you have been through have made you the person you are today." Addiction recovery is a transformative process that often involves confronting personal struggles and past traumas. Recognizing that these experiences contribute to personal growth and resilience is a source of empowerment.

Persisting Through Challenges

"Whenever you think about giving up, think about why you've kept going for this long." Persistence is a key factor in behavior change. In recovery, individuals must reflect on their motivation for change and use it as a driving force to overcome setbacks and continue moving forward.

Attitude as the Source of Happiness

"A happy person is not a person in a certain set of circumstances, but rather a person with a certain set of attitudes." Positive attitudes can significantly impact the recovery process. Maintaining a hopeful and optimistic mindset, even in the face of adversity, fosters resilience and promotes overall well-being.

A Journey of Transformation

The Power of Empathy and Helping Hands

"A person's most useful asset is not the head full of knowledge, but a heart full of love, an ear ready to listen, and a hand willing to help." Recovery often involves seeking support from others, and empathy and a willingness to help can be invaluable resources. Building connections and receiving support from those who understand and care can facilitate positive change.

Letting Go of Yesterday for a Brighter Tomorrow

"You can't reach for anything new if your hands are still full of yesterday's junk. So NEVER start your day off with broken pieces of YESTERDAY; it will destroy your wonderful TODAY and will ruin your great TOMORROW." Letting go of the past is a fundamental aspect of behavior change. Acknowledging past mistakes and focusing on the present and future is essential for lasting recovery.

Self-Reflection Questions:

Reflect on your daily commitment to facing another day in your recovery journey. How has your faith and determination been instrumental in your progress, and how can you continue to draw strength from each day?

Consider your transition from problem talk to solution thinking in recovery. How have you shifted your mindset toward seeking solutions, and how can you continue to prioritize problem-solving on your journey?

Reflect on the struggles you have faced and the growth you have experienced in recovery. How have these experiences shaped the person you are today, and how can you further harness them as sources of strength?

Think about the importance of persistence in your recovery. What motivates you to keep going, even when faced with challenges, and how can you use this motivation as a driving force for lasting change?

Reflect on the role of attitude in your recovery journey. How has maintaining a positive attitude contributed to your resilience and well-being, and how can you continue to cultivate this mindset?

Consider the significance of empathy, support, and helping hands in your recovery. How have these resources been valuable to your journey, and how can you maintain and foster connections with those who offer support?

Reflect on the concept of letting go of the past for a brighter tomorrow. What past experiences or habits have you needed to release in your recovery, and how can you ensure that your focus remains on the present and future?

The science of behavior change is a multifaceted journey that involves faith, solution thinking, strength through struggles, persistence, attitude, empathy, support, and letting go of the past. By understanding and embracing these principles, individuals can navigate the complexities of addiction recovery, foster lasting change, and embrace a brighter future. Through self-reflection and unwavering determination, individuals can continue to harness the transformative power of these influences on their path to lasting recovery.

The Psychology Behind Change:
Navigating the Path to Long-Term Recovery from Addiction

The journey to long-term recovery from addiction is a deeply psychological process, marked by self-discovery, resilience, and transformation. This book delves into the psychology behind change in the context of addiction recovery, drawing inspiration from motivational statements. It emphasizes the importance of self-understanding, embracing the journey, confronting fears, building resilience, and finding joy in life. By comprehending the psychological aspects of change, individuals can navigate their recovery journey with greater insight, adaptability, and fulfillment.

Understanding Ourselves: The Foundation of Change

"The most difficult phase of our life is not when no one understands us. It's when we don't understand ourselves." Addiction recovery often begins with introspection and self-understanding. Recognizing the underlying causes and triggers of addiction is essential for initiating meaningful change. Self-awareness forms the foundation upon which lasting recovery can be built.

Embracing the Journey: A Paradigm Shift

"So often we become so focused on the finish line that we fail to enjoy the journey." Recovery is not merely about reaching the end goal of sobriety but also about savoring the transformative journey itself. Embracing each step, with its ups and downs, fosters resilience and a deeper appreciation for the path to recovery.

Confronting Fears and Living Authentically

"Too many of us are not living our dreams because we are living our fears." Addiction recovery often entails confronting deeply rooted fears and insecurities. The decision to live authentically and pursue one's dreams is an act of courage that can propel individuals toward lasting change.

Becoming Stronger in Response to Life's Challenges

"When life changes to be harder, change yourself to be stronger." The psychology of change involves adapting to life's challenges by fortifying one's inner strength. In recovery, individuals must develop resilience to cope with adversity, thereby fostering personal growth and transformation.

A Journey of Transformation

The Importance of Enjoying Life

"The trick is to enjoy life. Don't wish away your days waiting for better ones ahead. DO WHAT YOU LOVE AND LOVE WHAT YOU DO!!!!" Recovery is not just about abstaining from substance abuse but also about finding joy and fulfillment in life. Engaging in activities that bring happiness and embracing a positive attitude can be instrumental in maintaining long-term recovery.

Self-Reflection Questions:

> Reflect on the phase of your life when you may not have fully understood yourself. How has self-awareness played a role in your addiction recovery journey, and how can you continue to deepen your self-understanding?

> Consider your focus on the finish line versus enjoying the journey in your recovery. How has this shift in perspective affected your resilience and appreciation for the recovery process, and how can you further embrace the journey?

> Reflect on the fears that may have hindered you from living your dreams in the past. How have you confronted these fears on your recovery journey, and what steps can you take to continue living authentically?

> Think about how you have become stronger in response to life's challenges during your recovery. How has resilience played a role in your personal growth, and how can you continue to nurture this strength?

> Consider the importance of enjoying life and pursuing activities you love. How have these elements contributed to your recovery, and how can you maintain a positive attitude and a sense of fulfillment in your life moving forward?

> What strategies or practices have helped you navigate the psychological aspects of change in your recovery journey? Are there specific techniques or resources that have been particularly helpful?

The psychology behind change is a multifaceted journey of self-understanding, embracing the journey, confronting fears, building resilience, and finding joy in life. By comprehending and embracing these psychological principles, individuals can navigate their recovery journey with greater insight, adaptability, and fulfillment. Through self-reflection and a commitment to personal growth, individuals can continue to harness the transformative power of these psychological influences on their path to lasting recovery.

Understanding Behavior Change Models and Theories: The Power to Shape Your Recovery

Long-term recovery from addiction is a journey that involves understanding the intricacies of behavior change. This book explores the importance of comprehending behavior change models and theories within the context of addiction recovery, drawing inspiration from motivational statements. It underscores the significance of self-belief, self-determination, self-worth, setting high standards, and the willingness to make necessary changes. By understanding these models and theories, individuals can navigate their recovery journey with clarity and resilience.

The Belief in Self-Choice

"Believe that we are who we choose to be. Nobody is going to come and save you. You've got to save yourself." Recovery begins with the belief that individuals have the power to choose their path. No one else can make this decision for them. Understanding this fundamental aspect of behavior change empowers individuals to take control of their recovery journey.

The Fight for What You Want

"Nobody is going to give you anything you've got to go out and fight for it." Recovery is not a passive process; it requires determination and effort. Acknowledging that individuals must actively work toward their goals reinforces the importance of self-determination in the recovery journey.

The Importance of Self-Knowledge

"Nobody knows what you want except you, and nobody will be as sorry as you if you don't get it." Understanding one's desires, needs, and motivations is central to recovery. Behavior change models emphasize the importance of self-knowledge as a catalyst for lasting change.

Raising the Bar and Setting High Standards

"We only get what we believe we deserve. Raise the bar, raise your standards, and you will receive a better outcome." Behavior change theories suggest that setting high standards and believing in one's worth can lead to more positive outcomes. Recovery often involves elevating one's self-worth and expecting better results.

Overcoming External Opinions

"You'll always believe that you're broken if you always let opinions tell you what needs to be fixed." External opinions and judgments can hinder recovery progress. Understanding behavior change models involves recognizing the impact of external influences and learning to overcome them.

A Journey of Transformation

The Willingness to Make Changes

"Too many people want change without having to make changes. In order to move up, there's some things you must be willing to give up." Behavior change often requires letting go of old habits and embracing new ones. Understanding the necessity of change is a crucial aspect of the recovery journey.

Navigating Changing Relationships

"Just because they say they're praying for you in your face, doesn't mean they aren't laughing at your struggle behind your back." Recovery can strain existing relationships, and some individuals may not fully support the journey. Behavior change models can provide insight into navigating changing dynamics in personal relationships.

Embracing Success Despite Opposition

"They want you to do better as long as you don't do better than them. Don't be surprised if your success turns friends into strangers. Everybody loves you until you become competition." Recovery often leads to personal growth and success. Understanding that not everyone will support these positive changes can help individuals maintain focus and resilience.

Accepting What Is Needed

"Sometimes it's not what you expect, and it's not what you want, but it's exactly what you need. You can't always control what someone gives you, but you're always in control of what you accept." Behavior change models acknowledge that individuals may encounter unexpected challenges and circumstances in recovery. The ability to adapt and accept what is needed is a valuable skill.

Self-Reflection Questions:

> Reflect on your belief in self-choice in your recovery journey. How has the realization that you have the power to choose your path impacted your recovery efforts, and how can you further reinforce this belief?

> Consider the fight you've put into your recovery. How has your determination and effort played a role in your progress, and how can you continue to actively work toward your goals?

> Reflect on your self-knowledge and understanding of your desires and motivations in recovery. How has self-awareness been instrumental in your journey, and how can you deepen your understanding of your own needs and aspirations?

> Think about the standards you have set for yourself in recovery. How have high standards and self-worth contributed to your outcomes, and how can you raise the bar even further?

Reflect on the influence of external opinions in your recovery journey. How have you navigated the impact of external judgments, and what strategies can you employ to overcome external influences more effectively?

Consider the willingness to make changes in your recovery. How have you embraced necessary changes, and what areas of your recovery might require further adaptation and transformation?

Reflect on how your recovery journey has affected your relationships with others. How have changing dynamics influenced your journey, and how can you continue to navigate these changes while staying focused on your recovery goals?

Think about the challenges and successes you have encountered in recovery. How have you managed opposition and maintained your focus on personal growth and success, and how can you continue to do so?

Consider your ability to accept what is needed in your recovery journey. How have you adapted to unexpected challenges, and how can you continue to embrace change and accept what is necessary for your recovery?

Understanding behavior change models and theories is fundamental to navigating the complexities of addiction recovery. These models emphasize the importance of self-belief, self-determination, self-worth, high standards, adaptation, and resilience. Through self-reflection and a commitment to personal growth, individuals can continue to harness the transformative power of these models and theories on their path to lasting recovery.

Factors That Drive and Hinder Behavioral Shifts: Navigating the Path to Recovery

Recovery from addiction is a journey marked by significant behavioral shifts, driven by various factors while often hindered by others. This book explores the dynamics of these factors, drawing inspiration from motivational statements that emphasize non-judgment, the importance of letting go of the past, embracing the present, and maintaining a positive mindset. By understanding what drives and hinders behavioral shifts, individuals can navigate their recovery journey with greater clarity and resilience.

Non-Judgment and Acceptance

"Do not judge people by the scriptures of their faith or the scars from their past, embrace them by the content of their hearts." Recovery requires a non-judgmental attitude towards oneself and others. Judging based on past actions can hinder progress. Instead, focusing on the present and the content of one's heart fosters acceptance and growth.

A Journey of Transformation

The Burden of the Past

"No one can control what happened in the past. It's gone and it's over. Don't allow the past to hinder us from getting to the place in life where we want to be." Past mistakes and experiences can weigh heavily on individuals in recovery. Understanding that the past cannot be changed and should not dictate the future is vital for behavioral shifts.

Embracing the Present

"Life becomes more meaningful when we realize the simple fact that we'll never get the same moment twice." Recovery is a journey of self-discovery and transformation. Embracing the present moment allows individuals to fully engage in their recovery process, making each moment meaningful.

Overcoming Worry About the Future

"Worrying about the future is tempting but useless. Do the best we can with what's right in front of us and the future will fall into place." Excessive worry about the future can hinder recovery progress. Focusing on the here and now and making the best of the present moment can pave the way for positive behavioral shifts.

Staying Strong and Positive

"Stay strong, be positive. We all struggle sometimes... and that's okay." Recovery is not always a smooth path, and setbacks can occur. Understanding that struggles are a natural part of the process and maintaining a positive mindset can be instrumental in driving behavioral shifts.

The Perils of Overthinking

"Overthinking is the biggest cause of our unhappiness. Keep ourselves occupied. Keep our mind off things that don't help us. Think positive." Overthinking can lead to stress and anxiety, hindering recovery efforts. Occupying the mind with positive thoughts and productive activities can help individuals overcome this obstacle.

Self-Reflection Questions:

> Reflect on instances where judgment, whether of yourself or others, has impacted your recovery journey. How can you cultivate a more non-judgmental attitude to promote growth and understanding?

> Consider the weight of the past on your recovery journey. How have you let go of past mistakes and experiences, and how can you further release their hold on your future?

> Reflect on your ability to embrace the present moment in your recovery. How has living in the moment enhanced your journey, and how can you continue to make each moment more meaningful?
>
> Think about your worries regarding the future and their impact on your recovery. How have you focused on the present to alleviate such worries, and how can you further prioritize the here and now?
>
> Consider your strength and positivity during moments of struggle in your recovery. How have these qualities supported your journey, and how can you continue to stay strong and positive in the face of challenges?
>
> Reflect on instances of overthinking and how they have affected your happiness. How have you managed overthinking, and what strategies can you employ to maintain a positive and occupied mind?

Behavioral shifts in addiction recovery are influenced by factors such as non-judgment, releasing the burden of the past, embracing the present, and maintaining positivity. By understanding what drives and hinders these shifts, individuals can navigate their recovery journey with clarity and resilience. Through self-reflection and a commitment to personal growth, individuals can continue to harness the transformative power of these factors on their path to lasting recovery.

Practical Strategies for Changing Habits and Behaviors:
A Path to Lasting Recovery

Long-term recovery from addiction often hinges on changing habits and behaviors. This book explores practical strategies for initiating and sustaining these changes, inspired by motivational statements that underscore the importance of embracing one's wounds, finding happiness in simplicity, and living an honest and hopeful life. By implementing these strategies, individuals can navigate the challenging journey of recovery with resilience and the potential for lasting transformation.

Embracing Our Wounds

"Our wounds are often the openings into the best and most beautiful part of us." Recovery begins with acknowledging and embracing our wounds, which are often the result of past struggles and trauma. Understanding that these wounds can be transformative openings empowers individuals to use their pain as a catalyst for growth.

Finding Happiness in Less

"Learning to find happiness with less is true wealth." Addiction often leads to a pursuit of excess and instant gratification. A critical strategy for behavioral change is to shift the focus from acquiring

A Journey of Transformation

material possessions to finding contentment in simplicity. This shift in perspective can lead to greater overall well-being.

Valuing Experiences Over Belongings

"Ultimately we are the sum of our experiences and not the sum of our belongings." In recovery, the emphasis shifts from material possessions to life experiences. Valuing moments, connections, and personal growth over material acquisitions fosters lasting behavioral change.

The Importance of Honesty

"We've found that growing up means being honest. About what we want. What we need. What we feel. Who we are." Honesty is a cornerstone of recovery. Individuals must be honest with themselves and others about their desires, needs, emotions, and identities. This authenticity is crucial for lasting behavioral change.

Living in the Present

"The trick is to enjoy life. Don't wish away our days, waiting for better ones ahead. We're not promised tomorrow. Today is our best day." Recovery is a journey best lived in the present moment. Practicing mindfulness and embracing the current day's opportunities can lead to sustained changes in habits and behaviors.

Hope as a Driving Force

"Hope is not pretending that troubles don't exist. It is the hope that they won't last forever. That hurts will be healed and difficulties overcome. That we will be led out of the darkness and into the sunshine." Hope is a powerful motivator in recovery. Believing that challenges are temporary and that healing and transformation are possible can drive individuals to change their behaviors and habits.

Self-Reflection Questions:

> Reflect on the wounds and challenges you have faced in your life and recovery journey. How have these experiences shaped you, and how can you use them as openings for personal growth?

> Consider your relationship with material possessions and excess. How can you shift your focus toward finding happiness in simplicity, and what steps can you take to embrace a more minimalist lifestyle?

> Reflect on the importance of valuing experiences over belongings. How can you prioritize moments, connections, and personal growth in your life, and what changes in behavior might be necessary to achieve this shift?

Think about your commitment to honesty in recovery. How have you practiced honesty with yourself and others, and what further steps can you take to ensure authenticity and transparency in your journey?

Consider your ability to live in the present moment. How has mindfulness and embracing the current day's opportunities impacted your recovery, and how can you continue to prioritize the present?

Reflect on the role of hope in your recovery journey. How has hope driven your behavioral changes, and how can you maintain a hopeful outlook, especially during challenging times?

Practical strategies for changing habits and behaviors in addiction recovery include embracing wounds, finding happiness in simplicity, valuing experiences, practicing honesty, living in the present, and nurturing hope. These strategies can empower individuals to navigate the journey of recovery with resilience and the potential for lasting transformation. Through self-reflection and a commitment to personal growth, individuals can continue to harness the transformative power of these strategies on their path to lasting recovery.

Setting Clear Goals and Intentions: A Path to Lasting Recovery

Long-term recovery from addiction is a journey that requires setting clear goals and intentions. This book explores the significance of goal setting in recovery, drawing inspiration from motivational statements that emphasize the importance of non-judgment, letting go of the past, living in the present, and maintaining a positive mindset. By setting and pursuing clear goals, individuals can navigate the challenges of recovery with purpose and determination.

Embracing Non-Judgment

"Do not judge people by the scriptures of their faith or the scars from their past, embrace them by the content of their hearts." Recovery often involves self-reflection and self-acceptance. Setting goals should be a non-judgmental process, allowing individuals to acknowledge their past without dwelling on it.

Releasing the Past

"No one can control what happened in the past. It's gone and it's over. Don't allow the past to hinder us from getting to the place in life where we want to be." Past mistakes and regrets can hold individuals back in recovery. Setting goals requires letting go of the past and focusing on the future and the possibilities it holds.

A Journey of Transformation

Seizing the Present

"Life becomes more meaningful when we realize the simple fact that we'll never get the same moment twice." In recovery, each moment presents an opportunity for change and growth. Setting goals and intentions in the present moment allows individuals to make the most of their journey.

Overcoming Worry About the Future

"Worrying about the future is tempting but useless. Do the best we can with what's right in front of us and the future will fall into place." Setting clear goals requires a focus on the present, as worrying about the future can be counterproductive. By doing their best in the present, individuals pave the way for a brighter future.

Staying Strong and Positive

"Stay strong, be positive. We all struggle sometimes... and that's okay. Overthinking is the biggest cause of our unhappiness. Keep ourselves occupied. Keep our mind off things that don't help us. Think positive." Maintaining a positive mindset and staying strong during recovery is essential. Setting goals that align with positivity and personal growth empowers individuals to overcome challenges.

Self-Reflection Questions:

Reflect on your judgment of yourself and others in your recovery journey. How can you cultivate a non-judgmental attitude when setting and pursuing goals?

Consider how your past has influenced your recovery goals. How can you release the past and focus on future possibilities when setting intentions for your journey?

Reflect on your ability to seize the present moment in your recovery. How has living in the moment impacted your goal-setting process, and how can you continue to make the most of each moment?

Think about your worries concerning the future and their impact on your recovery goals. How can you shift your focus to the present and do your best with what is right in front of you?

Consider your strength and positivity during moments of struggle in your recovery. How has a positive mindset influenced your goal setting, and how can you maintain that positivity in the face of challenges?

Reflect on the role of overthinking in your recovery journey. How has keeping occupied and thinking positively contributed to your progress, and how can you continue to apply these strategies in your goal-setting process?

Setting clear goals and intentions in addiction recovery is a powerful tool for personal growth and transformation. By embracing non-judgment, releasing the past, seizing the present, overcoming worries about the future, and maintaining strength and positivity, individuals can navigate their recovery journey with purpose and determination. Through self-reflection and a commitment to personal growth, individuals can continue to set and pursue goals that lead to lasting recovery.

Techniques for Breaking Old Habits and Forming New Ones: A Path to Lasting Recovery

Long-term recovery from addiction often involves the challenging process of breaking old habits and forming new ones. This book explores practical techniques for achieving this transformation, inspired by motivational statements that highlight the importance of resilience during challenging times, focusing on personal growth, appreciating intangible beauty, embracing patience, and nurturing determination. By implementing these techniques, individuals can overcome the grip of addiction and pave the way for lasting recovery.

Resilience in Dark Moments

"It is during our darkest moments that we must focus to see the light." Recovery is a journey with ups and downs. To break old habits, individuals must cultivate resilience and determination during their darkest moments. Recognizing that these moments are opportunities for growth is the first step toward change.

Focusing on Personal Growth

"Don't judge each day by the harvest you reap but by the seeds that you plant." Breaking old habits and forming new ones requires a shift in perspective. Rather than expecting immediate results, individuals should focus on the process of personal growth. Each day presents a chance to plant the seeds of positive change.

Appreciating Intangible Beauty

"The best and most beautiful things in the world cannot be seen or even touched, they must be felt with the heart." Recovery is not just about breaking harmful habits but also about discovering the beauty in life. By appreciating intangible qualities like love, joy, and inner peace, individuals can find motivation to change their behavior.

Embracing Patience

"The keys to being patience are acceptance and faith. Accept things as they are, and look realistically at the world around you. Have faith in yourself and in the direction you have chosen." Patience is a crucial element in the process of forming new habits. Accepting that change takes time and having faith in one's chosen path can sustain motivation and resilience.

A Journey of Transformation

Determining the Depth of Desire

"It doesn't matter how much you want. What really matters is how much you want it." Breaking old habits requires a deep and unwavering desire for change. Individuals must assess the depth of their desire and use it as a driving force to overcome obstacles and temptations.

Willingness to Solve the Problem

"The extent and complexity of the problem does not matter as much as does the willingness to solve it." A crucial technique for breaking old habits is the willingness to confront the problem head-on. Regardless of the challenges, individuals who are committed to change can find the strength to overcome their addiction.

Self-Reflection Questions:

Reflect on the darkest moments you have faced in your recovery journey. How have these moments shaped your resilience and determination to overcome old habits?

Consider your perspective on daily progress in recovery. How can you shift your focus from immediate results to the process of personal growth and the seeds you are planting?

Reflect on the intangible beauty you have found in life since starting your recovery journey. How has this appreciation motivated you to change your habits and behavior?

Think about your patience in the face of challenges. How can you enhance your acceptance of the time required for change and maintain faith in your chosen path?

Reflect on the depth of your desire for recovery. How can you assess and strengthen your determination to break old habits and form new ones?

Consider your willingness to solve the problem of addiction. How has this willingness influenced your recovery journey, and how can you maintain it in the face of challenges?

Breaking old habits and forming new ones in addiction recovery is a transformative process that requires resilience, focus on personal growth, appreciation of intangible beauty, patience, a deep desire for change, and a strong willingness to confront the problem. By implementing these techniques and engaging in self-reflection, individuals can overcome addiction and pave the way for lasting recovery.

The Stages of Change

Long-term recovery from addiction is a multifaceted journey that involves various stages of change. This book explores the significance of these stages, drawing inspiration from motivational statements that emphasize the importance of embracing challenges, learning from mistakes, and maintaining resilience. By understanding and navigating the stages of change, individuals can build a strong foundation for lasting recovery.

Embracing Challenges and Hurt

"We can't be brave if we don't get hurt. We can't learn if we don't make mistakes. We can't be successful if we don't encounter failure." Recovery is a brave and transformative journey that requires individuals to confront their challenges, even if it means getting hurt along the way. Embracing these challenges is essential for growth and change.

Learning from Mistakes

"When we take risks we learn that there will be times when we succeed and there will be times when we fail, and both are equally as important." Mistakes and failures are valuable learning experiences in the recovery process. They provide insight into what works and what doesn't, helping individuals refine their approach to change.

Resilience in the Face of Adversity

"Don't let circumstances pull us down. No matter what comes our way, let's get up and over it and keep moving forward." Recovery is often marked by setbacks and obstacles. Maintaining resilience and a forward-moving mindset, regardless of circumstances, is crucial for staying on the path to lasting change.

Consistency as the Key

"Consistency is the key! If we can't be consistent, then we can't be anything." The stages of change require a consistent commitment to the journey. Success in recovery depends on maintaining consistency in one's efforts, routines, and goals.

Taking Life Day by Day

"Life is tough. We just have to learn to take it day by day and have faith that in the end, everything is going to be okay." Recovery can feel overwhelming, especially when looking at the big picture. Focusing on each day as it comes and having faith in the ultimate outcome can alleviate anxiety and help individuals stay on course.

A Journey of Transformation

Self-Reflection Questions:

Reflect on the challenges you have faced in your recovery journey. How have these challenges contributed to your growth and transformation?

Consider the mistakes and failures you've encountered along the way. How have these experiences shaped your understanding of change and recovery?

Think about your resilience in the face of adversity. How have you managed to stay committed to your recovery goals despite setbacks and obstacles?

Reflect on the role of consistency in your journey. How have your efforts to maintain consistency impacted your progress in recovery?

Consider your approach to taking life day by day. How has this perspective helped you cope with the challenges of recovery and maintain faith in the process?

Reflect on your overall experience with the stages of change in recovery. What insights have you gained, and how do you plan to continue navigating these stages on your path to lasting recovery?

The stages of change in addiction recovery are integral to building a strong foundation for lasting transformation. By embracing challenges, learning from mistakes, maintaining resilience, prioritizing consistency, and taking life day by day, individuals can navigate the complexities of recovery with determination and faith in the ultimate outcome. Through self-reflection and a commitment to personal growth, individuals can continue their journey towards lasting recovery.

Navigating the Stages of Change:
A Journey to Self-Discovery and Lasting Recovery

Long-term recovery from addiction is a profound journey that involves navigating various stages of change. This book delves into the significance of these stages, drawing inspiration from motivational statements that emphasize the importance of finding balance, self-worth, and embracing change. By exploring and understanding these stages, individuals can embark on a transformative path towards lasting recovery.

Finding Balance

"Find balance in our life. Work hard but don't let work take over our life, we will lose ourselves." Recovery often requires a delicate balance between dedication to sobriety and maintaining a well-rounded life. It's essential to avoid letting one aspect of life consume us and lead to imbalance.

Love for the Right Reasons

"Love, but love for the right reasons. Life is too short for anything mediocre." Building and maintaining healthy relationships are crucial in recovery. Individuals should strive for love and connections that uplift and support their journey rather than settling for mediocrity.

Embracing Self-Worth

"Know who we are and know that we are worthy of reaching our dreams and that it is never too late to start creating that life we have always dreamed of." Self-worth is a cornerstone of lasting recovery. Understanding that we are deserving of a fulfilling life and that it's never too late to pursue our dreams can be a powerful motivator for change.

Avoiding Comparison

"Do not compare ourselves to others, that's just deadly. No two souls are the same. We are our own person, we are beautiful and we are unique." Comparing ourselves to others can be detrimental to our recovery journey. Recognizing our uniqueness and focusing on our own progress is essential for personal growth.

Trusting the Universe

"Put your trust in the universe. Some things are just meant to happen, and some are not. Let go of whatever is stealing our happiness, it's hard but it is worth it. Embrace change. Embrace life." Trusting in the universe and relinquishing control over everything can be liberating. It allows us to let go of what no longer serves us, embrace change, and find happiness in the unpredictability of life.

Self-Reflection Questions:

> Reflect on the balance in your life during your recovery journey. How do you manage to work hard towards your sobriety while also maintaining other aspects of your life?

> Consider your relationships and love life in recovery. How have you learned to differentiate between healthy and mediocre connections?

> Reflect on your self-worth and dreams. How has recognizing your worthiness influenced your pursuit of a fulfilling life in recovery?

> Think about the role of comparison in your journey. How have you avoided the trap of comparing yourself to others, focusing instead on your uniqueness and progress?

A Journey of Transformation

> Consider your ability to trust in the universe and embrace change. How has relinquishing control and trusting in the unfolding of life affected your overall happiness and recovery journey?
>
> Reflect on the stages of change you have experienced in your recovery. How do these insights inspire you to continue navigating the journey towards lasting recovery?

The stages of change in addiction recovery encompass finding balance, pursuing love for the right reasons, embracing self-worth, avoiding comparison, and trusting the universe. By exploring and understanding these stages, individuals can embark on a transformative journey towards lasting recovery while finding purpose and fulfillment in their lives. Through self-reflection and an openness to change, individuals can navigate these stages with grace and resilience.

Pre-contemplation:
The Starting Point of Self-Discovery in Recovery

The journey to long-term recovery from addiction is often characterized by various stages, and pre-contemplation marks the beginning of this transformative process. This book explores the significance of the pre-contemplation stage, drawing inspiration from motivational statements that emphasize the importance of self-discovery, trusting one's feelings, and embracing change. By reflecting on this stage, individuals can lay the foundation for a successful recovery journey.

Finding Direction Through Loss

"Sometimes we have to lose our way to find out what we really want, because we often ignore our needs until we are lost." The pre-contemplation stage often begins with a sense of being lost or uncertain. It is during this time that individuals may start to question their current path and recognize the need for change. Loss and confusion can be the catalysts for self-discovery.

Understanding Through Experience

"We have to experience what you don't want in life to come to a full understanding of what you do want." The pre-contemplation stage allows individuals to experience the negative consequences of addiction, which can lead to a deeper understanding of their desires and aspirations. It is through this contrast that individuals may begin to contemplate the possibility of change.

Letting Go of the Unnecessary

"Let go of the needless, let go of everything that does not serve your soul, let go of your need for solutions and let life be life." In pre-contemplation, individuals may still hold on to elements of their addiction or patterns that no longer serve them. Letting go of these unnecessary burdens is a crucial step toward acknowledging the need for change.

Embracing Trust and Faith

"Life is about trusting your feelings and taking chances, losing and finding happiness, appreciating the memories, learning from the past, and realizing." Trusting one's feelings and having faith in the recovery journey are foundational aspects of pre-contemplation. It is through this trust and faith that individuals can begin to explore the possibility of change.

Believing in the Possibilities

"You don't have to figure it all out. All you have to do is believe and have faith. When you believe, all things are possible." Pre-contemplation is a time to believe in the potential for change, even when the path ahead may not be fully clear. It is a stage marked by hope and the recognition that transformation is possible.

Self-Reflection Questions:

> Reflect on a time in your life when you felt lost or uncertain, similar to the pre-contemplation stage in recovery. How did this experience influence your subsequent decisions and actions?

> Consider the lessons you've learned from past experiences, particularly those related to your addiction. How have these lessons contributed to your understanding of what you truly want in life?

> Reflect on aspects of your life that may no longer serve your well-being. How can you begin to let go of these unnecessary burdens to create space for positive change?

> Think about the role of trust and faith in your recovery journey. How have these qualities allowed you to embrace the possibility of change?

> Consider your beliefs about the possibilities of recovery. How does your belief in the potential for change impact your motivation and commitment to the recovery process?

> Reflect on your current stage in the recovery journey. How can you use the principles of pre-contemplation to lay a strong foundation for your continued progress?

The pre-contemplation stage in recovery is a critical starting point marked by self-discovery, trust, and belief in the possibility of change. It is during this stage that individuals may begin to recognize the need for transformation and embark on the path to lasting recovery. Through self-reflection and a willingness to embrace change, individuals can set themselves up for success in their recovery journey.

A Journey of Transformation

Contemplation: Harnessing Inner Strength for Recovery

In the journey towards long-term recovery from addiction, the contemplation stage represents a pivotal moment of self-reflection and inner strength. This book explores the significance of contemplation, drawing inspiration from motivational statements that emphasize the power of positivity, resilience, and confidence. By delving into this stage, individuals can prepare themselves for the challenges and decisions that lie ahead on the path to recovery.

Smile Through Adversity

"To everyone battling a difficulty or under attack right now: smile, keep your head up, keep moving and stay positive, you'll get through it." Contemplation is a stage where individuals confront the reality of their addiction and the obstacles ahead. Despite the challenges, maintaining a positive outlook can be a source of strength. Smiling in the face of adversity signifies resilience and the determination to overcome.

The Power of Hope

"Whenever there is a great battle ahead of us, we should allow ourselves to smile and hope, because these two are the most powerful weapons we can carry." Hope is a potent force in the contemplation stage. It is hope that allows individuals to imagine a life free from addiction, sparking the desire for change. Hope fuels the determination to embark on the journey to recovery.

Strength in Positivity

"Being positive means being strong. The ability to keep your head up in times of need is an essential surviving skill." Contemplation demands a positive mindset, as it sets the stage for future actions. Positivity breeds resilience and the capacity to weather the storms of addiction and recovery. It is the foundation upon which individuals can build their strength.

Standing Up for Yourself

"When things get tough there is nothing more important than to find that inner strength that allows you to fight anything. The world doesn't take you seriously until you learn to stand up for yourself and hold your head high." Contemplation involves recognizing the need for change and acknowledging one's worth. It is a time to stand up for oneself and declare the intent to break free from addiction. Confidence in one's strength is key to successful recovery.

Bow to Your Confidence

"If you are convinced of your strength, the world will bow to your confidence. This is the secret of all successful people." Contemplation is a stage where individuals must believe in their ability to recover. Confidence in one's strength and the conviction that change is possible can serve as a driving force throughout the recovery journey. It is this inner assurance that leads to success.

Self-Reflection Questions:

Recall a time when maintaining a positive outlook helped you navigate a challenging situation. How can you apply this resilience to your contemplation stage in recovery?

Reflect on the role of hope in your contemplation process. What does hope look like for you in the context of overcoming addiction?

Consider moments when you demonstrated inner strength in the face of adversity. How can you draw upon this strength during the contemplation stage to fuel your motivation for recovery?

Reflect on the importance of self-worth and confidence in the recovery process. How can you cultivate a sense of self-worth as you contemplate your journey to sobriety?

Think about the power of confidence in achieving success. How can you build and strengthen your belief in your ability to overcome addiction and embrace a healthier future?

Reflect on your current stage in the contemplation journey. How can you harness the power of positivity and inner strength to propel yourself forward in your recovery journey?

The contemplation stage in recovery represents a critical phase marked by self-reflection, positivity, and inner strength. It is a time when individuals can prepare themselves mentally and emotionally for the challenges of recovery. By recognizing the potential for change, maintaining a positive outlook, and believing in their own strength, individuals can set the stage for a successful and transformative recovery journey.

Preparation: Expanding Horizons for a Fulfilling Recovery

As individuals embark on the path to long-term recovery from addiction, the stage of preparation is marked by transformation and the widening of horizons. This book explores the importance of preparation and draws inspiration from motivational statements that emphasize the significance of thinking big, fulfilling one's purpose, and changing thoughts to change one's world. By delving into this stage, individuals can lay a strong foundation for their recovery journey.

Thinking Beyond Limits

"We think too small. Like a frog at the bottom of a well. He thinks the sky is only as big as the top of the well. If he surfaced, he would have an entirely different view." Preparation involves transcending limitations and recognizing that recovery can lead to a life beyond addiction's constraints. Just as the frog's perspective changes when it emerges from the well, so too can individuals envision a future free from addiction.

A Journey of Transformation

Living with Purpose

"The great and glorious masterpiece of a person is to know how to live and fulfill their purpose." In the preparation stage, individuals begin to explore their purpose and the meaning of life beyond addiction. Discovering one's purpose can be a driving force for recovery, as it provides a compelling reason to change and grow.

Converting Ideas into Reality

"The ability to convert ideas to things is the secret to outward success." Preparation involves translating the desire for recovery into concrete actions and plans. It's a time to set goals, create strategies, and establish a roadmap for the journey ahead. Transforming aspirations into tangible steps is essential for a successful recovery.

Changing Thoughts, Changing Worlds

"Change your thoughts and you change your world." The preparation stage is an opportunity to reframe one's mindset. By challenging negative thought patterns and embracing positivity, individuals can alter their perceptions and attitudes toward recovery. A shift in thinking can pave the way for a more optimistic and successful journey.

Self-Reflection Questions:

Reflect on a time when you realized you were thinking too small or limiting your potential. How did you overcome this mindset, and how can you apply this lesson to your recovery journey?

Consider your purpose in life and how it aligns with your desire for recovery. How can your purpose serve as a motivating force in preparing for a life free from addiction?

Explore the ideas and aspirations you have for your recovery journey. How can you convert these ideas into concrete plans and actionable steps?

Reflect on the power of changing your thoughts and its potential impact on your recovery. Are there specific negative thought patterns you need to address or positive affirmations you can adopt?

Think about the transformative potential of preparation. How can you use this stage to set the stage for a successful and fulfilling recovery?

Consider the importance of broadening your perspective. What new possibilities and opportunities can you envision for yourself once you emerge from the "well" of addiction?

The preparation stage of recovery is a critical phase characterized by a shift in perspective, purposeful planning, and mindset transformation. It is a time when individuals can break free from limiting beliefs, define their purpose, set concrete goals, and embrace a positive outlook. By preparing effectively, individuals can lay the groundwork for a successful and fulfilling recovery journey.

Action: Taking the Leap Towards Recovery

The stage of action in the journey towards long-term recovery from addiction is marked by courage, resilience, and the determination to break free from the chains of dependency. This book explores the significance of taking action, drawing inspiration from motivational statements that emphasize the importance of facing fear, learning from the past, prioritizing what truly matters, and practicing unconditional love and patience. By embracing action, individuals can propel themselves forward on the path to recovery.

Confronting Fear

"When it feels scary to jump, that's exactly when we jump. Otherwise, we end up staying in the same place our whole life." The action stage requires individuals to confront their fears head-on. Recovery can be intimidating, and change can be frightening, but it is only by taking that initial leap of faith that individuals can escape the cycle of addiction. Staying stagnant is not an option when growth and healing are within reach.

Learning from Mistakes

"We needed our past and we needed our mistakes to get us to where we are today." Recognizing the value of past experiences, both positive and negative, is crucial in the action stage. It is through these lessons that individuals can gain insight and resilience, propelling them forward on their recovery journey. Mistakes do not define us; they guide us toward growth and self-improvement.

Prioritizing What Matters

"Every day, the world will drag us by the hand, yelling, 'This is important! And this is important! And this is important!' We need to worry about this! And this! And this!' And each day, it's up to us to yank our hand back, put it on our heart and say, 'No. This is what's important.'" Action entails prioritizing recovery and well-being above all else. It requires individuals to resist distractions and external pressures and focus on what truly matters—their path to healing and sobriety.

Unconditional Love and Patience

"Learn to love without condition. Talk without bad intention. Give without any reason. And most of all, care for people without expectation." In the action stage, it is essential to extend love and care to oneself and others without conditions or expectations. This includes self-compassion and

A Journey of Transformation

patience as individuals navigate the challenges of recovery. Recovery is a journey, and progress may be gradual; however, having faith that it will work out and being patient with oneself is vital.

Self-Reflection Questions:

Recall a time when fear held you back from taking an important step in your recovery journey. How did you eventually find the courage to overcome that fear, and what were the results?

Reflect on the lessons you have learned from your past, especially from mistakes or setbacks. How have these experiences contributed to your growth and determination in the action stage of recovery?

Consider the daily distractions and external pressures that can divert your focus from recovery. How can you practice prioritizing what truly matters and yanking your hand back from unnecessary distractions?

Explore the concept of unconditional love and patience, both for yourself and for others. How can you incorporate these principles into your daily life to support your recovery journey?

Think about the importance of taking action and the decision to jump when it feels scary. What motivates you to take these leaps of faith, and how do they propel you forward in your recovery?

Consider the idea of having faith and being patient with the recovery process. How can you cultivate patience and trust that your efforts will lead to positive outcomes over time?

The action stage of recovery is a pivotal phase marked by the courage to confront fear, the ability to learn from the past, the dedication to prioritize recovery, and the practice of unconditional love and patience. By taking action, individuals propel themselves forward on their journey towards long-term recovery, embracing the opportunity for growth, healing, and a brighter future.

Maintenance: The Key to Long-Term Recovery

The maintenance stage of recovery is a critical phase that often follows the initial steps of acknowledging addiction, seeking help, and taking action. During this phase, individuals must focus on sustaining their progress, avoiding relapse, and continually working towards a healthier, addiction-free life. This book delves into the significance of maintenance, drawing inspiration from statements that underscore the importance of learning from mistakes, doing one's best, and managing regrets. By embracing maintenance, individuals can solidify their journey towards long-term recovery.

Learning from Mistakes

"Regret for the things we did can be tempered by time; it is regret for the things we did not do that is inconsolable." The maintenance phase is an opportunity to reflect on the past, particularly on the mistakes and regrets that may have arisen during the addiction years. Rather than dwelling on these regrets, individuals should use them as valuable lessons. By acknowledging past mistakes and learning from them, individuals can strengthen their commitment to recovery and avoid repeating the same errors.

Avoiding Carrying Regrets Forward

"We should regret our mistakes but learn from them, and never carry them forward into the future with us." It is natural to have regrets, especially when confronting the consequences of addiction. However, the maintenance stage encourages individuals to avoid carrying these regrets as burdens into their future. Instead, they should focus on self-improvement, forgiveness, and growth. By doing so, they can break free from the shackles of past mistakes and continue their journey towards a brighter, addiction-free future.

Always Doing Your Best

"Always Do Your Best. Your best is going to change from moment to moment; it will be different when you are healthy as opposed to sick. Under any circumstance, simply do your best, and you will avoid self-judgment, self-abuse, and REGRET." Maintaining recovery requires a commitment to always do one's best, recognizing that this effort may vary depending on the circumstances. Self-judgment and regret can hinder progress, but by focusing on consistent effort and self-compassion, individuals can navigate the challenges of the maintenance phase with resilience.

Self-Reflection Questions:

> Reflect on a specific regret from your past related to your addiction. How can you transform this regret into a valuable lesson that supports your maintenance efforts in recovery?

> Consider the importance of not carrying regrets forward into the future. How can you cultivate forgiveness and self-compassion to release the burden of past mistakes and focus on your recovery journey?

> Explore the concept of always doing your best in recovery. How has your understanding of "your best" evolved over time, and how can you apply it to different circumstances in your life?

> Think about the challenges you may encounter during the maintenance stage of recovery. How can you maintain a resilient mindset and avoid self-judgment and self-abuse in the face of setbacks?

A Journey of Transformation

> Reflect on the statement, "Regret for the things we did not do is inconsolable." Are there specific actions or steps in your recovery journey that you regret not taking? How can you use this insight to drive positive changes in your maintenance phase?
>
> Consider the role of self-acceptance in maintaining recovery. How can you practice self-acceptance and embrace the idea that your best effort is enough, regardless of the circumstances?

The maintenance stage of recovery is a pivotal phase that requires individuals to learn from their mistakes, avoid carrying regrets forward, and always do their best. By focusing on self-improvement, forgiveness, and consistent effort, individuals can solidify their commitment to long-term recovery and navigate the challenges that may arise on their journey. The maintenance phase is an opportunity for growth, resilience, and a brighter, addiction-free future.

Navigating the Challenges and Opportunities at Each Stage

Recovery from addiction is a journey that unfolds in various stages, each presenting unique challenges and opportunities. This book explores the significance of these stages, drawing inspiration from statements that emphasize determination, gratitude, and the transformative power of optimism. By understanding and addressing the challenges at each stage while embracing the opportunities, individuals can navigate the path to long-term recovery with greater resilience and success.

Starting the Day with Positivity

"One small positive thought in the morning can change your whole day." The journey to recovery often begins with a commitment to positive change. Starting each day with a positive mindset can be transformative. By acknowledging the potential for a fresh start, individuals set the tone for their recovery journey. Positivity fosters hope, which is a powerful motivator, especially during challenging times.

Determination and Satisfaction

"You've got to get up every morning with determination if you're going to go to bed with satisfaction." The road to recovery can be demanding, requiring unwavering determination. Challenges and setbacks are inevitable, but by approaching each day with resolve, individuals build the foundation for long-term success. Satisfaction comes from recognizing the progress made and the effort invested in the journey.

Replacing Excuses with Effort

"Replace Excuses With Effort, Laziness With Determination & choose to see the world through optimistic eyes. Everything Will Fall Into Place!" Recovery demands a shift from excuses to effort, from complacency to determination. Excuses can hinder progress, while effort propels individuals forward. Viewing the world through optimistic eyes not only fosters a positive outlook but also attracts opportunities for growth and healing.

Gratitude and Blessings

"Life is a blessing, stop stressing. Some people don't understand how blessed they truly are. Be thankful for what you have rather than focusing on what you don't have." Gratitude is a powerful tool in recovery. Recognizing the blessings in life, such as the opportunity for recovery itself, can provide motivation and perspective. Gratitude helps individuals appreciate the journey and find strength in their blessings.

Embracing Challenges as Blessings

"Hard times are sometimes blessings in disguise. Let it go and let it make you better." Recovery is not without its challenges, but these difficulties can be transformative. By embracing adversity as an opportunity for growth, individuals can extract valuable lessons from their struggles. Challenges, when navigated with determination, become stepping stones towards lasting recovery.

Self-Reflection Questions:

Reflect on the power of positive thinking and its role in your recovery journey. How can you cultivate one small positive thought each morning to change your day for the better?

Consider the concept of determination and its significance in maintaining long-term recovery. How do you stay determined even when facing obstacles, setbacks, or cravings?

Explore the idea of replacing excuses with effort. Are there any excuses that have held you back from progress in your recovery? How can you shift your mindset to prioritize effort over excuses?

Reflect on the role of gratitude in your recovery. What blessings can you identify in your life, and how can you express gratitude for them?

Think about the challenges you have encountered in your recovery journey. How have these challenges contributed to your growth and personal development?

Consider the transformative power of optimism. How can you choose to see the world through optimistic eyes and attract positive opportunities on your path to recovery?

The journey of recovery is marked by various stages, each with its challenges and opportunities. By approaching each day with positivity and determination, by replacing excuses with effort, and by cultivating gratitude and optimism, individuals can navigate these stages with resilience and embrace the blessings that arise from their journey towards long-term recovery.

A Journey of Transformation

Common Experiences and Emotions During Each Stage

The journey to long-term recovery from addiction is a path fraught with challenges and emotions that are universal among those seeking change. This book explores the common experiences and emotions individuals often encounter at each stage of their recovery journey. Drawing inspiration from statements that emphasize the importance of courage, hope, and personal growth, we will shed light on the transformative power of embracing these shared experiences.

The Fear of Letting Go

"The biggest obstacle to our future success is the fear of letting go of the comfort of today." In the initial stages of recovery, it's common to fear the unknown. Letting go of the familiar, even if it's harmful, can be daunting. Individuals may experience anxiety and uncertainty as they confront the need for change. This fear often serves as the first hurdle to overcome.

Embracing Mistakes and Imperfections

"The most valuable thing you can make is a mistake – you can't learn anything from being perfect." Early in recovery, individuals may grapple with feelings of shame and regret for past actions. However, understanding that making mistakes is an essential part of growth can help alleviate these negative emotions. It's crucial to recognize that nobody is perfect, and learning from missteps is a valuable process.

Becoming the Courageous Self

"You must be the person you have never had the courage to be. Gradually, you will discover that you are that person." As individuals progress in their recovery journey, they often undergo a transformation. They gain the courage to confront their addiction, face their true selves, and work towards becoming the person they aspire to be. This shift can be accompanied by moments of self-discovery and empowerment.

Expanding Dreams and Potential

"Your potential is measured by the size of your dreams. Know this and you will control any outcome you desire." In the middle stages of recovery, individuals begin to dream bigger and realize the potential for a brighter future. As they work through their addiction, they start setting goals and envisioning a life free from substance dependency. This newfound hope becomes a driving force for change.

Navigating Pain and Lessons

"Hope is wishing something would happen. Faith is believing something will happen. Courage is making something happen." Recovery is not without its share of pain and challenges. Individuals may face relapses, cravings, and emotional struggles. However, these experiences are opportunities for growth and learning. With hope, faith, and courage, individuals can navigate these difficulties and emerge stronger.

The Journey Towards Victory

"All things pass and pain is temporary. It comes to teach a lesson and when the lesson is understood it disappears into the night." Finally, individuals in recovery come to understand that pain, like addiction itself, is temporary. It serves as a teacher, imparting valuable lessons along the way. With resilience and determination, they move forward on their journey, guided by the promise of victory over their addiction.

Self-Reflection Questions:

> Reflect on the fear of letting go. What comfort zones or habits are you reluctant to release in your pursuit of recovery? How can you overcome this fear?

> Consider the idea of embracing mistakes and imperfections. Have past mistakes hindered your progress in recovery? How can you reframe these experiences as valuable lessons?

> Explore the concept of becoming the courageous self. What aspects of your true self have you discovered or rekindled during your recovery journey? How has courage played a role in this process?

> Reflect on the expansion of dreams and potential. What aspirations do you have for your future in recovery? How can you harness these dreams to propel yourself forward?

> Consider the pain and lessons you've encountered in recovery. What lessons have you learned from your challenges and setbacks? How have they contributed to your growth and resilience?

> Reflect on the idea of victory in recovery. What does victory over addiction mean to you? How can you stay motivated and focused on the journey ahead?

The path to recovery is marked by common experiences and emotions that individuals share as they work towards lasting change. By acknowledging and embracing these stages, individuals can find strength and inspiration in their journey towards a life free from addiction.

Strategies for Progressing Through the Stages of Recovery Effectively

The journey to long-term recovery from addiction is a challenging but profoundly rewarding process. Navigating the stages of recovery requires determination, self-respect, and resilience. In this book, we will explore strategies for progressing through these stages effectively, drawing

A Journey of Transformation

inspiration from statements that emphasize the importance of self-belief, positive attitude, and personal transformation.

Embrace Your Uniqueness

"If you desire to make a difference in the world, you must be different from the world." Recovery is a personal journey, and it's essential to embrace your uniqueness. Recognize that your path to recovery may differ from others, and that's perfectly okay. Tailor your recovery plan to your specific needs, preferences, and circumstances.

> Self-Reflection Question: How can you celebrate your uniqueness and use it as a source of strength In your recovery journey?

Cultivate Self-Respect

"Respect yourself and others will follow suit." Self-respect is the foundation of a successful recovery. Treat yourself with kindness, compassion, and dignity. When you respect yourself, you set the standard for how others should treat you. Surround yourself with supportive individuals who value your journey to recovery.

> Self-Reflection Question: In what ways can you practice self-respect and set healthy boundaries in your interactions with others?

Eliminate Excuses and Persist

"Don't make excuses and never give up. Believe it's possible, find a way and make it happen." Recovery is a commitment to change, and it requires a resolute mindset. Eliminate excuses that may hinder your progress. When challenges arise, view them as opportunities to grow stronger and more determined in your recovery journey.

> Self-Reflection Question: What excuses or self-limiting beliefs have held you back in the past, and how can you overcome them to persist in your recovery?

Focus on Positivity

"You'll never know if you stop now. You may have had a negative past, but you don't have to have a negative future. Leave it behind you and stay positive." Maintaining a positive attitude is crucial in each stage of recovery. Let go of the negativity from your past and focus on the possibilities of the future. Cultivate optimism, even when faced with setbacks.

> Self-Reflection Question: How can you cultivate a more positive outlook on your recovery journey? What strategies can you use to stay focused on the positive aspects of your life?

Progressing through the stages of recovery requires commitment, self-respect, and a positive attitude. Embracing your uniqueness, cultivating self-respect, eliminating excuses, and staying positive are essential strategies for effectively navigating these stages. Remember that your recovery journey is a transformative process, and with the right mindset and determination, you can achieve lasting change.

Self-Reflection Questions:

How can you celebrate your uniqueness and use it as a source of strength in your recovery journey?

In what ways can you practice self-respect and set healthy boundaries in your interactions with others?

What excuses or self-limiting beliefs have held you back in the past, and how can you overcome them to persist in your recovery?

How can you cultivate a more positive outlook on your recovery journey? What strategies can you use to stay focused on the positive aspects of your life?

The Role of Beliefs and Mindset

Recovery from addiction is a challenging and ongoing journey that requires more than just breaking physical dependence on a substance. It necessitates a profound transformation of beliefs and mindset. Addiction often stems from a combination of genetic, environmental, and psychological factors, making it crucial to address the underlying beliefs and thought patterns that perpetuate substance abuse. This book explores the significance of beliefs and mindset in achieving long-term recovery and offers insights into the transformative power of one's convictions and outlook on life.

The Power of Positive Beliefs:

One of the first steps towards long-term recovery from addiction is cultivating positive beliefs about oneself and the possibility of change. Believing in one's capacity to overcome addiction is essential for progress. It's not merely about saying the right things; it's about truly believing in the potential for a healthier, drug-free life.

Overcoming Fear of Failure:

Many individuals battling addiction fear the prospect of relapse. However, the fear of failure can sometimes overshadow the desire for success. It's crucial to recognize that setbacks can occur on the path to recovery, but they should not deter one from pursuing sobriety. Embracing the possibility of failure should never overshadow the need to succeed.

Self-Compassion and Non-Judgment:

Addiction often carries a heavy burden of self-blame and judgment. To foster long-term recovery, it's vital to shift from being a judge of oneself to becoming a compassionate witness. Self-compassion and self-forgiveness can replace self-criticism, making room for healing and growth.

Focusing Inward:

Recovery is an individual journey. While support from others is valuable, true transformation begins with focusing on oneself. It involves introspection, self-awareness, and a commitment to personal growth. It's about listening to your heart and inner wisdom rather than being swayed by external pressures or the opinions of others.

Embracing Change:

Change is a constant in life, and embracing personal growth is an integral part of recovery. We are not the same people we were in the past, and recovery provides an opportunity for positive change. Recognizing and accepting this evolution is crucial for long-term success.

A Journey of Transformation

Pursuing Dreams and Goals:

Recovery is not just about abstaining from substances; it's about rebuilding one's life. If you never pursue your dreams and goals, you may never truly experience the fulfillment of recovery. It's about striving for a life that aligns with your aspirations and values.

Resilience and Gratitude:

The road to recovery is often filled with challenges, but resilience is the key to overcoming them. Embracing the hard times and remaining grateful for the good moments can provide the strength needed to persevere.

Seeking Guidance and Support:

In moments of doubt or difficulty, turning to a higher power, or taking a moment to pray, can provide comfort and guidance. For many, spirituality plays a significant role in addiction recovery.

Self-Reflection Questions:

What beliefs have I held about myself and my ability to overcome addiction? Are they empowering or limiting?

How can I shift my mindset from fearing failure to focusing on the need to succeed in my recovery journey?

In what ways can I practice self-compassion and replace self-judgment with self-acceptance?

Am I truly focusing on my personal growth and recovery, or am I overly influenced by external factors?

How can I embrace change in my life and use it as a tool for personal transformation in recovery?

What are my dreams and goals for a drug-free life, and how can I work towards achieving them?

How can I cultivate resilience and maintain gratitude during both the challenging and joyful moments of my recovery journey?

Do I find solace in seeking guidance and support from a higher power or through spiritual practices as part of my recovery process?

Achieving long-term recovery from addiction goes beyond physical abstinence; it involves a profound transformation of beliefs and mindset. By adopting positive beliefs, embracing change, and focusing on personal growth, individuals can increase their chances of sustained sobriety. Recovery is a journey of self-discovery, resilience, and self-compassion, and it is through these aspects that the dream of a drug-free life becomes not only possible but achievable.

The Power of Beliefs in Shaping Long-Term Recovery from Addiction

Recovery from addiction is a demanding journey that hinges not only on physical abstinence but also on the transformation of deeply ingrained beliefs. The power of beliefs in shaping behaviors and actions cannot be overstated. This book delves into the significance of beliefs in the context of addiction recovery and how fostering positive convictions can pave the way for long-term sobriety. Drawing inspiration from motivational statements, we will explore how one's beliefs can drive change, resilience, and a brighter future.

Overcoming Failure:

Addiction recovery often involves confronting past failures and relapses. It's essential to recognize that these setbacks are events, not definitions of who you are. You may have failed, but you are not a failure. Believing in your capacity to learn from past mistakes is a powerful tool for change.

Positive Possibilities:

Believing in positive possibilities is a cornerstone of recovery. While addiction can make individuals feel trapped, it's essential to redirect the energy of frustration towards determination. See the potential for change, and you can turn frustration into a driving force for transformation.

Cultivating a Positive Attitude:

Maintaining a positive attitude is crucial for long-term recovery. Believing in the possibility of overcoming immediate challenges and striving to give your best effort can lead to incremental progress. With a positive mindset, you become better equipped to face the obstacles on your journey to sobriety.

Finding the Light at the End of the Tunnel:

Addiction recovery can feel like a long, arduous journey, with moments of doubt and despair. However, it's crucial to remember that there is always a light at the end of the tunnel. Believing in this light, even when it seems distant, can provide the motivation to persevere.

A Journey of Transformation

Focusing on the Positive Side:

Dwelling on the negative aspects of addiction can hinder progress. Instead, it's important to shift your beliefs toward finding the positive side of things. Recognize the personal growth, strength, and resilience you gain through recovery.

Continuous Self-Belief:

Acknowledge that you've faced challenges and obstacles before and emerged stronger. This history of resilience and strength can be a powerful belief in your ability to succeed in addiction recovery.

Self-Reflection Questions:

How have past failures and relapses shaped my beliefs about myself and my ability to recover from addiction?

What strategies can I employ to redirect the energy of frustration towards positive determination in my recovery journey?

Do I maintain a positive attitude and strive to give my best effort in overcoming immediate challenges in my recovery process?

How can I remind myself of the light at the end of the tunnel when I face moments of doubt or despair in my recovery?

What are some ways in which I can shift my focus from the negative aspects of addiction to the positive aspects of personal growth and resilience?

How can I harness the belief in my past successes and resilience to reinforce my determination in overcoming addiction for the long term?

The power of beliefs in shaping behaviors and actions cannot be underestimated in the context of addiction recovery. By fostering positive convictions, individuals can transcend past failures, maintain a positive attitude, and persist in their journey toward long-term sobriety. Belief in the potential for positive change and personal growth is the driving force that empowers individuals to overcome addiction and embrace a brighter future.

Identifying Limiting Beliefs
That Hinder Change in Addiction Recovery

In the journey towards long-term recovery from addiction, one of the most critical yet often overlooked aspects is identifying and addressing limiting beliefs. These beliefs can act as formidable barriers to change, hindering progress and personal growth. This book explores the significance of recognizing and overcoming these limiting beliefs to create a more fulfilling and sustainable recovery. Drawing inspiration from motivational statements, we will delve into the idea that happiness, greatness, and transformation are achievable by challenging our own beliefs and dispositions.

The Power of Disposition:

"Be determined to be cheerful and happy in whatever situation you may find yourself." Our disposition, rather than external circumstances, often determines our happiness. Many individuals struggling with addiction hold limiting beliefs that happiness is unattainable without substances. Recognizing and challenging this belief is essential for sustained recovery.

Taking Ownership of Happiness:

"Happiness is not something ready-made. It comes from your own actions." Limiting beliefs can lead to the misconception that external factors must align for happiness to be achievable. In recovery, it's vital to realize that happiness is a choice, rooted in our actions and mindset.

Embracing Creativity and Greatness:

"Creativity means believing you have greatness." Limiting beliefs may convince individuals that they lack the capacity for creativity and greatness. However, it's crucial to challenge these beliefs and recognize that creativity and greatness can emerge when we change our perspective and embrace new possibilities.

The Fear of Greatness:

"Don't be afraid of greatness; some are born great, some achieve greatness, and others have greatness thrust upon them." Limiting beliefs can also manifest as a fear of success or greatness. Confronting this fear is essential for realizing one's full potential in recovery.

No One Lives in Vain:

"No great person lives in vain. The history of the world is but the biography of great people." Limiting beliefs can make individuals feel insignificant or unworthy of change. It's important to remember that every individual has the potential to make a meaningful impact and leave a positive legacy, even in the context of addiction recovery.

Self-Reflection Questions:

> What limiting beliefs have influenced my perception of happiness and its relationship to substances or addictive behaviors?

> How can I take ownership of my happiness and recognize that it is a result of my own actions and mindset, rather than external circumstances?

A Journey of Transformation

> Do I believe that creativity and greatness are attainable in my life, or have I been hindered by limiting beliefs that I lack these qualities?

> Have I ever felt a fear of success or greatness in my recovery journey, and if so, how can I confront and overcome this fear?

> How can I challenge the belief that my life is insignificant or that my recovery journey is in vain, recognizing that I have the potential to make a positive impact?

Identifying and addressing limiting beliefs is a crucial step towards achieving long-term recovery from addiction. By challenging these beliefs, individuals can change their disposition, take ownership of their happiness, and embrace creativity and greatness in their lives. It is through this transformation that sustainable recovery becomes not only possible but also a path to a more fulfilling and purposeful life.

Cultivating Empowering Beliefs
That Support Long-Term Recovery from Addiction

Long-term recovery from addiction is a transformative journey that requires not only overcoming substance dependence but also nurturing empowering beliefs that support change. These beliefs act as a foundation for personal growth, resilience, and lasting sobriety. In this book, we will explore the significance of cultivating empowering beliefs in addiction recovery, drawing inspiration from motivational statements that emphasize personal responsibility, perseverance, and the power of faith.

Taking Personal Responsibility:

"You must take personal responsibility. You cannot change the circumstances, the seasons, or the wind, but you can change yourself. That is something you are in charge of." Empowering beliefs start with taking ownership of one's actions and decisions. Acknowledging personal responsibility is the first step towards meaningful change in recovery.

Embracing Failure as a Stepping Stone:

"A failure is not always a mistake; it may simply be the best one can do under the circumstances. The real mistake is to stop trying." Empowering beliefs reject the notion that failure is permanent. Instead, they see it as a natural part of the journey and an opportunity to learn, grow, and persevere.

Maintaining Emotional Resilience:

"Nothing gives one person so much advantage over another as to remain always cool and unruffled under all circumstances." Empowering beliefs encourage emotional resilience. In recovery, it's essential to remain calm and composed, even in the face of challenges, triggers, and setbacks.

The Power of Persistence:

"NEVER EVER GIVE UP trying to do what you really want. Stand tall, be strong, take chances, be committed not interested." Empowering beliefs emphasize the importance of persistence. They recognize that the path to recovery may be challenging, but commitment and determination are the keys to success.

Letting Go of What Cannot Be Changed:

"You can't stress about the things you can't change. Obstacles can't stop you, problems can't stop you, most of all other people can't stop you. Only you are in control of your future." Empowering beliefs encourage letting go of what cannot be changed and focusing on what can be controlled: one's own actions and choices.

The Realism of Dreams:

"No dream is unrealistic. It's a matter of you doing what it takes to make it come true." Empowering beliefs inspire individuals to pursue their dreams and aspirations. They recognize that with dedication and effort, even the most ambitious goals can be achieved.

Faith and Endurance:

"If patience is worth anything to you, it must endure to the end of time. True faith will last in the midst of the blackest storm. Faith is the strength by which a shattered world shall emerge into the light. Keep having faith and never give up hope." Empowering beliefs emphasize the enduring power of faith and hope. They provide the strength to weather the storms of addiction recovery and emerge into a brighter future.

Self-Reflection Questions:

How can I take personal responsibility for my addiction and my journey towards recovery?

Do I view failure as a permanent setback, or can I embrace it as a stepping stone towards growth and change?

How can I work on maintaining emotional resilience in the face of challenges and triggers during my recovery?

What strategies can I employ to persist in my recovery journey, even when faced with difficulties or temptations?

In what ways can I let go of factors beyond my control and focus on the choices and actions that lead to a healthier future?

A Journey of Transformation

> Am I pursuing my dreams and aspirations in recovery, and if not, what steps can I take to make them a reality?

> How can I strengthen my faith and hope as sources of strength during the darkest moments of my recovery journey?

Cultivating empowering beliefs is a fundamental aspect of long-term recovery from addiction. These beliefs provide the foundation for taking responsibility, embracing failure as a learning opportunity, and maintaining resilience and perseverance. With the support of empowering beliefs, individuals can overcome addiction and move towards a brighter and more fulfilling future.

Nurturing a Growth Mindset for Long-Term Recovery from Addiction

In the journey toward long-term recovery from addiction, nurturing a growth mindset can be a transformative tool. A growth mindset is the belief that challenges and setbacks are opportunities for growth and learning. This book explores the importance of adopting a growth mindset in addiction recovery, inspired by motivational statements that emphasize the value of experiencing both good and bad days as integral parts of the journey toward happiness and success.

Embracing the Variability of Life:

"Some days are just bad days, that's all." In addiction recovery, it's important to understand that not every day will be smooth sailing. Accepting the variability of life, including the occasional bad days, is a crucial aspect of nurturing a growth mindset.

Learning from Adversity:

"You have to experience sadness to know happiness." Adversity and sadness can serve as teachers in recovery. They offer opportunities to learn, grow, and appreciate the moments of happiness that follow. Nurturing a growth mindset involves embracing these experiences as part of the process.

Finding Strength in Challenges:

"The hard days are what make you stronger. The bad days make you realize what a good day is." Challenges and bad days can be stepping stones to personal growth. They test your resilience and provide the motivation to strive for better days. Recognizing this strength is essential in nurturing a growth mindset.

Achieving a Sense of Accomplishment:

"If you never had any bad days, you would never have that sense of accomplishment!" Overcoming challenges and addiction-related difficulties can lead to a profound sense of accomplishment. Nurturing a growth mindset involves recognizing and celebrating these achievements.

Taking Control of Your Happiness:

"You're in control of your happiness." A growth mindset acknowledges that happiness is not solely dependent on external circumstances but is influenced by one's perspective and attitude. Taking control of your happiness is a powerful tool in recovery.

Gratitude for Every Day:

"Every day is a good day to be alive, whether the sun's shining or not." Nurturing a growth mindset involves finding gratitude in the simple fact of being alive and having the opportunity to work towards recovery, regardless of the external conditions.

Self-Reflection Questions:

> How do I typically respond to bad days or setbacks in my recovery journey? Do I view them as opportunities for growth and learning?
>
> Have I recognized the valuable lessons and strength that can be gained from experiencing challenges and adversity in my recovery process?
>
> What sense of accomplishment have I experienced in my recovery journey, and how can I celebrate these achievements?
>
> Am I actively taking control of my happiness and attitude in recovery, or do I often let external factors dictate my emotional state?
>
> In what ways can I cultivate gratitude for each day and the opportunity to continue my recovery journey, regardless of the external circumstances?
>
> Have I ever considered the value of experiencing both good and bad days in my life and how they contribute to my personal growth and happiness?

Nurturing a growth mindset is a valuable approach in the pursuit of long-term recovery from addiction. It involves embracing the variability of life, learning from adversity, finding strength in challenges, and recognizing the sense of accomplishment that comes from overcoming difficulties. By taking control of one's happiness and practicing gratitude, individuals can foster a growth mindset that supports their journey toward lasting sobriety and a fulfilling life.

Embracing Challenges and Setbacks as Opportunities for Growth in Addiction Recovery

In the journey towards long-term recovery from addiction, embracing challenges and setbacks as opportunities for growth is a powerful mindset shift. This book explores the importance of adopting this mindset, drawing inspiration from motivational statements that emphasize the true meaning of wealth and strength. It encourages individuals in recovery to find value and transformation in the face of adversity, rather than seeking it in external factors like money.

True Wealth and Happiness:

"Wealth is the ability to fully experience life." True wealth is not measured by the size of one's bank account but by the richness of life experiences. In recovery, it's crucial to understand that lasting happiness comes from within, not from external substances or material possessions.

Money and Happiness:

"Money has never made a person happy, nor will it, there is nothing in its nature to produce happiness." Addiction can often be driven by a pursuit of happiness through substances. Embracing challenges in recovery involves recognizing that true happiness cannot be bought.

The Insatiable Nature of Desires:

"The more of it one has, the more one wants." Addiction can be characterized by a never-ending craving for more. In recovery, individuals must come to terms with the insatiable nature of desires and shift their focus toward inner growth and fulfillment.

Money's Limitations:

"Money cannot buy peace of mind. It cannot heal ruptured relationships or build meaning into a life that has none." Money has its limitations when it comes to addressing the deep emotional and psychological wounds that often underlie addiction. Recovery offers the opportunity to find peace, heal relationships, and create a meaningful life.

True Wealth as Inner Strength:

"Real wealth and strength are decisions that can be found within each of us." True wealth is not found in external possessions but within one's own decisions and choices. In recovery, individuals have the chance to tap into their inner strength and resilience.

Strength in Relationships:

"It takes strength to be in a loving relationship, raise a family, be yourself, and allow others to be themselves." Recovery provides the opportunity to build and nurture meaningful relationships, which require inner strength, empathy, and authenticity.

The Value of Thought and Kindness:

"A little thought and a little kindness are often worth more than a great deal of money." Small acts of thoughtfulness and kindness can have a profound impact on one's well-being and relationships. In recovery, these actions can be transformative.

Self-Reflection Questions:

How has my pursuit of external desires, such as substances, impacted my perception of happiness and wealth?

Have I recognized the limitations of money and external possessions in addressing the deeper challenges and emotional wounds associated with addiction?

In what ways can I tap into my inner strength and resilience to find true wealth and happiness in my recovery journey?

How can I apply the lessons of recovery, such as building meaningful relationships and practicing empathy, in my daily life to find strength and fulfillment?

Do I understand the value of small acts of thoughtfulness and kindness in my recovery and life in general?

What steps can I take to embrace challenges and setbacks as opportunities for personal growth and transformation in my addiction recovery?

Embracing challenges and setbacks as opportunities for growth is a crucial mindset shift for long-term recovery from addiction. By recognizing the limitations of external pursuits, finding strength within, and valuing meaningful relationships and kindness, individuals can unlock true wealth and fulfillment in their recovery journey and in life as a whole.

Cultivating Self-Efficacy and Confidence in the Journey of Addiction Recovery

In the pursuit of long-term recovery from addiction, cultivating self-efficacy and confidence in change efforts is essential. Self-efficacy, the belief in one's ability to achieve goals, and confidence, a sense of self-assurance, are the cornerstones of successful recovery. This book explores the importance of nurturing these qualities, inspired by motivational statements that highlight the need to overcome fear, let go of the past, and embrace self-acceptance in the journey towards lasting sobriety.

A Journey of Transformation

Overcoming Fear of Change:

"Change can be scary, but you know what's scarier? Allowing fear to stop you from growing, evolving, and progressing." In addiction recovery, fear of change can be a significant obstacle. Cultivating self-efficacy involves recognizing that growth and progress require stepping out of one's comfort zone.

Leaving the Past Behind:

"The best can't find you until you put the worst behind you." To build self-efficacy and confidence, individuals must learn to leave the past, including past failures and mistakes, behind. Recovery is an opportunity for a fresh start.

Unfolding Your Best Self:

"The art of being yourself at your best is the art of unfolding your personality into the person you want to be." Cultivating self-efficacy means actively working on becoming the person you aspire to be in recovery. It involves setting goals and working towards personal growth.

Self-Love and Forgiveness:

"Be gentle with yourself, learn to love yourself, to forgive yourself, for only as we have the right attitude toward ourselves can we have the right attitude toward others." Self-efficacy and confidence are built on a foundation of self-love and self-forgiveness. These qualities allow individuals to approach recovery with kindness and resilience.

Strength Through Suffering:

"Out of suffering have emerged the strongest souls; the most massive characters are seared with scars." Recognizing that adversity and suffering can be sources of strength is a key element in building self-efficacy. It involves viewing challenges as opportunities for growth and resilience.

Courage in Small Steps:

"Courage is only the accumulation of small steps." Building self-efficacy and confidence doesn't require giant leaps. Instead, it involves taking small, consistent steps towards recovery goals. Each step is an affirmation of one's capability.

Strength in Facing Change:

"To keep our faces toward change and behave like free spirits in the presence of fate is strength undefeatable." Cultivating self-efficacy involves embracing change as a natural part of the recovery journey. It means facing challenges with a sense of resilience and adaptability.

Self-Reflection Questions:

How does fear of change impact my recovery efforts, and what steps can I take to overcome this fear and build self-efficacy?

What aspects of my past am I holding onto that may be hindering my recovery progress, and how can I let go of them to move forward?

How can I actively work on becoming the person I aspire to be in my recovery journey, and what goals can I set to facilitate personal growth?

Do I practice self-love and forgiveness in my recovery, and if not, how can I develop a more compassionate attitude towards myself?

Have I recognized the strength and resilience that can emerge from adversity and suffering in my recovery journey?

What small steps can I take to build courage and self-efficacy in my daily efforts towards lasting sobriety?

How can I embrace change as an opportunity for growth and resilience, rather than resisting it in my recovery journey?

Cultivating self-efficacy and confidence is vital in the process of long-term recovery from addiction. These qualities enable individuals to overcome fear, let go of the past, and embrace change with resilience and adaptability. By actively working on self-love, setting goals, and viewing challenges as opportunities for growth, individuals can build the inner strength needed to achieve lasting sobriety and a brighter future.

The Connection Between Emotions and Change

The path to long-term recovery from addiction is often a challenging and emotional journey. Emotions play a significant role in our ability to change and grow during recovery. This book explores the profound connection between emotions and change, drawing inspiration from motivational statements that encourage resilience, self-compassion, and the importance of learning from life's ups and downs.

The Connection Between Emotions and Change:
Challenging Our Beliefs and Limits:

"We create rules for ourselves that tell us 'This is as far as I can go in this direction' or 'This is just how life is.' We accept the limits of our vision for the limits of the world." Emotions are often tied to our beliefs and limitations. In recovery, it's essential to challenge these beliefs and open ourselves up to the possibility of change.

Resilience in the Face of Adversity:

"In life, many things don't go according to plan. If you fall, get back up. If you stumble, regain your balance but, never give up." Emotions can be intense during recovery, especially when facing setbacks. Resilience involves acknowledging these emotions, regaining balance, and continuing the journey toward sobriety.

Acceptance of Life's Uncertainties:

"You may never understand why something happened the way it did so don't drive yourself crazy trying." Emotions can be triggered by the unpredictability of life. Acceptance is a crucial component of recovery, allowing individuals to make peace with uncertainties and focus on the present.

Readiness for Change:

"If something hasn't happened for you, it doesn't mean it's never going to happen. It might mean that you're not ready for it." Emotions can signal readiness for change. Recognizing when you're emotionally prepared for certain shifts in recovery can guide your decisions and actions.

Learning from Choices:

"Life is all about making choices. Always do your best to make the right ones, and always do your best to learn from the wrong ones." Emotions often accompany the choices we make. Recovery involves making conscious choices and learning from both successes and setbacks.

A Journey of Transformation

Honesty and Accountability:

"The most honorable people of all are not those who never make mistakes, but those who admit to them when they do, and then go on to do their best to make right the wrongs they made." Emotions can be powerful motivators for honesty and accountability. Acknowledging mistakes and taking responsibility are essential steps in recovery.

Authentic Motivation:

"If people are good only because they fear punishment and hope for reward, then we are a sorry lot indeed." Emotions drive authentic motivation for change. True transformation in recovery comes from a genuine desire to lead a healthier, happier life.

The Perseverance of Hope:

"Remember, hope is a good thing, maybe the best of things, and no good thing ever dies." Emotions, particularly hope, play a central role in recovery. Hope provides the strength to persevere through the challenges and uncertainties of the recovery journey.

Self-Reflection Questions:

How have my beliefs and limitations influenced my emotions in the context of addiction recovery, and how can I challenge and expand my vision for change?

How do I respond to setbacks and challenging emotions in my recovery journey, and what strategies can I employ to regain balance and resilience?

Have I accepted the uncertainties of life and recovery, and how can I cultivate a mindset of acceptance and present-focused awareness?

How can I recognize the emotional readiness for change and make informed decisions in my recovery?

Do I view my choices in recovery as opportunities for growth and learning, and how can I embrace both successes and mistakes as valuable lessons?

Am I honest and accountable for my actions in recovery, and what steps can I take to make amends and make right any wrongs?

What genuinely motivates me to pursue long-term recovery, and how can I ensure that my motivation is authentic and not driven solely by fear or external rewards?

How does hope influence my perseverance in recovery, and how can I maintain a sense of hope even in the face of challenges and setbacks?

The connection between emotions and change is profound in the journey of addiction recovery. By embracing challenging emotions, learning from choices, and staying motivated by authentic desires, individuals can navigate the ups and downs of recovery with resilience and hope, ultimately achieving lasting sobriety and personal growth.

The Emotional Landscape of Change in Long-Term Addiction Recovery

Long-term recovery from addiction is a transformative journey that takes individuals through a complex emotional landscape. This book explores the emotional aspects of change in recovery, drawing inspiration from motivational statements that emphasize the process of letting go, self-discovery, and embracing the evolving emotional landscape. It sheds light on the significance of trusting one's feelings, taking chances, and nurturing positive habits to achieve lasting sobriety.

Letting Go to Grow:

"Anytime you're gonna grow, you're gonna lose something. You're losing what you're hanging onto to keep safe." Change in recovery often involves letting go of familiar but unhealthy habits and patterns. This process can be emotionally challenging as individuals release what they have clung to for comfort.

Rediscovering Needs:

"You're losing habits that you're comfortable with; you're losing familiarity." Addiction can numb or mask underlying emotional needs. In recovery, individuals begin to rediscover their true needs and emotions, which may have been neglected for a long time.

Finding Direction in Being Lost:

"Sometimes we have to lose our way to find out what we really want because we often ignore our needs until we are lost." The emotional landscape of recovery may involve moments of feeling lost or uncertain. However, these moments can be powerful opportunities for self-discovery and personal growth.

Trusting Feelings and Taking Chances:

"Life is about trusting your feelings and taking chances." Recovery is a journey of self-trust and taking chances on a healthier, sober life. Embracing one's emotions and taking calculated risks are integral components of this process.

A Journey of Transformation

Learning from the Past:

"Losing and finding happiness, appreciating the memories, learning from the past, and realizing people change." The emotional landscape includes reflecting on past experiences, both positive and negative, to gain insights and wisdom for a better future.

Spiritual and Emotional Practices:

"Pray, forgive yourself, appreciate others, listen to your gut, do things you enjoy, and remind yourself that we are all loved and connected." Nurturing positive emotional practices, such as prayer, forgiveness, gratitude, and self-care, can be immensely beneficial in managing the emotional ups and downs of recovery.

Self-Reflection Questions:

> How have I experienced the emotional challenges of letting go in my recovery journey, and how can I find the strength to release unhealthy habits and patterns?
>
> What emotions have I rediscovered in recovery that were previously masked by addiction, and how can I address my unmet emotional needs?
>
> Have I embraced moments of feeling lost or uncertain as opportunities for self-discovery and personal growth, and what strategies can I employ to navigate these moments effectively?
>
> How can I build trust in my own feelings and emotions and use them as a guide in making positive changes in my recovery journey?
>
> What lessons have I learned from my past experiences, and how can I apply this wisdom to foster a healthier, happier future?
>
> Do I engage in spiritual and emotional practices that support my emotional well-being in recovery, and how can I incorporate more positive habits into my daily life?

The emotional landscape of change in long-term addiction recovery is both challenging and rewarding. By recognizing the importance of letting go, rediscovering needs, and trusting emotions, individuals can navigate this landscape with resilience and self-discovery. Embracing the emotional journey of recovery ultimately leads to lasting sobriety and a richer, more fulfilling life.

Understanding the Emotions Associated with Change in Long-Term Addiction Recovery

Long-term recovery from addiction is a transformative process that involves significant emotional shifts and self-discovery. This book delves into the complex emotional landscape of change in recovery, inspired by motivational statements emphasizing the importance of self-happiness, setting ambitious goals, and recognizing the power of the mind. It explores the emotions linked to the recovery journey and the significance of focusing on hopes, dreams, and unfulfilled potential.

Prioritizing Self-Happiness:

"It's so important to make someone happy. More important to start with yourself." In the journey of recovery, understanding the emotions associated with change begins with prioritizing one's own happiness and well-being. Self-care is a crucial foundation for lasting sobriety.

Setting Ambitious Goals:

"Set goals beyond your reach so you always have something to reach for." Change in recovery often involves setting ambitious goals for personal growth and sobriety. These goals can inspire motivation and a sense of purpose.

The Significance of Little Things:

"It is the little things in life that are vital. Little things make big things happen." Recovery is not just about monumental milestones; it's about appreciating the small victories and the positive changes that accumulate over time.

Protecting the Mind:

"All the water in the world cannot sink a ship unless it gets inside of it. All the worry, frustration, anxiety, and jealousy cannot sink a person unless it gets inside their mind." Understanding the emotions associated with change involves safeguarding the mind from negative thoughts and emotions that can undermine recovery progress.

Focusing on Hopes and Dreams:

"Consult not your fears but your hopes and your dreams. Think not about your frustrations but about your unfulfilled potential." Embracing change means shifting one's focus from fears and frustrations to the possibilities and potential for a brighter future.

Belief in What Is Still Possible:

"Concern yourself not with what you tried and failed in but with what it is still possible for you to do." Recovery is a journey of second chances and renewed hope. Understanding the emotions associated with change involves believing in the potential for personal growth and transformation.

A Journey of Transformation

Self-Reflection Questions:

How does my pursuit of happiness align with my recovery goals, and what self-care practices can I incorporate into my daily life to prioritize my well-being?

Have I set ambitious goals for my recovery journey, and how do these goals motivate and guide my efforts towards lasting sobriety?

Do I appreciate the significance of small victories and positive changes in my recovery, and how can I celebrate these accomplishments along the way?

How can I protect my mind from negative thoughts and emotions that may hinder my recovery progress, and what strategies can I employ to foster a more positive mindset?

What are my hopes and dreams for the future, and how can I shift my focus away from fears and frustrations to embrace the potential for personal growth?

Am I aware of the possibilities and opportunities that still lie ahead in my recovery journey, and how can I maintain a sense of belief in my ability to achieve them?

Understanding the emotions associated with change is essential in the long-term recovery from addiction. By prioritizing self-happiness, setting ambitious goals, and protecting the mind from negativity, individuals can navigate the emotional landscape of recovery with resilience and optimism. Focusing on hopes, dreams, and unfulfilled potential ultimately leads to lasting sobriety and a fulfilling life in recovery.

Coping with Fear, Resistance, and Uncertainty in Long-Term Addiction Recovery

The path to long-term recovery from addiction is often fraught with fear, resistance, and uncertainty. This book delves into the emotional challenges that individuals face in recovery, drawing inspiration from motivational statements that encourage resilience, self-awareness, and empowerment. It explores strategies for coping with these emotions and maintaining a positive mindset on the journey to lasting sobriety.

Overcoming the Draining Nature of Complaining:

"Complaining is draining. Complaining only takes away energy from today and never solves the problems for tomorrow." Recovery is a time to focus on positive actions and solutions rather than dwelling on past mistakes or complaining about current challenges. How we use our energy can greatly impact our progress.

Recognizing Hidden Pain:

"The sad thing is, nobody ever really knows how much anyone else is hurting. We could be standing next to somebody who is completely broken, and we wouldn't even know it." In recovery, it's important to acknowledge that others may be experiencing hidden pain and struggles. Compassion and empathy can foster a sense of connection and support.

The Impact of Thoughts on Emotions:

"Your thoughts affect your emotions. Your emotions affect your decisions. Your decisions affect your life." Understanding the interplay between thoughts, emotions, and decisions is essential in coping with fear and uncertainty in recovery. Positive thinking can lead to more constructive actions and outcomes.

Setting Boundaries with Love and Trust:

"Give but don't allow yourself to be used. Love but don't allow your heart to be abused. Trust but don't be naive." Coping with fear and uncertainty in recovery requires setting healthy boundaries in relationships. It's important to give support while also protecting one's own well-being.

Maintaining Personal Voice:

"Listen to others but don't lose your own voice." Recovery involves seeking guidance and support from others, but it's equally important to maintain one's own identity and voice. Assertiveness and self-expression play a crucial role in personal growth.

Pursuing What You Really Want:

"In life, what you really want never comes easy. Make it happen for yourself because no one else will." Coping with resistance and uncertainty means embracing the challenges and working tirelessly to achieve your recovery goals. Self-determination and perseverance are keys to success.

Self-Reflection Questions:

How has complaining or dwelling on past mistakes drained my energy and hindered my progress in recovery, and how can I shift my focus toward positive actions and solutions?

Am I aware of the hidden pain and struggles that others in my support network may be experiencing, and how can I foster empathy and compassion in my interactions with them?

How can I actively manage my thoughts and emotions in recovery to make more constructive decisions and positively influence the trajectory of my life?

A Journey of Transformation

> Do I set healthy boundaries in my relationships, balancing support and self-care, and what steps can I take to maintain these boundaries in a healthy way?

> Have I maintained my personal voice and identity in recovery, or have I allowed the opinions of others to overshadow my own needs and desires?

> Am I actively pursuing what I really want in my recovery journey, and how can I remain committed and determined in the face of resistance and uncertainty?

Coping with fear, resistance, and uncertainty is a significant part of the long-term recovery journey from addiction. By focusing on positive actions, fostering empathy, setting boundaries, and staying true to one's own voice and goals, individuals can navigate these challenges with resilience and determination. Ultimately, embracing the difficulties and working tirelessly to achieve sobriety leads to a brighter and more fulfilling future.

Emotional Intelligence in Navigating Change:
A Key to Long-Term Addiction Recovery

Long-term recovery from addiction is a journey filled with uncertainty and change, where emotional intelligence plays a pivotal role. Emotional intelligence involves recognizing, understanding, and managing our own emotions and the emotions of others. This book explores the significance of emotional intelligence in navigating the complexities of recovery, drawing inspiration from motivational statements that highlight faith, resilience, and the power of emotional control.

Faith in the Unknown:

"When you have come to the edge of all the light that you know and are about to drop off into the darkness of the unknown, faith is knowing one of two things will happen: there will be something solid to stand on, or you will be taught to fly." Emotional intelligence in recovery includes having faith in oneself and the process, even when facing the uncertainty of change. It means trusting that one can adapt and grow.

Treating Defeat as Temporary:

"Treat defeat as a temporary roadblock." Emotional intelligence allows individuals to view setbacks not as permanent failures but as temporary challenges. It involves managing emotions in the face of defeat and maintaining a positive outlook on the recovery journey.

Emotional Self-Control:

"Always stay in control of your emotions and never allow them to influence you in a negative way." Emotional intelligence involves recognizing and managing one's emotions in a healthy manner. It means avoiding impulsive or self-destructive behaviors that can hinder recovery progress.

Adjusting to Change:

"If something in your life is not going according to plan, make the necessary adjustments to put yourself back on track." Emotional intelligence includes the ability to adapt to change and make necessary adjustments in recovery. It means recognizing when a course correction is needed and taking action.

Embracing Life's Realities:

"Life isn't always sunshine and butterflies. Sometimes you've got to learn to smile through the pain because in the end, it's not going to matter how many breaths you have taken, but how many moments have taken your breath away." Emotional intelligence acknowledges the ups and downs of life and recovery. It involves finding strength and resilience to smile through the pain and cherish moments of personal growth and transformation.

Self-Reflection Questions:

> How do I demonstrate faith in myself and the recovery process when faced with the unknown and uncertainty?

> In what ways can I treat defeat and setbacks as temporary roadblocks rather than permanent failures, and how does this mindset benefit my recovery journey?

> Am I effectively managing my emotions in recovery, and how can I further develop my emotional self-control to avoid negative influences on my progress?

> Do I recognize when adjustments are needed in my recovery path, and how can I develop the ability to adapt to change and make necessary course corrections?

> How can I embrace the realities of life and recovery, acknowledging that challenges are a part of the journey, and find moments that take my breath away through resilience and personal growth?

Emotional intelligence is a crucial asset in the long-term recovery from addiction. By fostering faith in the unknown, treating defeat as temporary, practicing emotional self-control, adjusting to change, and embracing life's realities, individuals can navigate the challenges of recovery with resilience and grace. Developing emotional intelligence empowers individuals to maintain a positive outlook and achieve lasting sobriety.

Managing Emotions Effectively During the Change Process in Long-Term Addiction Recovery

Long-term recovery from addiction is a transformative journey filled with change and emotional challenges. This book delves into the importance of managing emotions effectively during this

A Journey of Transformation

process, drawing inspiration from motivational statements that underscore the value of discipline, time, self-improvement, and personal responsibility. It explores how individuals can harness their emotions to navigate the complexities of recovery successfully.

Choosing the Pain of Discipline:

"We must all suffer one of two things: the pain of discipline or the pain of regret and disappointment." Managing emotions effectively in recovery often involves choosing the discipline required to stay on the path of sobriety. This choice can be emotionally taxing but ultimately leads to lasting fulfillment.

Recognizing the Value of Time:

"Time is more value than money. You can get more money, but you cannot get more time." Effective emotional management in recovery means recognizing the preciousness of time and making the most of each moment. Time spent in addiction cannot be regained, emphasizing the importance of recovery.

Leading a Purposeful Life:

"Let others lead small lives, argue over small things, cry over small hurts, and leave their future in someone else's hands, but not you." Managing emotions involves leading a purposeful life in recovery, where individuals take control of their destiny and prioritize their well-being over trivial matters.

Embracing Personal Growth:

"Don't wish for life to be easier; wish you were better. Don't place mistakes over your head; their weight may crush you. Instead, place them under your feet and use them as a platform to view your horizons." Effective emotional management includes using mistakes and challenges as opportunities for personal growth. Embracing resilience in the face of adversity is key to successful recovery.

Taking Control of One's Future:

"We have to make plans for ourselves as a CEO would for a company. If we don't make plans for ourselves, someone else will. Those plans will most likely not be our desires." Managing emotions involves taking control of one's future in recovery, setting clear goals, and making choices aligned with personal desires rather than succumbing to external influences.

Seizing the Moment:

"Time to step it up. We live once, and time is ticking..." Effective emotional management means recognizing the urgency of taking action in recovery. Seizing the moment and committing to lasting sobriety are vital steps toward a fulfilling life.

Self-Reflection Questions:

> Am I willing to endure the short-term pain of discipline to achieve long-term recovery, and how can I better manage my emotions during moments of temptation or weakness?
>
> Do I value time as a precious resource in my recovery journey, and how can I make the most of each day to stay committed to my sobriety goals?
>
> Am I leading a purposeful life in recovery, or do I find myself getting caught up in small, trivial matters? How can I prioritize my well-being and personal growth instead?
>
> How do I view mistakes and challenges in my recovery, and how can I shift my perspective to use them as stepping stones toward personal growth and resilience?
>
> Have I taken control of my future in recovery by setting clear goals and making choices aligned with my desires? If not, what steps can I take to regain control?
>
> Do I recognize the urgency of committing to lasting sobriety and taking action in my recovery, or am I procrastinating? How can I harness this sense of urgency to drive positive change in my life?

Managing emotions effectively during the change process of long-term addiction recovery is crucial for success. By choosing discipline over regret, valuing time, leading purposeful lives, embracing personal growth, taking control of their future, and seizing the moment, individuals can navigate the emotional challenges of recovery with determination and resilience. Effective emotional management leads to lasting sobriety and a brighter future.

Leveraging Positive Emotions as Drivers of Change in Long-Term Addiction Recovery

Long-term recovery from addiction is a transformative journey where emotions play a pivotal role. This book explores the significance of leveraging positive emotions as drivers of change, drawing inspiration from motivational statements that emphasize living in the present, self-worth, learning from mistakes, and embracing the journey. It highlights how positive emotions can be powerful catalysts for lasting sobriety.

A Journey of Transformation

Embracing the Present:

"We waste so many days waiting for the weekend. So many nights wanting morning. Our lust for future comfort is the biggest thief of life." In addiction recovery, positive emotions are harnessed by embracing the present moment. Instead of longing for the future, individuals focus on the opportunities for growth and happiness today.

Individualizing the Journey:

"Let us not compare our situation to somebody else's. We are not running their race. We are running our own race." Positive emotions flourish when individuals recognize that their recovery journey is unique. Comparisons to others can be counterproductive; self-compassion and self-acceptance are key.

Seeking Strength in Challenges:

"Don't pray for an easy life, pray for the strength to endure a hard one." Positive emotions serve as a wellspring of strength when individuals face challenges in recovery. Rather than avoiding difficulties, they use them as opportunities for personal growth and resilience.

Learning from Mistakes:

"Mistakes are meant for learning, not repeating. Don't be afraid to make mistakes; just be afraid of not learning from them." Positive emotions drive change when individuals view mistakes as stepping stones toward improvement. Each misstep becomes a chance for growth and self-discovery.

Embracing the Journey:

"Life is all about learning from yesterday, living for today, and hoping for tomorrow." Positive emotions are potent drivers of change when individuals fully engage with the journey of recovery. By learning from the past, living purposefully in the present, and embracing hope for the future, they sustain motivation for lasting sobriety.

Recognizing Self-Worth:

"Our value doesn't decrease based on someone's inability to see our worth. We are not what we have done; we are what we have overcome." Leveraging positive emotions involves recognizing one's intrinsic self-worth. Self-esteem and self-compassion are essential for a resilient recovery.

Viewing Failure as a New Beginning:

"Failure is not final; it is a chance to start again with the knowledge gained from what went before. We must go through the worst to arrive at our best." Positive emotions drive change when individuals view failure as a stepping stone to a fresh start. Every setback is an opportunity to apply newfound wisdom and resilience.

Self-Reflection Questions:

How can I better embrace the present moment in my recovery journey and leverage the positive emotions that arise from living in the now?

Do I find myself comparing my recovery progress to others, and how can I shift my focus toward recognizing the uniqueness of my journey and valuing my individual experience?

Am I seeking strength in the face of challenges, or do I often wish for an easier path? How can I cultivate positive emotions to endure and grow through adversity?

How do I currently approach mistakes in my recovery, and how can I harness positive emotions to ensure that I learn from them rather than repeat them?

Do I fully embrace the journey of recovery, with a balance of learning from the past, living purposefully in the present, and nurturing hope for the future?

Have I recognized my self-worth in the context of my recovery journey, and how can I cultivate self-esteem and self-compassion to drive positive change?

Do I view failure as a finality, or am I open to the idea that it can be a stepping stone to a fresh start? How can I use positive emotions to approach setbacks with resilience and growth in mind?

Leveraging positive emotions as drivers of change is essential in the long-term recovery from addiction. By embracing the present, individualizing the journey, seeking strength in challenges, learning from mistakes, embracing the journey, recognizing self-worth, and viewing failure as a new beginning, individuals can harness the power of positive emotions to sustain motivation and achieve lasting sobriety.

The Importance of Self-Reflection

Self-reflection is a powerful tool on the journey to long-term recovery from addiction. It allows individuals to examine their thoughts, behaviors, and emotions, gaining insights into the path they've walked and the road ahead. This book explores the importance of self-reflection in recovery, drawing inspiration from motivational statements that underscore the value of patience, letting go of temporary happiness, and cultivating positivity.

Gaining Perspective:

"Remember that time when we felt hopeless, got lost, and didn't know where to go? But here we are today. We survived." Self-reflection provides an opportunity to gain perspective on the progress made in recovery. It reminds individuals of their resilience and the journey they've undertaken.

Letting Go of Temporary Happiness:

"We get attached to temporary things, then wonder why our happiness never lasts. We ignored truths for temporary happiness." Self-reflection prompts individuals to examine their attachments to temporary sources of happiness, such as substances, and encourages them to seek deeper, lasting sources of fulfillment.

Cultivating Patience:

"Sometimes we need patience in order to find true happiness. It won't come fast and it won't come easy, but it will be worth it." Self-reflection reinforces the idea that lasting happiness and recovery require patience. It helps individuals appreciate the slow but meaningful progress they make.

Taking Responsibility:

"Life is going to give us just what we put into it. So we have to put our whole heart in everything we do." Self-reflection encourages individuals to take responsibility for their actions and decisions. It reminds them that recovery is an active process that requires their full commitment.

Overpowering Negativity with Positivity:

"It takes but one positive thought when given a chance to survive and thrive to overpower an entire army of negative thoughts." Self-reflection empowers individuals to combat negativity with positivity. By examining their thought patterns, they can shift their focus toward hope, resilience, and optimism.

A Journey of Transformation

Self-Reflection Questions:

> How has self-reflection helped me gain perspective on my recovery journey, and what progress have I made that I can be proud of?
>
> Do I find myself clinging to temporary sources of happiness or unhealthy attachments in recovery, and how can self-reflection guide me toward seeking deeper, lasting sources of fulfillment?
>
> Have I cultivated patience in my recovery, recognizing that lasting happiness takes time, and how can I continue to develop this trait?
>
> Am I taking full responsibility for my actions and decisions in the recovery process, and how can self-reflection motivate me to put my whole heart into my journey?
>
> How do I currently manage negative thoughts and emotions in recovery, and how can self-reflection help me shift toward a more positive and hopeful mindset?

Self-reflection is a vital component of long-term recovery from addiction. It provides individuals with perspective, encourages them to let go of temporary happiness, cultivates patience, promotes personal responsibility, and empowers them to overcome negativity with positivity. By regularly engaging in self-reflection, individuals can navigate their recovery journey with greater insight and determination, ultimately achieving lasting sobriety.

The Role of Self-Awareness in Long-Term Addiction Recovery

Self-awareness is a fundamental aspect of personal growth and transformation in the context of long-term addiction recovery. This book explores the pivotal role of self-awareness in the recovery journey, drawing inspiration from motivational statements that emphasize self-belief, overcoming limitations, learning from failures, and having faith in the process.

Believing in Oneself:

"Never let the negativity get to you. There are gonna be a lot of people you have to plow through, but as long you believe in yourself, that's all that matters." Self-awareness begins with believing in oneself. It means acknowledging one's worth and potential, regardless of external negativity or doubts.

Overcoming Limitations:

"When someone tells you it can't be done, it's more a reflection of their limitations, not yours." Self-awareness allows individuals to recognize that limitations imposed by others are not a reflection of their own potential. It empowers them to challenge and transcend those limitations.

Embracing Failure and Learning:

"Failures are part of life. If you don't fail, you don't learn. If you don't learn, you'll never change." Self-awareness involves embracing failure as a natural part of the learning process. It encourages individuals to view setbacks as opportunities for growth and transformation.

Having Faith in the Process:

"Have faith that things will work out, maybe not how you planned but how it's meant to be. Faith that it's not always in your hands or things don't always go the way you planned, but you have to have faith that there is a plan for you, and you must follow your heart and believe in yourself no matter what." Self-awareness is intertwined with faith in the recovery process. It means trusting that, even in the face of uncertainty and unexpected challenges, there is a path to healing and sobriety.

Self-Reflection Questions:

> How does self-awareness play a role in my belief in myself and my worth on the journey to long-term recovery from addiction?

> Do I allow external negativity and doubts to affect my self-belief, or am I able to plow through obstacles and maintain confidence in my abilities?

> How do I currently view limitations imposed by others, and how can self-awareness help me recognize that they do not define my potential?

> Am I open to embracing failure and using it as a catalyst for growth and change in my recovery journey, and how can I further develop this aspect of self-awareness?

> How does my faith in the recovery process influence my actions and mindset, and how can self-awareness strengthen my trust in the journey, even when it doesn't go as planned?

Self-awareness is a cornerstone of long-term addiction recovery. By believing in oneself, overcoming external limitations, embracing failure as a learning opportunity, and having faith in the process, individuals can harness the power of self-awareness to drive positive change and achieve lasting sobriety. Self-reflection and self-awareness are key components of this transformative journey.

Reflecting on Motivations and Desires in Long-Term Addiction Recovery

In the journey towards long-term recovery from addiction, self-reflection on motivations and desires is essential for sustained growth and transformation. This book delves into the significance of reflecting on one's motivations and desires, drawing inspiration from motivational statements

A Journey of Transformation

that highlight the development of courage through adversity, the advantages of facing challenges, and the continuous nature of personal growth.

Developing Courage through Adversity:

"We don't develop courage by being happy every day. We develop it by surviving difficult times and challenging adversity." Self-reflection on motivations begins with acknowledging that recovery is not always a smooth path. It requires the courage to face adversity, learn from it, and grow stronger as a result.

Embracing Adversity as an Advantage:

"We should never view our challenges as a disadvantage. Instead, it's important for us to understand that our experience of facing and overcoming adversity is actually one of our biggest advantages." Reflecting on motivations involves recognizing that adversity is not a setback but an opportunity. It teaches resilience, determination, and the ability to adapt.

Learning from Defeat and Loss:

"There is nothing better than adversity. Every defeat, every heartbreak, every loss, contains its own seed, its own lesson on how to improve our performance the next time." Self-reflection prompts individuals to learn from their defeats and losses. By examining these experiences, they can identify valuable lessons that guide their future actions and decisions.

Embracing Continuous Growth:

"The journey is never ending. There's always gonna be growth, improvement, adversity; we just gotta take it all in and do what's right, continue to grow, continue to live in the moment." Reflecting on desires and motivations involves understanding that personal growth is an ongoing process. It requires embracing the present, staying committed to improvement, and adapting to the challenges that arise.

Self-Reflection Questions:

> How has adversity in my recovery journey contributed to the development of courage, and how can I continue to draw strength from challenging times?

> Do I view challenges and setbacks as disadvantages, or am I able to recognize the advantages they bring in terms of personal growth and resilience?

> What lessons have I learned from past defeats, heartbreaks, or losses in my recovery journey, and how have these experiences shaped my determination to improve?

How can I maintain a mindset of continuous growth, acknowledging that there will always be challenges and opportunities for improvement along the path to lasting sobriety?

Reflecting on motivations and desires is a vital aspect of long-term addiction recovery. By developing courage through adversity, embracing challenges as advantages, learning from defeat and loss, and recognizing the continuous nature of personal growth, individuals can navigate their recovery journey with resilience and determination. Self-reflection and self-awareness are key components of this transformative process.

Identifying Areas in Need of Transformation on the Road to Recovery

The journey towards long-term recovery from addiction is marked by self-awareness and the identification of areas in need of transformation. This book explores the significance of recognizing these areas, drawing inspiration from motivational statements that emphasize self-worth, acknowledging progress, and the transformative potential inherent in life's challenges.

Recognizing Self-Worth:

"Your value doesn't decrease based on someone's inability to see your worth." Self-reflection plays a crucial role in identifying areas that need transformation. It begins with recognizing one's intrinsic value and self-worth, irrespective of external judgments or opinions.

Acknowledging Progress:

"Remember how far you've come. Not just how far you have to go. You are not where you want to be, but neither are you where you used to be." Identifying areas for transformation involves acknowledging the progress made in recovery. By reflecting on how far one has come, individuals can appreciate their capacity for change.

Learning from Life's Tests:

"Every test in our life makes us bitter or better, every problem comes to break us or make us. The choice is ours whether we become victims or victors." Self-awareness helps individuals recognize that life's challenges are opportunities for transformation. They can choose to view these challenges as chances for personal growth and resilience rather than as obstacles.

Self-Reflection Questions:

How do I currently perceive my self-worth, and how can I use self-reflection to reinforce my intrinsic value?

In what ways have I progressed on my journey to recovery, and how can I leverage this progress to identify areas in need of further transformation?

A Journey of Transformation

> How have I responded to life's tests and challenges in my recovery journey, and how can I shift my mindset toward viewing them as opportunities for growth and resilience?

Identifying areas in need of transformation is a crucial aspect of long-term addiction recovery. By recognizing their intrinsic self-worth, acknowledging their progress, and embracing life's challenges as opportunities for growth, individuals can harness the power of self-reflection to facilitate positive change and achieve lasting sobriety. Self-awareness and self-reflection are essential tools on this transformative journey.

Self-Assessment and Introspection:
Catalysts for Change in Addiction Recovery

In the journey towards long-term recovery from addiction, self-assessment and introspection are powerful tools for fostering personal growth and transformation. This book explores the significance of self-assessment and introspection in recovery, drawing inspiration from motivational statements that highlight the importance of experiencing life, defining oneself through patience and attitude, embracing positivity, and the resilience to endure and restart.

Self-Assessment and Introspection as Catalysts for Change:

Embracing Life's Mystery:

"The mystery of life is not a problem to be solved; it is a reality to be experienced." Self-assessment begins with the recognition that life is a complex and ever-changing journey. Instead of seeking to solve life's mysteries, individuals in recovery can embrace the experience of living, including the challenges it presents.

Defining Oneself:

"Two things define you: Your patience when you have nothing, and your attitude when you have everything." Introspection encourages individuals to define themselves through their patience and attitude. By reflecting on these attributes, individuals can uncover the qualities that contribute to their personal growth and resilience.

Focusing on Positives:

"You are always stronger than you think you are. Focus on the positives, and soon the negatives will disappear." Self-assessment prompts individuals to focus on their strengths and resilience. By concentrating on the positives in their recovery journey, individuals can gradually diminish the impact of negative influences.

Embracing Understanding Over Fear:

"The day you let go of fear and instead embrace understanding, is the day you begin to live." Introspection encourages individuals to shift from fear to understanding. By exploring their thoughts and emotions, they can gain a deeper understanding of their addiction and recovery process, ultimately leading to more meaningful and fulfilling lives.

Embracing Change and Resilience:

"Every time it rains, it stops raining. Every time we hurt, we heal. After darkness, there is always light, and we get reminded of this every morning, but still, we choose to believe that the night will last forever. Nothing lasts forever. Not the good or the bad. So we might as well smile while we're here." Self-assessment and introspection highlight the cyclical nature of life, including recovery. They encourage individuals to embrace change, practice resilience, and find solace in the knowledge that challenges are temporary.

Cultivating Happiness:

"Happiness cannot be traveled to, owned, earned, or worn. It is the spiritual experience of living every minute with love, grace, and gratitude." Self-assessment promotes the cultivation of happiness by emphasizing the spiritual experience of living in the present moment with love, grace, and gratitude.

Restarting the Day:

"I hope we all remember today that if we slip up, we can restart our day at any time. We don't have to wait until the next day to start over. Just sit down, breathe for a few minutes, and start again." Introspection encourages individuals to acknowledge that setbacks are part of the journey. They can restart their recovery journey at any moment by practicing self-compassion and resilience.

Endurance and Resilience:

"At the end of the day, we can endure much more than we think we can." Self-assessment and introspection foster endurance and resilience. By reflecting on their inner strength, individuals can draw on their capacity to face and overcome challenges in recovery.

Self-Reflection Questions:

> How can I use self-assessment and introspection to embrace the mysteries of life and fully experience my recovery journey?

> What defines me in terms of patience and attitude, and how can I use introspection to refine these attributes for personal growth?

A Journey of Transformation

> How can I shift my focus from the negatives to the positives in my recovery journey through self-assessment and introspection?
>
> How can I transition from fear to understanding in my recovery, and how does introspection guide me in this process?
>
> How can I better embrace change and resilience in my recovery, and how does self-assessment help me recognize the cyclical nature of challenges?
>
> What steps can I take to cultivate happiness through self-assessment and introspection, focusing on love, grace, and gratitude in my daily life?
>
> How can I practice self-compassion and resilience to restart my recovery journey when setbacks occur?
>
> How does self-assessment and introspection empower me to recognize and tap into my endurance and resilience in recovery?

Self-assessment and introspection are essential tools for long-term addiction recovery. By embracing life's mysteries, defining oneself through patience and attitude, focusing on positives, shifting from fear to understanding, and practicing resilience and happiness, individuals can navigate their recovery journey with greater self-awareness, personal growth, and transformation. Self-reflection plays a pivotal role in this transformative process.

Gaining Insights into Strengths and Weaknesses:
A Path to Long-Term Recovery

Long-term recovery from addiction is a journey of self-discovery and growth. This book delves into the importance of gaining insights into one's strengths and weaknesses as a means to foster personal development and sustained recovery. Drawing inspiration from motivational statements, we explore the significance of living in alignment with one's identity, avoiding self-imposed limitations, believing in oneself, and the importance of resilience and positivity.

Consistency with Identity:

"The strongest force in the universe is a human being living consistently with their identity." Gaining insights into strengths and weaknesses begins with understanding one's true identity. It involves recognizing who one is, free from the grip of addiction, and striving to live in alignment with that identity.

Breaking Self-Limitations:

"Don't limit yourself. Many people limit themselves to what they think they can do. You can go as far as your mind lets you. What you believe you can achieve." Gaining insights into strengths involves breaking self-imposed limitations. By shifting the mindset from doubt to belief, individuals in recovery can unleash their full potential.

Embracing Hard Work and Courage:

"Work hard for what you want because it won't come to you without a fight. You have to be strong and courageous and know that you can do anything you put your mind to." Recognizing strengths requires dedication and courage. It means being willing to put in the effort and fight for one's recovery goals.

Turning Criticism into Positivity:

"If somebody puts you down or criticizes you, just keep on believing in yourself and turn it into something positive." Acknowledging weaknesses involves resilience in the face of criticism. It means learning from feedback, embracing constructive criticism, and using it as a catalyst for personal growth.

Staying Positive and Hopeful:

"Stay positive and happy. Work hard and don't give up hope." Recognizing both strengths and weaknesses requires maintaining a positive and hopeful attitude. Positivity fosters resilience and provides the motivation needed to overcome challenges in recovery.

Being Open to Criticism:

"Be open to criticism and keep learning." Gaining insights into weaknesses involves a willingness to be open to criticism. By seeking feedback and learning from mistakes, individuals can continually improve on their journey to recovery.

Surrounding Oneself with Positivity:

"Surround yourself with happy, warm and genuine people." Recognizing strengths and weaknesses is influenced by one's environment. Surrounding oneself with supportive and positive individuals can contribute to personal growth and recovery.

Recognizing the Nature of Achievement:

"It is easy to hate and it is difficult to love. This is how the whole scheme of things works. All good things are difficult to achieve; and bad things are very easy to get." Gaining insights into strengths and weaknesses involves recognizing the nature of achievement. It requires acknowledging that personal growth and recovery are challenging but ultimately rewarding endeavors.

A Journey of Transformation

Self-Reflection Questions:

How can I gain a deeper understanding of my true identity and live consistently with it on my path to recovery?

In what ways have I imposed self-limitations on my potential, and how can I shift my mindset to believe in my abilities?

What steps can I take to work hard and summon the courage needed to achieve my recovery goals?

How can I cultivate resilience in the face of criticism and use it as a source of personal growth?

How do I maintain a positive and hopeful attitude in my recovery journey, and how does this positivity impact my recognition of strengths and weaknesses?

Am I open to criticism and feedback, and how can I use them as tools for continuous learning and improvement?

How does the environment and the people I surround myself with influence my journey of recognizing strengths and weaknesses?

What motivates me to embrace the challenges of personal growth and recovery, knowing that they require effort and resilience?

Gaining insights into one's strengths and weaknesses is a pivotal aspect of long-term addiction recovery. By living in alignment with one's identity, breaking self-imposed limitations, embracing hard work and courage, and maintaining positivity and resilience, individuals can navigate their recovery journey with a deeper understanding of themselves and a stronger foundation for lasting sobriety. Self-reflection and self-awareness are essential components of this transformative process.

Fostering a Deeper Understanding of Oneself in the Journey of Addiction Recovery

Long-term recovery from addiction is a transformative journey that hinges on self-discovery and self-understanding. This book delves into the importance of fostering a deeper understanding of oneself as a catalyst for personal growth and lasting recovery. Drawing inspiration from motivational statements, we explore the significance of reconnecting with one's authentic self, pursuing dreams, seizing opportunities, learning from mistakes, and taking actions aligned with one's future self.

Reconnecting with Authenticity:

"Can you remember who you were before the world told you who you should be?" Fostering self-understanding begins with a reconnection to one's authentic self—the person they were before societal influences and addiction shaped their identity.

Pursuing Dreams and Aspirations:

"Happy are those who dream dreams and are ready to pay the price to make them come true." A deeper understanding of oneself involves identifying dreams and aspirations that may have been suppressed during addiction. It requires the willingness to pursue these dreams, even if it means overcoming obstacles.

Seizing Common Occasions:

"Don't wait for extraordinary opportunities. Seize common occasions and make them great." Self-discovery is not solely about grand revelations. It can also occur in everyday experiences. Recognizing the value of common occasions and using them to learn more about oneself is a crucial aspect of recovery.

Learning from Mistakes:

"People mess up. People mess up a lot. We allow our own selfishness to overpower us at times. It happens. But you can't allow that to tear you down. You can't keep dwelling on your past choices, and your past actions, or else you'll never learn from them." A deeper understanding of oneself acknowledges past mistakes and allows them to serve as lessons rather than sources of shame or regret.

Taking Actions Aligned with Future Self:

"Do something now that will make the person you'll be tomorrow proud to have been the person you are today." Self-discovery is an ongoing process that involves taking actions aligned with one's future self. It requires making choices today that contribute to a more fulfilling and purpose-driven life in recovery.

Self-Reflection Questions:

>How can I reconnect with my authentic self and rediscover the person I was before addiction influenced my identity?

>What dreams and aspirations did I suppress during my addiction, and how can I begin to pursue them on my journey to recovery?

A Journey of Transformation

> How can I recognize the value of everyday experiences and seize common occasions to learn more about myself and foster self-understanding?
>
> What past mistakes have I made in my addiction, and how can I shift my perspective to view them as opportunities for growth and learning?
>
> What actions can I take today that align with the person I aspire to be in the future, and how do these actions contribute to my journey of self-discovery and recovery?

Fostering a deeper understanding of oneself is a fundamental aspect of long-term addiction recovery. By reconnecting with one's authentic self, pursuing dreams, seizing everyday opportunities, learning from mistakes, and taking actions aligned with one's future self, individuals can embark on a transformative journey of self-discovery and personal growth. Self-reflection and self-awareness are essential components of this process, guiding individuals toward lasting recovery and a more fulfilling life.

Summarizing Key Insights into the How and Why of Personal Change

Long-term recovery from addiction is a profound journey of transformation that involves understanding the dynamics of personal change. This book summarizes key insights into how and why individuals change as they navigate the challenging path of recovery. Drawing inspiration from motivational statements, we explore the importance of embracing pain, accepting the process, and living authentically to foster lasting change.

Key Insights into How and Why We Change:

Embracing Pain and Hopelessness:

"Remember that time when we felt hopeless, got lost, and didn't know where to go? But here we are today. We survived." Change often begins in moments of hopelessness. It is when we acknowledge our brokenness that we become open to the possibility of rebirth and transformation.

Accepting Pain as a Teacher:

"When we were broken, we need to be reborn. Do not fight the pain; embrace it. Accept it. Live it." Pain can be a powerful catalyst for change. Rather than resisting or avoiding it, individuals in recovery must accept pain as a teacher and a necessary part of their growth.

Patience and Resilience:

"Don't rush the process; we need to swim in the deep end of life for a while to build our muscles. Learn. Keep swimming. We will be stronger for it." Change is not an overnight process. It requires patience and resilience. Just as one builds physical strength through consistent effort, emotional and mental strength is developed by enduring life's challenges.

Self-Centered Recovery:

"Tell yourself every day I gotta do this for me. This is for me. This isn't about anybody. Live for me. Honor me. Never lose sight of that." Recovery is a deeply personal journey. It is essential to prioritize one's own well-being and self-growth. Only by taking care of oneself can individuals truly honor their journey to change.

Resilience and Survival:

"We've survived 100% of everything in our life so far, so there's a pretty good chance that we'll survive whatever is next." Recognizing one's resilience and ability to endure past challenges can instill the confidence needed to face future obstacles. Change is possible because individuals have a track record of survival and resilience.

Whole-Hearted Commitment:

"Life is going to give us just what we put into it. So put our whole heart in everything we do." Lasting change requires whole-hearted commitment. It involves investing one's full self in recovery and approaching each aspect of life with sincerity and dedication.

Self-Reflection Questions:

> Have I embraced moments of hopelessness as opportunities for personal growth and transformation in my recovery journey?
>
> How can I better accept pain as a teacher and a catalyst for change, rather than resisting or avoiding it?
>
> What strategies can I employ to cultivate patience and resilience as I navigate the process of change?
>
> In my recovery journey, am I prioritizing self-care and self-centered growth, or am I too focused on external influences?
>
> How can I draw on my past experiences of survival and resilience to boost my confidence in overcoming future challenges?
>
> What steps can I take to commit whole-heartedly to my recovery and approach life with sincerity and dedication?

A Journey of Transformation

Understanding the dynamics of personal change is integral to long-term recovery from addiction. Embracing pain, accepting the process, and living authentically are key insights that underpin the transformational journey. By practicing patience, resilience, and self-centered recovery, individuals can foster lasting change and find strength in their survival and resilience. Self-reflection and self-awareness are instrumental in this transformative process, guiding individuals towards a more fulfilling life in recovery.

Emphasizing the Multifaceted Nature of Change in Addiction Recovery

Long-term recovery from addiction is a complex journey that involves multifaceted changes—physical, emotional, psychological, and social. This book explores the various aspects of change in the context of addiction recovery and highlights the significance of embracing transformation as a dynamic process. Drawing inspiration from motivational statements, we delve into the importance of optimism, personal growth, and resisting the judgments of those who resist change.

Emphasizing the Multifaceted Nature of Change:

Overcoming Negative Thinking:

"Overthinking is the biggest cause of our unhappiness." Addiction recovery often begins with a shift away from negative thought patterns. Acknowledging and addressing these negative thoughts can pave the way for emotional healing and personal growth.

Staying Occupied and Optimistic:

"Keep yourself occupied. Keep your mind off things that don't help you. Be optimistic. Things work out best for those who make the best out of how things work out." Recovery is not just about quitting substances; it's about embracing a healthier lifestyle. Staying busy and maintaining a positive outlook can support this process.

Adaptation and Strength:

"When life becomes difficult, you must change yourself to become stronger." Addiction recovery often requires individuals to adapt to new challenges and develop resilience. Strength emerges from the willingness to change and grow in response to adversity.

Embracing Growth:

"People who are comfortable with remaining stagnant will always say 'you've changed.' The cycle of life is supposed to include growth and transformation." Recovery involves profound personal growth and transformation. Those who resist change may not understand the necessity of this evolution.

Blooming in the Face of Resistance:

"Don't allow those who are stuck in a bud to make you feel less for blooming." Recovery can be met with resistance from others who may not be ready for change themselves. It's important to stay true to one's path and not let the judgments of others hinder personal growth.

Self-Reflection Questions:

How do negative thought patterns impact my recovery journey, and what strategies can I use to overcome them?

What activities or hobbies can I engage in to keep my mind occupied and maintain a positive outlook during recovery?

In what ways have I adapted and grown stronger in response to the difficulties I've faced in my recovery journey?

How do I view personal growth and transformation in the context of my recovery, and how can I embrace these changes more fully?

Have I encountered resistance or judgment from others in my recovery journey, and how do I respond to such challenges while staying true to my path of growth?

Addiction recovery is a multidimensional process that encompasses various facets of change. Overcoming negative thinking, staying optimistic, adapting to challenges, embracing personal growth, and resisting external resistance are integral components of this transformative journey. Self-reflection and self-awareness are essential tools for navigating these changes and maintaining a path of lasting recovery.

In conclusion, our exploration of the mechanisms and motivations behind personal change has provided a comprehensive understanding of the intricacies of this transformative process. We have delved into the intrinsic motivations that drive change, including the desire for personal growth, happiness, and alignment with values and beliefs. We've also examined the influence of extrinsic factors, recognizing the impact of life events, social influences, and external support systems.

The science of behavior change has shed light on the psychology behind transformation, offering practical strategies for breaking old habits and forming new ones. Furthermore, we've navigated the various stages individuals go through during change, from pre-contemplation to maintenance, understanding the challenges and opportunities at each stage.

Beliefs and mindset have emerged as powerful drivers of change, with a focus on identifying limiting beliefs and nurturing a growth mindset. We've explored the emotional landscape of change, learning to cope with fear, resistance, and uncertainty while harnessing emotional intelligence as a tool for navigating transformation effectively.

A Journey of Transformation

Self-reflection and self-awareness have been highlighted as essential elements in the change process, guiding individuals to gain insights into their strengths and weaknesses, fostering a deeper understanding of themselves.

As we wrap up this journey through the dynamics of personal change, we encourage you, the reader, to embark on your own transformation journey. Take a moment to reflect on your motivations and desires, recognizing the multifaceted nature of change. Embrace change as a dynamic process, and remember that your path to personal growth and fulfillment is uniquely yours to navigate. With self-awareness, determination, and the insights gained from this exploration, you can embark on a transformative journey that leads to a more empowered and fulfilling life.

Conclusion

The journey of transformation is ongoing, and it is our hope that you continue to explore the multifaceted nature of change, nurture your own motivations for transformation, and embark on your personal journey of self-discovery, empowerment, and positive change. May this voyage serve as a guiding light on your path to becoming the change maker you are destined to be.

In conclusion, "The Change Maker- We Do Recover- The Journey of Transformation" has been a profound expedition, specifically tailored for individuals seeking long-term recovery from addiction. We embarked on this tailored journey to help you understand and embrace the change maker within, with a focus on your unique path to recovery.

Our journey began by laying a solid foundation for change, emphasizing the pivotal role it plays in your recovery journey. We explored the diverse facets of change, its inevitability in life, and how it manifests in various forms, all with the aim of helping you recognize its significance in your recovery process.

We dove deep into understanding the dynamics of change as it relates to addiction recovery. We discussed the internal and external drivers that can motivate your journey towards sobriety and the triggers that may prompt you to seek change, often propelled by life events and adversities that are intimately tied to addiction.

We took a close look at the psychological impact of change, acknowledging the stress and anxiety that can accompany recovery, but also emphasizing the immense potential for personal growth and resilience in your quest for sobriety. We provided strategies and coping mechanisms to help you navigate these challenges, encouraging you to see change as an opportunity for personal transformation.

The paradox of resistance and acceptance was explored in the context of addiction recovery, recognizing that it's natural to encounter resistance on this path. We discussed common barriers and provided strategies for overcoming them, emphasizing the importance of cultivating a mindset of acceptance and adaptability, which is crucial in the recovery journey.

We then applied these insights to the specific stages of change in addiction recovery, helping you understand the emotional and experiential aspects of each stage. We offered strategies to assist you in progressing through these stages effectively and maintaining your commitment to long-term recovery.

Throughout our journey, we highlighted the immense potential for personal growth and positive change that recovery from addiction offers. We encouraged you to embrace this transformational opportunity and recognize the strength within you to overcome addiction.

A Journey of Transformation

In the second part of our tailored journey, we delved into the principles of being a change maker in the context of addiction recovery. We discussed the importance of self-awareness, empathy, resilience, and authenticity in your recovery journey, providing you with a comprehensive toolkit to navigate the challenges you may face.

The third part of our tailored expedition took you through the essential steps of transformation specifically tailored for long-term recovery from addiction. We highlighted the significance of self-reflection, goal setting, vision, and personal well-being in your recovery journey, emphasizing that recovery is an ongoing commitment and a lifelong journey.

Finally, we explored the intricacies of how and why you change in the context of addiction recovery. We examined the intrinsic and extrinsic motivations that drive your desire for sobriety, the psychology behind behavioral changes, and the emotional and belief systems that play a role in your recovery process.

As we conclude this journey, tailored to your unique path towards long-term recovery from addiction, we want to remind you that you are not alone in this endeavor. The path to recovery is challenging, but it is also profoundly rewarding. Embrace change as your ally in this journey, and recognize the incredible strength within you to overcome addiction and lead a life of sobriety.

Your journey to long-term recovery is ongoing, and we encourage you to continue exploring the multifaceted nature of change in the context of addiction recovery. Nurture your intrinsic motivations, seek support from your community, and keep moving forward with resilience and determination. May this tailored journey serve as a guiding light on your path to achieving and maintaining long-term recovery.

Best wishes,
C. Michael Welsh

www.ingramcontent.com/pod-product-compliance
Lightning Source LLC
Chambersburg PA
CBHW081213170426
43198CB00017B/2603